A FALSE TREE OF LIBERTY

A FALSE TREE OF LIBERTY

HUMAN RIGHTS IN RADICAL THOUGHT

SUSAN MARKS

OXFORD
UNIVERSITY PRESS

OXFORD
UNIVERSITY PRESS

Great Clarendon Street, Oxford, OX2 6DP,
United Kingdom

Oxford University Press is a department of the University of Oxford.
It furthers the University's objective of excellence in research, scholarship,
and education by publishing worldwide. Oxford is a registered trade mark of
Oxford University Press in the UK and in certain other countries

First Edition published in 2019

Published in the United States of America by Oxford University Press
198 Madison Avenue, New York, NY 10016, United States of America

British Library Cataloguing in Publication Data

Data available

Library of Congress Control Number: 2019946546

ISBN 978–0–19–967545–6

for Philip

now dream
of that sweet
equal republic
where the juniper
talks to the oak,
the thistle,
the bandaged elm,
and the jolly jolly chestnut.

from: Tom Paulin, 'The Book of Juniper'
in *Liberty Tree* (London: Faber & Faber Ltd, 1983)

Acknowledgements

An early inspiration for this book came from Noel Thompson's *The Real Rights of Man*.[1] It was from Thompson that I first learned of the 'false tree of liberty'.[2] In learning more, I profited from the scholarship of many authors, but perhaps especially Alastair Bonnett and Malcolm Chase.

I want to acknowledge the enormous importance for my understanding of the issues I discuss in this book of work by Peter Linebaugh and James Holstun. Footnotes are supposed to convey influence, but what I have learned from their writing goes well beyond that which any footnote could capture.

Huge thanks go to my former student Victoria Adelmant for invaluable help in preparing the text for publication. I look forward to reading her books one day. I am immensely grateful to Matt Craven and Tor Krever, who generously read and commented on the manuscript. I also wish to record my thanks for the unstinting support of Rosemary Marzio and Guy Marks.

Philip Green inhabits a very different world from the one in which I have made my professional home, but it has been my extraordinarily good fortune that he has dwelled with me here, encouraging, listening, discussing, reading, commenting, rallying and affirming. This book is dedicated to him with love and deep gratitude.

1. Noel Thompson, *The Real Rights of Man: Political Economies for the Working Class 1775–1850* (London: Pluto Press, 1998).
2. See chap. 9 below.

Contents

Illustrations xiii

1. Introduction 1
2. Enclosure and its Critics 21
3. Two Early Modern Revolts 45
4. Rights in the English Revolution 71
5. The French Revolution Controversy 95
6. In the Shadow of Dearth 121
7. Improvement and the Real Rights of Man 153
8. Does Nature Confer Rights? 183
9. Trees and Liberty 211
10. Afterword 241

Index 267

Illustrations

1. Thomas Gainsborough, *Mr and Mrs Andrews*, portrait, (c. 1750), incamerastock / Alamy Stock Photo 9
2. Thomas Gainsborough, *The Cottage Door*, Cincinnati Art Museum, (c. 1778), The Artchives / Alamy Stock Photo 10
3. *The Diggers of Warwickshire to all other Diggers* © The British Library Board, Harley MS 787/11 61
4. James Gillray, *Smelling out a rat*, Chronicle / Alamy Stock Photo 100
5. *Tom Paine's Nightly Pest*, published by Hannah Humphrey in 1792 (hand-coloured etching), Gillray, James (1757–1815) / Courtesy of the Warden and Scholars of New College, Oxford / Bridgeman Images 111
6. Byron, Frederick George, *Contrasted Opinions of Paine's Pamphlet* 1791 © Fitzwilliam Museum, Cambridge 117
7. *The Republican attack*. James Gillray 1795. Art Collection 2 / Alamy Stock Photo 126
8. *Copenhagen House* published by H. Humphrey, 1795 (print), Gillray, James (1757–1815) / London Metropolitan Archives, City of London / Bridgeman Images 143
9. Thomas Spence, *cat token*, 1796. ©The Trustees of the British Museum. All rights reserved 178

   Thomas Spence, *token*, 1795. © The Trustees of the British Museum. All rights reserved 179
10. Philip Dawe, *The Bostonians Paying the Excise-Man, or Tarring & Feathering*, 1774, Pictorial Press Ltd / Alamy Stock Photo 213
11. *A foreign tree*, subitarius Engraving, Musée de la Révolution française. Inv. MRF 1988.72.2, © Coll. Musée de la Révolution française / Domaine de Vizille 228

    British tree of true Liberty, stabilissimus Engraving, Musée de la Révolution française. Inv. MRF 1988.72.1, © Coll. Musée de la Révolution française / Domaine de Vizille 229

12. REUTERS, *An opposition supporter with pieces of bread taped onto his head shouts slogans during anti-government protest in Sanaa* 3 February 2011 242

13. *New path after autumn shower, Newcastle Town Moor*, October 2004. Jacky Longstaff 247

1

Introduction

'And live with all the rights of man'

Who was the first person to use the English phrase 'the rights of man'? Thomas Spence, a little remembered but once notable figure on the London radical scene of the late eighteenth and early nineteenth centuries, claims that it was him.[1] The occasion was a visit which Spence made one day around 1780 to a man and woman who were living in a cave opposite Marsden Rock — an outcrop off the north-eastern coast of England.[2] Marsden Rock is near Newcastle upon Tyne, which is where Spence was born and where he lived until his move to London some years later.

According to Spence, the man and woman had been 'ill-used by [their] landlords'.[3] Spence does not go into detail, but whatever happened, we may guess that it involved eviction, perhaps repeated evictions, after which the couple had got fed up and decided to make a home for themselves in this cave. As the cave was quite small when they first found it, the man, who was a retired miner and has since been identified as one Jack Bates, had enlarged it by blasting the rock with explosives, in the process earning the nickname which Spence uses to refer to him: 'Jack the Blaster'. Spence gives us to understand that Jack the Blaster's unusual dwelling had become something of a tourist

1. See Alastair Bonnett, 'The Other Rights of Man: The Revolutionary Plan of Thomas Spence', *History Today* 57(9) (2007) 42, 44–45.
2. Marsden Rock is a column of rock or 'stack' lying just out to sea at Marsden in South Shields.
3. Quoted in Alastair Bonnett, 'The Other Rights of Man: The Revolutionary Plan of Thomas Spence', *History Today* 57(9) (2007) 42, 44.

A False Tree of Liberty. Susan Marks, Oxford University Press (2019). © Susan Marks.
DOI: 10.1093/oso/9780199675456.003.0001

attraction by the time he visited it. Jack and his wife Jessie made a little money by supplying refreshments to those who came on day-trips to see them.

We don't know what the other visitors thought, but where Spence is concerned, it is clear that he was absolutely delighted to meet Jack and Jessie, and thrilled by their decision to move out of the reach of any landlord and by what that seemed to him to represent. In his words, he '[exulted] in the idea of a human being who had bravely emancipated himself from the iron fangs of aristocracy, to live free from impost' — by which he meant, primarily, rent. It was in this state of exultation that Spence was inspired, as he explains, to write 'extempore with chaulk above the fire place of this free man' the lines which are said to justify his claim to be the first to make 'use of the phrase "[the] rights of man"':

> Ye landlords vile, whose man's peace mar
> Come levy rents here if you can;
> Your stewards and lawyers I defy,
> And live with all the RIGHTS OF MAN.[4]

The site of Jack and Jessie's cave is now a pub called The Marsden Grotto. You can still see their fireplace behind the bar, though Spence's chalk marks on the wall above have long gone. That may not be such a great loss, as, in fact, he was not the first person to use the English phrase 'the rights of man'. There exists textual evidence for its use going back at least to the beginning of the eighteenth century.[5] Yet the phrase's occurrence was undeniably rare before 1780, and from another perspective, those extemporaneous lines of verse do seem significant as an early invocation of a quite distinctive kind.

Note how Spence frames the rights of man as a matter of emancipation from the clutches of rapacious landlords and their henchmen stewards and lawyers. If we reflect on today's human rights, that is hardly the way anyone would be likely to frame what they are about. To be sure, our twenty-first-century human rights include the right to adequate housing, with implications for eviction. But protection of the right to adequate housing is compatible with subjection to landlordly rapacity. As many have observed, international human rights law carries forward a tradition of which the right to property has always been a cardinal principle.

4. Quoted ibid, 45.
5. See Peter de Bolla, *The Architecture of Concepts: The Historical Formation of Human Rights* (New York: Fordham University Press, 2013), esp. 50, 102, 111 et seq. See also Lynn Hunt, *Inventing Human Rights* (New York: W.W. Norton, 2007), 22–24.

Against that background, Spence's story opens up an intriguing vista — a vista of another tradition, in which what is important is not the right to property, but instead the dispossession of the unpropertied. With Spence, the focus of attention shifts to the rights that needed to be taken away in order that private property could arise, and to the demands and actions by which those dispossessed have sought, and might again seek, to remake their future on a different basis. As he tells it, Jack and Jessie Bates 'lived with all the rights of man' because they had thrown off their dependence on the men of property, who could not now continue to exploit and oppress them.

This book investigates the conditions in which such an idea of the rights of man arose, its relation to prior currents of activism and thought, and its place in the wider discourse of the rights of man of late eighteenth-century England. For if the phrase 'the rights of man' had occurred only rarely before 1780, things, of course, changed dramatically barely a decade after Spence composed his ditty. With the French Revolution came a remarkable debate about the significance of the events in France for England, thanks to which the rights of man became, for a time, an essential and unignorable theme of public political discussion. Edmund Burke's *Reflections on the Revolution in France* and Thomas Paine's *Rights of Man* are just the best known of very many publications associated with that development.

No straight line

Before going further, I need to address an important question. I have been talking about eighteenth-century conceptualisations of the rights of man and human rights as we know them today as though they have something to do with one another and even belong in the same historical narrative. But do they? To refer to human rights in the twenty-first century is to refer to a worldwide social movement, area of governmental and intergovernmental activity, field of professional practice, and multidisciplinary terrain of academic enquiry. Our human rights nowadays are protected by international law. We have procedures for invoking that law, courts and committees to interpret and apply it, and fora in which it is developed, promoted, evaluated, and continuously amended and institutionally reformed. None of this existed in the eighteenth century.

In his book *The Last Utopia*, published in 2010, Samuel Moyn emphasises the novelty of the phenomena I have just mentioned, and debunks as a 'myth' the notion that human rights have 'deep roots' which connect them with the revolutionary declarations of the eighteenth century.[6] The search for precursors is misconceived, he writes, because the project in the eighteenth century was to create a new kind of popular sovereignty and nation-state, 'not [as in the case of human rights, to] move beyond sovereignty and the state altogether'.[7] Put differently, '[f]ar from being sources of appeal that transcended the state and nation, the rights asserted in early modern political revolutions . . . were central to the construction of state and nation, and led nowhere beyond' them.[8] Those rights were about 'a whole people incorporating itself in a state, not a few foreign people criticizing another state for its wrongdoings', 'a politics of citizenship at home, [rather than] a politics of suffering abroad'.[9]

Critics of this argument have pointed out that the distinctions made here are overdrawn.[10] Human rights do not transcend the state or move beyond sovereignty. International human rights law is made by states, and is hence an expression of state sovereignty. The state is the main focus of efforts to secure the implementation of internationally protected human rights. Domestic remedies are central to — the front line of — human rights enforcement. Certainly, evidence abounds of human rights being treated as though they were about suffering abroad and foreign people criticising other states for wrongdoing. Yet it is notable that government officials and others in turn face criticism for that approach, evincing as it seems to do a belief that arrangements within their own country give rise to no issues of human rights. As for the eighteenth century, its politics of citizenship at home may prove on closer inspection also to have been a complex matter, incorporating internationalist or universalist dimensions, along with sub-national and local-customary ones.[11]

These things said, it is plainly the case that any 'search for precursors', or attempt to connect concepts from widely disparate epochs, must be handled with care. Concepts gain sense from the historically specific conditions

6. Samuel Moyn, *The Last Utopia* (Cambridge, MA: Harvard University Press, 2010), 12.
7. Ibid, 23.
8. Ibid, 12.
9. Ibid, 26, 12.
10. See, e.g., Philip Alston, 'Does the Past Matter? On the Origins of Human Rights', *Harvard Law Review* 126(7) (2013) 2043, esp. 2069–2070, 2072.
11. See further chaps. 7 and 8 below and the references there cited.

in which they are deployed. While human rights are often represented as natural rights, birthrights, or rights inherent in human existence, that representation itself has a history, and cannot provide a basis for treating them as positioned beyond or outside time.[12] But the point here is not just that, even if similar words are used,[13] and even if cognate ideas are involved, our twenty-first-century human rights necessarily, and manifestly, differ in their meaning from the eighteenth-century rights of man. It is also that our twenty-first-century human rights and the eighteenth-century rights of man differ in their meaning from *themselves*, so to speak. There is now, and (as this book will discuss at some length) was also then, contestation over how these rights should be conceptualised. No straight line can link the present with the age of revolutions because no fixed point stands at either end.

Their proprietary attitude

Let me now say something about my interest in that period of history, and specifically, in late eighteenth-century England. In the first place, and bracketing for a moment the question of why England, it was during the late eighteenth century that the rights of man entered public consciousness and began to circulate and become familiar as a concept, discourse and problematic. Where the English-speaking world is concerned, the publication of Paine's two-part *Rights of Man* in 1791 and 1792 had a lot to do with that. Estimates vary as to how many copies of Paine's book were printed and sold, how many people read it or had it read to them, and how widely the book circulated in the cities, towns and countryside of Britain and Ireland. Paine claimed for himself colossal sales figures and vast dissemination, and some historians argue that he exaggerated his influence, encouraged by a hostile government that was grateful for the help he thereby provided in affirming the scale of the threat which the authorities professed to confront.[14]

12. See further Martti Koskenniemi, 'Foreword: History of Human Rights as Political Intervention in the Present', in Pamela Slotte and Miia Halme-Tuomisaari (eds.), *Revisiting the Origins of Human Rights* (Cambridge: Cambridge University Press, 2015), ix.
13. Sometimes the very same words were used. Regarding the incidence and significance of the phrase 'human rights' during the eighteenth century, see Peter de Bolla, *The Architecture of Concepts: the Historical Formation of Human Rights* (New York: Fordham University Press, 2013), 48 et seq.; and Lynn Hunt, *Inventing Human Rights* (New York: W.W. Norton, 2007), 22–23.
14. See, e.g., Peter de Bolla, *The Architecture of Concepts: the Historical Formation of Human Rights* (New York: Fordham University Press, 2013), 209.

There is general agreement, however, that an exceptionally large number of copies of *Rights of Man* were sold in the years that followed its first appearance, that the book achieved an uncommonly high level of penetration both in and outside the British capital, and that among contemporaries it was widely perceived as a publishing sensation. It seems that the book's title may have been a key element in its reception, though, by a small misreading, it began almost immediately to be referred to as 'The Rights of Man'.[15] A recent analysis of the database of *Eighteenth-Century Collections Online* shows an exponential increase in the usage of the phrase 'the rights of man' in 1791 — Part I of *Rights of Man* appeared in March of that year, and Part II the next February — and especially 1792.[16] The archival materials that support this finding include other books, pamphlets, book reviews, digests, poems, songs and commentary in periodicals such as newspapers, broadsheets and journals. Dating back to a time when the cartoon was gaining significance as a mode of communication about public affairs, they also include political cartoons, as well as images of legend-bearing everyday objects.

But, of course, this is not just about one book, and nor is it just about a phrase and its uptake in public culture. Harold Laski is said to have characterised the 1790s as the 'last great period in British history of open debate about the fundamentals of civil government'.[17] When Laski lived, and for many decades thereafter, scholarly writing about the controversy over the implications for England of the French Revolution and its declaration of the rights of man mostly focused on the conflict between supporters and opponents of the continuation of monarchical government and aristocratic oligarchy. Thus, the arguments of members of the political establishment were counterposed to those of Paine and such other Jacobin sympathisers as William Godwin, Mary Wollstonecraft and John Thelwall. In more recent work, attention is concentrated as well on divisions within the radical camp. Part of the impetus for this has come from research into less 'respectable' figures, including Spence, but also Richard Brothers, Robert Wedderburn and Richard Lee, who have come to be understood as forming a 'radical underworld' in London at the time.[18]

15. See ibid, 210–11.
16. See ibid, 273 (Table 27).
17. Quoted in Kenneth Johnston, *Unusual Suspects: Pitt's Reign of Alarm and the Lost Generation of the 1790s* (Oxford: Oxford University Press, 2013), 5.
18. See, esp., Iain McCalman, *Radical Underworld: Prophets, Revolutionaries and Pornographers in London, 1795-1840* (Cambridge: Cambridge University Press, 1988). It should be noted that Laski does touch in passing on Spence, though he brackets him with Paine, and says that, together with others, they 'are responsible for a special current of their own in the great tide of protest against

By way of example, Gregory Claeys concludes the introduction to a collection of eighteenth-century British utopian texts with the observation that '[t]wo roads . . . emerged from the utopianism of the 1790s'. One 'led from a new democratic form of commercial republicanism towards the more welfare-oriented forms of liberal democracy'. The second, 'scouted by Godwin and Spence, pointed towards socialist proposals . . . [designed] to abolish vice and poverty, and to efforts to eliminate political conflict altogether'.[19] In a study of William Blake (who had some connection to polite society, while also having affinities with the underground milieu), Saree Makdisi contrasts what, for his part, he terms the 'hegemonic liberal-radicalism' of Paine and the organised fora of 1790s English radicalism with the 'plebeian radicalism' of Blake and others, among them again Spence.[20] As it happens, neither Blake nor Godwin (nor Brothers, Wedderburn or Lee) was very voluble on the subject of the rights of man, but in foregrounding that theme, this book will likewise highlight a divergence between positions to which it will eventually attach the labels 'Paineite' and 'Spencean'.

I pass now to a second factor that underlies my interest in late eighteenth-century England, which is that this was not only an important moment in the history of the rights of man. It was also, and far more generally, an important moment in the history of the modern world. For this time and this place saw the culmination of the developments that brought humanity capitalism. I will touch very briefly below on something of the complicated debate about the origins of capitalism, but for now it suffices to recall that most accounts tell of a system that reached its evolved form in later eighteenth- and nineteenth-century England. A defining feature of capitalism is the phenomenon of market compulsion — the systemic obligation to carry out the activities that sustain life in and through the market — and it has long been understood that, in the case of people who are self-sustaining, the establishment of market compulsion depends on separating them from their livelihoods and hence disabling them from providing for themselves. In that connection, one aspect of what transpired in late eighteenth-century England was the near-completion of the long-running enclosure of the English commons.

the unjust situation of labour [and] build their system upon natural rights' (156). See Harold Laski, *Political Thought in England from Locke to Bentham* (Oxford: Oxford University Press, 1920), 16, 156.

19. Gregory Claeys (ed.), *Utopias of the British Enlightenment* (Cambridge: Cambridge University Press, 1994), xxviii.

20. Saree Makdisi, *William Blake and the Impossible History of the 1790s* (London: University of Chicago Press, 2003), esp. 21–23.

Enclosure refers to the process by which large sections of the peasantry and many others who derived their subsistence wholly or partly from land were deprived of access to land and its resources. The other side of that is that it is the process by which those who owned, or were able to buy, land acquired rights of exclusive possession — that is to say, rights that were no longer subject to the cooperative agricultural arrangements and customary use-rights that had traditionally been in place.[21] Janette Neeson reports that '[m]uch of England was still open in 1700; but most of it was enclosed by 1840', following a marked acceleration in the pace of enclosure that occurred in the later eighteenth century.[22] In *The Making of the English Working Class* and *Customs in Common,* E. P. Thompson depicts the effects of this.[23] He writes of the struggles associated with the establishment of market society and industrialised production, and of the emergence of a new kind of working class consciousness. He also locates in this period the beginnings of the later middle class sensibility that preached to the proletariat about thrift, frugality, sobriety, forbearance and hard work.

Underpinning these developments was a distinctive ideology in which private profit became identified with the public good, and social progress came to mean increasing the productivity of land and labour. Science and culture were part of this too. Within the still predominantly agrarian economy of late eighteenth-century England, a new agricultural science lent support for 'improved' estate management, while a new landscape aesthetics exhibited and reinforced the power of the propertied. In *Ways of Seeing* John Berger highlights the memorialisation of that power in works of art. Indeed, ever since his exploration of the 'special relation between oil painting and property', his example of Thomas Gainsborough's *Mr and Mrs Andrews* (fig. 1) has been held to epitomise the privatisation of landscape and land.[24] The handsomely dressed pair under an oak tree in a setting of rich farmland with well-tended wheat fields and a large flock of sheep are not, in Berger's words, 'a couple in Nature as Rousseau imagined nature. They are landowners and

21. See further below, esp. chaps. 2, 3, 7 and 10.
22. J. M. Neeson, *Commoners: Common Right, Enclosure and Social Change in England, 1700–1820* (Cambridge: Cambridge University Press, 1993), 5.
23. E. P. Thompson, *The Making of the English Working Class* (New York: Vintage, 1966) and *Customs in Common* (Pontypool: Merlin Press, 1991).
24. See John Berger, *Ways of Seeing* (London: BBC and Penguin, 1972), 106, and, for a recent restatement of this, Raj Patel and Jason Moore, *A History of the World in Seven Cheap Things* (London: Verso, 2018), 122 et seq.

Figure 1 Thomas Gainsborough, *Mr and Mrs Andrews*, portrait, (c. 1750), incamerastock / Alamy Stock Photo

their proprietary attitude towards what surrounds them is visible in their stance and their expressions.'[25]

It is often observed that there is, in this painting, no sign of any of the people who would actually have worked the land for Robert and Frances Andrews. The painting that bears their name was made around 1750. John Barrell directs attention to another painting by Gainsborough, made almost thirty years later.[26] *Cottage Door with Children Playing* (fig. 2) depicts a modest cottage in the countryside. Children merrily play in front of the door, while a group of women look on, lit by a shaft of sunshine. As Barrell emphasises, however, this scene has a 'dark side'. On the sunless, left-hand side of the painting, a man is bent under a heavy bundle of sticks that he is bringing home to fuel the family's fire. 'That deformed and struggling labourer blights the landscape', and, now quite explicitly, invites consideration of 'the relations between rich and poor, consumer and producer', and of the changing roles and relationships of men and women.[27]

25. John Berger, *Ways of Seeing* (London: BBC and Penguin, 1972), 107.
26. John Barrell, *The Dark Side of the Landscape: The Rural Poor in English Painting 1730–1840* (Cambridge: Cambridge University Press, 1980), 70 et seq.
27. Ibid, 71. Barrell's discussion is actually of how the painting works 'to resist or to deny' (73) the creation of the working class consciousness of which Thompson writes. The labourer is portrayed as suffering, but dutiful and uncomplaining, and there is no hint in the painting of any 'social energy' (72) exuding from him and his extended family.

Figure 2 Thomas Gainsborough, *The Cottage Door*, Cincinnati Art Museum, (c. 1778), The Artchives / Alamy Stock Photo

This brings forward a further aspect of the significance of late eighteenth-century England, and the last I shall mention here. '[F]or the first time', writes Gareth Stedman Jones, 'contemporaries [began] to discuss the meaning and implications of living in a commercial society, or what would now be called "capitalism"'.[28] They raised new questions about poverty, its nature and extent, its causes and consequences, its exacerbation and remediation, engendering also new (or rather, renewed) anxieties on the part of the property-owning classes that, in the words of one prominent contemporary, 'gratitude' was going, and the 'claim of poverty on Riches . . . is taken as a right'.[29]

28. Gareth Stedman Jones, *An End to Poverty?* (London: Profile Books, 2004), 10.
29. George Onesiphorus Paul, 7 August 1795, PC 1/29/A64. Quoted in John Bohstedt, *The Politics of Provisions: Food Riots, Moral Economy and Market Transition* (London: Routledge, 2016), 261.

Right names, rights claims

If an important moment in the history of the rights of man coincides with an important moment in the development of capitalism (understood not only as an economic system, but as a system that has shaped the modern world in all its dimensions), it seems appropriate to ask about the connection between those two things. In particular, it seems worthwhile to examine whether and how such phenomena as enclosure informed debate over the French Revolution and the rights of man, and vice versa.

The historical literature about enclosure invariably stresses that the enclosure of the English commons did not begin in the eighteenth century. As already indicated, it was a long-running process, and dates back to the late fifteenth and early sixteenth centuries. This literature also stresses that the destruction of the English peasantry was brought about by a variety of factors, of which expropriation was only one. Nonetheless, enclosure became an emblem of the changes that were transforming life in the English countryside. Michael Perelman writes of how exclusion from access to land 'cut through traditional lifeways like scissors'.[30] One blade undermined established means of securing the necessities of life. The other blade kept those affected from finding alternative survival strategies that did not involve proletarianisation.

It is well known that enclosers took a long time to get the state on board, and that, from the outset, the enclosure of England's common and waste land encountered very considerable popular resistance. It also formed the basis of a large literature of (to use the technical term) complaint. What were the terms in which this hostility was expressed? Especially in the initial period, enclosers were denounced as 'rogues', 'villains' and 'knaves', and were condemned for their 'wickedness', 'ungodliness', 'avarice' and 'greed'. If this vocabulary is unfamiliar to us, R. H. Tawney, writing almost a century ago, found it 'important to observe that [people in those days] called these vices by their right names, and had not learned to persuade themselves that greed was enterprise and avarice economy'.[31]

30. Michael Perelman, *The Invention of Capitalism* (Durham, NC and London: Duke University Press, 2000), 14.
31. R. H. Tawney, *Religion and the Rise of Capitalism* (London: Penguin, 1938), 72. (The book's first edition appeared in 1926.) For a recent discussion of the 'moral' dimensions of Tawney's analysis, as of the analysis of Karl Polanyi and E. P. Thompson (touched on in later chapters of this book), see Tim Rogan, *The Moral Economists: R. H. Tawney, Karl Polanyi, E. P. Thompson and the Critique of Capitalism* (Princeton, NJ: Princeton University Press, 2017).

For present purposes, what is even more important to observe is that, in doing so, they asserted rights. They insisted on, and sought to defend, the rights of common upon which the livelihoods and independence of the rural poor wholly or partly depended. Quite different from the rights of man, these rights arose under local custom or by local prescription, and another thing stressed in the historical literature about enclosure is that rights of common were immensely variable across the country. Yet it is striking that, in asserting these emphatically localised rights, the sixteenth- and seventeenth-century opponents of enclosure also made more general claims. They pointed to the common humanity of rich and poor. They claimed a fundamental right of subsistence. They said they gave voice to the experience of the dispossessed everywhere. A big debate in the English Revolution of the seventeenth century centred on the 'native rights of freeborn Englishmen', but again the discursive picture is blurry as, for native rights, the forces of conservatism kept hearing 'natural rights'.

I take — or, at any rate, in writing this book, have taken — all this to signal that the story of another tradition of thought about the rights of man in the eighteenth century must stretch back to earlier times. With that in mind, the next three chapters are devoted to texts and events of the sixteenth and seventeenth centuries. Chapter 2 considers three contributions to the sixteenth-century literature of complaint. Chapter 3 examines two early modern revolts. Chapter 4 looks at some writings that have come down to us from the Levellers and Diggers of the English Civil War. Most of the remainder of the book then addresses the rights of man debates of the 1790s. Chapter 5 introduces those debates. Chapter 6 foregrounds food insecurity as part of the context in which they unfolded. Chapter 7 relates them to land reorganisation and the ideology associated with it. Chapter 8 explores the intersection of nature and history in eighteenth-century thinking about the rights of man. Chapter 9 retraces the book's path with specific reference to the imagery and actuality of its eponymous tree. Chapter 10 is concerned with the present day. Linking the historical periods I discuss will be, in part, the collective memory, and knowledge of the past, of contemporaries themselves, but, in part also, a lineage of which they were not aware, and which can only be reconstructed in retrospect.

The chapters that follow (with the exception of chapter 10) are limited in their focus to England. Even then, the ambit is narrow, in that I have put to one side the whole huge and properly inseparable topic of empire, for the sake of dwelling on domestic controversies. As will be clear by now, the investigation here involves situating the rights of man within the history of capitalism. The origins of capitalism are, and have long been, the subject of great debate. A key preoccupation within that debate has been the question of how to account for the transition from feudalism to capitalism.[32] To what extent was it determined by factors internal to feudalism (lord/peasant relations, seigneurial powers, patterns of landowning), and to what extent was it determined by external factors having to do with changes in the sphere of trade and commerce? Different answers to those questions have yielded different portrayals of the historical geography of capitalism. In 1991 Ellen Wood opened a book with the words: 'The capitalist system was born in England.'[33] Others disagree,[34] though generally without denying that the capitalist system was very substantially raised there. But I want to mention another consideration as well, which bears on human rights. It is the surprising geometry according to which, at a certain point, universalism and localism — and much of the material to be reviewed below will be intensely local — curve around from their divergent trajectories and touch.

The historical turn

This book comes on the heels of an 'historical turn' in writing about human rights, evinced by a spate of publications dealing with the history of human rights that appeared in the later 2000s and 2010s. Miia Halme-Tuomisaari and Pamela Slotte remark on the salutary effect of this body of work in prompting a reconsideration of what they term the 'textbook narrative of origins' — so-called because it, or something like it, is recounted in the opening chapters of many international protection of human rights textbooks.[35] As Halme-Tuomisaari and Slotte characterise it, the textbook narrative of origins has two variants.

One variant presents the Enlightenment as the 'moment of birth' of human rights, and emphasises the importance of the American and French

32. See, e.g., Rodney Hilton (ed.), *The Transition from Feudalism to Capitalism* (London: Verso, 1976).
33. Ellen Meiksins Wood, *The Pristine Culture of Capitalism* (London: Verso, 1991), 1. See also Ellen Meiksins Wood, *The Origin of Capitalism: A Longer View* (London: Verso, 2002).
34. See, e.g., Henry Heller, *The Birth of Capitalism* (London: Pluto Press, 2011); and Alexander Anievas and Kerem Nişancıoğlu, *How the West Came to Rule* (London: Pluto Press, 2015).
35. Miia Halme-Tuomisaari and Pamela Slotte, 'Revisiting the Origins of Human Rights: Introduction', in Pamela Slotte and Miia Halme-Tuomisaari (eds.), *Revisiting the Origins of Human Rights* (Cambridge: Cambridge University Press, 2015), 1.

Revolutions and of the declarations of rights they respectively inspired. According to this account, the influence of human rights then grew and spread over the succeeding centuries, leading eventually to the adoption of the Universal Declaration of Human Rights in 1948, and thence to the various legal and institutional developments and the changes in policy and practice that have followed it. The other variant instead celebrates the Universal Declaration of Human Rights as itself the foundational moment of the phenomenon of human rights. Portraying the interwar period as a time devoid of rights initiatives, this account tells of the advent of a new era that could begin only once the world's conscience had been awakened by the Holocaust, and by the need to ensure that such atrocities would never occur again.[36]

Halme-Tuomisaari and Slotte observe that, '[d]espite their differences', both versions 'convey the same message . . . [of] unilinear progress and global improvement'. Both variants (and most explicitly the first) also depict human rights as having their roots in Euro-American experience, so that 'the textbook narrative becomes simultaneously [a] story of the inevitable ideological triumph of the Western, liberal world'.[37] This creates problems for the legitimacy of the international human rights regime, and fuels perceptions that that regime is the latest iteration of the 'civilising mission' deployed to rationalise colonial rule. To address these perceptions, scholars and interested organisations have undertaken to show that basic tenets of human rights can be found throughout the world in diverse traditions. However, as Halme-Tuomisaari and Slotte again note, that writing does not stray very far from the textbook narrative of origins, inasmuch as it uses 'cross-cultural' history to affirm and extol the steady rise of human rights.[38]

A forceful challenge to human rights history-writing in this mode was put forward by Samuel Moyn in *The Last Utopia*, mentioned above. The use of 'world history as raw material for the progressive ascent of international human rights . . . [cannot] reveal the true origins' of human rights, he writes. It simply provides 'recent enthusiasms with uplifting backstories'.[39] And

36. See ibid, 5–6.
37. Ibid, 6–7. See also Joseph Slaughter, 'Hijacking Human Rights: Neoliberalism, the New Historiography, and the End of the Third World', *Human Rights Quarterly* 40(4) (2018) 735 (arguing that the Euro-American 'rediscovery' of human rights in the 1970s is instead a neoliberal 'hijacking' of human rights).
38. Miia Halme-Tuomisaari and Pamela Slotte, 'Revisiting the Origins of Human Rights: Introduction', in Pamela Slotte and Miia Halme-Tuomisaari (eds.), *Revisiting the Origins of Human Rights* (Cambridge: Cambridge University Press, 2015), 1, 9.
39. Samuel Moyn, *The Last Utopia* (Cambridge, MA: Harvard University Press, 2010), 5.

again, in a later work, 'human rights history should turn away from ransacking the past as if it provided good support for the astonishingly specific international movement of the last few decades'.[40] It was Moyn's argument that 'human rights . . . emerged in the 1970s', and they emerged 'seemingly from nowhere'.[41] This claim sparked extensive debate, and has been an immensely significant stimulus for the recent reconsideration of the textbook narrative of origins. For the most part, the disagreement revolves around the theme of continuity and discontinuity. Thus, in Christopher McCrudden's summary, scholars are divided over 'continuity and rupture: to what extent is our understanding of human rights a reflection of past uses or is it something new, representing a radical break from these past uses?'[42]

McCrudden's own answer is that this is a 'false dichotomy'; 'the history of human rights is both one of continuity and discontinuity'. And while Moyn is 'correct to identify several important discontinuities', and more generally, to criticise representations of human rights as the inevitable triumph of enlightened consciousness (or awakened conscience), he 'underestimates several critically important continuities'.[43] Likewise, for Philip Alston, Moyn 'exaggerates the discontinuities'.[44] In response, Moyn has said that he 'never denied continuities absolutely', but that in this context, what is paramount to grasp is the contingency of relevant developments, and their often accidental character, stop-start temporality, and mostly very recent date. It follows that the 'discontinuities are both more massive and more interesting' than the continuities.[45]

In these discussions of the genesis or 'moment of birth' of human rights, there is a common pattern reflected in the work of both exponents and critics of the textbook narrative of origins, in which authors canvass a range of possibilities, often going back to antiquity, and then set out the case for their proposed start-date. Yet, as Michael Freeman observes, '[b]efore we can study

40. Samuel Moyn, *Human Rights and the Uses of History* (London: Verso, 2014), xiii.
41. Samuel Moyn, *The Last Utopia* (Cambridge, MA: Harvard University Press, 2010), 3. On this time-frame, see also Jan Eckel and Samuel Moyn (eds.), *The Breakthrough: Human Rights in the 1970s* (Philadelphia: University of Pennsylvania Press, 2014).
42. Christopher McCrudden, 'Human Rights Histories', *Oxford Journal of Legal Studies* 35(1) (2015) 179, 180.
43. Ibid, 181 (emphasis omitted), 187.
44. Philip Alston, 'Does the Past Matter? On the Origins of Human Rights', *Harvard Law Review* 126(7) (2013) 2043, 2078.
45. Samuel Moyn, 'The Continuing Perplexities of Human Rights', *Qui Parle* 22(1) (2013) 95, 96. Exploring the interrelation of human rights to the history of social justice, Samuel Moyn, *Not Enough: Human Rights in an Unequal World* (Cambridge, MA: Harvard University Press, 2018) traces a wider arc than *The Last Utopia*.

the history of human rights . . ., we have to know what it is the history of'.[46] Similarly, Alston charges that those writing human rights histories all too frequently 'fail to provide any meaningful definition to confine the scope of the inquiry'.[47] Are they writing a history of the human rights 'movement', the human rights 'regime', the human rights 'legal system', or the human rights 'idea'?

There can be no singular history, no unitary origin, of human rights because human rights are not one thing. Importantly, however, this is not just a matter of complexity, but also of the self-otherness to which I made reference earlier. As indeed in the case of capitalism, the debate over origins is in part a debate over the essential characteristics or defining properties of that which originated — what it is to 'know' that phenomenon (to use Freeman's word). Stefan-Ludwig Hoffmann writes that '[o]nly in the second half of the twentieth century did human rights develop into a political and legal vocabulary for confronting abuses of disciplinary state power',[48] without registering that the most controversial element of that sentence may be the identification of human rights with a political and legal vocabulary for confronting abuses of disciplinary state power.

This book investigates sources from the past that are pertinent to our understanding of human rights, but it does not seek to answer the question of when (or where and why) human rights began. It focuses on the late eighteenth century as the moment when the rights of man 'arrived' in English politics and culture, in the sense of entering the stream of public discourse in the country and becoming a topic on which people staked out positions. In using the phrase 'the rights of man', it keeps open the question of that concept's relation, both to earlier notions of rights, humanity, and their connectedness (which, as indicated, the book also explores), and to human rights in the present.

The story I have to tell bears on the history of an idea and its relationship to change in the material conditions of life. I can concretise what I mean by

46. Michael Freeman, *Human Rights* (Cambridge: Polity Press, 2002), 14.
47. Philip Alston, 'Does the Past Matter? On the Origins of Human Rights', *Harvard Law Review* 126(7) (2013) 2043, 2071.
48. Stefan-Ludwig Hoffmann, 'Introduction: Genealogies of Human Rights', in Stefan-Ludwig Hoffmann (ed.), *Human Rights in the Twentieth Century* (Cambridge: Cambridge University Press, 2011), 1–2. See also Stefan-Ludwig Hoffmann, 'Human Rights and History', *Past and Present* 232 (2016) 279 ('[pushing] the historical revisionism of Moyn and others even further [with the argument] that we can first speak of individual human rights as a basic concept . . ., that is, a contested, irreplaceable and consequential concept of global politics, only in the 1990s, after the end of the Cold War' (282)).

that by touching on another of the works that formed part of the historical turn in writing about human rights of the later 2000s and 2010s. In *Inventing Human Rights*, Lynn Hunt advances an interesting argument about how the emergence of the novel as a literary form in the eighteenth century was crucial to the development of the idea of human rights, in that it helped to foster the experience of empathy.[49] Early epistolatory novels such as Samuel Richardson's *Pamela* (1740) and *Clarissa* (1747–8) 'reinforced the notion of a community based on autonomous, empathetic individuals who could relate beyond their immediate families, religious affiliations, or even nations to greater universal values', she maintains. 'Readers learned to appreciate the emotional intensity of the ordinary and the capacity of people like themselves to create on their own a moral world. Human rights grew out of the seedbed sowed by these feelings.'[50]

If human rights grew out of the seedbed sowed by the novel, what was the seedbed out of which, for its part, the novel grew? In *The Country and the City*, Raymond Williams also points to developments of the eighteenth century in England.[51] He writes of the heightened pressure on the remaining peasantry, and of 'an increasingly regular structure of tenant farmers and wage-labourers: the social relationships that we can properly call those of agrarian capitalism'. He comments that the 'transition from feudal and immediately post-feudal arrangements to this developing agrarian capitalism is of course immensely complicated', but that its consequences were clear enough. Landowners, though outwardly and in political terms still an aristocracy, now lived 'by a calculation of rents'. No longer simply inheritances with fixed incomes, landed estates became opportunities for investment. 'Social relations which stood in the way of this . . . were then steadily and at times ruthlessly broken down.'[52]

Williams argues that the 'crisis of values which resulted from these changes [was] enacted in varying ways in eighteenth-century literature'. He refers to the appearance in poetry of 'a deep and melancholy consciousness of change and loss'. But he says that, before that came to light, 'there was a lively engagement with the human consequences of the new institutions and emphases', and that 'it was in just this interest that the novel emerged as the most creative form of the time'. The novels of Richardson and others took up in new

49. Lynn Hunt, *Inventing Human Rights* (New York: W.W. Norton, 2007).
50. Ibid, 32, 58.
51. Raymond Williams, *The Country and the City* (Nottingham: Spokesman, 2011).
52. Ibid, 60–61.

ways '[t]he problems of love and marriage, in a society dominated by issues of property in land'. 'What is dramatised' in these novels, writes Williams, 'is the long process of choice between economic advantage and other ideas of value'.[53]

Money and death

Late in his life, and many years after the day he scrawled on the wall of a cave in the cliffs facing Marsden Rock, Spence published a collection of his songs, with a prefatory note that spoke of the 'miscarriage of the mighty struggle made in our day against oppression'. He went on: 'Let us then gather up the fragments . . . and let the wellwishers of the human race, bind up such valuable tracts as fall in their way', so that 'future generations . . . [may] profit more by them than we have done, and avoid our mistakes'.[54] I close this introductory chapter with a final word about the background to my own effort, at another moment of miscarried emancipation, to 'gather up the fragments' in the pages that follow.

I am not an historian. My connection to human rights comes from the study of international human rights law. In particular, and inspired by a rich and ever expanding critical literature, it comes from the study of the contradictoriness and double-edged effects of human rights, and of the difficulty that international law and institutions seem to have in grappling with the conditions in which abuses occur and recur. By contradictoriness and double-edged effects, I have in mind the degree to which, and the ways in which, human rights are at once pivotal and marginal, potent and ineffective, subversive and hegemonic. As Raj Patel suggests, reprising an old theme, if you have no money, the main human rights you seem to have in today's 'market society . . . [are] to do nothing, to have very little and to die young'.[55]

The final chapter of this book will refer to the play *Bingo* by Edward Bond, first performed in 1973.[56] In introducing the play, Bond underlines

53. Ibid, 61. Hunt alludes to discussions like Williams's, explaining that 'whatever the reasons for the rise of the novel', she is 'concerned with its psychological effects and how they connect to the emergence of human rights'. See Lynn Hunt, *Inventing Human Rights* (New York: W.W. Norton, 2007), 41.
54. Thomas Spence, *Spence's Songs* (London: Seale and Bates, 1807), 1, reprinted in H.T. Dickinson, *The Political Works of Thomas Spence* (Newcastle upon Tyne: Avero, 1982), 130.
55. Raj Patel, *The Value of Nothing* (London: Portobello, 2011), 112–13.
56. See chap. 10 below.

its subtitle — *Scenes of money and death* — and remarks that '[w]e live in a closed society where you need money to live. You earn it, borrow it, or steal it . . . [T]here's no greenwood to escape into any more, it's been cut down'. As Bond sees it, '[w]e have no natural rights, only rights granted and protected by money', and 'when you live by money you must live by [its laws and conventions]'.[57] I quote these passages now because they bring together in a few short lines the matters that will preoccupy us in this book — money, death, enclosure, trees, natural rights and living. And with that, the playwright sends us on our way.

57. Edward Bond, *Plays: 3* (London: Methuen Drama, 1987), 6–7.

2

Enclosure and its Critics

New social criticism

Thomas More's *Utopia*, first published in 1516, is well known for its description of the 'no place' that is also a 'good place'.[1] His fictional island has come to name a whole genre of writing about ideal societies and alternative worlds. But if More's text inaugurated a new and still flourishing literary genre, historians tell us that it also stands at the beginning of a new kind of social thought. As Ellen Wood and Neal Wood explain, 'for the first time in history, there emerged [in sixteenth-century England] a large and detailed body of social criticism which scathingly denounced the plight of the impoverished majority'.[2] More than that, this body of social criticism 'did not just commiserate with the poor but boldly and in forthright language assigned responsibility for their appalling circumstances to the greed and power of acquisitive' others.[3] Wood and Wood are quick to point out that the writers in question were by no means revolutionaries. These critics did not seek to overturn the established order. Rather, they developed an analysis which aimed to highlight practices and processes that were endangering that order and threatening to break it apart.

This chapter takes up the work of some of these early English social critics. Their writing was a response to, and reflection of, great changes that were afoot in their country at the time, and we will need to begin with brief reference to those changes, or at least to the ones they took to be most consequential.

1. Thomas More, *Utopia*, in George Logan and Robert Adams (eds.), *Thomas More: Utopia* (Cambridge: Cambridge University Press, rev. ed., 2002), 1. On *Utopia* today, see chap. 10 below.
2. Ellen Meiksins Wood and Neal Wood, *A Trumpet of Sedition: Political Theory and the Rise of Capitalism 1509–1688* (London: Pluto Press, 1997), 27.
3. Ibid.

A False Tree of Liberty. Susan Marks, Oxford University Press (2019). © Susan Marks.
DOI: 10.1093/oso/9780199675456.003.0002

We will then consider More's *Utopia*, along with Edmund Dudley's earlier *The Tree of Commonwealth* and Robert Crowley's later *The Way to Wealth* and other works. Writing in 1510, Dudley was the first of the 'new' social critics, or maybe a late precursor.[4] He gestures towards the themes that will be of interest to us, rather than doing much to elaborate them. Crowley wrote in the 1540s and 50s, and produced some of the most biting social commentary of his age. He was among the so-called 'Commonwealthmen' of mid-Tudor England, the group of prominent clerics and polemicists that barred (almost) no holds in their diagnosis of the state of the nation, and became, for a time, the scourge of, or at any rate purveyor of unwelcome truths to, the English ruling classes. Read together, these texts testify to a gathering unease about the direction in which their authors' society was going, linked to a very specific set of concerns about what this meant and where it would lead.

Neither fully capitalist nor feudal

To Karl Marx, as to many later analysts, late fifteenth- and early sixteenth-century England was where the prelude was played to the foundation of the capitalist mode of production.[5] If capitalism did not assume its 'developed' form until much later (in the eighteenth or early nineteenth century), and if feudalism had come to an end around the late fourteenth or early fifteenth century, then '[w]e are left', Jane Whittle writes, 'with a lengthy period of time which is neither fully capitalist nor feudal'.[6] Debate on England's transition to capitalism — on how, why and exactly when it occurred, and on its relation to changes elsewhere — is, as already noted, intense and ongoing.[7] For our purposes, it will be sufficient to notice developments which were striking at the time, even if their enmeshment with long-term trends and structural transformations could not at that stage be known. In particular, our three authors were exercised, as we shall see, by a series of developments affecting access to land — that then being, in one way or another, the basis of most livelihoods.

Access to land was organised during this period at manorial level. Manors were villages in which land was worked by people who held tenancies from

4. Neal Wood, *Foundations of Political Economy: Some Early Tudor Views on State and Society* (Berkeley: University of California Press, 1994), 70.
5. See Karl Marx, *Capital, Vol. 1* (London: Penguin, 1976), 878.
6. Jane Whittle, *The Development of Agrarian Capitalism: Land and Labour in Norfolk 1440–1580* (Oxford: Clarendon Press, 2000), 11.
7. See chap. 1 above.

a lord. For their part, lords had long ceased to be a warrior aristocracy; their earlier military capabilities were now firmly centralised in the state. At the same time, since serfdom had been largely abolished, they had disengaged from agricultural production. Instead, they had become landlords, making their living from the collection of rent. Under the established system of land tenure, tenancies were of three principal types: freehold, leasehold and copyhold. Freehold tenants had relatively secure tenure and paid only nominal rent. Leasehold tenants held their land for periods of years, or for lives, and sometimes from year to year ('at will'); their rent could be increased, and additional charges ('fines') also levied, upon renewal or fresh grant. Copyhold tenants were, in most places, the vast bulk of the tenantry at the end of the fifteenth century. They were so called because a copy of their admission to tenancy was inscribed in the manor court roll. Copyhold tenants occupied what was known as 'customary land', and they did so, as it was said, 'according to the customs of the manor'. Customs varied from manor to manor, but in many cases the rents and fines associated with copyhold tenancies were fixed; in some cases they remained fixed even upon inheritance. Moreover, unlike leasehold rents, copyhold rents were set at a rate designed to monetise earlier feudal obligations and did not reflect the value of the land as a source of rental income.

Against this background, one development of the late fifteenth and early sixteenth centuries was the conversion of copyhold tenancies into leasehold tenancies. Lords found a variety of expedients for doing this, but however it was accomplished, the effect was to enable the rents and fines of more tenants to be increased more easily and quickly, and to whatever rates the lord could command. Where tenancies were converted to leasehold, customary rights and expectations could be set aside, and the custom of the manor dismissed as an archaic relic of earlier times, outmoded and inoperative. A second development of the period was the rent hikes and evictions that then followed. Contemporaries complained of the 'racking' of rents — the charging of an annual rent that was equivalent to the whole value of a landholding — and of the exaction of exorbitant fines upon the granting or renewal of leases. They also complained of 'lease-mongering' — the buying up of leases for subletting at higher rents.

Part of the context for these unwelcome practices was a third development which compounded the changes affecting tenements: rising prices. Of course, the price of grain had always fluctuated according to the harvest, but historical research has shown that sixteenth-century England saw for the first time the phenomenon of sustained inflation. To contemporaries, high prices were a sign of recourse to the manipulative market practices of 'forestalling' (keeping goods away from the market in order to make them scarce and boost their price), 'regrating' (buying up goods in order to sell them at a higher price in the same or a nearby market) and 'engrossing' (cornering the market in a good and using the resultant monopoly power to increase its price). In fact, engrossing referred not only to an abusive practice in the market for grain and other daily necessities. Within the emergent market in land, it also referred to the expansion or amalgamation of landholdings to create large farms — that is to say, farms which could be the basis of profitable businesses. This was a fourth development that caused widespread consternation, contributing as it did to driving into landlessness poorer tenants who got edged out in the newly competitive conditions.

A final, crucial development was, and still is, sometimes invoked as a shorthand for all the rest: enclosure.[8] The phenomenon of enclosure has a long and complicated history in England, with different phases and considerable regional divergences. To understand its broad lines in this early period, it is necessary to recall something of the structure of agricultural activity in medieval times. Most villages had some arable fields and meadows, along with areas of permanent pasture ('commons') and rougher, marginal land known as 'waste'. Under the 'open-field system', the arable fields were divided into long rectangles or 'strips', and individuals worked particular strips scattered across the unfenced — 'open' — fields. After the harvest, the strips were available to all the villagers, who had the right to gather leftover grain ('glean'). Arrangements varied, but in some places there was also a right to graze animals on the open fields and meadows after the harvest and during fallow periods. Further use-rights applied to the commons and wastes. These were shared areas under village control which provided the main land for keeping animals and served additionally as sources of fuel, animal feed, building materials, artisanal supplies and supplementary food.

Depending on the locality, villagers might have rights with respect to the commons and wastes that included, alongside their right of grazing, the right to take wood, cut turf and dig peat for fuel, the right to gather acorns and

8. See, e.g., Roger Manning, *Village Revolts: Social Protest and Popular Disturbances in England, 1509–1640* (Oxford: Clarendon Press, 1988), 33 (on contemporaries' use of the term as shorthand), and Christopher Hill, *Liberty Against the Law* (London: Allen Lane, 1996), 326 (for an example of 'shorthand' use in recent historical scholarship).

beech-mast as feed for pigs, the right to collect stone, gravel, slate, or clay for repairing houses, barns and roads, the right to take rushes and sticks for making baskets and brooms, and the right to collect berries, herbs and fruits in season. Insofar as the available resources were limited, these rights were subject to restriction ('stinting'), for instance, on the number of animals each person was allowed to keep on the commons and wastes, or the days on which each person could gather wood. The open-field system was not used in all parts of the country. Whether because the system had never been used, or because earlier generations had considered that it no longer met their needs, land was, in some places, held 'in severalty', rather than wholly or partly in common. In such areas, fields were typically enclosed by hedges or walls, and access was controlled by individual owners. From the late fifteenth and early sixteenth centuries, however, the nature and scale of what came to be called 'enclosure' altered significantly, as did its social consequences.

Village lands began to be enclosed for the sake of commercial farming by upwardly mobile peasants in collaboration with lords, who gained by virtue of the greater rents which such peasants would then be able to pay. This often occurred as part of a scheme of land engrossment, though both enclosure and engrossment were also carried out separately. Owing to the high price of English wool on international markets, an initial focus was sheep farming. Indeed, it has been suggested that the 'most striking single aspect of the English landscape [in this period] was that there were about three sheep to every human being'.[9] On the one hand, arable land was enclosed and converted into sheep pasture. On the other hand, commons and wastes were also filled with sheep and wholly or partially enclosed. Again, a variety of expedients were used. Where open-field land was concerned, an encloser might buy or exchange strips with a view to acquiring contiguous holdings, which could then be removed from the open-field system. Where commons and wastes were concerned, an encloser might simply appropriate land to his own use, disregarding restrictive stints and then securing village approval to regularise this situation, with or without the provision of compensatory land elsewhere. Whatever method was deployed, the significance of enclosure was to extinguish the use-rights — 'rights of common' or 'common rights' — that had previously applied to the land and reallocate it for exclusive possession by the encloser.

9. The human population at this time was around two and a half to three million. See W. G. Hoskins, *The Making of the English Landscape* (London: Pelican, 2nd ed., 1970), 137.

Enclosure brought with it, or reinforced the advent of, two fateful things. One was social differentiation. Out of the earlier medieval triad of clergy, nobility and peasantry or commonalty, there emerged the beginnings of a new triad, made up of an increasingly aggressive rentier class and a peasantry that was splitting into a class of entrepreneurial tenant-farmers and a class of wholly or partly landless poor. The latter — the vast bulk of the population — were enclosure's losers. The extent of their loss remains a matter of debate among historians, but what is clear is that, to contemporaries, the combined effect of conversion to leasehold tenure, rent and fine rises, engrossment of farms and enclosure was to produce novel and alarming levels of destitution, dislocation and, in the language of the day, 'depopulation'. Peasants had long used wage-labour as a means of supplementing household income, but once access to land was gone, 'vagabondage' in search of work became a desperate necessity.

The second thing that came with enclosure was a new way of thinking about collective life (including both social relationships and the relationships between people and the world around them), along with new concepts and new legal forms. We will return to amplify on this later. For the moment, historian Joan Thirsk will hold the place. She writes: '[a]fter enclosure, when every man could fence his own piece of territory and warn his neighbours off, the discipline of sharing things fairly with one's neighbours was relaxed, and every household became an island unto itself. This was the great revolution in men's lives, greater than all the economic changes following enclosure.'[10] Contemporaries saw this too, though they had their own idiom for capturing it. To gain a sense of that idiom, and of approaches to the upheavals of the age more generally, let us turn now to our three authors.

A core right dangerous

Edmund Dudley was a prominent lawyer and high official who lost royal favour when Henry VIII acceded to the English throne in 1509. After conviction for treason, he composed *The Tree of Commonwealth* whilst awaiting execution in the Tower of London.[11] The text stands in the tradition of political

10. Joan Thirsk, 'Enclosing and Engrossing', in Joan Thirsk (ed.), *Agrarian History of England and Wales, Vol. IV 1500–1640* (Cambridge: Cambridge University Press, 1967), 200, 255.
11. D. M. Brodie (ed.), *The Tree of Commonwealth: A Treatise Written by Edmund Dudley* (Cambridge: Cambridge University Press, 1948). Neal Wood suggests that Dudley wrote the text 'perhaps in a last desperate bid to save himself'; see Neal Wood, *Foundations of Political*

advice-books or manuals for the prince. Dudley's only surviving publication, it sets out his views on good government and the particular challenges he saw it as facing in contemporary conditions. In putting 'commonwealth' in his title, he seems to have wanted to emphasise that his discussion dealt with the people as a whole, rather than only the most powerful and privileged persons or groups within it. His intention seems to have been to signal that good government was necessarily government in the collective interest and for the common good. It is believed that he was among the first to use the word 'commonwealth' in that way.[12] The now archaic phrase 'common weal' was well established in his time, though it had acquired an awkward, if fascinating, ambiguity.[13] On the one hand, it too referred to the people considered as a whole. On the other hand, it had also taken on a more subversive meaning, coming to be associated with the abolition of distinctions between social groups, the unification of the people. That latter meaning is at odds with Dudley's explicit argument, so we may presume that he did not intend it. Perhaps something of it clung to his 'commonwealth' nonetheless.

Dudley delivers his advice in the form of an allegory, in which his meaning is conveyed through some rather elaborate imagery involving a tree. He begins by proposing that the 'comon wealth of this realme . . . may be resemblid to a faier and mighte tree'.[14] We are invited to picture the tree 'growing in a faier feild or pasture, under the . . . shade wherof all beastes . . . are protectyd and comfortyd from heate and cold as the tyme requireth'.[15] Dudley suggests that '[i]n like maner all the subjectes of that realme wher this tree of comon welth doth sewerly [surely] growe are ther by holpen [helped] and relyved [relieved] from the highest degre to the lowest'.[16] Commentators observe that Dudley took for granted an hierarchical social order in which the population was divided into 'degrees' or 'estates', each with its distinctive place, status and characteristics. The question for him was how to achieve harmony between these

Economy: Some Early Tudor Views on State and Society (Berkeley: University of California Press, 1994), 70.

12. D. M. Brodie (ed.), *The Tree of Commonwealth: A Treatise Written by Edmund Dudley* (Cambridge: Cambridge University Press, 1948), 79.
13. See David Rollison, 'The Specter of the Commonalty: Class Struggle and the Commonweal in England before the Atlantic World', *William and Mary Quarterly* 63(2) (2006) 221, and *A Commonwealth of the People: Popular Politics and England's Long Social Revolution* (Cambridge: Cambridge University Press, 2010), esp. chap. 5.
14. Edmund Dudley, *The Tree of Commonwealth*, in D. M. Brodie (ed.), *The Tree of Commonwealth: A Treatise Written by Edmund Dudley* (Cambridge: Cambridge University Press, 1948), 21, 31.
15. Ibid.
16. Ibid, 31–32.

different social groups and weld them together into a prosperous and stable whole.[17] What would be necessary to strengthen the commonwealth — to make the tree grow *surely* — so that everyone would fulfil their responsibilities and be satisfied according to their rank?

Less than fifteen years earlier, a large-scale popular rebellion had broken out in Cornwall against the imposition of additional taxes, and Dudley was aware that his country's problems by no means ended there.[18] In the first place, then, he highlights the need for strong roots, of which the 'principall and cheif roote . . . in every Christen realme must be the love of god'.[19] Dudley adhered to the medieval vision of a Christian community in which good government meant first and foremost deepening the faith. Beyond that, he declares that the tree of commonwealth depends for its flourishing on four other roots: the fair administration of justice; honest dealing and the keeping of promises; concord among the inhabitants; and finally, peace in relations with other princes and realms. Regarding the third root (concord), he touches on the implications for the different social groups. Under the conventional scheme, the two main non-clerical groups were, as earlier recalled, the nobility and the common people or 'commonalty'.

Where the lords are concerned, Dudley emphasises the need for them not to be 'at variance one with an other'[20] and not to oppress their social inferiors. Disputes were obviously inimical to civil peace, and abuses of power likewise fostered insubordination and crime. As for the commonalty, he holds that their contribution to concord was not to 'grudge nor murmure to lyve in labor and pain, and the most parte of there tyme with the swete of ther face'.[21] 'Lett not them presume above ther owne degree', he writes, nor 'cloth them selfes in Lyverie of lordes', nor neglect 'ther rentes and paimentes [that] thei must make'.[22] At the same time, he warns that the 'chief of theis folke' — 'the substanciall marchauntes, the welthie grasiers and farmers' — should 'not use or covett greate lucre [money] of them [that] be lesse then thei'.[23] These wealthier members of the commonalty should not charge prices or pay rates

17. See Keith Wrightson, *Earthly Necessities: Economic Lives in Early Modern Britain* (New Haven, Yale University Press, 2000), 27–28.
18. On the Cornish rebellion of 1497, see Mark Stoyle, 'Cornish Rebellions, 1497–1648', *History Today* 47(5) (1997) 22.
19. Edmund Dudley, *The Tree of Commonwealth*, in D. M. Brodie (ed.), *The Tree of Commonwealth: A Treatise Written by Edmund Dudley* (Cambridge: Cambridge University Press, 1948), 21, 32.
20. Ibid, 41.
21. Ibid, 45.
22. Ibid, 45–46.
23. Ibid, 46.

that bring excessive profit, and they should refrain from usury and deceitful commercial practices. '[I]f your gaines be reasonable', he advises them, 'the Better [they] will abyde'.[24]

Dudley next explains that each of these four roots (after the love of God) bears a particular fruit. From the fair administration of justice is borne honourable dignity; from honest dealing and the keeping of promises, worldly prosperity; from concord among the inhabitants, tranquillity; and from external peace, good example.[25] Further developing his metaphor, he proposes that, in turn, each of those fruits has a 'perillous [core] within [it that] may in no wise be tochid [touched] but of necessytie be utterly refusyd'.[26] Again, there are four: unreasonable elation, vain delectation, lewd enterprise and glorification.[27] We can leave aside the first and last of these, which revolve primarily around spiritual transgressions. Turning then to the other two, vain delectation — the 'core righte dangerous' of the fruit of worldly prosperity[28] — is what happens 'when a man settyth his love greatly or howgely [hugely] on a thing'.[29] That is to say, it is an over-investment in things, a fetishism of possessions.

Dudley describes how this produces a pathology in which the prosperous man becomes alienated not only from God, but also from mankind and from himself. The man forgets that '[f]or all his prosperitie, what is he better [than] a mysarable man, having and suffering all the passions, disseases and infyrmities, aswell of the soule as of the bodie, equall [with] the poore ploughman, and oftentymes mutche worsse'.[30] 'Will any of thies diseases, passions or infyrmities forebere hym any moment of an hower [hour] for all his worldly prosperite', he rhetorically asks, 'or what beast, fowle or fysshe will obey [him] more therfore, or what beast or worme in his furie will forbere hym more then the poorest begger [that] goith?'[31] Dudley insists on this point. 'Loke', he says, 'when our glorious garmentes be don off, and we nakyd, what differens is then betwene us and the poore laborers . . . Also loke whether our naturall mother brought us not into this world with like sorrowes and

24. Ibid, 47.
25. Ibid, 51–59.
26. Ibid, 60.
27. Ibid, 68–92
28. Ibid, 77.
29. Ibid, 78.
30. Ibid, 81.
31. Ibid.

paines . . . [and look how, when] death comyth . . . all the treasure in the tower can not intreate hym for one daie.'[32]

The main point he wants to make is that, where worldly prosperity has a man in its thrall, it can so cloud his consciousness that he will stop at nothing to increase it. In the author's words, it can make him 'so gredy and desiorous [of wealth that] he forcyth not what pain or labor he takyth or doith to have [it]'.[33] What then of lewd enterprise, the perilous core of the fruit of tranquillity, itself the outgrowth of the root of concord within the realm? Here Dudley addresses particularly the commonalty, on the grounds that they form 'the greate nomber',[34] and hence most affect, and are affected by, the prospects for civil peace. 'Lewd' in his time meant ignorant, foolish or wicked, and Dudley seems to have intended by 'lewd enterprise', essentially, rebellion. He urges the poor to recognise that the will to insurrection rests on false promises. In their own interest, they should accept the established order, for the world, with all its inequalities, is as it must be. '[Y]e good comyners', he writes, 'for your owne eas dele not with this false core, but be contentyd with the fruite of tranquilitie.'[35]

We began this chapter by referring to a new breed of social critics that emerged in sixteenth-century England. On the evidence of *The Tree of Commonwealth*, it seems difficult to conceive of Edmund Dudley as anything other than a traditionalist and conservative. He adheres to the medieval idea of society as a divinely ordained hierarchy. He assumes that, within that hierarchy, there exist three estates which allocate to their members particular social roles and forms of life — the clergy, with their pre-eminent position in spiritual affairs, and the lay population comprising the nobility and commonalty. He treats good government as a matter of promoting harmony among the various estates, and ensuring that each plays its part. He holds that, to that end, the status quo must be identified with the interest of all, including those at the bottom of the social hierarchy. And he is in no doubt that it is incumbent upon those at the bottom of the social hierarchy to remain dutiful, obedient, and reconciled to their inferior status, despite their privations and indignities. Plainly there is not yet denunciation of the plight of the impoverished majority here. Nonetheless, in at least three ways, Dudley lays an important part of the basis for such a perspective.

32. Ibid, 81–82.
33. Ibid, 84.
34. Ibid, 55.
35. Ibid, 90.

First, he makes clear that a distinction must be drawn between the common people and the poor. Not all the common people are poor. It will be recalled that he has separate words for the 'chief of this folk', in which category he places substantial merchants and wealthy graziers and farmers. His analysis points to the development of fissures within the commonalty, and to the emergence of a new class of commercial men who are doing very well indeed — and not only from trade, but also from agriculture. Secondly, he brings into focus something of the preconditions and effects of this. Although he does not provide details, his account alludes to forms of excessive profit-taking that bear down grievously on the poor. Dudley worries that within worldly prosperity is a perilous core that can make those who have riches 'set their love greatly or hugely on a thing'. And once they have set their love on a thing, he is concerned that worldly prosperity can drive such people to a point where they become estranged from their humanity and indifferent to the 'pain or labour they take or do' to accumulate more things. Thirdly, and in consequence, he highlights that wealth may pose a problem for society, just as much as poverty. Or rather, he highlights that wealth and poverty may be linked. Thus, he counsels that 'reasonable gains' are sustainable, but a prudent prince should see to it that his subjects do not 'use or covet great lucre of them that be less than they'.

Sheep devouring men

It is said that Thomas More spoke to Edmund Dudley when the latter was on his way to the scaffold on Tower Hill.[36] More was himself to be executed in the same place and at the behest of the same king some twenty-five years later. A prolific author and prominent statesman and intellectual, he began *Utopia* in 1515 whilst in Flanders on a diplomatic mission to renegotiate the terms of trade in English wool for the Flemish cloth industry. The work was completed upon his return to London the following year, and was written in Latin, appearing only after his death in the first English translation.[37] The

36. Neal Wood, *Foundations of Political Economy: Some Early Tudor Views on State and Society* (Berkeley: University of California Press, 1994), 71.

37. More died in 1535. The first English translation of *Utopia*, by Ralph Robinson, appeared in 1551: see *A fruteful / and pleasaunt worke of the beste state of a publyue weale, and of the newe yle called Utopia: written in Lattine by Syr Thomas More knight, and translated into Englyshe by Raphe Robynson* (London: Alsop, 1624).

text is framed as an encounter between the narrator (whom he calls Thomas More), his friend Peter Giles (secretary to the municipality of Antwerp) and the mysterious Raphael Hythloday (a Portuguese traveller and philosopher). In the garden of the narrator's house in Antwerp, the three '[sit] down on a bench covered with grassy turf to talk together'.[38]

Hythloday's travels have taken him to many places, including the island of Utopia, and in the best known sections of the book he relates to Giles and the narrator his impressions of that island, and describes the institutions that make its inhabitants the happiest, healthiest and most enlightened people in the whole world. Before getting to that, however, Hythloday tells of a visit to another island, England, and of a conversation he had there over dinner on the subject of administration of justice. An English lawyer was defending the use of harsh punishments for theft. Hythloday reports that he questioned both the justice and the efficacy of such punishments, and invited the lawyer to consider why people commit theft. Hythloday's argument was that they commit theft because they are destitute, '[a]nd a man of courage is more easily persuaded to steal than to beg'.[39] Why then were people destitute? Hythloday says that he put to the lawyer a reason particular 'to you Englishmen', namely that '[y]our sheep . . . that commonly are so meek and eat so little; now . . . have become so greedy and fierce that they devour human beings themselves. They devastate and depopulate fields, houses and towns.'[40] In other words, his suggestion was that people in England were destitute because they were being dispossessed of land to make way for sheep; in *Utopia*'s now famous image, sheep were devouring human beings. In the passages that follow, More has Hythloday present a withering account of why and how this was occurring.

The general problem, Hythloday contends, is that 'the nobility and gentry . . . are not content with the old rents that the land yielded to their predecessors. Living in idleness and luxury without doing society any good no longer satisfies them; they have to do positive harm.' Specifically, their mission is to 'leave no land free for the plough'. They 'enclose every acre for pasture; they destroy houses and abolish towns, keeping the churches — but only for sheep-barns'. He explains that when land is enclosed, 'tenants are ejected; and some are stripped of their belongings by trickery or brute force,

38. Thomas More, *Utopia*, in George Logan and Robert Adams (eds.), *Thomas More: Utopia* (Cambridge: Cambridge University Press, rev. ed., 2002), 1, 11.
39. Ibid, 20.
40. Ibid, 18.

or, wearied by constant harassment, are driven to sell them'. Whatever the course of events, the poor are 'forced to move out', and 'what finally remains for them but to steal . . . or to wander and beg?'[41] Their livelihoods have been taken away, and there is no other work by which they might sustain themselves. Sheep farms cannot avail them, as animal husbandry requires little labour compared to the cultivation of crops: '[o]ne herdsman or shepherd can look after a flock of beasts large enough to stock an area that used to require many hands to make it grow crops'.[42] Nor is it only peasants who are affected. The 'enclosing has led to sharply rising food prices'. And because the wool trade is 'concentrated in so few hands . . ., and these so rich, that the owners are never pressed to sell until they have a mind to', the 'price of raw wool has risen' too, so that poor people 'who used to make cloth can no longer afford it, and so great numbers are forced from work to idleness'.[43]

All this is leading to a situation, continues Hythloday, whereby 'your island' — England — 'which seemed specially fortunate . . . will be ruined by the crass avarice of a few'.[44] And that ruination will be all the greater to the extent that 'poverty and scarcity . . . exist side by side with wanton luxury', reflected in 'ostentatious dress and gourmandising'. If the earlier felicity of the English is to be brought back, it will be necessary to '[b]anish these blights, [and] make those who have ruined farmhouses and villages restore them'. '[T]he right of the rich to buy up anything and everything, and then to exercise a kind of monopoly' will have to be restricted. 'Let agriculture be restored, and the wool-manfacture revived as an honest trade.'[45] Hythloday concludes the tale of his visit to England with a warning he professes to have given to his legal interlocutor: '[U]nless you cure these evils it is futile to boast of your justice in punishing theft. Your policy may look superficially like justice, but in reality it is neither just nor expedient.' For 'you first [make] [the poor] thieves and then [punish] them for it'.[46]

Life in Utopia, of course, is quite different to this. As Hythloday goes on to describe it, there is universal plenty, and civil peace reigns. An important tenet of Utopian society is that there is no private property. Hythloday comments that, 'wherever you have private property, and money is the measure

41. Ibid, 18–19.
42. Ibid, 19.
43. Ibid.
44. Ibid, 20.
45. Ibid.
46. Ibid.

of all things, it is hardly ever possible for a commonwealth to be just or prosperous — unless you . . . suppose happiness can be found where the good things of life are divided among the very few'. For '[h]owever abundant goods may be, . . . a handful of men end up sharing the whole pile, and the rest are left in poverty'.[47] Without private property, Utopians enjoy a 'fair [and] just distribution of goods'.[48] They cooperate to bring in the harvest, and everyone practises a trade. At the market-place no-one asks for more than he or she needs, and everyone receives what they ask for; no money changes hands, and nothing else is given in exchange. The people of Utopia are energetic, industrious and learned. Everyone works, but normal working hours are not long, and profitable use is made of leisure time. Slavery exists rather as a penalty upon (rare) conviction of a crime than as a form of property or mode of production.

In general, and thanks to the fact that everyone in Utopia works 'at useful trades', 'there is an abundance of everything'.[49] But when 'a barren year of failed harvests' arrives, the available grain is equitably divided among the population as a whole, rather than being kept in the 'barns of the rich'.[50] Hythloday says that the Utopians have achieved 'this republic which I wish all mankind would imitate. Through the plan of living which they have adopted, they have laid the foundations of a commonwealth that is not only very happy but also, as far as human prescience can tell, likely to last for ever', inasmuch as they have 'torn up the seeds of ambition and faction at home', and created 'institutions healthy' enough to withstand pressures from abroad.[51]

After Hythloday has finished speaking, the narrator commends the constitution of the Utopians and the account which Hythloday has given of it, and tells his company that he will find 'some other time for thinking of these matters more deeply, and for talking them over in more detail'. He then adds as an aside that Hythloday clearly has great knowledge of the world, but 'I can hardly agree with everything he said'. At the same time — and with this the book closes — 'I freely confess that in the Utopian commonwealth there are very many features that in our own societies I would wish rather than expect to see'.[52]

47. Ibid, 37–38.
48. Ibid, 38.
49. Ibid, 53.
50. Ibid, 105.
51. Ibid, 106.
52. Ibid, 107.

To speak of expectation is to evoke real possibilities, even if ones that do not, in the event, come to pass. Wish, on the other hand, is the language of counterfactual desire. More's narrator leaves us, then, with the thought that there can be no Utopia. Yet he also proposes that that does not put the subject to an end; as he says, time needs to be found for reflecting on these matters more deeply and talking them over in more detail. It is not difficult to imagine the narrator expressing the author's own opinion when he makes that final proposal. But to what extent are we to identify the narrator's perspective with More's more generally? To what extent are we to appraise Hythloday's views as worthy of serious consideration? (Just as the word 'utopia' evokes the Greek for both 'no place' and its near-homonym 'a good place', so Hythloday's name hovers between 'purveyor of nonsense' and 'destroyer of nonsense'.)[53] Is More inviting his early sixteenth-century English countrymen — or rather, the Latin-literate elite among them — to admire the steady, disciplined and well-ordered Utopia, or is he inviting them to criticise or deride it?[54] How is the relation between Hythloday's two island stories to be understood? If More's text is shrouded in ambiguity, what is clear is that it raises important issues of his day concerning politics, society and economy.

In particular, it raises issues to do with property ownership and with the phenomena of enclosure and engrossment. As noted earlier, a key aspect of the context for these phenomena in late fifteenth- and early sixteenth-century England was the high price of wool on international markets. The main markets were in Flanders, which was at that time a leading centre for the dyeing and finishing of cloth. Sent to Antwerp as part of a wool trade delegation, More was well placed to observe the significance of commercial sheep farming and the wealth it was generating for his country. At the same time, there could be no mistaking that this came at a cost. In *Utopia* he gives voice to the view that it came at a very considerable cost. As Andrew McRae explains, More's image of sheep devouring human beings suggests a 'vision of an agrarian world turned upside down'.[55] The point was not just that human beings should be eating sheep, rather than sheep eating — consuming the livelihoods, and laying waste to the lives, of — human beings. It was also that, for More and his contemporaries, a 'powerful ideal of socio-economic

53. See Nigel Wilson, 'The Name Hythlodaeus', *Moreana* 29(110, 2) (1992) 33.
54. *Utopia* was first published in Leuven, under the editorship of More's friend Erasmus. Accordingly, it had from the outset a wider, European readership.
55. Andrew McRae, *God Speed the Plough: The Representation of Agrarian England 1500–1660* (Cambridge: Cambridge University Press, 1996), 10.

order in the countryside' laid down that 'sheep-rearing [should be] universally subordinated to the production of grain', rather than grain-production being subordinated to sheep-rearing.[56] The main product of sheep-rearing was wool, and grain was the staple food — how could anything matter more than food? Likewise part of that ideal was that landlords '[acknowledged] a moral duty towards their tenants'.[57] This too was reversed when tenants were dispossessed of their holdings and deprived of their rights to make way for profitable animal husbandry. How could these things happen?

Like Dudley, More presents an analysis that emphasises the greed of the nobility and gentry ('not content with the old rents that the land yielded to their predecessors'), along with their corruption by luxury ('ostentatious dress and gourmandising'). He also highlights the exploitative relation according to which, as he puts it in another section of the text, landlords 'live idly like drones off the labour of others, their tenants whom they bleed white by constantly raising their rents'.[58] And, of course, with Hythloday's famous description of Utopia, he provides a revealing foil that prompts critical scrutiny of the conceptual framework within which households were being reconstituted as metaphorical islands. Set against the background of a society in which there is no private property, the people enjoy a fair and just distribution of goods, and the public interest is pursued by all, enclosure — the eclipse of common right by individual property — could scarcely appear more starkly. The question then was how the agrarian world might be put aright. Insofar as the nobility and gentry were leaving tillage to decay, destroying houses and even whole towns, and turning decent people into beggars and thieves, More lays out the argument that good order depends on undoing all of this. It is necessary to reopen the enclosures, he argues, restrain the engrossments, and rebuild the villages that have been depopulated through the actions of the rich.

Cormorants, greedy gulls

Robert Crowley belongs to the generation following Dudley and More that was active during the reign of Henry VIII's son, Edward VI (from 1537 to 1553). A printer, pamphleteer, and eventually clergyman, he is among the

56. Ibid, 23.
57. Ibid.
58. Thomas More, *Utopia*, in George Logan and Robert Adams (eds.), *Thomas More: Utopia* (Cambridge: Cambridge University Press, rev. ed., 2002), 16.

reformists of this period who became known to their critics, and later to historians, as the 'Commonwealthmen' (or, sometimes, 'Commonwealthsmen'). Like their predecessors, but now with heightened vehemence and explicitness, the Commonwealthmen denounced the dispossession and immiseration of ordinary people due to enclosure and related practices, and called on those responsible to alter their ways. Crowley was a gifted writer and preacher, and was especially trenchant in his criticism. We can gain a sense of his perspective by considering in the first place a couple of short texts written in verse ('epigrams') that form part of his *One and Thyrtye Epigrammes, wherein are bryefly touched so many Abuses that maye and ought to be put away.*[59] Under the spotlight in these two epigrams are, respectively, the figure of the 'rente rayser' and the 'unsaciable [insatiable] purchaser'.

Of Rente Raysers tells the story of a landlord who racks his rent, and is then warned that it is dangerous to oppress his tenants in this way. The landlord pays no heed to the warning, insisting that he can do as he likes with his own property: 'For thys thynge, he sayde, / full certayne he wyste, / That wyth hys owne he myghte / alwayes do as he lyste.' But then divine retribution strikes, and the oppressing landlord falls sick: 'immediatelye . . . / thys oppressoure fyl sicke / Of a voyce that he harde, / "geve accountes of thy baliwicke"'.[60] That last word 'bailiwick' is a reference to the office of bailiff. In Crowley's time, a bailiwick was the area with respect to which a bailiff had the duties and responsibilities of 'bailieship' or stewardship. So the voice which the landlord hears as he falls providentially ill is challenging him to give an account of himself as steward of the land and resources he owns. The landlord's claim that he can always do as he likes with his own property contradicts the responsible stewardship which — the author seems to be suggesting — is a landowner's proper role.

In the second epigram, Crowley's 'unsaciable purchaser' is an 'unreasonable ryche man' who is out riding one day with a boy named Jack. As they pass by a pasture 'most pleasaunte to se', the rich man remarks to the boy that he has recently purchased that land. Jack unguardedly replies: '[M]aister . . . / men saye over all, / That your purchase is greate, / but your householde is small.' The man then asks: 'Why, Jacke . . . / Woulde they have me to purchase / and kepe greate house to?' The boy's response is that he does not know, but

59. Joseph Cowper (ed.), *The Select Works of Robert Crowley* (London: Trübner & Co, 1872), 1. (In fact there are thirty-three epigrams.)
60. Robert Crowley, *Of Rente Raysers*, in Joseph Cowper (ed.), *The Select Works of Robert Crowley* (London: Trübner & Co, 1872), 46, 47.

that 'they saye that ye purchase / the Devill, his dame, and all'.[61] Faced with the disparity between great purchases and small households, Crowley has the young innocent deliver a damning judgement. In the eyes of others, the rich man's acquisition of large tracts of land for pasture — the engrossment of his estate — is a diabolical act of greed and rapacity.

These themes continue in Crowley's later *Informacion and peticion against the oppressours of the pore Commons of this Realme.* Addressed to Parliament, the text invites the country's landowners to 'consyder whoe gave them theyr possessions, and howe they ought to bestowe them'.[62] Crowley writes that it was God who ultimately gave them their possessions, and it is God to whom they must answer for the way they bestow those possessions. The point is not, he explains, that 'all thynges [should be] made commune'. It is, rather, that landowners should conceive themselves as stewards of their holdings, rather than lords: 'the possessioners [should] consyder them selves to be but stuardes, and not Lordes over theyr possessions'. Were that crucial shift in the mindset of landowners to occur, Crowley maintains that 'thys oppression woulde sone be redressed'. But 'so longe as thys perswasion styketh in theyr myndes, — "It is myne owne; whoe shall warne me to do wyth myne owne as me selfe lysteth?" — it shall not bee possible to have any redresse at all'. The problem, as he characterises it, is that, if landlords can treat their land as exclusively their own and do with it whatever they like, then they may equally set rents at whatever rate they like and throw onto the street tenants who cannot pay; even their own brother will not be safe, should he live and work on land they own. In his words, 'if I may do wyth myne owne as me lysteth, then maye I suffer my brother, hys wyfe, and hys chyldrene to lye in the strete, excepte [unless] he wyll geve me more rent for myne house then ever he shal be able to paye'.[63]

A final text, and Crowley's best known, shows where this argument takes him. In *The Way to Wealth*, Crowley discusses the causes of civil unrest — 'sedition' — in his time. The text purports to present the alternative analyses that would be proffered respectively by a poor man from the country and a wealthy landowner. He proposes that a poor man from the country would

61. Robert Crowley, *Of Unsaciable Purchasers*, in Joseph Cowper (ed.), *The Select Works of Robert Crowley* (London: Trübner & Co, 1872), 48, 48–49.
62. Robert Crowley, *Informacion and peticion against the oppressours of the pore Commons of this Realme*, in Joseph Cowper (ed.), *The Select Works of Robert Crowley* (London: Trübner & Co, 1872), 151, 157.
63. Ibid.

say that the causes of sedition lie with the great farmers, the graziers, the rich butchers, the men of law, the merchants, the gentlemen, the knights, the lords, and other men he could not name — indeed, 'men that have no name because they are doares in al thinges that ani gaine hangeth upon'.[64] These doers in all things that any gain hangs upon were '[m]en that would have all in their owne handes' and 'leave nothyng for others; men that would be alone on the earth; men that bee never satisfied'. Drawing on a popular symbol of edacity and greed, Crowley imagines that the poor man would dub these nameless, shameless profit-seekers '[c]ormerauntes [cormorants], gredye gulles'.

'Yea,' he would declare, 'men that would eate up menne, women, & chyldren, are the causes of Sedition!'[65] He would go on: '[t]hey take our houses over our headdes, they bye our growndes out of our handes, they reyse our rentes, they leavie great (yea unreasonable) fines, they enclose our commens! . . . We knowe not whyche waye to turne us to lyve.'[66] The poor man would lament that no custom, no law or statute, can restrain such men from oppression, and he would conclude that, out of necessity, he and his fellows must 'stand up agaynst them'. Otherwise, he would say, 'we must be theyr slaves and laboure tyll our hertes brast [burst], and then they must have al'.[67]

What then of the great farmers and graziers and others themselves? Crowley imagines them exclaiming in horror at 'paisant knaves . . . [who] would not have us maisters of that which is our owne!'[68] Just as the poor would see the causes of sedition as lying with the profit-seeking rich, so he proposes that the rich would see the causes of sedition as lying with the unruly, upstart poor. They would complain that the common people 'knowe not them selves, they knowe no obedience, they regard no lawes, . . . they would have al thinges commune'.[69] 'We wyll tech [teach] them to know theyr betters', the well-off men would retort. 'And because they wold have al commone, we wil leave them nothing.' 'Shall we suffer the vilaines to disprove our doynges?', the rich men would rhetorically ask. 'No, we wil be lordes of our own & use it as we shal thinke good!'[70]

64. Robert Crowley, *The Way to Wealth*, in Joseph Cowper (ed.), *The Select Works of Robert Crowley* (London: Trübner & Co, 1872), 129, 132.
65. Ibid.
66. Ibid, 132–33.
67. Ibid, 133.
68. Ibid, 142.
69. Ibid, 142.
70. Ibid, 143.

After rehearsing each side of this argument, Crowley gives his own view, though it is already plain where his sympathies fall. To be sure, he has harsh words for the idea that the poor should 'stand up agaynst' the rich. He believes that they should exercise patience and leave God to punish those who, far from oppressing them, should be their protectors and defenders. To his mind, rebellion is the sinful result of greed as much on the part of the poor as on the part of the rich. He is, however, clear that the rich are the origin of the problem. If he depicts them as reacting with comic horror to those who resist their extravagant claims, he also berates them explicitly for 'al maner of oppression & extortion'.[71] They accuse the poor of disobedience, yet it is they who were 'firste disobedient'. Contrary to conscience and law, they 'enclosed frome the pore theire due commones, leavied greater fines then heretofore have been leavied, put them from the liberties . . . that they held by custome, & reised theire rentes'. And even when the king and his commissioners ordered the laying open of their enclosures, they 'lefte not of to enclose stil'.[72] Addressing them directly, Crowley warns these 'ungentle gentlemen'[73]: 'You shall never the soner [sooner] be gentlemen for your stout oppression, nor the later have thynges in private for that ye let youre tenauntes lyve by you upon theyre laboure.'[74]

The orders for laying open enclosures to which Crowley refers here are a series of statutes and proclamations aimed at arresting the depopulation of villages and towns and curbing the conversion of arable land to pasture. The statutes and proclamations were first enacted during the reign of Henry VII, in the late fifteenth century, and re-enacted with broader application by subsequent monarchs. Beginning in the sixteenth century, commissions of inquiry were also appointed to investigate, and determine action to be taken with respect to, enclosure and the related phenomena of emparkment (enclosure for the creation of private hunting grounds) and engrossment.[75] Crowley reproaches the 'ungentle gentlemen' engaged in enclosure, emparkment and engrossment for arrogantly and unlawfully disregarding both these royal measures and the customary rights of common which the measures were designed to protect. More fundamentally, however, he condemns the worldview which that disregard reflected, comprising, as he portrays it, three key elements.

71. Ibid, 144.
72. Ibid.
73. Ibid, 143.
74. Ibid, 146.
75. See Joan Thirsk, *Tudor Enclosures* (London: Historical Association, 1958), 10 et seq.

First, there was the limitless drive to accumulate, the aspiration to 'have all in [one's] own hands' and the willingness, in pursuit of that aim, to do 'all things that any gain hangs upon'. For Crowley, as we saw with the insatiable purchaser, this is the devil's work. Equally, the rent raiser is cursed. The world is to be shared, yet these unnatural men were bent on '[leaving] nothing for others'; they would not be satisfied until they were 'alone on the earth', the sole possessors of land and all its bounty. Second, there was the idea that an owner can 'with his own . . . always do as he likes'. The great farmers and graziers claim to be 'masters of that which is [their] own'; they hold themselves out as 'lords' of their possessions, to 'use . . . as [they] shall think good'. Yet, as Crowley's rent raiser discovers to his cost, God gave men their possessions, and accordingly men must account to God for their use of them. Rejecting absolute ownership as a smokescreen for irresponsibility and inhumanity, Crowley argues instead for a notion of responsible stewardship. 'Possessioners should consider themselves to be but stewards, and not lords over their possessions', he writes.

A third element completed the enclosers' worldview. This was the vision, still embryonic and far from fully formed, of a society divided between property-owners and others who worked for them. Whilst, as we have noted, wage-labour had long been used to supplement peasant income, paid work took on new significance for those deprived of access to land. Dispossession of land and rights left those affected with no means of surviving independently, and hence with the need to accept whatever work for whatever pay they were offered. For the first time, poverty became not just a matter of bad harvests, but also of working poverty or unemployment.[76] Crowley's message to the ruling elite is that this is a recipe for class war. *The Way to Wealth* dramatises the potential for such conflict with its speeches by the presumptive antagonists. On the one side, the wealthy landowner expresses hatred for the poor and, after misattributing to them a wish to 'have all things common', vows to 'leave them nothing'. On the other side, the poor man from the country exhorts his fellows to 'stand up against' the expropriators, lest he and they end up the rich men's 'slaves'.

76. See further Keith Wrightson, *Earthly Necessities: Economic Lives in Early Modern Britain* (New Haven: Yale University Press, 2000), 148.

The way to poverty

Our starting point in this chapter was a new kind of social thought that both denounced the plight of the impoverished majority and assigned responsibility for their circumstances to the greed and power of acquisitive others. The works we have considered represent a small sample of the much larger literature that evidences that new thinking. Nonetheless, these works have a potency of their own on which we have been able to draw. It has emerged that each of our three authors uses allegory and other literary devices to tell a troubling tale of social dislocation in sixteenth-century England. Rent rises and evictions, enclosure and engrossment, tenurial fines and high prices — Crowley's poor man from the country does not know which way to turn so as to live. More and Crowley, if not Dudley, appear to have perceived that the changes to which they were witness went 'beyond the normal range of mutability in human affairs'.[77] Why were these things happening? The recurrent answer we have heard is moral degeneracy, and specifically cupidity. Worldly prosperity is among the fruits of the tree of commonwealth, but it has a perilous core that holds men in its thrall and makes them set their love hugely or greatly on things. Greedy landowners are allowing sheep to devour human beings, and to devastate and depopulate fields, houses and towns. Like cormorants whose hunger can never be satisfied, insatiable purchasers, rent raisers and their ilk crave to have all in their own hands and are willing to do anything for gain. Fruit, sheep and a bird hold the mirror of nature up to a society in urgent need of moral renewal.

And if our authors called for moral renewal on the part of the avaricious rich, they were equally insistent that the poor must know their place and leave God to do his work. There should be no grudging or murmuring, no clothing of peasants in the livery of lords. The common people should be contented with the fruit of tranquillity. Rebellion is the sinful result of greed as much on the part of the poor as on the part of the rich. As emphasised at the beginning of this chapter, the primary concern of these writers was to preserve the established order against the threat they took it to face. What was that threat? Crowley articulates it clearly when he describes how the 'way to wealth' is also the way to poverty — and the way to oppression, resistance and strife. Confronted with the wealthy landowner who will leave nothing

77. Ibid, 3.

to the poor, the poor man urges fighting back, for fear that those in his position will otherwise become compelled to labour until their hearts burst. Of course, the story Crowley tells of the proletarianisation of small producers in the English countryside is also the one Karl Marx tells in the final chapters of the first volume of *Capital*.[78] Andy Wood reports that, in fact, Marx based his account on mid-sixteenth-century material he found in the British Library, and especially on texts by Commonwealthmen such as Crowley.[79] Later historical knowledge has led to many refinements of Marx's account but, as the next chapter will discuss, he was not wrong to listen to the likes of Crowley on the subject of class war.

78. Karl Marx, *Capital, Vol. 1* (London: Penguin 1976), chaps. 26–32.
79. See Andy Wood, *The 1549 Rebellions and the Making of Early Modern England* (Cambridge: Cambridge University Press, 2007), 15.

3

Two Early Modern Revolts

When Adam delved and Eve span

In medieval England there was a well-known proverb that took the form of a rhetorical question: 'When Adam delved and Eve span, who was then a Gentleman?'[1] The earliest extant record of the proverb is in an account of a sermon by the preacher John Ball during the Peasants' Revolt of 1381.[2] One of several contemporary chroniclers of the revolt, Thomas Walsingham, tells of how, on 12 June of that year, Ball addressed a crowd of 'two hundred thousand of the commons' who were then gathered at Blackheath, outside London.[3] According to Walsingham, Ball 'began a sermon in this fashion: "When Adam dalf and Eve span, / Wo was thanne a gentilman?"' (Although Walsingham wrote in Latin, he rendered this bit in the vernacular.) It is related that the rest of Ball's sermon was an attempt 'to prove by the words of the proverb that he had taken for his text, that from the beginning all men were created equal by nature, and that servitude had been introduced by the unjust and evil oppression of men, against the will of God, who, if it had pleased Him to create serfs, surely in the beginning of the world would have appointed who should be a serf and who a lord'. Walsingham further reports that Ball told the assembly

1. It seems that a similar saying existed during the same period in some other parts of Europe: see Sylvia Resnikow, 'The Cultural History of a Democratic Proverb', *Journal of English and Germanic Philology* 36(3) (1937) 391.
2. See Thomas Walsingham, *Historia Anglicana*, II, 32–33, translated and reprinted in Richard Dobson, *The Peasants' Revolt of 1381* (London: Macmillan, 2nd ed., 1983), 373–75.
3. The contemporary chroniclers' figures are believed to be exaggerated. See, e.g., Christopher Dyer, 'The Social and Economic Background to the Rural Revolt of 1381', in Rodney Hilton and Trevor Aston (eds.), *The English Rising of 1381* (Cambridge: Cambridge University Press, 1984), 9, 11.

A False Tree of Liberty. Susan Marks, Oxford University Press (2019).
DOI: 10.1093/oso/9780199675456.003.0003

that God had now 'appointed the time wherein, laying aside the yoke of long servitude, they might, if they wished, enjoy their liberty so long desired'.[4]

Ball had earlier been excommunicated for his radical claims, and banned from preaching in churches. But he had carried on preaching outdoors, and another contemporary chronicler, Jean Froissart (who wrote in French), fills in the background to the Blackheath sermon with an account of 'the kinds of things which John Ball usually preached in the villages on Sundays, when the congregations came out from mass'. 'Good people', Ball would say, 'things cannot go right in England and never will, until goods are held in common and there are no more villeins and gentlefolk, but we are all one and the same'. He would ask, 'In what way are those whom we call lords greater masters than ourselves? How have they deserved it? . . . If we all spring from a single father and mother, Adam and Eve, how can they claim or prove that they are lords more than us, except by making us produce and grow the wealth which they spend?' Ball would remind his listeners that '[t]hey are clad in velvet and camlet lined with squirrel and ermine, while we go dressed in coarse cloth. They have the wines, the spices and the good bread: we have the rye, the husks and the straw, and we drink water. They have shelter and ease in their fine manors, and we have hardship and toil, the wind and the rain in the fields.' 'And', Ball would re-emphasise, 'from us must come, from our labour, the things which keep them in luxury'. 'Let us go to the King', Ball would propose in concluding, 'and tell him that we want things to be changed, or else we will change them ourselves'.[5] In a series of letters written in Ball's name or believed likely to be attributable to him, a recurrent phrase is 'nowe is tyme'.[6]

Needless to say, change did eventually come to England's feudal peasantry. At any rate, servile villeinage ended. Yet the practice of rebellion, and with that, Ball's millenarian vision of a world organised in the interests of all, very much endured, to be repurposed for the new and differently exploitative circumstances of later times. We get some hint of this a century afterwards from a 'seditious bill' that was reported to have been nailed to a church door in Coventry in July 1496.[7] The author of the bill complains that 'The cyte

4. Thomas Walsingham, *Historia Anglicana*, II, 32–33, translated and reprinted in Richard Dobson, *The Peasants' Revolt of 1381* (London: Macmillan, 2nd ed., 1983), 373–75.
5. Jean Froissart (Geoffrey Brereton, trans. and ed.), *Chronicles* (London: Penguin, 1968), 213, 212.
6. See Richard Dobson, *The Peasants' Revolt of 1381* (London: Macmillan, 2nd ed., 1983), 381–83. (Some of these letters are written under what are considered probable pseudonyms for Ball.)
7. See R.H. Tawney and Eileen Power (eds.), *Tudor Economic Documents, Vol. III* (London: Longmans, Green & Co, 1924), 12–13. This text is also reproduced in Mary Dormer Harris, 'Laurence Saunders, Citizen of Coventry', *English Historical Review* 9(36) (1894) 633, 650. Harris explains

[city] is bond that shuld be fre / The right is holden from the Cominalte.' Lammas, the harvest festival, marked the traditional day on which the fields and meadows of England were opened up for the exercise of common rights of pasture and gleaning. But instead of that happening, the local land that would normally have been opened up was 'closed in and hegged [hedged] full fast'. Worse, the man who 'speketh for our right' — one Laurence Saunders, the leader of the struggle to have the land reopened — lay 'in the hall', by which was meant that he had been imprisoned. The anonymous rhymster ended by issuing a warning to the town's elite: 'Cherish the Cominalte and se they have their right / For drede of a worse chaunce be day or be nyght.'

Laurence Saunders is said to have stirred up 'commotions' among the people.[8] The precise form of those commotions is not specified by the author of the bill, but if they adhered to the usual pattern, they would have involved destruction of the physical barriers erected around the enclosed land. These were sometimes fences, walls or trenches, but the typical barrier, and the one that had evidently been put up in Coventry, was a quickset hedge. Hedge-breaking allowed cattle to enter the land and graze, while also carrying a symbolic charge which was sometimes intensified by burning the broken hedge and burying the ash. Re-erection was made difficult by digging up the hedge roots and filling in the ditches that had been created to plant them.[9] Other modes of direct action against enclosure and related developments included land occupation, rent strikes, and attacks on pounds to which livestock found straying onto enclosed land were taken. Keith Wrightson argues that, whereas these activities have sometimes been portrayed as the 'desperate spasms of an oppressed and immiserated peasantry', they are better understood as the 'truculent resistance of self-confident . . . communities determined to fend off any encroachment upon the customary rights which secured their relatively advantageous position'.[10]

The action led by Laurence Saunders remained small in scale and essentially reactive, a response to particular enclosures and other parochial grievances. In a few instances, however, the century or so that followed the commoners'

(at 647) that it was the custom in Coventry at the time to affix to church doors announcements which a town crier would not, or could not be expected to, proclaim.

8. Mary Dormer Harris, 'Laurence Saunders, Citizen of Coventry', *English Historical Review* 9(36) (1894) 633.
9. See Nicholas Blomley, 'Making Private Property: Enclosure, Common Right and the Work of Hedges', *Rural History* 18(1) (2007) 1, 14.
10. Keith Wrightson, *Earthly Necessities: Economic Lives in Early Modern Britain* (New Haven: Yale University Press, 2000), 152.

campaign in Coventry saw the staging of major uprisings over large areas with more ambitious programmes of reconstruction and reform — uprisings that 'shook the established order to its core', in the way the late medieval Peasants' Revolt did.[11] This chapter extends our discussion of early English social criticism with a consideration of two such uprisings which formed part of its evolving context: Kett's Rebellion and the Midland Rising. Kett's Rebellion took place in Norfolk over seven weeks in 1549. It was what prompted Crowley's denunciation of the 'greedy cormorants' and 'ungentle gentlemen' in *The Way to Wealth*, which we encountered in the previous chapter. The Midland Rising was a set of disturbances occurring at sites in Northamptonshire, Warwickshire and Leicestershire in the spring of 1607. The two revolts are the subject of a variety of surviving contemporary texts — *inter alia*, chronicles, letters, manifestos, sermons, and literary reworkings (among them, in the case of the Midland Rising, an apparent reworking by William Shakespeare) — brought together and assessed in modern historical scholarship. Reviewing something of this material will enable us to observe how a 'worse chance' was indeed felt to threaten England's rulers at this time, just as Saunders's supporter warned. On the other hand, it will also reveal how a new appreciation of right-holding arose among commoners willing to fight to 'see they have their right'.

No man shall enclose any more

The story of Kett's Rebellion first appears in three works composed in the 1570s: an unpublished account by Nicholas Sotherton;[12] a pamphlet by Alexander Neville;[13] and the multi-author *Holinshed's Chronicles of England, Scotland and Ireland*.[14] The first modern history of the rebellion was written by Frederic Russell in 1859,[15] and there exists a more recent body of research and

11. David Horspool, *The English Rebel* (London: Penguin Books, 2010), 121.
12. Nicholas Sotherton, *The Commoyson in Norfolk 1549* (Harley MS 1576, fos. 251–59).
13. Alexander Neville, *De furoribus Norfolciensium Ketto duce* (London: Henry Binneman, 1575). Neville's work was translated by the Reverend Rich Woods in 1623. It is that translation from which I quote below: Alexander Neville (Rich Wood, trans.), *Norfolke Furies, and their Foyle under Kett* (London: Casson, 1623).
14. Raphael Holinshed, *Holinshed's Chronicles of England, Scotlande, and Irelande* 3 vols. (London: Imprinted for John Harrison, 1577).
15. Frederic Russell, *Kett's Rebellion in Norfolk: Being a History of the Great Civil Commotion that Occurred at the Time of the Reformation, in the Reign of Edward VI* (London: Longman, Brown Green, Longmans & Roberts, 1859).

debate on it that was initiated in the late 1970s.[16] What the sources disclose is that on 6 July 1549 a large crowd gathered in the town of Wymondham in Norfolk to attend the annual performance of a play celebrating the life of Thomas à Becket. Wymondham had an abbey dedicated to Thomas à Becket which had been dissolved eleven years earlier in pursuance of Henry VIII's programme of monastery dissolutions. This had caused much grief among the local population. There was also enduring anger at corrupt handling of the sale of assets belonging to the abbey by the man charged with overseeing the process, a landowner from the neighbouring village of Hethersett named John Flowerdew.

By tradition, the play and associated festivities ran over two days and two nights. It seems that, at some point during this time, a group of townspeople formulated a plan to vent their ire on Flowerdew. He had recently enclosed common land, and their plan was to throw down his enclosures. On 9 July, the group set out for Hethersett. However, when they arrived at Flowerdew's estate, he managed to talk them around. Furthermore, he paid them to head back to Wymondham to break the hedges of a landowner and encloser from that town who had been one of his chief critics in the business over the dissolution, a man by the name of Robert Kett. This the group of townspeople did, and an unexpected thing then happened. Instead of resisting, Kett joined the hedge-breakers in throwing down his own enclosures, and offered to serve as their leader in a wider effort to reclaim the people's rights of common. In Neville's words, Kett promised to pursue justice for the 'hurts don unto the Weale publike [the 'public weal' or commonwealth] and common Pasture by the importunate Lords therof', and said that 'he would doe his indevour, that what lands soever he had inclosed, should againe be made common unto them, and all men, and that his owne hands should first performe it'.[17]

In the days that followed, Kett and his Wymondham companions marched to the nearby city of Norwich, breaking hedges and levelling ditches as they went (including, needless to say, Flowerdew's at Hethersett). Along the way, they were joined by a growing band of sympathisers. In Norwich the group destroyed fences on the Town Close, an area of common pasture that had recently been enclosed, before moving on to Mousehold Heath on the other side of the city. Mousehold Heath was an historic place, redolent of popular

16. Julian Cornwall, *Revolt of the Peasantry, 1549* (London: Routledge and Kegan Paul, 1977), 140; Stephen Land, *Kett's Rebellion: The Norfolk Rising of 1549* (Woodbridge: Boydell & Brewer, 1977).
17. Alexander Neville (Rich Wood, trans.), *Norfolke Furies, and their Foyle under Kett* (London: Casson, 1623), sig. B3r.

rebellion. More than 250 years earlier, on 17 June 1381, rebels from Norfolk held a huge meeting there in the week that preceded an important battle of the Peasants' Revolt. Froissart's chronicle includes a vivid description, albeit one believed to have been largely invented, of the circumstances in which a knight, Robert Salle, was killed at the meeting.[18] (Though the Peasants' Revolt began in the south-east of the country and, in most accounts, culminated with the death of the leader of the Kent and Essex rebels, Wat Tyler, in London on 15 June 1381, it also encompassed the country's eastern counties of Cambridgeshire, Suffolk and Norfolk. The eastern rebellion was put down in a battle waged at North Walsham, around 25 kilometres north of Mousehold Heath, on 25 or 26 June of that year.)[19]

Once on the heath, Kett and those with him set up camp. They were to remain encamped there for the next six weeks, during which their numbers continued to swell, reaching by some accounts an unprecedented 20,000 people. To defend and govern themselves, they established an army and a decision-making council comprising representatives of the various localities from which participants came. They also established a court, designating as its site a tree — according to Neville, 'an old Oke [oak] with great spred boughes' that could support boards to make a rough roof[20] — which they dubbed the 'Oke of Reformation' (or, as some other chroniclers have it, the 'Tree of Reformation'). For use as a prison, they requisitioned a large house belonging to a member of the local gentry. And they arranged for a chaplain to lead daily prayers. Fairly early on, Kett and other leaders drew up a document setting out the demands of those assembled on Mousehold Heath for the attention of the king, Edward VI. (As the latter was a child, in practice it was the attention of the country's 'Lord Protector', the Duke of Somerset, who had been appointed to exercise royal powers during the king's minority, that was sought.) Their document still survives and is known by the title 'Kett's Demands. Being in Rebellion'.[21]

Evidently drafted by committee, the text comprises twenty-nine articles, and deals with an assortment of grievances of varying degrees of importance and in no particular order. That said, the very first article could scarcely be

18. Jean Froissart (Geoffrey Brereton, trans. and ed.), *Chronicles* (London: Penguin, 1968), 222–24.
19. For a discussion that brings together the 1381 Peasants' Revolt and Kett's Rebellion, see Jane Whittle, 'Peasant Politics and Class Consciousness: the Norfolk Rebellions of 1381 and 1549 Compared', *Past and Present* 195, Supp. 2 (2007) 233.
20. Alexander Neville (Rich Wood, trans.), *Norfolke Furies, and their Foyle under Kett* (London: Casson, 1623), sig. C3v.
21. *Kett's Demands: Being in Rebellion* (Harley MS 304, ff. 75r–78v).

more arresting: 'from hensforth noman shall enclose any more'. The succeeding articles reflect both concerns in some way linked to this, as outlined in the previous chapter, and a range of unrelated controversies. The articles call for, among other things, a return to reasonable rents, regulation of the land market in the interest of the poor, a prohibition on commercial sheep and cattle farming, the curtailment of lordly abuses of customary rights, and the definitive abolition of feudal tenures involving the status of bondsman (still residually existing in some places, and under threat of reinstatement in others). In modern commentary, the article on the last mentioned issue is perhaps the document's most often quoted passage: 'all bonde men may be made ffre for god made all ffre with his precious blode sheddyng'. The historian of feudalism Rodney Hilton makes this the epigraph to his book *Bond Men Made Free*, adding that the clause, 'though late in date', epitomised the 'chief desire of rebellious serfs throughout medieval Europe'.[22] Forty representatives gave their names as subscribers to the text, and there are also signatures appended at the end.

It seems that Protector Somerset was — or, at any rate, was popularly believed to be — broadly favourable to the campmen's demands. However, their actions caused great alarm, and after they attacked and occupied Norwich, forces were dispatched in the name of the king to overcome them. The royal forces initially proved inadequate, but a greatly enlarged contingent was then sent, which defeated the campmen in a bloody battle at Dussindale, just outside Norwich, on 27 August 1549. Between 2,000 and 3,500 people are believed to have been killed.[23] Kett, along with a number of others, was captured and hanged. As with the Peasants' Revolt of 1381, there exists no record of these events by anyone who took part in the rebellion, and all chroniclers of the period adopted a perspective that was strongly hostile to it. (In the case of the Peasants' Revolt, Ball was condemned as a 'crack-brained priest', whose 'ravings' encouraged 'wickness', and found favour with common people 'envious of the nobles and the rich'.)[24] Neville, who wrote in Latin, entitled his pamphlet '*De Furoribus Norfolciensium* (Norfolk's Furies)', and denounced the rebels as the 'vilest of all that ever lived'.[25] Sotherton and Holinshed

22. Rodney Hilton, *Bond Men Made Free* (London: Routledge, new ed., 2003), viii.
23. Jane Whittle, 'Lords and Tenants in Kett's Rebellion 1549', *Past and Present* 207 (2010) 3, 21.
24. Jean Froissart (Geoffrey Brereton, trans. and ed.), *Chronicles* (London: Penguin, 1968), 212–13; Thomas Walsingham, *Historia Anglicana*, II, 32–33, reprinted in Richard Dobson, *The Peasants' Revolt of 1381* (London: Macmillan, 2nd ed., 1983), 375.
25. Alexander Neville (Rich Wood, trans.), *Norfolke Furies, and their Foyle under Kett* (London: Casson, 1623), sig. B3v.

likewise portrayed the campmen as mindless, violent, and impelled by hatred and envy of their social superiors — a mob inflamed by Kett's 'sinister will' (Sotherton) and engaged in an 'ungodlie enterprise' with a 'malicious purpose' (Holinshed).[26] Yet in the midst of the invective, hints can be found that there was also another side to this story.

Neville, in particular, begins his narrative by recounting that in 1549 'many grievously complained unto king Edward the sixt, that their Commons were taken from them and enclosed by certaine private persons'. Readers are given to understand that it is out of dissatisfactions such as these that the troubles in Norfolk arose. In a passage reminiscent of the speech by the poor man from the country in Crowley's *The Way to Wealth*, Neville writes of what people were saying. As he tells it, people were saying that the nobility and gentry 'thirst only after gaine'. Meanwhile, the common folk are 'themselves almost killed with labor'. As their tenure of land has become insecure, they also suffer the indignity of '[holding] all at the pleasure of great men'. '[A]s soone as any man offend any of these gorgious Gentlemen, he is put out, deprived.' At the same time, the poor are excluded from common lands. 'The common pastures left by our predecessours for the reliefe of us, and our children, are taken away.' 'Whatsoever fowles of the ayre, or fishes of the water, and increase of the earth, all these do they devoure, consume and swallow up . . .; while we in the meane time eat hearbs and roots.'

Neville dwells on this aspect, linking it directly to the rebellion. Echoing now Dudley, he reports a perception that '[n]ature hath provided for us [the common people], as well as for them [the gentry and nobility]'. All have 'the same forme, and the same condition of birth'. '[W]hy [then] should they have a life so unlike unto ours?' 'Shall they, as they have brought hedges about common Pastures, inclose . . . also, all the commodities and pleasure of this life'? Shall we 'leave the Commonwealth unto our posteritie, mourning, and miserable, and much worse then [than] we received it of our fathers'? No, such a state of affairs could not be allowed to go on. 'We desire liberty, and an indifferent use of all things: this will we have, otherwise these tumults, and our lives shall end together.'[27] Of course, Neville may have misstated popular views. Some parts of his reportage seem, at the least, overstated for

26. Nicholas Sotherton, *The Commoyson in Norfolk 1549* (Harley MS 1576, fos. 251–59); Raphael Holinshed, *Holinshed's Chronicles of England, Scotlande, and Irelande, Vol. 3* (London: John Harrison 1577), 966.
27. Alexander Neville (Rich Wood, trans.), *Norfolke Furies, and their Foyle under Kett* (London: Casson, 1623), sig. B2.

discrediting effect. Nonetheless, it is hard to avoid the sense that he was not without ambivalence towards the rebels, and we perhaps hear something of their voice in his account, just as we seem to hear something of the voice of John Ball in the chronicles that otherwise denigrate him as a crack-brained rabble-rouser.

Opposition to enclosure was evidently a major theme of the complaints registered here. In that connection, it needs to be noted that popular opinion was not uniformly negative towards enclosure. Attitudes were complex, and where there was conflict, it was sometimes the privileged members of a community who were the ones opposed. This was especially the case in Norfolk, owing to its distinctive agrarian structure. Broadly speaking, the region was divided into areas of light soil used for growing corn and raising sheep, and areas of heavier soil that were used mostly for pasture and also contained abundant woodland.[28] In the areas of light soil, a special regional custom known as the 'foldcourse' system was followed, under which the lord of the manor had exclusive rights to raise sheep. The effect of this system was that it was often in the interests of tenants, including poorer tenants, to enclose their land, both to protect their corn from damage by large flocks of sheep, and also to keep in cattle used to fertilise ground during fallow periods where there were no sheep. Conversely, it was often in the interests of landlords to oppose enclosure. The foldcourse system did not apply to the areas of heavier soil, which included Wymondham, Hethersett, Norwich, and the other places where hedge-breaking occurred.

If, despite this complexity, Neville could represent the rebels as opposed to enclosure, and they themselves could demand that 'from henceforth no man shall enclose any more',[29] we may infer that, for them, it went without saying that the enclosure to be stopped was 'offensive', rather than 'defensive' enclosure. The working people gathered on Mousehold Heath and the minor landowners like Kett who were with them were not troubled by enclosure of the kind undertaken by smallholders in the sheep-corn areas of Norfolk. The problem was enclosure by wealthy landlords and tenant-farmers, as Neville puts it, 'thirsting only after gain'. The problem was extinguishment of the

28. Diarmaid MacCulloch, 'Kett's Rebellion in Context', *Past and Present* 84 (1979) 36, 50 et seq.
29. The first article reads: 'We pray your grace that where it is enacted for inclosyng that it be not hurtfull to suche as have enclosed saffren grounds for they be gretly chargeablye to them and that ffrome hensforth noman shall enclose eny more.' Some historians consider 'saffren' a solecism; others contend that the rebels were referring to 'saffron', a profitable crop. Either way, the meaning of that part of the article is somewhat obscure.

rights of common upon which ordinary people depended. Hence Neville's reference to the taking away of 'common pastures left by our predecessors for the reliefe of us, and our children', and hence too his question, 'Shall they, as they have brought hedges about common Pastures, inclose . . . also, all the commodities and pleasure of this life?'

The question is particularly interesting because it suggests that enclosure had begun to take on a metaphorical, or perhaps synecdochic, dimension. The establishment of exclusive access to land was being experienced as an effort to establish exclusive access to social resources and opportunities more generally. No-one doubted that the immediate issue for the poor was that, as Neville again puts it in another passage in *Norfolk's Furies*, 'lands which in the memory of our fathers were common, those are ditched and hedged in, and made severall [private]; the Pastures are inclosed, and we shut out'.[30] But beyond that, there seemed to loom a larger and greater danger, a more comprehensive shutting out. With enclosure, participation by the poor in *all* the 'commodities' — benefits, advantages, rewards — and pleasure of this life seemed at risk.

Narratives of Kett's Rebellion invariably include discussion of the quarrel which the Wymondham villagers had with the man in charge of the sell-off of assets belonging to Wymondham abbey, John Flowerdew. Insofar as this was part of the rebellion's context, it was, of course, only the most superficial part, and explains little of what really aggrieved the rebels or unfolded among them. Even so, the dissolution of the English monasteries that was an outcome of the Henrician Reformation of the late 1530s was a hugely significant event in the country's economic history. After initially coming into Crown hands, monasteries were in many instances quickly sold off to fund military adventures, and a land boom followed of mammoth proportions. As monastic lands became available for private purchase, new modes of finance developed, enabling landlords and wealthy tenant-farmers to expand their holdings on a scale not previously possible. It was in this context that many of the Norfolk gentry are believed to have acquired their large estates and invoked seigneurial foldcourse rights to maintain huge flocks of sheep, to the detriment of others in their communities. There, as elsewhere, the infusion of monastic lands greatly contributed to the project of increasing landed income already underway.

30. Alexander Neville (Rich Wood trans.), *Norfolke Furies, and their Foyle under Kett* (London: Casson, 1623), sig. B2.

Historians use the term 'fiscal seigneurialism' to refer to such aspects of that project as the raising of rents and other charges, enclosure and engrossment, the assertion of customary rights for non-customary purposes, and the 'overstocking' of common land, that is to say, its use for grazing excessive numbers of sheep and cattle in disregard of customary expectations or applicable communal stints. These practices were all in some way linked to the commercial exploitation of land, whether because (as in the case of rent increases) they depended upon it, or because (as in the other cases) they facilitated or stemmed from it. Along with commercial exploitation itself, each was contested in the Mousehold articles. I touched on the demand for a return to reasonable rents. The rebels demanded a return of rents to their levels prior to the ascension of King Henry VIII, and hence prior to the property transfers associated with his religious and political Reformation.[31] Specifically, they stipulated as the appropriate date the first year of the reign of Henry VIII's predecessor and father, Henry VII, that is to say, 1485 — a very significant alteration of the terms of tenure, and hence of the nature of property relations, as they had developed in the intervening period.[32]

I referred to the prohibition on commercial sheep and cattle farming, and the curtailment of lordly abuses of customary rights. The rebels demanded that no-one should be able to graze sheep or cows if they earned more than a small producer would earn ('more than fforty pounds a yere') from their lands, except for their own household needs.[33] They also demanded that no lord of the manor should graze his own animals on village commons,[34] and that lords should not take for themselves the profits to be derived from common lands; those, they maintained, belonged to the freeholders and copyholders.[35] And to enable redress against landlordly abuses, they demanded that manorial ('leet') courts be removed from the control of local landlords and placed under royal control.[36] In another demand, they called for an extension of the commissions of enquiry which Protector Somerset had set up to investigate the scale and effects of enclosure. Under the rebels' proposal, '[s]uche comyssioners as your pore comons hath chosyn', or at any rate, as many of them as the king may think suitable, would be appointed to bring to light and consider all laws,

31. *Kett's Demands: Being in Rebellion* (Harley MS 304, ff. 75r–78v), article 14.
32. See James Holstun, 'Utopia Pre-Empted: Kett's Rebellion, Commoning, and the Hysterical Sublime', *Historical Materialism* 16 (2008) 3, 12.
33. *Kett's Demands: Being in Rebellion* (Harley MS 304, ff. 75r–78v), article 29.
34. Ibid, article 3.
35. Ibid, article 11.
36. Ibid, article 13.

statutes, proclamations, and other proceedings that had been introduced since the first year of the reign of Henry VII, and to 'redresse and refourme' those laws, statutes, proclamations, and other proceedings.[37] Finally, the rebels addressed the land market. It should not be lawful, they wrote, for the lord of any manor to 'purchase londes frely and to lett [them] out ageyn . . . to ther gret advaunchement and to the undoyng of your pore subjects'.[38]

From Hampton field in haste

To gain further perspective on the challenge to developments that were 'greatly advancing' some, while 'undoing' others, let us turn now from Kett's Rebellion to the Midland Rising. No detailed chronicle survives of this like the ones produced a generation after the events about Kett's Rebellion. What is known of it comes mainly from a series of letters written in June 1607 by Gilbert Talbot, seventh Earl of Shrewsbury, and from a short account in the 1615 edition by Edmund Howes of *Stow's Annals or General Chronicle of England*.[39] These and other sources were first brought together and assessed in a paper by Edwin Gay published in 1904.[40] More recent scholarship has identified further sources and connections.[41]

From Talbot, we learn that, on 30 April 1607, a 'tumultuous rabble of people' assembled in Northamptonshire. Similar assemblies later occurred in Warwickshire and Leicestershire.[42] Howes reports that these 'common persons . . . cut and brake downe hedges, filled up ditches, and laid open all such enclosures of Commons, and other grounds as they found enclosed, which of ancient time hadde bin open and imploied to tillage'.[43] In some places, there

37. Ibid, article 27.
38. Ibid, article 21.
39. See Letter from Gilbert Talbot, Earl of Shrewsbury, to the Earl of Kent, 2 June 1607, reprinted in Edwin Gay, 'The Midland Revolt and the Inquisitions of Depopulation of 1607', *Transactions of the Royal Historical Society* 18 (1904) 195, 240; Letter from Gilbert Talbot, Earl of Shrewsbury, to Sir John Manners, Sir Francis Leake and Sir John Harper, 11 June 1607, reprinted in John Nichols, *The History and Antiquities of the County of Leicester, Vol. IV* (London: John Nichols, 1807), 83; and Edmund Howes, *Stow's Annals or General Chronicle of England* (London: T. Adams, 1615), 889–90.
40. Edwin Gay, 'The Midland Revolt and the Inquisitions of Depopulation of 1607', *Transactions of the Royal Historical Society* 18 (1904) 195.
41. See Steve Hindle, 'Imagining Insurrection in Seventeenth-Century England: Representations of the Midland Rising of 1607', *History Workshop Journal* 66 (2008) 21.
42. Letter from Gilbert Talbot, Earl of Shrewsbury, to the Earl of Kent, 2 June 1607, reprinted in Edwin Gay, 'The Midland Revolt and the Inquisitions of Depopulation of 1607', *Transactions of the Royal Historical Society* 18 (1904) 195, 240.
43. Edmund Howes, *Stow's Annals or General Chronicle of England* (London: T. Adams, 1615), 889.

were 'a thousand' men, women and children; in a few, even more — 'three thousand' at Hillmorton in Warwickshire, and 'five thousand' at Cotesbach in Leicestershire.[44] Local residents provided 'not only many cartes laden with victuall, but also good store of spades and shovells for speedy performance, of their present enterprize'.[45] According to Howes, 'these riotous persons bente all their strength to leavell and lay open enclosures without exercising any manner of . . . violence upon any mans person goods or cattell'. He says that at a certain point the protesters began to follow the directions of one of their number, a man named John Reynolds, who commanded them 'not to sweare, nor to offer violence to any person: but to ply their busines and to make fare worke'. Reynolds went by the moniker Captain Pouch. Howes explains that he got this name from a great leather pouch he wore by his side in which he claimed to hold magical stuff that would 'defend . . . against all commers'. When Reynolds was apprehended, the stuff turned out to be 'onely a peece of greene [i.e. mouldy] cheese'.[46]

However orderly the protests, Talbot expresses the propertied classes' view that the local authorities did not deal with them with sufficient firmness. Local law officers should have apprehended the leaders and subdued or dispersed the rest. Instead, they attempted to rely on persuasion. He mentions in particular a situation that arose in Warwickshire. The sheriff and justices there met with a 'great number', urging them to depart and desist, and warning them of the consequences if they did not. The people's response was to ask the sheriff and justices to tell the king that the cause of their rising was in no way lack of loyalty. What they sought was 'reformation of thos late inclosures which made them of the porest sorte reddy to pyne for wante'. The people said that, if within six days they received an answer from the king that he would reform these abuses, they would all go home and wait for the performance of his promise. Talbot indicates that this was duly communicated to the king's council (the privy council), of which he was a member. He says that the council regarded it as a 'course very strange to expostulate with

44. Ibid. On the long-running enclosure dispute at Cotesbach, see L. A. Parker, 'The Agrarian Revolution at Cotesbach 1501–1612', in William Hoskins (ed.), *Studies in Leicestershire Agrarian History* (Leicestershire Archaeological Society, 1949), 41.

45. Edmund Howes, *Stow's Annals or General Chronicle of England* (London: T. Adams, 1615), 889.

46. Ibid.

suche insolent, base and rebelllious people'.[47] A royal proclamation was subsequently issued, ordering the use of force should the risings continue or spread.

It seems that things came to a head in early June 1607 in the village of Newton in Northamptonshire. Talbot writes that a thousand people gathered there and set about digging up hedges and fences that had recently been erected on common land by the owner of an estate at nearby Rushton, Thomas Tresham. By Talbot's account, the crowd were armed with primitive weapons, including half-pikes, pikestaffs, stones, and bows and arrows, and despite the royal proclamation, the county soldiers were ill-prepared (or perhaps, in reality, unwilling) to confront them. Seeing this, Tresham and other members of the local gentry put together a private militia, made up of 'their owne servants and followers . . . they could trust'. Talbot tells of how this private militia 'charged [the protesters] thoroughlie both with their horse and foote', killing forty or fifty and wounding many more.[48] A number of the survivors were subsequently put on trial. Howes says that they spoke in their defence of their determination to resist further depopulation through enclosure, and to maintain tillage so that they could continue to support their families. Having made 'warre against the King', however, they were hanged, and Howes reports that an example was made of Captain Pouch.[49]

On the occasion of these trials, a sermon was preached by Robert Wilkinson, chaplain to the lord lieutenant of Northamptonshire, before the lord lieutenant and other county officials.[50] Wilkinson took as his text for the sermon Matthew 4:4: '. . . Man shall not live by bread onely, but by every word that proceedeth out off the mouth of God.' The sermon was later published, and in a dedicatory passage, Wilkinson writes of the 'tempestous and troublesome times, wherein the excessive covetousnesse of some hath caused extreame want to other, and that want not well digested hath riotted to the hazard of all'. In making this observation, he forewarns readers that there will be no simple denunciation of the rebellion. To be sure, he will condemn the 'Rebellion of the manie', but he will also condemn the 'Oppression of the

47. Letter from Gilbert Talbot, Earl of Shrewsbury, to the Earl of Kent, 2 June 1607, reprinted in Edwin Gay, 'The Midland Revolt and the Inquisitions of Depopulation of 1607', *Transactions of the Royal Historical Society* 18 (1904) 195, 240–41.

48. Letter from Gilbert Talbot, Earl of Shrewsbury, to Sir John Manners, Sir Francis Leake and Sir John Harper, 11 June 1607, reprinted in John Nichols, *The History and Antiquities of the County of Leicester, Vol. IV* (London: John Nichols, 1807), 83.

49. Edmund Howes, *Stow's Annals or General Chronicle of England* (London: T. Adams, 1615), 889–90.

50. Robert Wilkinson, *A Sermon Preached at North-Hampton the 21 of June Last Past, Before the Lord Lieutenant of the County and the Rest of the Commissioners There Assembled Upon Occasion of the Late Rebellion and Riots in Those Parts Committed* (London: John Flasket, 1607), sigs. C4v, F1r–1v.

mighty'. His 'judgement looketh both wayes' — both at the offenders and at those 'by whose covetousness and cruelty the offence cometh'.[51] When the sermon begins, it becomes clear what Wilkinson means and how his biblical theme serves him.

He declares that the rebels acted impatiently and wickedly, neglecting the word of God. They need to 'learne with Christian wisdome and patience to temper themselves in want', for man does not live by bread alone. But equally — and now he addresses their landed adversaries — man lives by bread. Invoking now the Book of Isaiah, he declares that the rich should not 'grind the faces of the poore'.[52] The master should so 'wage his servant that he may live'. Likewise, the landlord should charge rent that enables his tenant to live. God enjoined Adam and Eve to fill the earth with their descendants; the 'rich and greedy' should not seek, through enclosure and engrossment ('by joyning house to house, and land to land'), to 'bee alone upon the earth'.[53] Wilkinson warns that for the ruling powers to ignore all this is not only wrong, but perilous. 'Marke', he says, 'the course of this creeping conspiracie'. First the people 'come forth with shovels and spades' to till the land. Then they turn their 'spades into swords'. Or rather 'they come with weapons in one hand, and working tooles in another, to professe themselves as ready to fight as to work'. First they 'professe nothing, but [an intention] to throw downe enclosures'. Then 'afterward they will reckon for other matters'. They will 'kill up gentlemen' and 'will levell all states [estates, social classes] as they levelled bankes and ditches'.[54]

Wilkinson perhaps alludes to the name by which, according to both Talbot and Howes, the participants in the Midland Rising chose to be known: 'Levellers'. Some also called themselves 'Diggers'. Just as 'leveller' came from the activity of levelling hedges, so 'digger' referred to the activity of digging up hedges, though in that case there was also another association. Andy Wood explains that, by the beginning of the seventeenth century, 'digger' had become a synonym for day-labourer, and 'carried with it a nasty

51. Ibid, The Epistle and Dedicatory.
52. Isaiah 3:15 'What mean ye that ye beat my people to pieces, and grind the faces of the poor?'; see Robert Wilkinson, *A Sermon Preached at North-Hampton the 21 of June Last Past Before the Lord Lieutenant of the County and the Rest of the Commissioners There Assembled Upon Occasion of the Late Rebellion and Riots in Those Parts Committed* (London: John Flasket, 1607), sig. D2.
53. Isaiah 5:8.
54. Robert Wilkinson, *A Sermon Preached at North-Hampton the 21 of June Last Past Before the Lord Lieutenant of the County and the Rest of the Commissioners There Assembled Upon Occasion of the Late Rebellion and Riots in Those Parts Committed* (London: John Flasket, 1607), F2v.

sneer of contempt'.[55] To re-code the term for use as a badge of honour, or at any rate a confident self-description, was thus a powerful act of defiance in itself. But the Midland protesters may have had something else in mind as well. Recall the proverb with which this chapter began: 'When Adam delved and Eve span, who was then a gentleman?' To 'delve' here is to dig, in the sense of tilling the soil to raise crops. As Walsingham observes in his account of the Peasants' Revolt, the idea being put across was that, in the Garden of Eden, there were no social hierarchies. Adam cultivated the land, while Eve was busy at her work, and if an exploitative (non-labouring) class of gentlemen — a gentry and nobility — had come into existence, that was not part of God's plan, but was rather the unjust result of oppression on its part. The proverb lent the word 'digger' (or 'delver') an unmistakeable radicality, which is forcefully articulated in a document that has come down to us from the Diggers — or, as they sign off, 'poore Delvers and Daylabourers' — of 1607 (fig. 3).[56]

The document is believed to have been written in June of that year, and is marked 'ffrom Hampton field in hast'. It appears to be the draft of a manifesto circulated by the Diggers of Warwickshire 'to all other Diggers'. Lambasting enclosers for their violence and rapacity, the Warwickshire Diggers proclaim: 'Wee, as members of the whole, doe feele the smarte of these incroaching Tirants.' They 'grind our flesh upon the whetstone of poverty' — the Diggers evoke the same verse from the Book of Isaiah as Wilkinson — so that they may enjoy the wealth to be derived from their great flocks of sheep. 'It is not unknowne', the Diggers go on, 'why these mercyless men doe resist with force against our good intents.' They do not do so for the good of the king, nor for the benefit of the people, but 'only for theyr own private gaine'. 'They have depopulated and overthrown whole townes, and made thereof sheep pastures.' In doing so, they have brought 'nothing profitable for our Commonwealth'. On the contrary, their actions have brought the risk of 'fearfull dearth'. The Warwickshire Diggers conclude by declaring that they would rather 'manfully dye' than 'be pined to death for want of that which these devouring encroachers do serve theyr fatt hogges and sheep'. As already mentioned, they sign off as 'poore Delvers and Daylabourers', adding 'for the good of the Commonwelth till death'.

55. Andy Wood, *Riot, Rebellion and Popular Politics in Early Modern England* (Basingstoke: Palgrave, 2002), 109.
56. *The Diggers of Warwickshire to all other Diggers* (1607) (Harley MS 787/11).

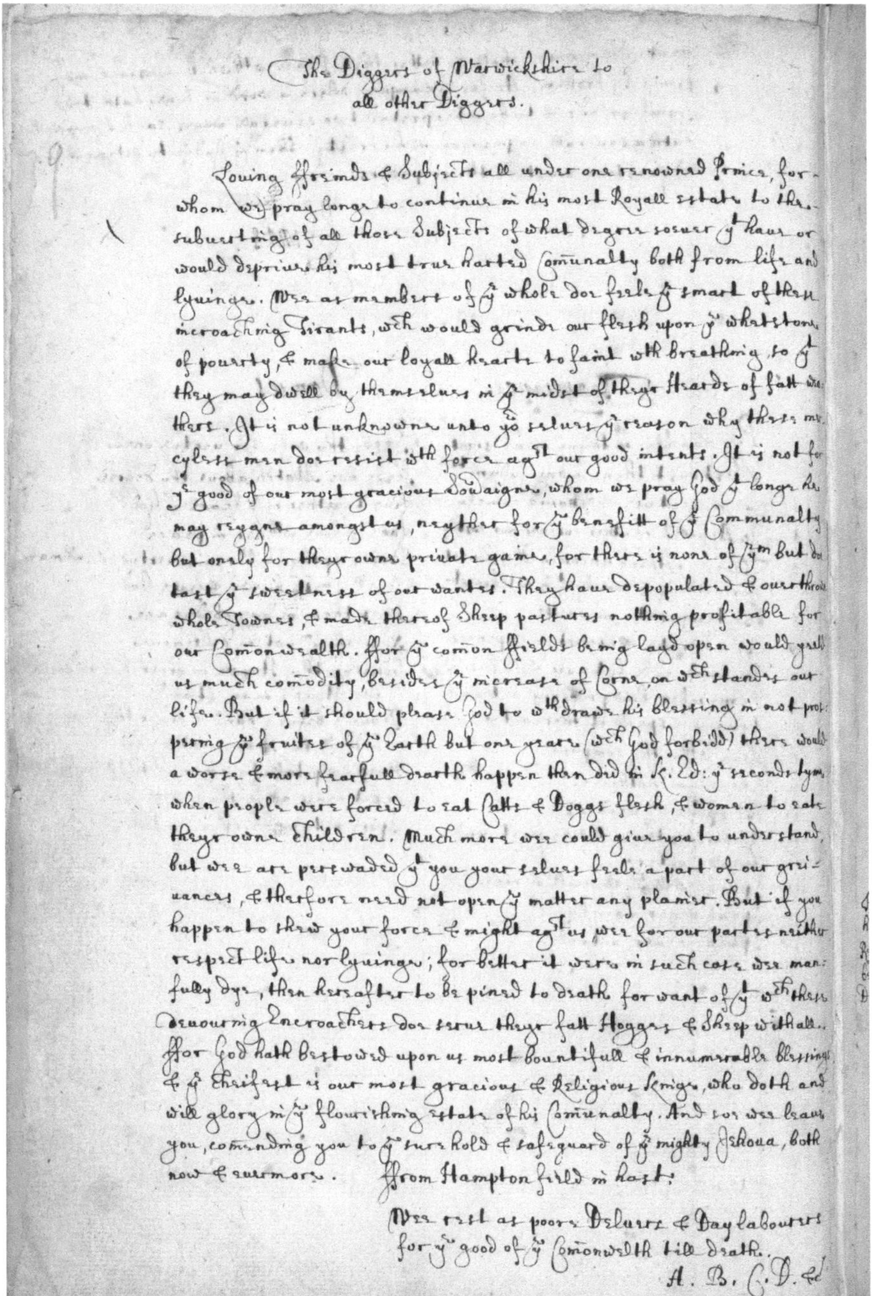

The Diggers of Warwickshire to all other Diggers.

Louing ffreinds & Subjects all under one renowned Prince, for whom wee pray longe to continue in his most Royall estate to the subuerting of all those Subjects of what degree soeuer yt haue or would depriue his most true harted Comunalty both from life and lyuinge. Wee as members of ye whole doe feele ye smart of these incroaching Tirants, wch would grinde our flesh upon ye whetstone of pouerty, & make our loyall hearts to faint wth breathing, so yt they may dwell by themselues in ye midst of theyr Heards of fatt wethers. It is not unknowne unto yo selues ye reason why these mercylesse men doe resist wth force agt our good intents. It is not for ye good of our most gracious Souaigne, whom wee pray God yt longe hee may reygne amongst us, neyther for ye benefitt of ye Communalty but onely for theyr owne priuate gaine, for there is none of ym but doe tast ye sweetness of our wantes. They haue depopulated & ouerthrowne whole Townes, & made thereof Sheep pastures nothing profitable for our Comonwealth. ffor ye comon ffields being layd open would yeild us much comodity, besides ye increase of Corne, on wch stands our life. But if it should please God to withdrawe his blessing in not prospering ye fruites of ye Earth but one yeare (wch God forbidd) there would a worse & more fearfull dearth happen then did in K. Ed: ye seconds tyme, when people were forced to eat Catts & Doggs flesh, & women to eate theyr owne Children. Much more wee could giue you to understand, but wee are perswaded yt you your selues feele a part of our grieuances, & therfore need not open ye matter any plainer. But if you happen to shew your force & might agt us, wee for our partes neither respect life nor lyuinge; for better it were in such case wee manfully dye, then hereafter to be pined to death for want of yt wch these deuouring Encroachers doe serue theyr fatt Hoggs & Sheep withall. ffor God hath bestowed upon us most bountifull & innumerable blessings & ye cheifest is our most gracious & Religious Kinge, who doth and will glory in ye flourishing estate of his Comunalty. And soe wee leaue you, comending you to ye sure hold & safeguard of ye mighty Iehoua, both now & euermore. ffrom Hampton field in hast.

Wee rest as poore Deluers & Day labourers for ye good of ye Comonwealth till death.

A. B. C. D. &c

Figure 3 *The Diggers of Warwickshire to all other Diggers* © The British Library Board, Harley MS 787/11

There is evidence that the Diggers' fear of famine indeed coincided with a spike in enclosures in the Midlands counties, consequential upon a relaxation of statutory curbs on 'depopulating' enclosure and the conversion of tillage to pasture.[57] Whatever the significance of this spike relative to climatic conditions and demographic and other changes, more people than ever before were dependent on the market for food. Hence more people than ever before were vulnerable to distributive distortions and inequities. That famine was building at the time of the Midland Rising may be confirmed by the reissue in the following year of the 'Book of Orders'. The Book of Orders was a set of directions issued by the Crown to local officials in times of food shortage. It formalised traditional arrangements for ensuring that as much grain as possible would reach the market, and that grain would be available to the poor at affordable prices and in sufficient quantities. The focus was mostly on restraining presumed profiteers — both middlemen ('regraters, forestallers and engrossers') and producers. The first Book of Orders was issued in 1587, and it was repeatedly reissued on the recurrence of dearth until the system lapsed in 1630.

The fact that depopulating enclosure was depriving more and more people of the capacity to produce their own food was an important part of the context for this system. Buchanan Sharp shows that, where food riots occurred, it was generally those dependent on the market for their food — landless or near-landless artisans and others — who were at the forefront.[58] Officials and elites tended to depict food-related unrest as a manifestation of pure desperation and visceral need. The favoured maxims were 'necessity has no law' and 'an empty belly has no ears'. However, R. H. Tawney writes of the persistence at this time of the medieval idea that every transaction may be '[tried] by a rule of right', to which 'considerations of economic expediency must be subordinated'.[59] By 'tried' is here meant that transactions could be judged or evaluated according to these criteria. As he explains it, the rule of right did not mean that reduced levels of supply had to be ignored in price-setting, but it did bring with it an expectation that prices should not 'vary with individual necessity or individual opportunity'.[60] And when, against that expectation,

57. Keith Wrightson, *Earthly Necessities: Economic Lives in Early Modern Britain* (New Haven: Yale University Press, 2000), 209.
58. See Buchanan Sharp, *In Contempt of All Authority: Rural Artisans and Riot in the West of England, 1586–1660* (Berkeley: University of California, Press).
59. R. H. Tawney, *Religion and the Rise of Capitalism* (London: Penguin, 1938), 52.
60. Ibid.

prices were raised to take advantage of necessity or opportunity, the practice of popular price-setting, or *taxation populaire*, saw a crowd determine the just price for basic provisions and defy sellers by insisting on buying the provisions at that price.

To gain a sense of these phenomena, we might consider the opening scene of Shakespeare's play *Coriolanus*.[61] Though the setting is ancient Rome, the editor of a recent edition of the play explains that, to its first audiences, this scene would have provided an immediate signal that, despite the togas, the subject-matter of the drama was 'anything but "ancient history"'.[62] A 'company of mutinous citizens' has gathered, ready for a fight. Even dogs must eat, they shout. The gods did not send corn for rich men alone. Addressing the crowd, First Citizen asks whether his fellow plebeians are all resolved 'rather to die than to famish'. They reply that they are. First Citizen then declares: 'we'll have corn at our own price'. The crowd responds, 'No more talking on't. Let it be done.' Clearly there is a grain shortage, but if prices have spiralled, First Citizen proposes that the real problem is that the plebeians 'are accounted poor citizens, the patricians good'. He continues: 'What authority surfeits on would relieve us. If they would yield us but the superfluity while it were wholesome, we might guess they relieved us humanely. But they think we are too dear. The leanness that afflicts us, the object of our misery, is an inventory to particularise their abundance; our sufferance is a gain to them.'[63]

Like Shakespeare's other plays set in classical antiquity, *Coriolanus* was drawn mainly from a story which the playwright found in Thomas North's English translation of Plutarch's *Lives of the Noble Greeks and Romans*.[64] However, in 1950 Ernest Pettet pointed out that the opening scene of a food riot is not in Plutarch's story.[65] That scene was added by Shakespeare, and Pettet believed that it was framed with reference to the Midland Rising. Shakespeare, of course, was himself born and, during his adult life, still partly lived, in Warwickshire, in the town of Stratford-upon-Avon. It seems that he may

61. William Shakespeare (Lee Bliss, ed.), *Coriolanus* (Cambridge: Cambridge University Press, 2014).
62. Lee Bliss, 'Introduction', in William Shakespeare (Lee Bliss, ed.), *Coriolanus* (Cambridge: Cambridge University Press, 2014), 1, 25. See further James Holstun, 'Tragic Superfluity in *Coriolanus*', *ELH* 50(3) (1983) 485.
63. William Shakespeare (Lee Bliss, ed.), *Coriolanus* (Cambridge: Cambridge University Press, 2014), I.i.3, 8, 10, 12–17.
64. Plutarch (Thomas North, trans. and ed.), *Lives of the Noble Grecians and Romanes* (London: Vautroullier & Wight, 1579).
65. See E. C. Pettet, 'Coriolanus and the Midlands Insurrection of 1607', in Allardyce Nicoll (ed.), *Shakespeare Survey 3: The Man and the Writer* (Cambridge: Cambridge University Press, 1950), 34, 35–36.

actually have been there at the time of the protests for his daughter's wedding on 5 June 1607.[66] At the least, it is believed that he would have had personal knowledge of the events and of individual participants in them.[67] And while the exact date of *Coriolanus*'s composition is not known, scholars building on Pettet's work have confirmed that it is likely to have been written around 1608, that is, the year following the Midland Rising. So when First Citizen asks the assembled crowd whether they are all resolved rather to die than to famish, and the response comes that they are, the plebeians may be heard to line up with the Midlands rebels.[68] And when First Citizen then says, 'we'll have corn at our own price', he may be heard to refer to a price set according to the rule of right as the plebeians conceive it.

It seems that price-setting by the crowd was in fact a rarity in England at this time, but Shakespeare perhaps reflects an anxiety on the part of the country's ruling establishment that, in the circumstances of famine or threatened famine, the poor might resort to such an expedient.[69] Alongside that aspect of *taxation populaire*, the rule of right is also in evidence when First Citizen tells his fellows 'they think we are too dear', too expensive. The patricians are content to allow the 'leanness that afflicts' the plebeians to become an inventory, or record, of their own 'abundance'. They stay well fed while — or rather, by — leaving the plebeians to starve; 'our sufferance is a gain to them'. First Citizen may be heard to engage here in a considered process of 'trying' the transactions through which the poor are being priced out of the corn market, and censuring the rich for prioritising considerations of self-interest and economic expediency. The argument then moves a step further when some of the patricians — first Menenius, friend to the great soldier Coriolanus, and then Coriolanus himself — enter the stage. Menenius advises the mutinous citizens to entrust their 'charitable care' to their betters. Why do they rail against the 'helms o'th'state, who care for you like fathers'? Famine is a natural disaster. The plebeians are wrong to blame the patricians: 'For the dearth, / The gods, not the patricians, make it', he says.[70]

66. Lee Bliss, 'Introduction', in William Shakespeare (Lee Bliss, ed.), *Coriolanus* (Cambridge: Cambridge University Press, 2014), 1, 19.
67. Ibid. See further chap. 10 below.
68. 'Hampton-field' (today's Hampton-in-Arden), from where the Warwickshire Diggers issued their draft manifesto, is 25 km from Stratford-upon-Avon.
69. See Buchanan Sharp, *In Contempt of All Authority: Rural Artisans and Riot in the West of England, 1586–1660* (Berkeley: University of California Press, 1980), 33.
70. William Shakespeare (Lee Bliss, ed.), *Coriolanus* (Cambridge: Cambridge University Press, 2014), I.i.51, 63, 58–59.

But the plebeians will have none of it. 'Care for us?', cries Second Citizen, incredulously. They '[s]uffer us to famish, and their storehouses crammed with grain; . . . repeal daily any wholesome act established against the rich, and provide more piercing statutes daily to chain up and restrain the poor'. He concludes: 'If the wars eat us not up, they will'.[71] Like the 'devouring encroachers' denounced by the Midlands rebels, the patricians of Shakespeare's play are portrayed in this speech as feeding off the plebeians — and not only by using them as cannon fodder in wars. Menenius makes one further attempt to win over the plebeians with a fable based on the conventional image of the political community as akin to a human body. Whereas the plebeians condemn the patricians for being like parasites, living inside the belly of the body politic and draining its nutrients away, the drift of his fable is that the patricians should, on the contrary, be thought of as the body politic's 'good belly', feeding, energising, and sustaining the rest. A 'cormorant belly' is Second Citizen's bitter retort. The exchange comes to an abrupt end when Coriolanus arrives. Informed by Menenius that the people demand to have 'corn at their own rates, whereof they say / The city is well stored', his response is 'Hang 'em!' He calls the rebels 'rats', and urges their violent suppression.[72] Later in the play, the wheel of fortune turns, and he is himself likened to an animal. A plebeian tribune asks: 'Where is this viper / That would depopulate the city and / Be every man himself?'[73]

It is not difficult to imagine that, to a contemporary audience, Coriolanus might have called to mind Talbot and his kind, frustrated that the Midlands protest was not put down at the outset with force. Equally, Menenius might have been felt to echo Howes's later message that the protesters were gullible fools, following a leader with a mystical charisma that depended on mouldy cheese. Menenius declares what Howes leaves unstated when he tells the plebeians that they would be best advised to rely on the charity and paternalism of their betters. But if, as Dudley, More, and Crowley had earlier done, he urges passivity, that is only because, like them, he knows that God will not — and in truth cannot — be left to do his work in his own time. For their part, the plebeians may have been seen to resemble the protesters themselves in their struggle against the 'tyrants' who, like Coriolanus, depopulate their localities. So too the plebeians may have recalled the protesters in their knowledge that

71. Ibid, I.i.65–70.
72. Ibid, I.i.131, 104, 172–73, 233.
73. Ibid, III.i.265–67.

the gods bring bad weather and harvest failure, but hunger is a man-made affliction. After all, the Warwickshire Diggers did not fear pining to death from hunger. What they feared was *being* 'pined to death for want of that which these devouring encroachers do serve theyr fatt hogges and sheep'.

A different reformation

If the Henrician Reformation remade the English state and church, we have seen that the men and women who took part in Kett's Rebellion and the Midland Rising proposed a different sort of reformation — a 'reformation of enclosures', a wholesale 'redress and reform' of laws, a 'Tree of Reformation' that would — and for a time did — give expression to the claim of ordinary people to define and administer justice for themselves.[74] Andrew Hopper writes of the creation on Mousehold Heath of a 'functioning alternative local government'.[75] Stanley Bindoff characterises the campmen's demands as a 'radical programme' which, if implemented, would have 'clipped the wings of rural capitalism'.[76] As Diarmaid MacCulloch interprets it, Kett's Rebellion was an effort to 'keep the company of gentlemen at arm's length'. The rebel leaders made manifest the 'sense of alienation [they] felt . . . from their immediate social superiors' and the rebels' shared desire to 'exclude the gentry and the clergy from their world'.[77] To James Holstun, it was 'not so much a rebellion as the greatest practical utopian project of Tudor England'.[78] Likewise, in Roger Manning's assessment, the Midland Rising saw an exceptionally 'explicit articulation of social conflict'.[79] Lee Bliss comments that the grievances expressed by the Warwickshire Diggers passed beyond what, in the eyes of the authorities, were 'legitimate' reasons to protest. They 'evinced

74. On the contested meanings of 'reformation', see Andy Wood, *The 1549 Rebellions and the Making of Early Modern England* (Cambridge: Cambridge University Press, 2007), 143 et seq.
75. Andrew Hopper, 'Introduction: Rebel Politics and Organisation', *1549: Kett's Rebellion*, Virtual Norfolk project (on file with the author).
76. Stanley Bindoff, *Ket's Rebellion 1549* (London: George Philip, 1949), 9.
77. Diarmaid MacCulloch, 'Kett's Rebellion in Context', *Past and Present* 84 (1979) 36, 47.
78. James Holstun, 'Utopia Pre-Empted: Kett's Rebellion, Commoning, and the Hysterical Sublime', *Historical Materialism* 16 (2008) 3, 5. Holstun also characterises Kett's rebellion as 'a smallholders' constitutional revolution' (11) and the 'greatest anticapitalist rising in English history' (5), observing that the 'Peasant's Revolt of 1381 aimed at feudalism, not capitalism, while the English Revolution of 1642–60 was largely capitalist . . . More recent anticapitalist risings have lacked the campmen's concentrated forces and their ally in a *de facto* head of state' (5, fn 8).
79. Roger Manning, *Village Revolts: Social Protest and Popular Disturbances in England 1509–1640* (Oxford: Clarendon Press, 1988), 235.

glimmerings of a political awareness that basic social conflict lay behind the immediate economic difficulties'.[80] Thus, Steve Hindle writes, 'the masks of paternalism and deference slipped', and a 'counter-theatre of social relations' emerged to impart the reality of 'class-based antagonism'.[81]

Speaking of the mid-sixteenth-century Commonwealthmen, R. H. Tawney tells us that they were 'shocked . . . [b]y the material misery of their age' and by its 'repudiation of the principles by which alone, as it seemed, human society is distinguished from a pack of wolves'. But, he adds, they were 'at once incurious and ill-informed as to the large and impersonal causes which were hurrying forward the reorganisation of agriculture on a commercial basis'.[82] As Neal Wood puts it, '[w]hy [a] . . . wave of greed and egoism should so suddenly sweep the country, they did not explain'.[83] In our own time, an influential analysis accounts for the changes that occurred in early modern England in terms of the distinctive character of English feudalism and the increasingly limited possibilities open to landed elites for sustaining their position by extra-economic, as distinct from economic, means.[84] That sort of perspective was unavailable to contemporaries. Nonetheless, it is evident that, to the rebels on Mousehold Heath, as also to those who took part in the Midland Rising, the moral degeneration of which they bore fearful witness had arisen in, and helped to consolidate, specific historical conditions. Far from any timeless conflict between rich and poor, what these activists apprehended were mutable developments, not brute social facts. Their efforts at popular reformation faced tremendous resistance, but clearly signalled their belief that there was no need to pursue change only within the limits of the existing order.

For the authors discussed in the previous chapter, change was a top-down process, with no room for popular initiative. Anti-enclosure protest was as morally reprehensible as enclosure itself, and they counselled the poor to know their place, be patient, and leave God to do his work. Of the same mind, Wilkinson said that the Midlands rebels 'reformed wickedness, but with far greater wickedness'. Captain Pouch was reputed to earn his living

80. Lee Bliss, 'Introduction', in William Shakespeare (Lee Bliss, ed.), *Coriolanus* (Cambridge: Cambridge University Press, 2000), 1, 22.
81. Steve Hindle, 'Imagining Insurrection in Seventeenth Century England: Representations of the Midland Rising of 1607', *History Workshop Journal* 66 (2008) 21, 50.
82. R. H. Tawney, *Religion and the Rise of Capitalism* (London: Penguin, 1938), 151.
83. Neal Wood, *Foundations of Political Economy: Some Early Tudor Views on State and Society* (Berkeley: University of California Press, 1994), 177.
84. See, e.g., Ellen Meiksins Wood, *The Origins of Capitalism* (London: Verso, 2002).

as an itinerant tinsmith, and in another part of his sermon Wilkinson remarked on the scandal that 'a king of three great kingdomes must capitulate with a Tinker . . . and . . . this is called Reforming'.[85] Indeed, that *was* part of what the rebels called reforming. Kett's Rebellion brought together minor gentry and people without property in a striking demonstration of non-elite agency, imagination and entitlement. The later Midland Rising had no, or no significant, gentry participation. (By the early seventeenth century, the alliance of artisans, labourers, smallholders, and landowners like Kett had become unattainable, leaving the poor to pursue their struggle alone.) Yet the point here was not just that the poor acted, rather than waiting. More's *Utopia* was written in Latin. In contrast, Kett and his companions, like the authors of the Warwickshire manifesto, used a language everyone in the country could understand.[86]

Wilkinson '[looked] both ways' in his sermon, but his ultimate message was that a 'creeping conspiracy', if not halted, would one day lead to a 'killing up [of] gentlemen' and a 'levelling of all [e]states'. Neville also stoked gentry fears by projecting hatred and envy onto the Mousehold rebels, and by mispresenting them as committed to 'an indifferent use of all things'. As we saw, Froissart ascribed to John Ball a similar belief that 'things cannot go right in England . . . until goods are held in common'. That too is considered likely to have been a misrepresentation; rather, what seems to have been envisaged by those engaged in the Peasants' Revolt, or at any rate their leaders, was 'family ownership of peasant holdings and artisan workshops, with the large scale landed property of the church and the aristocracy divided among the peasants'.[87] On the other hand, Howes's account of Captain Pouch commanding the Midlands protesters 'not to sweare, nor to offer violence to any person, but to ply their business and to make fare works' underscored the dignity of the rebels and their resolve that incivility and violence should remain strictly on the side of the enclosers.[88] Neville's account of Kett's Rebellion contextualised this with reference to the acutely felt indignity that came with the increasing insecurity of

85. Robert Wilkinson, *A Sermon Preached at North-Hampton the 21 of June Last Past, Before the Lord Lieutenant of the County and the Rest of the Commissioners There Assembled Upon Occasion of the Late Rebellion and Riots in Those Parts Committed* (London: John Flasket, 1607), sig. F.
86. Christopher Hill, 'Introduction', in Christopher Hill (ed.), *Winstanley: The Law of Freedom and Other Writings* (London: Penguin, 1973), 10.
87. See Rodney Hilton, *Bond Men Made Free* (London: Routledge, new ed., 2003), 229.
88. See John Walter, 'Reynolds, John (*alias* Captain Pouch) (d. 1607)', in *Oxford Dictionary of Biography* (Oxford: Oxford University Press, 2004).

the poor — their 'holding all at the pleasure of great men', their being liable to eviction at any moment by those who would 'be alone upon the earth'.

Neville posed the question of 'why [the rich] should . . . have a life so unlike [the poor]' when all have 'the same form, and the same condition of birth'. I suggested earlier that, in this respect, he echoed Dudley, who emphasised that, after all, the rich suffer the same passions, diseases and infirmities as the poor, the rich look the same as the poor when their glorious garments are taken off, and the rich were born in the same manner as the poor and, like the poor too, they will one day die.[89] For Neville, however, the gap between common humanity and widely disparate life circumstances was not simply the way things were, as it was for Dudley; it was a defining problem of the age. Kett's demands registered in the rebels' own words their strategy for tackling that problem. 'From henceforth no man shall enclose any more', they declared, expressing a universal right in the canonical style of a prohibition. It shall not be lawful to 'purchase lands freely and to let them out again . . . to the undoing' of the poor. 'Such commissioners as your poor commoners hath chosen' shall be appointed to review and rewrite statutes, proclamations and other legislative proceedings. And 'all bond men [shall] be made free for god made all free with his precious blood shedding'. Through these demands, freedom as an unbonded tenurial status was linked to the larger claims of Christian egalitarianism articulated already in the late fourteenth century by John Ball.

The two rebellions on which we have focused in this chapter are among the period's most formidable episodes of organised resistance, but they are by no means its only known episodes.[90] They need to be situated within a wider geography of protest, just as they need to be placed within a longer history of insurrection. In that latter regard, it is striking that Kett and his companions chose to make their encampment on Mousehold Heath, where in 1381 a meeting had taken place as part of the Peasants' Revolt. Moreover, it is notable that some of the Midlands protesters chose to call themselves Diggers, a word similarly reminiscent of the Peasants' Revolt insofar as it recalled Ball's evocation of Adam as the proverbial digger living among equals.[91] And if the past

89. See chap. 2 above.
90. Study of court records has shown that Kett's Rebellion was itself part of a wider rising that encompassed not only Norfolk, but other parts of the east of England as well. See Diarmaid MacCulloch, 'Kett's Rebellion in Context', *Past and Present* 84 (1979) 36.
91. Richard Dobson writes that the Norfolk rebels 'presumably had no conception that they were re-echoing sentiments of John Ball's sermon'. See Richard Dobson, *The Peasants' Revolt of 1381* (London: Macmillan, 2nd ed., 1983), 30. In contrast, Andy Wood highlights the importance

was significant in these rebellions, so too was the future. In Neville's chronicle, the Mousehold rebels' fear was that they would be compelled to 'leave the Commonwealth unto our posterity, mourning, and miserable, and much worse than we received it from our fathers'. Thus the chronicler lays stress at once on the temporariness of the current generation and on the permanence of its legacy, the sense that if it loses rights, the loss will be mourned by generations to come. In attempting to hold onto their livelihoods, the participants in Kett's Rebellion and the Midland Rising were crushed and defeated. So which later generations would mourn, and seek to recover, the rights they lost? In the next chapter, we pass from the Levellers and Diggers of 1607 to the very much better known Levellers and Diggers of the English Revolution.

of social memory to early modern popular politics. See Andy Wood, *The Memory of the People: Custom and Popular Senses of the Past in Early Modern England* (Cambridge: Cambridge University Press, 2013).

4

Rights in the English Revolution

Revolt within the revolution

'It started', writes Christopher Hill, 'as so much seventeenth century thinking did, with a vision.'[1] Writing in January 1649, Gerrard Winstanley tells of how he fell into a trance one day. Strange things appeared in front of his eyes, and a voice spoke to him with 'these words, *Worke together. Eat bread together;* declare this all abroad'.[2] Winstanley refers to the voice variously as that of 'the Spirit' and of 'the Law', and explains that, having obeyed its command to declare this message 'by word of mouth' and 'by my pen', he decided that he needed to 'go forth and declare it in my action'.[3] His moment for doing so arrived a few months later. On 1 April 1649, Winstanley and four other men gathered on uncultivated common land at St George's Hill, now part of Weybridge, in Surrey, and began digging the ground and sowing vegetables.[4] Within a week, the group had grown to twenty or thirty, and a small communal settlement was taking shape. Further Digger settlements or 'colonies' were established at a number of other locations in south-central England in the ensuing months. The movement lasted for a little over a year.[5] There was

1. Christopher Hill, *A Nation of Change and Novelty* (London: Bookmarks, 1993), 136.
2. Gerrard Winstanley, *The New Law of Righteousnes*, in Thomas Corns, Ann Hughes and David Loewenstein (eds.), *The Complete Works of Gerrard Winstanley, Vol. I* (Oxford: Oxford University Press, 2009), 472, 513 (emphasis in original).
3. Ibid, 517.
4. See, esp., John Gurney, *Brave Community: the Digger Movement in the English Revolution* (Manchester: Manchester University Press, 2007).
5. The movement always remained modest in size. In 1969 it was reported that ninety Diggers had been identified by name, though more people were certainly with them. See Keith Thomas, 'Another Digger Broadside', *Past and Present* 42 (1969) 57, 60.

A False Tree of Liberty. Susan Marks, Oxford University Press (2019).
DOI: 10.1093/oso/9780199675456.003.0004

persistent harassment by local landowners, wealthy farmers and clergy, both in the courts and through the use of physical violence against individuals and the destruction of crops and shelters, and by May 1650, the last remaining Digger colony had been forcibly dispersed.[6]

Perhaps because the colonies faced harassment from the very beginning, it was a feature of the Digger movement that its participants made repeated attempts to explain and justify their enterprise in print. Manifestos, open letters, and tracts are among the many kinds of publication that survive, a large number of them written or co-written by Winstanley. This was, of course, the period of the English Civil War, and historians have shown that one aspect of the turmoil was a breakdown of press censorship. With the availability of relatively cheap printing equipment, publishing suddenly became open to everyone with something to say and the capacity to express it in writing.[7] The Diggers' first manifesto appeared just a few weeks after Winstanley and his companions arrived at St George's Hill. It was entitled *The True Levellers Standard Advanced*. We shall return to consider this and other Digger texts later on. For now, it is enough to notice that the authors claim the mantle of 'true' Levellers. The Levellers were a largely London-based movement that had emerged some years earlier out of struggles within the parliamentary army in the Civil War, the New Model Army. The movement encompassed a range of positions, but in broad terms it reflected and informed the outlook of ordinary people in the army, or at any rate, those who did not belong to the landed elite, whether rank and file or officers. The Leveller leaders were civilians with connections to military radicals.

In his book *The World Turned Upside Down*, Hill famously proposed that '[t]here were, we may oversimplify, two revolutions in mid-seventeenth-century England'. 'The one which succeeded established the sacred rights of property . . ., gave political power to the propertied . . ., and removed all impediments to the triumph of the ideology of the men of property — the protestant ethic.'[8] At the same time, however, there was also 'another revolution which never happened, though from time to time it threatened'.[9] In Hill's assessment, the Levellers and Diggers, along with the Ranters, Quakers,

6. Regarding the sites associated with the Digger movement today, see chap. 10 below.
7. See Christopher Hill, *The World Turned Upside Down* (London: Penguin, 1972), 17, and James Holstun, 'Introduction', in James Holstun (ed.), *Pamphlet Wars: Prose in the English Revolution* (London: Routledge, 1992), 1.
8. Christopher Hill, *The World Turned Upside Down* (London: Penguin, 1972), 15.
9. Ibid.

Fifth Monarchists, Muggletonians and the profusion of other dissident groups that sprung up during this period, should be understood as having staged a 'revolt within the Revolution'.[10] One of the earliest verbal shots in that revolt was fired by the Leveller leader John Lilburne in 1646 when he declared that 'the poorest that lives, hath as true a right to give a vote, as well as the richest and greatest'.[11] This chapter takes Lilburne's statement as a point of departure for investigating rights — voting rights, but also other categories of rights — in Leveller and Digger thought. We look at the Putney Debates, where Leveller arguments came into contact with arguments on the side of senior officers ('grandees') in the parliamentary army. Then afterwards we trace the vicissitudes of rights in the visionary writings of Winstanley and other Diggers.

The poorest he

The Putney Debates were a series of discussions convened by the New Model Army in late October and early November 1647 and held in the church of St Mary the Virgin at Putney in what is today south-west London. In the absence of the army's commander-in-chief, Oliver Cromwell chaired the meetings as next in command. Participants included other army grandees, Leveller-aligned officers and 'agitators' (representatives of the rank and file), and some civilians. It bears emphasis that these were oral discussions. The Putney Debates did not form part of the outpouring of printed material to which I referred a moment ago. If there now exists a text, the circumstances in which it has come down to us make for a remarkable story. The army secretariat was tasked with keeping a record of the proceedings in shorthand. Among the record-keepers was William Clarke, a young assistant to the army's principal secretary. Some years after the event, Clarke transcribed into longhand the notes he had made on three days — 28 October, 29 October, and 1 November 1647. For more than two centuries, his manuscript lay undiscovered. Part of an archival bequest to Worcester College, Oxford, it was finally read in the late nineteenth century by an historian of the college,

10. Ibid, 14, 15.
11. John Lilburne, *The charters of London: or, The second part of Londons liberty in chaines discovered*, published 18 December 1646, reprinted in Don Wolfe, *Leveller Manifestoes of the Puritan Revolution* (New York: Nelson, 1944), 14.

Charles Firth. An edition prepared by Firth was published in 1891.[12] In 1938 Arthur Woodhouse re-edited the manuscript for publication in a volume entitled *Puritanism and Liberty*, now styling it 'the Putney Debates'.[13]

It seems that the purpose of the debates was to resolve, or at least ventilate, differences that had surfaced within the army over plans for the country's future governing structure, given the defeat of the king by Parliament. The differences had surfaced in a series of proposals and counter-proposals that had begun to circulate in the summer of 1647. Briefly stated, the grandees favoured relatively modest adjustments to the existing set-up, while the Leveller-aligned officers and agitators sought more far-reaching change. The specific focus of attention at Putney was a document that had been drafted by civilian Levellers for presentation to the Army Council. The document took the form of a constitution or 'Agreement of the People'.[14] On the side of the grandees, the main speaker in the debates was Cromwell's son-in-law, Henry Ireton, and very quickly, he made the key issue that of the franchise. Who should have the right to vote in parliamentary elections? The Agreement called for reorganisation of parliamentary constituencies on the grounds that, in its words, 'the people of England [are] . . . at this day very unequally distributed by counties, cities, and boroughs for the election of their deputies in parliament'.[15]

Referencing that passage, Ireton singled out the phrase 'the people of England'. '[T]his doth make me think that the meaning is, that every man that is an inhabitant is to be equally considered, and to have an equal voice in the election of those representers', he said, 'and if that be the meaning, then I have something to say against it.'[16] Ireton's position was that only those who have what he called a 'permanent fixed interest' or a 'permanent and a local interest' in the kingdom should be allowed to vote. As he put it, 'I think that no person hath a right to an interest or share in the disposing of the affairs of the kingdom, and in determining or choosing those that shall determine

12. C. H. Firth (ed.), *The Clarke Papers: Selections from the Papers of William Clarke, Vols. I–IV* (1894–1901) Camden New Series (Royal Historical Society, 1894).
13. A. S. P. Woodhouse (ed.), *Puritanism and Liberty: Being the Army Debates 1647–9 from the Clarke Manuscripts with Supplementary Documents* (London: J. M. Dent, 3rd ed. with preface by Ivan Roots, 1986).
14. See Andrew Sharp (ed.), *The English Levellers* (Cambridge: Cambridge University Press, 1998), 92.
15. 'An Agreement of the People', in Andrew Sharp (ed.), *The English Levellers* (Cambridge: Cambridge University Press, 1998), 92, 93.
16. A. S. P. Woodhouse (ed.), *Puritanism and Liberty: Being the Army Debates 1647–9 from the Clarke Manuscripts with Supplementary Documents* (London: J. M. Dent, 3rd ed. with preface by Ivan Roots, 1986), 52.

what laws we shall be ruled by here — no person hath a right to this, that hath not a permanent fixed interest in this kingdom.'[17] He explained that, by 'permanent fixed' or 'permanent and local' interest, he meant the kind of interest that freeholders of land or freemen of boroughs had — an interest that enabled people to live 'without dependence',[18] and that was 'not [able to be removed] anywhere else'.[19] To his mind, then, the franchise was a privilege that was necessarily linked to ownership of property (including the kind of hereditable trading rights possessed by freemen of boroughs); people without property had no right to take part in parliamentary elections.[20]

As we saw above, already in the previous year John Lilburne had signalled the Levellers' challenge to that aspect of the prevailing order. Lilburne's point was reiterated in the Putney Debates by Colonel Thomas Rainborough. In a celebrated speech, Rainborough declared, 'For really I think that the poorest he that is in England hath a life to live, as the greatest he.' He went on: '[A]nd therefore, sir, I think it's clear that every man that is to live under a government ought first by his own consent to put himself under that government'. It followed that 'the poorest man in England is not at all bound in a strict sense to that government that he hath not had a voice to put himself under'.[21] What could be the basis of such a principle, and what consequences would it have? Cromwell said that it would lead to 'anarchy . . . if you take away this [limit], that men that have no interest but the interest of breathing [may have no voice in elections]'.[22] Ireton elaborated on the particular form this anarchy would take: 'if you make this the rule I think you must fly for refuge to an absolute natural right, and you must deny all civil right'.[23] He clarified in a later speech that for 'civil right' should be read 'property'. To do away with the property qualification and institute universal manhood suffrage was 'to deny all property'.[24] How so?

17. Ibid, 53–54.
18. Ibid, 58.
19. Ibid, 57.
20. The rules excluded most men and virtually — though not quite — all women. At this time, women who were unmarried or widowed and met the property qualification, had the vote. See Patricia Crawford, '"The Poorest She": Women and Citizenship in Early Modern England', in Michael Mendle (ed.), *The Putney Debates of 1647: The Army, the Levellers and the English State* (Cambridge: Cambridge University Press, 2001), 197, 204.
21. A. S. P. Woodhouse (ed.), *Puritanism and Liberty: Being the Army Debates 1647–9 from the Clarke Manuscripts with Supplementary Documents* (London: J. M. Dent, 3rd ed. with preface by Ivan Roots, 1986), 53.
22. Ibid, 59.
23. Ibid, 53.
24. Ibid, 58.

Ireton reasoned that, if those without a permanent fixed interest were to be recognised as having a right to vote, that could only be either 'for the end of better being' or to comply with the 'Law of Nature'. Since 'that better being is not certain, and [what is] more, destructive to another', Rainborough's argument necessarily relied on the Law of Nature. That is to say, it relied on the idea that '[by the right of nature] we are free, we are equal', and hence 'one man must have as much voice as another'.[25] This then opened the way to the denial of all property because what was there to stop the unpropertied majority from voting to take the property of others for themselves? What was there to stop them from voting to abolish private ownership of property altogether? As Ireton put it to Rainborough, 'I would fain have any man show me [the] bounds [of that natural right], where you will end, and [why you should not] take away all property'. For 'if by . . . right of nature (whatever it be) . . . one man hath an equal right with another to the choosing of him that shall govern him', then 'by the same right of nature, he hath the same [equal] right in any goods he sees — meat, drink, clothes — to take and use them for his sustenance'. Likewise, he 'hath a freedom to the land, [to take] the ground, to exercise it, till it; he hath the [same] freedom to anything that any one doth account himself' to own.[26] Ireton concluded: 'let every man consider with himself that he do not go that way to take away all property. For here is the case of the most fundamental part of the constitution of the kingdom, which if you take away, you take away all by that.'[27]

While not disagreeing that property was a fundamental part of the country's constitution, Rainborough disputed that his argument implied a denial of property. To suppose that, he said, was 'to forget the Law of God'. 'That there's a property, the Law of God says it; else . . . God [would not have] made that law, *Thou shalt not steal*.'[28] The issue was not property. It was the relationship between property and sovereignty. Sovereignty belonged to the people, not to parliament, not to the wealthy few who had arrogated to themselves the right to rule by perpetuating unjust property-related voting qualifications. Why did Ireton assume that it was for Rainborough to justify the extension of the franchise? Why was it not for Ireton to justify the existing *restriction* of the franchise? 'I desire to know', said Rainborough, 'how this [the franchise] comes to be a property in some men, and not in others.'[29] Once again,

25. Ibid.
26. Ibid.
27. Ibid, 57.
28. Ibid, 59.
29. Ibid, 63.

there were limited logical options: 'either it must be the Law of God or the law of man that must prohibit the meanest man in the kingdom to have this benefit [the franchise] as well as the greatest'. He continued: 'I do not find anything in the Law of God, that a lord shall choose twenty burgesses,[30] and a gentleman but two, or a poor man shall choose none: I find no such thing in the Law of Nature, nor in the Law of Nations.'[31] It was purely English law that had created this state of affairs: 'the old law of England — and that which enslaves the people of England — that they should be bound by laws in which they have no voice at all!'[32]

Someone else in the debate said that if the poor were given the vote, property would be in jeopardy because 'five parts of the nation . . . would then come in'. To which Rainborough's response was: 'Then, I say, the one part shall make hewers of wood and drawers of water [i.e. labourers, menial drudges][33] of the other five, and so the greatest part of the nation be enslaved.'[34] With his references here to enslavement, Rainborough touched on a theme that was prominent in much radical thought of the time. This was the idea that the whole history of England since the Norman Conquest had been a history of slavery and subjugation. Before 1066 — so the story ran — the Anglo-Saxon inhabitants of England had lived as free and equal citizens, with self-governing institutions. Then William the Conqueror had come and taken away their freedom and disrupted their equality, and his tyranny had been maintained in force by each successive monarch and his or her loyal lieutenants, the aristocracy and clergy. However, the English people had never forgotten the rights and freedoms they once enjoyed, and the struggle to regain them went on.

It seems that, while some theory along these lines may have existed ever since 1066, there is little evidence of it before the sixteenth century, and it was, in any event, rediscovered and embraced with fresh vigour in the seventeenth century.[35] The 'Norman Yoke' was not a single, uniform theory, but one aspect

30. Burgesses were parliamentary representatives of urban constituencies or 'boroughs'.
31. A. S. P. Woodhouse (ed.), *Puritanism and Liberty: Being the Army Debates 1647–9 from the Clarke Manuscripts with Supplementary Documents* (London: J. M. Dent, 3rd ed. with preface by Ivan Roots, 1986), 56.
32. Ibid, 61.
33. See Hebrew Bible, Joshua 9:21: 'And the leaders said unto them, Let them live; but let them be hewers of wood and drawers of water unto all the congregation; as the leaders had promised them.'
34. A. S. P. Woodhouse (ed.), *Puritanism and Liberty: Being the Army Debates 1647–9 from the Clarke Manuscripts with Supplementary Documents* (London: J. M. Dent, 3rd ed. with preface by Ivan Roots, 1986), 67.
35. Christopher Hill, *Puritanism and Revolution* (London: Secker and Warburg, 1958), 57.

often emphasised in this period was the oppressive character of English law. At Putney the civilian Leveller John Wildman declared, 'we have been under slavery . . . Our very laws were made by our conquerors.'[36] In a similar vein, an earlier Leveller pamphlet denounced 'the laws of this nation' as 'unworthy a free people' and [in need of reconsideration] 'from first to last'.[37] According to the same pamphlet, even the occasional 'concessions' that had been wrung from the monarchs had done little or nothing to advance the people's effort to win back their rights and freedoms. Thus, Magna Carta was 'but a beggarly thing containing many marks of intolerable bondage'.[38] For the Leveller William Walwyn, it was 'that messe of pottage'.[39]

In likening the 'great charter of liberties' of 1215 to the meal for which, in the Book of Genesis, Esau sold his birthright to his younger brother Jacob, Walwyn reflected another theme of mid-seventeenth-century English radical thought, and one especially conspicuous in the Putney Debates. What had the New Model soldiers fought for? Thanks to them, the parliamentary side had emerged victorious in the Civil War. Were those without property, the thousands of men who made up the vast bulk of the various regiments, to remain excluded from the franchise? Did a parliamentary soldier fight, Rainborough asked, 'to enslave himself, to give power to men of riches, men of estates, to make him a perpetual slave'?[40] The Leveller-aligned agitator Edward Sexby said: 'We have . . . ventured our lives, and it was all for this: to recover our birthrights and privileges as Englishmen.' The army's rank and file 'have had little propriety [property] in the kingdom as to our estates', he continued, 'yet we have had a birthright. But it seems now, except a man hath a fixed estate in this kingdom, he hath no right in this kingdom. I wonder we were so much deceived.'[41]

To Sexby, then, as for Walwyn, any post-Civil War constitutional settlement that did not grant ordinary soldiers the vote irrespective of property holdings

36. A. S. P. Woodhouse (ed.), *Puritanism and Liberty: Being the Army Debates 1647–9 from the Clarke Manuscripts with Supplementary Documents* (London: J. M. Dent, 3rd ed. with preface by Ivan Roots, 1986), 65.
37. Richard Overton with William Walwyn, *A Remonstrance of Many Thousand Citizens*, in Andrew Sharp (ed.), *The English Levellers* (Cambridge: Cambridge University Press, 1998), 33, 46.
38. Ibid, 46–47.
39. William Walwyn, *Englands Lamentable Slaverie*, in Jack McMichael and Barbara Taft (eds.), *The Writings of William Walwyn* (Athens, Ga.: University of Georgia Press, 1989), 143, 148.
40. A. S. P. Woodhouse (ed.), *Puritanism and Liberty: Being the Army Debates 1647–9 from the Clarke Manuscripts with Supplementary Documents* (London: J. M. Dent, 3rd ed. with preface by Ivan Roots, 1986), 71.
41. Ibid, 69. As a contemporary term for property, 'propriety' denoted primarily ownership of an 'estate', that is to say, landed property (though see below for the idea of 'self-propriety').

was just another mess of pottage, just another illusory benefit accepted in exchange for precious birthrights. He would not allow this: 'I am resolved to give my birthright to none', he said, adding '[i]f we had not a right to the kingdom, we were mere mercenary soldiers'.[42] As that latter remark makes clear, there was more at stake for Sexby and others who shared his perspective than the Norman Yoke and the project of recovering lost rights. There was also the question of whether ordinary soldiers in the parliamentary army were to be regarded as mere wage-labourers — hired war-workers, like mercenaries — or whether they were instead to be regarded as owner-producers — people fighting their own cause, taking up arms in a country that belonged to them too. Sexby's determination to give his birthright to no-one was equally a determination to allow the fruits of his military labours to be appropriated by no-one. It was an insistence on sharing in ownership of what he and his fellow soldiers in the army's lower ranks had produced.[43]

In the background of this issue of the nature and significance of military labour was the broader issue of labour under conditions of developing agrarian capitalism. Enclosure, engrossment and related practices were continuing to drive more and more small independent proprietors into wage-labour. At the same time, more and more of those who used wage-labour to supplement their incomes were losing their land and their rights of common, and becoming wholly dependent on wages. Yet wages were rarely set at a rate that was sufficient to support a family, and there was little or no protection against employers who failed to pay their employees promptly or at all.[44] Hill writes that, in these circumstances, 'men fought desperately to avoid the abyss of wage labour'.[45] Until well into the industrial age, full-time wage work was seen 'as a kind of hell into which peasants may fall'.[46] Hill and others have shown that the Levellers and their allies in the army came mainly from the class of small independent producers who had hitherto managed to avoid that hell. They were farmers who rented their own land, or artisans who had their

42. Ibid. Sexby articulates here a theme elaborated by Walwyn. See Jack McMichael and Barbara Taft (eds.), *The Writings of William Walwyn* (Athens, Ga.: University of Georgia Press, 1989), 299.
43. On this aspect, see further James Holstun, *Ehud's Dagger: Class Struggle in the English Revolution* (London: Verso, 2000), esp. 240–41.
44. See Christopher Hill, 'Pottage for Freeborn Englishmen: Attitudes to Wage Labour in the Sixteenth and Seventeenth Centuries', in Charles Feinstein (ed.), *Socialism, Capitalism and Economic Growth: Essays Presented to Maurice Dobb* (Cambridge: Cambridge University Press, 1967), 338, 339.
45. Ibid, 340.
46. Ibid, 338.

own workshop and tools.[47] But the independence of such people was not secure; their future was now uncertain and full of fears.

'[W]eep and howl, ye Rich men', wrote the anonymous authors of one Leveller pamphlet, 'God will visit you for all your oppressions; You live on other mens labours, and give them their bran to eat, extorting extreme rents and taxes on your fellow-creatures.' But, the authors warned, 'now what will you do? for the People will no longer be enslaved by you'.[48] In another pamphlet, Richard Overton put forward the idea that all human beings have ownership of themselves. 'To every individual', he declared, 'in nature is given an individual property by nature not to be invaded or usurped by any. For every one, as he is himself, so he has a self-propriety, else could he not *be* himself.'[49] As described by Overton, self-propriety is a natural endowment that belongs equally to everyone: 'by natural birth all men are equally and alike born to like propriety, liberty and freedom'. It is inviolable: no-one 'may presume to deprive any of [it] without manifest violation and affront to the very principles of nature and of the rules of equity and justice between man and man'. And it logically precedes every particular claim to property ownership, which is accordingly contingent upon it: '[m]ine and thine cannot be, except this be'.[50] Considered from the standpoint of political community, self-propriety is popular sovereignty — the people's ownership of themselves — and their legitimate demand, as he expressed it, 'that we may be men and live like men'. 'It is but the just rights and prerogative of mankind (whereunto the people of England are heirs apparent as well as other nations) which we desire', Overton said.[51]

At Putney, Ireton may have put words into the Leveller speakers' mouths when he said they needed to fly for refuge to natural rights. They do not seem to have minded very much, conscious as they nonetheless were that nature had not established and maintained the domination of a property-owning elite. That was a product of history. Later in the century, John Locke would build on the ideas of Overton and others to develop a theory that wove together natural rights, self-propriety and private property.[52] For now,

47. See Brian Manning, *The Far Left in the English Revolution: 1640–1660* (London: Bookmarks, 1999), 15.
48. *Light shining in Buckinghamshire*, in George Sabine (ed.), *The Works of Gerrard Winstanley* (New York: Russell and Russell, 1965), 611, 616.
49. Richard Overton, *An Arrow to all Tyrants*, in Andrew Sharp (ed.), *The English Levellers* (Cambridge: Cambridge University Press, 1998), 54, 55 (emphasis in original).
50. Ibid.
51. Ibid, 57.
52. Brief further reference to Locke is made in chap. 8 below.

self-propriety gave little hint of its future in the explanation, or justification, of private property, and no-one — least of all Ireton — suggested that private property had anything to do with natural rights. In Ireton's words, 'The law of God doth not give me property, nor the Law of Nature, but property is of human constitution . . . Constitution founds property.'[53] The Levellers set up the 'Law of Nature against that constitution'. Ireton's final word on the subject of universal manhood suffrage was that '[l]iberty may be had and property not be destroyed', but it needed to be understood that the liberty which could be had was that of property-owners. Liberty could not 'be provided for in a general sense'.[54]

Events soon overtook the Levellers, and their activism did not continue much beyond 1650. In the immediate aftermath of the Putney Debates, however, the Agreement of the People was revised, and one compromise the Levellers made was a more qualified position on the franchise than Rainborough had expressed in his response to Ireton. The general principle that governmental authority depends on popular consent remained in place, but under the revised scheme of suffrage, alms-takers (those in receipt of poor relief) and 'servants' (those who worked for others, that is to say, wage-labourers) were to be excluded from the right to vote.[55] The Leveller leadership also sought to reassure the grandees at this time by putting on record their opposition to all measures aimed at 'abolishing propriety, levelling men's estates or making all things common'.[56] To many in the faction, the name by which they had become known had always been a slur, designed to discredit them by fixing them with a commitment to social parity they did not hold. The widely read pamphleteer Marchamont Nedham was felt to issue a particular provocation when he wrote of their 'endeavour to cast down and level the enclosures of nobility, gentry, and property, to make us all even: so that every Jack should vie with a gentleman, and every gentleman be made a

53. A. S. P. Woodhouse (ed.), *Puritanism and Liberty: Being the Army Debates 1647–9 from the Clarke Manuscripts with Supplementary Documents* (London: J. M. Dent, 3rd ed. with preface by Ivan Roots, 1986), 69.
54. Ibid, 72–73.
55. See John Lilburne, William Walwyn, Thomas Prince and Richard Overton, *An Agreement of the Free People of England*, in Andrew Sharp (ed.), *The English Levellers* (Cambridge: Cambridge University Press, 1998), 168, 170. On this, see further C. B. Macpherson, *The Political Theory of Possessive Individualism* (Oxford: Oxford University Press, 1962), chap. 3.
56. John Lilburne et al., *The Petition of 11 September 1648*, in Andrew Sharp (ed.), *The English Levellers* (Cambridge: Cambridge University Press, 1998), 131, 137.

Jack'.[57] But Nedham's contemptuous quip did not rattle everyone who advocated for 'liberty in a general sense', and let us turn now to those who instead embraced the Leveller name.

A common treasury

St George's Hill, where the first Digger colony was established in April 1649, is on the edge of Windsor Great Park at the intersection of the present counties of Berkshire and Surrey. Since the early 1640s the area had been the site of protests due to regulatory changes that curtailed rights of common and also brought an increase in the number of deer in the forest, endangering local farmers' crops. At the same time, rights of common were being more strictly enforced than previously against those who lacked customary entitlements. In 1646 a number of residents of the nearby village of Cobham were fined by a local manorial court for digging peat and cutting turves — valuable sources of fuel — on the village commons. Not holding manorial tenancies, they did not qualify for customary use-rights, and under prevailing law they could have access to such resources only at the will of the lord of the manor, who was no longer pleased to allow it. Among those fined was Gerrard Winstanley.[58]

Originally from Wigan in the north-west of the country, Winstanley had come to the Cobham area in 1643 from London, where he had run a small mercery business. Wartime disruption of the cloth trade had forced him to sell up, and he was now making a precarious living in the countryside as a herdsman or grazier. Historians report that the second half of the 1640s was an especially difficult time for people of modest means in England.[59] As well as bringing about a general economic downturn, the Civil War had imposed heavy burdens in the shape of requisitions, taxes and the obligation to provide free quarter to soldiers. Then, from 1646 to 1650 a series of calamitous harvest failures brought the recurrence of dearth, and with soaring grain prices, the purchasing power of the poor collapsed. In these circumstances, as Steve

57. Quoted in Blair Worden, 'The Levellers in History and Memory, c. 1660–1960', in Michael Mendle (ed.), *The Putney Debates of 1647: The Army, the Levellers and the English State* (Cambridge: Cambridge University Press, 2001), 256, 281.
58. On this episode, see John Gurney, *Brave Community: the Digger Movement in the English Revolution* (Manchester: Manchester University Press, 2007), 50.
59. See Steve Hindle, 'Dearth and the English Revolution: The Harvest Crisis of 1647–50' *Economic History Review* 61, S1 (2008) 64.

Hindle explains, the Levellers and their army allies might speak highmindedly of not selling birthrights for a mess of pottage, but for those further down the socio-economic scale, the pottage also mattered.[60] Or rather, the pottage was itself a birthright. Thus, Hindle writes of the assertion of 'the right to subsist', reflected in demands to '[purchase] grain at a reasonable price' so that poorer consumers would not lose the possibility of 'putting food on the table for their hungry families'.[61]

Traditional approaches to dearth emphasised market regulation, and although the late sixteenth- and early seventeenth-century practice of reissuing the Book of Orders on which we touched in the previous chapter had fallen out of favour, Hindle shows that, from about 1647, measures were put in place, initially by local magistrates and then eventually by Parliament, to manage the supply of grain.[62] The upshot seems to have been that starvation was largely, if not wholly, averted. But how did England's poor come to be so vulnerable to the effects of dearth in the first place? What were the social, economic and political conditions in which hunger and the threat of hunger arose? Those were the questions that interested Winstanley. He saw that the poor were losing non-market access to the means of subsistence. He also saw that compulsory market mediation forced the poor to compete with the rich. Yet the poor could not compete with the rich; those who could afford more would always have the possibility of getting more, and when prices rose, those who could afford less would be at risk in the satisfaction of their basic needs. Winstanley believed that things did not have to continue this way. In *The New Law of Righteousnes* he laid out the beginnings of a programme aimed at restoring direct access by the poor to the means of subsistence, but on the basis of a new system involving communal production and enhanced use of land.

The text was completed at a moment of unprecedented expectation or, at least, hope. The country's tyrannical king, Charles I, had been put on trial earlier in the same month, and would be executed just four days after the date recorded in Winstanley's preface (26 January 1649).[63] The central argument advanced in this work was that God had made the earth 'to be a common Treasury for all'.[64] That it had been converted into 'a particular

60. Ibid, 93–94.
61. Ibid, 93.
62. Ibid, 74 et seq.
63. Winstanley actually gave the date as 26 January 1648. Adjusting for the later shift from the Gregorian to the Julian calendar, however, the year to which he referred was 1649.
64. Gerrard Winstanley, *The New Law of Righteousnes*, in Thomas Corns, Ann Hughes and David Loewenstein (eds.), *The Complete Works of Gerrard Winstanley, Vol. I* (Oxford: Oxford University Press, 2009), 472, 520.

Treasury for some' was the true meaning of the Fall of Man.[65] Like earlier writers, Winstanley explained enclosure and the privatisation of land-holding in terms of moral turpitude. Covetousness had led the rich to 'lock up the treasures of the earth'.[66] A few 'unrighteous men' sat high and mighty in 'the chair of tyranny', while others were 'trod under the foot-stool of misery'.[67] However, with this moralising came also a striking political analysis that encompassed causes, consequences and remedies. As indicated in the passage just quoted, Winstanley recognised that tyranny had many faces. Not only a matter of the arbitrary rule of kings, it was a potentiality that belonged to relationships of power of all kinds. Thus, 'many husbands, parents, masters, magistrates . . . doe carry themselves like oppressing Lords over such as are under them; not knowing that their wives, children, servants, subjects are their fellow creatures, and hath an equall priviledge to share with them in the blessing of liberty'.[68]

Winstanley seems to have regarded it as self-evident that the patriarchal family was a structure of power and often tyranny, just as he understood that relations of domination and oppression were the social reality of wage-labour. Relatedly, he also comprehended that, under conditions of developing agrarian capitalism, the appropriation of the social surplus depended on the exploitation of labour. If a few unrighteous men had locked up the treasures of the earth and now sat in the chair of tyranny, that was ultimately because 'the common-people by their labours . . . have lifted up their Landlords and others to rule in tyranny and oppression over them'.[69] And if the common people by their labours had lifted up their landlords and others to rule in tyranny and oppression over them, might not the common people equally be able to *bring down* that tyranny and oppression by withdrawing their labour and redeploying it to sustain themselves? This was the wager from which Winstanley's programme proceeded. '[Y]ou dust of the earth, that are trod under foot', he wrote, 'you poor people, that [make] . . . rich men, your oppressours by your labours. Take notice of your priviledge, the Law of Righteousnesse is now declared.'[70]

65. Ibid.
66. Ibid, 504.
67. Ibid, 503, 482.
68. Ibid, 481.
69. Ibid, 482.
70. Ibid, 516.

Under the Law of Righteousness there would be no more buying and selling of land, no more working for hire, no more enclosure and private estate-holding. But 'if the rich wil stil hold fast this propriety of *Mine and thine*', then, he proposed, 'let them labour their own Land with their own hands'. And 'let the common-People . . . that say the earth is ours, not mine, let them labour together, and eat bread together upon the Commons, Mountains, and Hils'.[71] As he tells the story in *The New Law of Righteousnes*, Winstanley conceived — or rather, received in a trance — the idea of labour withdrawal and communal production before he had identified a 'place and manner' of implementing the programme.[72] That came, as already mentioned, some months later, with digging starting on St George's Hill on 1 April 1649. *The True Levellers Standard Advanced* appeared on 26 April 1649, and was subscribed with the names of fifteen men, including Winstanley. It was addressed 'to the Powers of England, and to all the powers of the world'.[73]

Again, the authors asserted that the Creator, which they now called 'Reason', had 'made the Earth to be a common Treasury'. And again, they used the language of original sin to indict the actions of those who 'hedged [the earth] into In-closures' so that it could be 'kept in the hands of a few'.[74] Private ownership of land — 'civill propriety' — was 'the curse the Creation groans under',[75] and the Diggers expressed their determination to break that curse and remake the earth into a 'common Store-house for all'.[76] There had been many 'good words from Pulpits and Councell Tables'. The common people waited and waited 'for good, and for deliverances, but none comes'. Indeed, 'while they wait for liberty, behold greater bondage comes insteed of it'.[77] Thus, the authors continued, now moving into the first person singular of revelation and ordinance, 'I do not intreat thee, for thou art not to be intreated . . . I Command thee, To *let Israel go free . . . hold [the people] no longer in bondage*.'[78] Evoking here the Book of Exodus, the Diggers also pinned their demands to the vernacular theory of the Norman Yoke, on which we

71. Ibid, 518.
72. Ibid, 517.
73. William Everard et al., *A Declaration to the Powers of England (The True Levellers Standard Advanced)*, in Thomas Corns, Ann Hughes and David Loewenstein (eds.), *The Complete Works of Gerrard Winstanley, Vol. II* (Oxford: Oxford University Press, 2009), 1, 4.
74. Ibid, 5.
75. Ibid, 6.
76. Ibid, 5.
77. Ibid, 17.
78. Ibid, 19.

touched in connection with earlier Leveller debates.[79] 'O what mighty delusion do you, who are the powers of England, live in!', they exclaimed. '[Y]ou pretend to throw down that Norman yoke . . . yet you still lift' it up.[80] For '[t]ake notice that England is not a free-people, till the poor that have no Land, have a free allowance to dig and labour the Commons and so live as comfortably as the Landlords that live in their Inclosures'.[81]

Winstanley elaborated on the significance for the Diggers' project of the Norman Yoke in a series of pamphlets published later in 1649 and in 1650. Going further than *The True Levellers Standard Advanced*, he argued that the right of landlords to control common and waste lands could not survive the beheading of the last in the line of 'Norman' kings, Charles I. As that right was dependent on law, which was in turn dependent on monarchical authority, it had lapsed with the execution of the king. In his words, 'all Lords of Mannors hold Title to the Commons by no stronger hold then the Kings Will'. '[N]ow if you cast off the King who was the Head of that power, surely the power of Lords of Mannors is the same'.[82] It was an idea that went to the heart of what Brian Manning has described as the 'head-on clash between the lords of manors and the main body of the peasantry' which was underway at this time in the English countryside. As Manning characterises it, the 'conflict was to decide whether the landlords and big farmers or the mass of the peasantry were to control and develop the wastes and commons'.[83] The Diggers were certainly aware of the need to develop these lands. They realised that, to feed a growing population, it was not enough simply to defend customary rights of common. Winstanley estimated that between half and two-thirds of England was not properly cultivated, and one third lay 'waste and barren'.[84] The question was by what modality common and waste land would be brought under more intensive cultivation, and for whose benefit.

79. Exodus 9:1: 'Then the Lord said to Moses, "Go in to Pharaoh and say to him, 'Thus says the Lord, the God of the Hebrews, "Let my people go, that they may serve me."'

80. William Everard et al., *A Declaration to the Powers of England (The True Levellers Standard Advanced)*, in Thomas Corns, Ann Hughes and David Loewenstein (eds.), *The Complete Works of Gerrard Winstanley, Vol. II* (Oxford: Oxford University Press, 2009), 1, 13 (emphasis omitted).

81. Ibid.

82. Gerrard Winstanley, *A New-yeers Gift*, in Thomas Corns, Ann Hughes and David Loewenstein (eds.), *The Complete Works of Gerrard Winstanley, Vol. II* (Oxford: Oxford University Press, 2009), 107, 114.

83. Brian Manning, *The English People and the English Revolution* (London: Penguin, 1978), 135.

84. Gerrard Winstanley, John Barker and Thomas Star, *An Appeal to the House of Commons*, in Thomas Corns, Ann Hughes and David Loewenstein (eds.), *The Complete Works of Gerrard Winstanley, Vol. II* (Oxford: Oxford University Press, 2009), 65, 69. See further Christopher Hill, 'Introduction', in Christopher Hill (ed.), *Winstanley: The Law of Freedom and Other Writings* (London: Penguin, 1973), 9, 23.

Hill writes that, in the long run, '[e]nclosure by men with capital, brutally disregarding rights of commoners did at least do the job; in the long run . . . it created more employment. But in the short run it disrupted a way of life, causing intense misery; and the employment which it did ultimately create was not of a sort to attract free commoners.'[85] The Diggers' alternative was common ownership. The people would lay collective claim to common and waste land, and would work it together, sharing its fruits. They would proceed one Digger colony at a time, and as more and more colonies were established, the area under common ownership would expand, so that eventually 'all the Commons and waste ground in England, and in the whole World' would be encompassed.[86] The system was to be voluntary, and hence, for the present, a bifurcated arrangement was envisaged. The rich could remain 'in their inclosures, saying This is mine', while the poor lived 'upon their Commons, saying This is ours'.[87] Attempts at expropriation were not part of the Diggers' programme. They simply relied on labour withdrawal to undermine the basis of private land ownership. Or, as Winstanley put it to the men of property, the Diggers would wait for the 'Spirit in you freely [to] give it [the land you have taken into private ownership] up'.[88] In the fullness of time, the 'universall spreading of the divine power' would bring universal participation in the new scheme of communal production, he believed.[89]

As already noted, Winstanley and his companions in fact faced very considerable hostility from local landowners and others. Forced off St George's Hill, they moved in August 1649 to nearby Little Heath at Cobham. In that same month, Winstanley wrote that he felt 'like a man in a storm, standing under shelter . . . [and] waiting till the storm be over to see the end of it'.[90] But he

85. Christopher Hill, *The World Turned Upside Down: Radical Ideas During the English Revolution* (London: Penguin, 1975), 130.
86. William Everard et al., *A Declaration to the Powers of England (The True Levellers Standard Advanced)*, in Thomas Corns, Ann Hughes and David Loewenstein (eds.), *The Complete Works of Gerrard Winstanley, Vol. II* (Oxford: Oxford University Press, 2009), 1, 14.
87. Gerrard Winstanley, *The New Law of Righteousnes*, in Thomas Corns, Ann Hughes and David Loewenstein (eds.), *The Complete Works of Gerrard Winstanley, Vol. I* (Oxford: Oxford University Press, 2009), 472, 519.
88. Gerrard Winstanley, *A Letter to the Lord Fairfax*, in Thomas Corns, Ann Hughes and David Loewenstein (eds.), *The Complete Works of Gerrard Winstanley, Vol. II* (Oxford: Oxford University Press, 2009), 43, 46.
89. Gerrard Winstanley, *The New Law of Righteousnes*, in Thomas Corns, Ann Hughes and David Loewenstein (eds.), *The Complete Works of Gerrard Winstanley, Vol. I* (Oxford: Oxford University Press, 2009), 472, 503–04.
90. Gerrard Winstanley, *A Watch-Word to the City of London and the Armie*, in Thomas Corns, Ann Hughes and David Loewenstein (eds.), *The Complete Works of Gerrard Winstanley, Vol. II* (Oxford: Oxford University Press, 2009), 79, 91–92.

also wrote, now alluding to the Acts of the Apostles and various other passages from the scriptures, that 'freedom is the man that will turn the world upside downe, therefore no wonder he hath enemies'.[91] In digging the commons and wastes, the Diggers were simultaneously '[digging] up . . . all that Art and Trade of darknesse' whereby the rich 'get money under couller of Law'.[92] The rebel colonists' activities had significance on multiple levels at once. Yet there was a literal level of collective sustenance or 'common preservation' of which they never lost sight. This received particular emphasis in manifestos that have come down to us from two of the ten or so further Digger communities that were established during the course of 1649 and 1650.

For the Diggers of Wellingborough in Northamptonshire[93] and of Iver in Buckinghamshire — localities at which large numbers of people were barely surviving on alms — digging seems to have been, first and foremost, a solution to the problem of hunger.[94] The earth had become a source of profit-taking for the rich, who 'drawe all the treasures and fruits of the earth into their nests and holes [like Ratts and Mice]'. 'Therefore', they wrote, 'you of the poorer sort, understand this, that nothing but the manuring [and, with that, cultivation] of the common Land, will reduce you into a comfortable condition.'[95] In another Digger pamphlet, Robert Coster — one of Winstanley's co-colonists in Surrey — made explicit the Diggers' belief that 'a Livelihood [is] . . . the right . . . of every man'.[96] If only the poor could reclaim the means of subsistence, rather than going 'with Cap in hand and bended knee, to Gentlemen Farmers, begging and intreating to work for them for [meagre

91. Ibid, 81. See Acts 17:6: 'And when they could not find them, they dragged Jason and some of the brothers before the city authorities, shouting, "These men who have turned the world upside down have come here also, and Jason has received them, and they are all acting against the decrees of Caesar, saying that there is another king, Jesus."' It seems that *The World Turned Upside Down* was the title of a broadside ballad which had appeared a few years earlier; see Christopher Hill, *The World Turned Upside Down* (London: Penguin, 1975), 380.

92. Gerrard Winstanley, *A Watch-Word to the City of London and the Armie*, in Thomas Corns, Ann Hughes and David Loewenstein (eds.), *The Complete Works of Gerrard Winstanley, Vol. II* (Oxford: Oxford University Press, 2009), 79, 97. On this metaphorical dimension, see Nigel Smith, 'Gerrard Winstanley and the Literature of Revolution', in Andrew Bradstock (ed.), *Winstanley and the Diggers, 1649–1999* (London: Frank Cass, 2000), 47, 51, 58.

93. On commemoration of the activities of the Wellingborough Diggers, see further chap. 10 below.

94. The Diggers of Wellingborough report that in one parish 1169 people were in receipt of alms. They write: 'our wives and children cry for bread . . . and we cannot get bread for one of them by our labour'. See *A Declaration by the Diggers of Wellingborough*, in Andrew Hopton, *Digger Tracts, 1649–50* (London: Aporia Press, 1989), 29.

95. *A Declaration by the Diggers of Iver*, in Andrew Hopton, *Digger Tracts, 1649–50* (London: Aporia Press, 1989), 31, 32.

96. Robert Coster, *A Mite Cast into the Common Treasury*, in Andrew Hopton, *Digger Tracts, 1649–50* (London: Aporia Press, 1989), 11, 13.

pay]', that right would be secure. Moreover, the gentlemen farmers would be deprived of an 'occasion to tyrannize over poor people', in collaboration with the landlords.[97] For if the surplus labour of the poor could no longer be exploited, the farmers would not have the possibility of running the kinds of commercial enterprise that enabled them to pay high rents to their landlords. And if the landlords could not command high rents, they would lack 'those great baggs of money . . . which are carried into them by their Tenants', and in turn, they too would be cut down to size. '[D]own would fall the Lordliness of their spirits', Coster predicted, 'and then poor men might speak to them; then there might be an acknowledging of one another to be fellow-Creatures.'[98]

According to John Gurney, it may have been evidence of growing support for the Diggers that eventually sealed their fate.[99] On 19 April 1650, the colony at Little Heath was burned down by men said to have been hired by local landowners. And while at least one of the other colonies is known to have carried on for a little longer, the whole experiment was over by the passing of spring. Winstanley's final text, entitled *The Law of Freedom in a Platform*, appeared almost two years later, in February 1652. Dedicated to Oliver Cromwell, it was an intervention in debates which had been initiated about reform in the post-monarchical 'Commonwealth and Free-State'. Would Cromwell and the other leaders of the new republic 'onely remove the Conquerors Power out of the Kings hand into other mens, maintaining the old Laws still', or would they 'set the Land free'?[100] Emancipation was a theme of all Winstanley's works, but in this text he dwelled at some length on the concept of freedom. Freedom could mean many things, he observed. There was freedom to trade, freedom of religion, sexual freedom of the sort advocated by Abiezer Coppe and other Ranters, and freedom to own private property. 'All these, and such like [were] Freedoms', but they were freedoms that left the people as a whole in bondage. They were forms of 'particular Freedom', whereas what was needed for true emancipation was 'common Freedom', which he also termed 'Foundation-Freedom'.[101]

97. Ibid, 12–13.
98. Ibid, 12.
99. See John Gurney, *Brave Community: the Digger Movement in the English Revolution* (Manchester: Manchester University Press, 2007), 185.
100. Gerrard Winstanley, *The Law of Freedom in a Platform*, in Thomas Corns, Ann Hughes and David Loewenstein (eds.), *The Complete Works of Gerrard Winstanley, Vol. II* (Oxford: Oxford University Press, 2009), 278, 279.
101. Ibid, 294–95.

For Winstanley, foundation-freedom depended on free access by all to the earth, that being the basis of human 'nourishment and preservation',[102] as also of peaceful and dignified life, and in the remainder of *The Law of Freedom in a Platform*, he laid out a detailed blueprint for reorganising the state so as to realise and sustain foundation-freedom. He called the form of government in such a state 'commonwealths' government, as distinct from 'kingly' government, and wrote that 'seeing England is declared to be a free Commonwealth, and the name thereof established by a Law; surely then the greatest work is now to be done, and that is to escape all Kingly cheats . . . [and bring it about] that the power and the name may agree together'.[103] Thinking back to the Levellers' discussions and the rights around which they revolved, it is evident that, from the perspective of the Diggers, something very important had been omitted. The right to subsist, the right to a livelihood, the right of access to the earth as a site of human sustenance and emancipation were, in their judgement, cardinal birthrights (to use a word which Winstanley also used, especially in *The Law of Freedom in a Platform*).

To be sure, Winstanley conversely passed over the right that had such prominence in official Leveller thought, especially at and after Putney — the right to vote. But if his list of freedoms did not include reference to political freedom, his belief was beyond doubt that the disenfranchisement of the unpropertied belonged with the pathology of kingly government. The point, for him, was that meaningful change depended on transforming the conditions within which property ownership could determine political participation. And he highlighted the agency and responsibility of the poor in bringing about that transformation. He also directed attention to the creativity of the poor, initiating with others a pattern of activities which took familiar practices and developed them in unfamiliar ways. Thus, the Diggers' programme bore some resemblance to anti-enclosure protest. They plainly sought to put a stop to enclosure, but unlike earlier (and later) anti-enclosure protesters, they did not attack particular enclosures or insist on the customary rights of access thereby extinguished. Instead, they claimed uncultivated land for the common people as a whole, and simply occupied the land and set about cultivating it.

In doing so, they can be seen as having carried forward a long tradition of squatting and encroachment on forests and wastes.[104] Yet again they also

102. Ibid, 295.
103. Ibid, 311–12.
104. See Keith Thomas, 'Another Digger Broadside', *Past and Present* 42 (1969) 57, 58.

departed from that tradition inasmuch as their endeavours were part of an organised collective project of communal production and labour withdrawal. The Diggers took possession of areas of common land in order to form communities that would work together, eat together, and cooperate in achieving better conditions of life for ordinary people. Finally, their approach to communal production, while quite different from what passed in official circles for 'improvement', overlapped in some respects with the concurrent activities of their entrepreneurial contemporaries.[105] The Diggers recognised the need for enhanced agricultural productivity, and they employed some modern techniques of cultivation. Crucially, however, they believed that improvement should be undertaken by, and for the benefit of, everyone.

Winstanley's approach to the Norman Yoke was also highly distinctive — and not only because of the way he used the theory to challenge the legal validity of landed property in the new republican order. What marked off his approach from that of most other radicals was that he refrained from hitching his anti-Normanism to philo-Saxonism.[106] For him, there was no golden age of Saxon freedom before the Norman conquest, no ancient constitution that could undo the subjugation of the intervening centuries if only it were restored. As he explained, '[t]he Reformation that England now is to endeavour, is not to remove the Norman Yoke only, and to bring us back to be governed by those Laws that were before William the Conqueror came in, as if that were the rule or marke we aime at'. 'No', he emphasised, 'that is not it.' The plan is 'Reformation . . . according to the Word of God, and that is the pure Law of righteousnesse before the fall'.[107]

It seems, then, that the society Winstanley envisioned was of a kind not yet known, a society without historical precedent that he nonetheless held to be latent in the circumstances of his own life and the life of those around him. The Diggers dug the earth to sustain themselves, but also to excavate the sources of transformative change. Furthermore, they dug to clear the way for such change, conscious that tyranny had not ended with the execution of the king and the abolition of the monarchy. As Winstanley memorably put it, 'that top-bow is lopped off the tree of Tyrannie, and Kingly power in that

105. On improvement, see further chap. 7 below.
106. On this point, see James Holstun, *Ehud's Dagger: Class Struggle in the English Revolution* (London: Verso, 2000), 395.
107. Gerrard Winstanley, *A Letter to the Lord Fairfax*, in Thomas Corns, Ann Hughes and David Loewenstein (eds.), *The Complete Works of Gerrard Winstanley, Vol. II* (Oxford: Oxford University Press, 2009), 43, 55 (emphasis omitted).

one particular is cast out; but alas oppression is a great tree still . . . [It] hath many branches and great roots which must be grub'd up' — that is to say, dug up — 'before every one can sing Sions songs in peace.'[108]

Two models

The revolt within the English Revolution took place against the backdrop of developments that consolidated and advanced the trends already highlighted in previous chapters. The earth, so alive for working people and so integral to their lives, was becoming inert matter to be instrumentalised for the generation of profit. The state, initially perturbed by enclosure, was undergoing capture by the emergent class of agrarian capitalists, whose interests as enclosers it increasingly defended. Private property, the once scandalous or at any rate highly contentious law of 'mine and thine', was turning into the norm, eclipsing the principle of shared use and the (formal and informal) rights of common through which that principle was known, experienced and enforced.[109] James Holstun writes of an epochal struggle between two models of the human relationship to land, the outcome of which must have seemed to contemporaries increasingly plain. On the one hand, there was a 'rights-based model that gave the direct producers some measure of immediate access to the agrarian means of production'. On the other hand, there was a 'model of absolute property that gave them such access only through the mediation of the capitalist wage form'.[110]

We have seen in this chapter that, at the Putney Debates, Ireton drew a distinction between civil rights and natural rights. To his way of thinking, property was itself a right, but importantly it was civil right, by which he meant that it was a legal institution established and recognised under the constitution. And just as under the constitution that right only belonged to some, so too the franchise could not belong to all. If you extend the franchise to those without property, he said, you must rely on a natural right, and then the outcome will be to put all private ownership at risk. Ellen Wood remarks that

108. Gerrard Winstanley, *A New-yeers Gift for the Parliament and Armie*, in Thomas Corns, Ann Hughes and David Loewenstein (eds.), *The Complete Works of Gerrard Winstanley, Vol. II* (Oxford: Oxford University Press, 2009), 107, 112.

109. See further Andrew McRae, *God Speed the Plough: The Representation of Agrarian England 1550–1660* (Cambridge: Cambridge University Press, 1996), esp. 10.

110. James Holstun, *Ehud's Dagger: Class Struggle in the English Revolution* (London: Verso, 2000), 378.

the later Lockean approach, which turned that argument around and used natural rights to account for private property, 'may seem the most powerful defence of propertied interests'. To Ireton and others of his time, however, it was considered less 'easy to explain and justify gross inequalities of property on the basis of a natural right vested in the individual' than on the basis of convention. Thus, the argument advanced was 'simply that the present system [had] existed as long as anyone [could] remember', that it was inseparable from the constitution, and that an attack on the constitution was 'a threat to any social order and peace'.[111]

From the perspective of the Levellers, the English constitution was a Norman Yoke. The law of England enslaved the people, said Rainborough, binding them to laws in which they had no say. Sexby declared that he would give his birthright to no-one. He had a right to the kingdom which he was determined to reclaim. According to Overton, it was the just rights and prerogative of mankind — rights and prerogative to which the people of England were heirs, along with the people of other nations — that the Levellers desired. As Wood reads these statements, the Levellers manifestly drew on the trope of historic subjugation, but at the same time, and whether or not in response to the claim ascribed to them by Ireton, 'something like a more universal conception of natural rights [kept] emerging from beneath [the] historical argument'. In their account, the Norman Yoke was illegitimate 'not just because it . . . destroyed a more ancient order in England but . . . also because it [violated] certain more basic principles'.[112] For Hill too, the Levellers 'made use of a version of the Anglo-Saxon past, but they also moved forward to a conception of natural rights'. 'It was a momentous transition', he suggests, 'from the recovery of rights which used to exist to the pursuit of rights because they ought to exist: from historical mythology to political philosophy'.[113]

Rainborough said that the poorest he had a life to live as much as the greatest he, and in the writings and activities of the Diggers, the corollary of that life to live was the rights-based model of the human relationship to land to which Holstun refers. Winstanley and his companions set about asserting their entitlement to some measure of immediate access to the agrarian means of production by occupying uncultivated common land and cultivating it.

111. Ellen Meiksins Wood, *Liberty and Property* (London: Verso, 2012), 237.
112. Ibid, 236–37.
113. Christopher Hill, *Puritanism and Revolution* (London: Secker and Warburg, 1958), 75 (emphasis omitted).

That the earth was a common treasury for all was axiomatic to him. If it had been made into a particular treasury for some, he related this to a broader contradiction between social privilege and common humanity. Many husbands, parents, masters and magistrates carry themselves like oppressive lords, he noted, unaware that their wives, children, servants and subjects are their fellow creatures, and have an equal right to share in the blessing of liberty. Coster encapsulated the Diggers' claim with the assertion that a livelihood is everyone's right, and he proposed that, if only the poor could reclaim their own means of subsistence, rather than having to go to gentlemen farmers with cap in hand and on bended knee to beg for work on inadequate pay, this right would be secure.

As this formulation makes clear, the Diggers thought of life not simply in terms of survival (Cromwell's 'interest in breathing'), but in terms of the conditions for a decent existence — sustenance and security, as well as dignity. On 20 April 1649 Winstanley and another Digger leader were brought before the Parliamentary commander-in-chief, General Thomas Fairfax, and required to explain what they were doing on St George's Hill. It is said that, as a symbol of their refusal of subservience, they kept their hats on in Fairfax's presence.[114] *The True Levellers Standard Advanced* was written by, and on behalf of, the 'poor despised People' of England, but Hill observes that, like Overton and other radicals, Winstanley framed his ideas with reference to humankind as a whole.[115] Andy Wood comments that the Diggers presented an analysis that was 'simultaneously local and panoramic'. Attentive to the 'intensely parochial character of English social conflict . . ., [they] moved with ease from an assessment of the micro-politics of the parish into a macro-analysis of English social relations',[116] and from there, to claims on 'all the powers' affecting all 'the commons and waste Grounds' of the entire world. Over a century later, a new concept would gain currency to describe, and delimit, claims on all powers and the just rights and prerogative of humankind. Let us turn to it now.

114. Christopher Hill, 'Introduction', in Christopher Hill (ed.), *Winstanley: The Law of Freedom and Other Writings* (London: Penguin, 1973), 9, 27.
115. See Christopher Hill, *The World Turned Upside Down* (London: Penguin, 1972), 138.
116. Andy Wood, *Riot, Rebellion and Popular Politics* (London: Palgrave, 2002), 159–60.

5

The French Revolution Controversy

The monstrous doctrine

In May 1794 a report was presented to the British Parliament which purported to reveal the existence of a conspiracy to overthrow the monarchy and turn Britain into a republic, as had recently happened in France.[1] In the debate convened to consider the report, Prime Minister William Pitt raised the question of how the country found itself in this predicament. What could account for such a conspiracy? According to the *New Annual Register*, it was his view that the 'whole system of insurrection was laid in the monstrous doctrine of the rights of man, which seduced the weak and ignorant to overturn government, law, property, security, and whatever was valuable'. That doctrine had already 'destroyed whatever was valuable in France', and now it 'endangered the safety, if not the existence, of every nation in Europe'.[2]

To those sitting in the House of Commons, this would have been a very familiar argument. It had been expounded at considerable length by the prominent Anglo-Irish writer and politician Edmund Burke in *Reflections on the Revolution in France,* published in November 1790. In Burke's assessment, the French Revolution was 'a great crisis, not of the affairs of France alone, but of all Europe, perhaps of more than Europe'.[3] And behind the crisis, putting 'every thing . . . out of nature', was 'that monstrous fiction', the rights of man.[4]

1. Report of 16 May 1794. See *The New Annual Register, or General Repository of History, Politics and Literature for the Year 1794* (London: G.G. and J. Robinson, 1795), 190.
2. Ibid.
3. Edmund Burke, *Reflections on the Revolution in France* (London: Penguin, 1968), 92.
4. Ibid, 92, 124.

A False Tree of Liberty. Susan Marks, Oxford University Press (2019). © Susan Marks.
DOI: 10.1093/oso/9780199675456.003.0005

Burke had first publicly intimated that this was how he saw things in a speech in Parliament in February 1790. Characterising the revolutionaries in France as the 'ablest architects of ruin that had hitherto existed in the world', he had spoken of the danger that 'the present distemper of France' would spread.[5]

Thomas Paine — an acquaintance from the days of their shared support for the American Revolution — was among many who were dismayed by Burke's reaction. Paine was in Paris at the time, and he wrote to Burke in an attempt to sway him towards a more positive appreciation of the revolutionaries' actions. Upon learning that Burke remained steadfast in his opinion and intended to set it out in writing, Paine later said that '[a]s the attack was made in a language but little studied and less understood in France, and as everything suffers by translation, I promised some of the friends of the Revolution in that country, that whenever Mr Burke's pamphlet came forth, I would answer it.'[6] Paine's answer was a huge, and soon legendary, publishing success.[7] And with Burke's 'monstrous fiction' right there on its title page, *Rights of Man* declared the analysis put forward by Burke to be itself 'marvellous and monstrous'.[8]

Burke and Paine were, and still remain, each other's most famous critics. But they were by no means each other's only critics. The 'Revolution controversy' of 1790s England saw the unfolding of a complex war of words (and images) that engaged many contributors and spanned an array of different perspectives.[9] That multifaceted clash will preoccupy us in one way or another for most of the rest of this book. In this chapter we take a preliminary look at some of the works associated with it. Of particular interest here and in the succeeding chapters will be the question of how the authors variously conceptualised the rights of man, what they had in mind when they spoke in that idiom or heard it. For if one issue in this controversy was whether the rights of man should be denounced or vindicated, another was what the rights of man should mean.

5. Edmund Burke, *Substance of the Speech of the Right Honourable Edmund Burke, in the Debate on the Army Estimates in the House of Commons, 9 February 1790* (London: J. Debrett, 1790), 7, 11.
6. Thomas Paine, *Rights of Man, Part I*, in Bruce Kuklick (ed.), *Paine: Political Writings* (Cambridge: Cambridge University Press, 2000), 57, 59.
7. As indicated in chap. 1 above, diverse sales figures appear in the historical literature, though there is general agreement that sales of the work were unprecedented. See, e.g., Marilyn Butler, *Burke, Paine, Godwin and the Revolution Controversy* (Cambridge: Cambridge University Press, 1984), 108.
8. Thomas Paine, *Rights of Man, Part I*, in Bruce Kuklick (ed.), *Paine: Political Writings* (Cambridge: Cambridge University Press, 2000), 57, 62.
9. The phrase 'Revolution controversy' comes from Marilyn Butler (ed.), *Burke, Paine, Godwin and the Revolution Controversy* (Cambridge: Cambridge University Press, 1984).

A general amendment

As a debate about the significance of the French Revolution for England, the Revolution controversy is generally dated to 4 November 1789. On that day Richard Price preached a sermon at an event held in London to commemorate England's 'Glorious Revolution' of 1688. Price was a Unitarian minister and public intellectual who led a congregation at Newington Green, just to the north of the city. A fervent supporter of the American Revolution and friend of Benjamin Franklin, Thomas Jefferson and John Adams, his *Observations on the Nature of Civil Liberty, the Principles of Government and the Justice and Policy of the War with America* had appeared to great acclaim in 1776. The sermon he preached on 4 November was originally scheduled for the centenary of the Glorious Revolution in 1788. Delayed by a year, Price gained the opportunity to react to the momentous developments by then underway across the Channel, as can be read in a text of the speech that was published shortly afterwards.

'What an eventful period is this!', he exclaims. '[T]he light [which set] America free [has] reflected to France, and there kindled into a blaze that lays despotism in ashes, and warms and illuminates Europe!'[10] Price was sixty-six at the time, and he expresses pleasure and gratitude that 'I have lived to see thirty millions of people, indignant and resolute . . . demanding liberty with an irresistible voice . . . an arbitrary monarch surrendering himself to his subjects.' He continues: 'I have lived to see the rights of men better understood than ever; and nations panting for liberty, which seemed to have lost the idea of it.'[11] And now, he says, 'methinks, I see the ardour for liberty catching and spreading; a general amendment beginning in human affairs; the dominion of kings changed for the dominion of laws, and the dominion of priests giving way to the dominion of reason and conscience'.[12]

Price speaks allusively about the implications of that 'general amendment' for England. The title of his published text is *A Discourse on the Love of Our Country*. Taking it for granted that those listening to him love, or should love, their country, he urges them to do so without 'any conviction of the superior value of [it] to other countries, or any particular preference of its laws and

10. Richard Price, *A Discourse on the Love of Our Country* (London: T. Cadell, 3rd ed., 1790), 50.
11. Ibid, 49.
12. Ibid, 49–50.

constitution of government'.[13] The question then arises of how, in that spirit, the events of 1688 should be remembered. How was the legacy of those events to be assessed, when viewed against the backdrop of recent developments in America and now France? His answer is that, 'though the [Glorious] Revolution was a great work, it was by no means a perfect work'.[14]

Certainly, he considers it a cause for celebration that James II was deposed and, in his stead, 'constitutional monarchy' instituted under 'a Sovereign of our own choice', William of Orange together with his wife Mary.[15] So too it is to be celebrated that '[s]ecurity was given to our property', 'our consciences were emancipated', and 'the volume in which are the words of eternal life was laid more open to our examination'.[16] At the same time, he writes that 'all was not . . . gained' in the settlement of 1688 (and by related subsequent arrangements) 'which was necessary to put the kingdom in the secure and complete possession of the blessings of liberty'.[17] Only limited religious toleration was achieved, and — 'the most important instance of the imperfect state in which the Revolution left our constitution'[18] — representation in the legislature remained unequal. Price understands the Glorious Revolution to have established the principle that the people have the 'right to chuse our own governors; to cashier them for misconduct; and to frame a government for ourselves'.[19] In turn, he maintains that that implies a right of fair and equal representation, and he calls for the renewal of efforts to realise that state of affairs.

Price was a man of wide interests, spanning not only theology and politics, but also mathematics, finance and 'political arithmetic' (the compilation and analysis of demographic and economic statistics). In earlier years, he had helped to lay a basis for the introduction of life insurance, publishing many papers on actuarial topics. At the same time, he was a high-profile critic of enclosure. We will take up the subject of enclosure in the eighteenth century in a later chapter.[20] For now, it suffices to note that, during this period, most of the remaining unenclosed land in England was enclosed, thanks to a Parliamentary process that dealt with specific localities in successive

13. Ibid, 3.
14. Ibid, 35.
15. Ibid, 32.
16. Ibid.
17. Ibid, 35.
18. Ibid, 39.
19. Ibid, 34.
20. See chap. 7 below.

Inclosure Acts. In one of his works of political arithmetic, Price writes that the effect of enclosure is that '[t]he circumstances of the lower ranks of men are altered in almost every respect for the worse'. 'From little occupiers of land, they are reduced to the state of day-labourers and hirelings', obliged to earn their subsistence by working for others, yet receiving wages that do not keep pace with the price of provisions.[21] 'How astonishing' then 'that our parliament', instead of remedying these evils, 'should chuse to promote them'.[22] He concludes that '[m]odern policy is, indeed, more favourable to the higher classes of people; and the consequences of it may in time prove, that the whole kingdom will consist only of gentry and beggars, or of grandees and slaves'.[23]

That lastmentioned passage later found its way into Karl Marx's *Capital*.[24] But Price was no social revolutionary, and when it came to reform, he advocated for relatively moderate changes designed to put an end to official discrimination against dissenting Christians and improve the quality of popular representation in the House of Commons. It seems that even his warm words about the revolution in France echoed much mainstream opinion in the months that followed the fall of the Bastille. However, mainstream opinion soon changed, and Price's speech took on greater retrospective importance after Edmund Burke made it the point of departure for his instant classic of the counter-revolutionary cause, *Reflections on the Revolution in France*.

Inheritance from our forefathers

In a satirical etching by the political cartoonist James Gillray (fig. 4), Price is shown seated at his desk with Burke looming up to startle him from behind. Entitled *Smelling out a Rat, or The Atheistical-Revolutionist disturbed in his Midnight "Calculations"*, the etching has Price working by candlelight to write a sermon 'On the Benefits of Anarchy, Regicide, Atheism'. Hanging on the wall next to him is a painting that depicts the execution of Charles I

21. Richard Price, *Observations on Reversionary Payments; on Schemes for providing Annuities to Widows, and for persons in old age; on the method of calculating the values of assurances on lives, and on the National Debt* (London: T. Cadell, 1773), 394 (emphasis omitted).
22. Ibid, 390.
23. Ibid, 393 (emphasis omitted).
24. See Karl Marx, *Capital, Vol. 1* (London: Penguin, 1976), 829.

during the English Civil War — an allusion to the idea that Price's 'predecessor' is the Civil War preacher Hugh Peters, who was himself executed after the Restoration for his part in the killing of the king.[25] Burke, meanwhile, is imagined as a monstrous apparition, all suspicious nose and gigantic spectacles, emerging out of the gloom to hold up before Price a crown in one hand and a cross in the other. A book labelled 'Reflections on the Revolution in France' lies open above the apparition's head. The cartoon vividly captures the sense that, for Burke, the dissenting reformism preached by Price is a recipe for anarchy, atheism, calculation, revolution, and the recurrence of regicide. From Price's perspective, conversely, Burke appears like an inquisitor at the trial of a heretic.[26] In the face of the crown and cross, there can be no dissenting religion and indeed no dissent at all, only the mutually sustaining power of the monarchy and church.

Figure 4 James Gillray, *Smelling out a rat*, Chronicle / Alamy Stock Photo

25. See Edmund Burke, *Reflections on the Revolution in France* (London: Penguin, 1968), 94 and 158. Hugh Peters was also known as Hugh Peter. Regarding the connection with Gillray's cartoon, see David Bindman, *The Shadow of the Guillotine: Britain and the French Revolution* (London: British Museum, 1989), 108.
26. For the idea that Gillray satirises Burke as a 'Jesuitical inquisitor', see David Bindman, *The Shadow of the Guillotine: Britain and the French Revolution* (London: British Museum, 1989), 107.

Reflections is composed in epistolatory form; Burke uses the conceit that the work is his reply to a 'very young gentleman at Paris' who has written to ask his opinion of what is happening in the latter's homeland. Burke's opinion is delivered with a mixture of horror and scorn. As he apprehends them, the events in France make for an unnatural and indeed 'monstrous tragi-comic scene',[27] in which 'publick measures are deformed into monsters', and legislation is the outcome of 'crude and desperate measures suggested by . . . a monstrous medley of all conditions, tongues and nations'.[28] 'I see the confiscators begin with' church property, he writes, but 'I do not see them end there'. 'I see [noblemen, the owners of large landed estates according to] the oldest usages of that kingdom', stripped of their possessions and reduced to the most abject poverty.[29] Contrasting this situation with England, he declares that the 'tenant-right of a cabbage-garden [and] a year's interest in a hovel . . . are more ceremoniously treated in our parliament than with you [in France] the oldest and most valuable landed possessions . . . or than the whole body of the monied and commercial interest of your country'.[30] He goes on: 'We entertain an high opinion of the legislative authority; but we have never dreamt that parliaments had any right whatever to violate property, to overrule prescription.'[31]

Yet it is about English institutions that Burke is most concerned, and here, as Gillray depicts, his immediate target is Price. At the time of the American Revolution, Burke and Price had been aligned in their views. Like Price, Burke had been a critic of British government policy in America and a supporter of those waging war for independence. Now, however, when what was at issue was the established order at home, their views diverged. With its 'manifest design of connecting the affairs of France with those of England', Price's sermon 'gave me a considerable degree of uneasiness', Burke writes.[32] On the question of the Glorious Revolution and its legacy, he argues that the 1688 settlement was made to preserve the time-honoured constitution 'which is our only security for law and liberty', and that the cardinal principle of that constitution is monarchical succession, not popular sovereignty.[33] As he reads the historical record, William and Mary of Orange (the grandson of Charles II and daughter of James II respectively) ascended the English throne

27. Edmund Burke, *Reflections on the Revolution in France* (London: Penguin, 1968), 92.
28. Ibid, 160.
29. Ibid, 260.
30. Ibid, 261.
31. Ibid. On this, see further chap. 7 below.
32. Ibid, 91.
33. Ibid, 117.

not because they were the people's choice, but to achieve an appropriate succession at a moment of constitutional crisis. Furthermore, the Bill of Rights of 1689 and other documents of the constitutional settlement did not, as Price claims, vest the people with the right to choose their own governors, cashier them for misconduct, and frame a government for themselves. On the contrary, the purpose was to stabilise hereditary monarchy and the people's allegiance to it. In his words, '[w]e wished at the period of the Revolution, and do now wish, to derive all we possess as *an inheritance from our forefathers*'.[34]

'Inheritance' is a word that recurs throughout Burke's text. He applies it not just to the 'inheritable crown', but to all the other parts of the constitution as he conceives it as well: 'an inheritable peerage; and an house of commons and a people inheriting privileges, franchises, and liberties, from a long line of ancestors'.[35] Thus, he writes, 'we receive, we hold, we transmit our government and our privileges, in the same manner in which we enjoy and transmit our property and our lives'.[36] Burke explains that what he values about the idea of inheritance is that it provides stability while also allowing for progressive change. As he puts it, inheritance 'furnishes a sure principle of conservation, and a sure principle of transmission; without at all excluding a principle of improvement'.[37] The underlying concerns that motivate this emphasis on security emerge clearly in his commentary on the revolution in France. In his judgement, the 'levellers' (as he calls them) of the revolution are compromising the 'edifice of society, by setting up in the air what the solidity of the structure requires to be on the ground'.[38]

Thus, unpropertied men — the likes of 'taylors and carpenters' and the holders of the 'occupation of an hairdresser, or of a working tallow-chandler' — are being elevated to a governing situation to which they cannot possibly be equal.[39] This imperils the nation and its institutions, in the same way as it also imperils national culture. For when the aristocracy and gentry are displaced from their proper role as society's 'protectors and guardians', 'all the good things which are connected with manners, and with civilization . . . will be . . . trodden down' — as Burke puts it in a much mocked passage — 'under the hoofs of a swinish multitude'.[40] Price, in his sermon, praises

34. Ibid (emphasis in original).
35. Ibid, 119.
36. Ibid, 120.
37. On improvement, see further chap. 7 below.
38. Edmund Burke, *Reflections on the Revolution in France* (London: Penguin, 1968), 138. On this use of the term 'levellers', see chap. 8 below.
39. Ibid.
40. Ibid, 173.

the French revolutionaries for their part in restoring to mankind its rights. Burke rejoins by comparing the rights supposedly restored to the 'freedom' of a convicted criminal to escape from gaol. 'Am I to congratulate an highwayman and murderer, who has broke prison, upon the recovery of his natural rights?', he asks.[41]

But to his mind, the problem also goes deeper than that. Talk of the rights of man 'serves only to aggravate and imbitter that real inequality which it can never remove'.[42] By inspiring 'false ideas and vain expectations into men destined to travel in the obscure walk of laborious life', the revolutionary ideologues fuel dissatisfaction with social arrangements that exist 'as much for the benefit of those whom it must leave in a humble state as [for the benefit of] those whom it is able to exalt to a condition more splendid but not more happy'.[43] Moreover, where there is misery, due, for example, to hunger or illness, '[w]hat is the use of discussing a man's abstract right to food or to medicine? The question is upon the method of procuring and administering them.' And '[i]n that deliberation', Burke maintains, 'I shall always advise to call in the aid of the farmer and the physician, rather than the professor of metaphysics.'[44]

To him, the revolutionaries in France and their admirers in England fail to grasp the complexity of nature and society. They ignore that '[t]hese metaphysic rights [of which they speak], entering into common life, like rays of light which pierce into a dense medium, are, by the laws of nature refracted from their straight line'. Indeed, these rights 'undergo such a variety of refractions and reflections, that it becomes absurd to talk of them as if they continued in the simplicity of their original direction'.[45] Given that the 'nature of man is intricate [and] the objects of society are of the greatest possible complexity', 'no simple disposition or direction of power can be suitable either to man's nature, or to the quality of his affairs'.[46] Burke considers that this rules out attempts abstractly and categorically to 'define' the rights of man. But it does not mean that the rights of man are 'impossible to be discerned'.[47] In his account, the 'real rights of men' are the advantages gained from living in such society, the claims that citizens in such society may justifiably make.[48]

41. Ibid, 90.
42. Ibid, 124.
43. Ibid.
44. Ibid, 151–52.
45. Ibid, 152.
46. Ibid, 152–53.
47. Ibid, 153.
48. Ibid, 149 (emphasis omitted).

For '[g]overnment is not made in virtue of natural rights'; rather, rights exist in virtue of government.[49] As he explains, '[i]f civil society be made for the advantage of man, all the advantages for which it is made become his right'.[50]

On this basis, Burke proposes that '[m]en have a right to live [according to law]; they have a right to justice', to the 'fruits of their industry; and to the means of making their industry fruitful'. They have a right to inherit from their parents and to raise their families. They have a right to 'a fair portion of all which society . . . can do in [their] favour'. And everything 'each man can separately do, without trespassing upon others, he has a right to do for himself'. A civic 'partnership' exists in which 'all men have equal rights'.[51] Importantly, however, the 'rights of men in governments'[52] do not include the right 'to equal things', and nor do they include the right to an equal 'share of power, authority, and direction . . . in the management of the state'.[53] Property and power are 'settled by convention'. They are not 'amongst the direct original rights of man in civil society', whatever may be imagined to have been the natural rights of human beings in the 'abstract perfection' of their pre-political existence.[54] When it comes to England, this entails that there can be no more equality of wealth and no greater diffusion of sovereignty than is accepted under the constitution, that being the established order by which the rights and freedoms of Englishmen are protected.[55]

Burke further contends that English governing institutions have done an excellent job of protecting native rights and freedoms. '[W]e have long prospered', he writes, under the 'old-fashioned constitution.' *Pace* Price, 'representation has been found perfectly adequate to all the purposes for which a representation of the people can be desired or devised'.[56] That is not only because these institutions have stood the test of time, but also because they operate by 'the disposition of a stupendous wisdom, moulding together the great mysterious incorporation of the human race'. Thus, '[o]ur political system is placed in a just correspondence and symmetry with the order of the world', and with the arrangement appropriate to a 'permanent body

49. Ibid, 150.
50. Ibid, 149.
51. Ibid, 149–50.
52. Ibid, 153.
53. Ibid, 150.
54. Ibid, 150–51.
55. On this form of ancient constitutionalism, see John Pocock, *The Ancient Constitution and the Feudal Law* (Cambridge: Cambridge University Press, 2nd ed., 1987), 319 and passim.
56. Edmund Burke, *Reflections on the Revolution in France* (London: Penguin, 1968), 146.

composed of transitory parts'. The parts come and go, while the whole remains 'in a condition of unchangeable constancy, [and] moves on through the varied tenour of perpetual decay, fall, renovation, and progression'. '[B]y preserving the method of nature', Burke contends that 'in what we improve we are never wholly new; in what we retain we are never wholly obsolete'.[57] As against both an 'obstinacy that rejects all improvement' and a 'levity that is fatigued and disgusted with every thing of which it is in possession', reform occurs slowly and with 'circumspection and caution', recognising that 'time is amongst the assistants'.[58]

The definition of English liberty

The publication of *Reflections* sparked a great flurry of responses and counter-responses — the pamphlet war that would later be celebrated as the last great episode in British history of open debate about the fundamentals of civil government.[59] Of the many authors who contributed in the succeeding months and years, Burke's first respondent was Mary Wollstonecraft. Her *A Vindication of the Rights of Men* was printed anonymously on 29 November 1790, and again under her own name on 18 December 1790. Wollstonecraft may have been especially impatient to defend Price against Burke's attack as, while not sharing Price's Unitarian faith, she regularly attended services at his church at Newington Green and appears to have regarded him as a sort of mentor.[60] Coming from a family of declining fortunes, she worked initially as a governess, lady's companion, and teacher, and at one stage ran a school for girls which she moved to Newington Green in 1784. Through Price she met the radical publisher Joseph Johnson, who published her early writings (a tract on the upbringing of girls, a novel entitled *Mary: A Fiction*, and a collection of children's stories). From 1788, Johnson employed her as a compiler of anthologies, French translator, and journalist on his new literary magazine, the *Analytical Review*. It was also he who published *A Vindication of the Rights of Men*, along with its today more famous sequel, A *Vindication of the Rights of Woman*, and her other subsequent works.

57. Ibid, 120.
58. Ibid, 280.
59. See chap. 1 above.
60. Price preached Rational Dissent, later known as Unitarianism.

A Vindication of the Rights of Men again takes the form of a letter, addressed now to Burke and focused squarely on what Wollstonecraft likewise terms the 'rights of men'. The question with which she begins is 'how far [are we] to go back to discover the rights of men?'[61] She observes that Burke venerates 'the rust of antiquity' and the 'vestiges of ancient days'.[62] So does he advise going back to 'the dark days of ignorance, when the minds of men were shackled by the grossest prejudices and most immoral superstition', and disagreements were settled by the power of the sword?[63] To her mind, as to Price's, the rights of men are not to be discovered in history. Rather, they are God-given attributes and hence natural endowments, made known through the application of reason. 'It is necessary emphatically to repeat', she declares, 'that there are rights which men inherit at their birth, as rational creatures.' These are 'natural rights', and they are received 'not from [our] forefathers, but, from God'.[64]

Why then do they remain unfulfilled? Wollstonecraft considers that, although Burke's cherished 'prescription' can neither confer nor cancel the rights of man, it can put obstacles in their way, and has persistently done so. In particular, 'the demon of property has ever been at hand to encroach on the sacred rights of men, and to fence round with awful pomp laws that war with justice'.[65] At any rate, she maintains that this has been the case in England, where the 'barbarous feudal institution' of primogeniture still persists,[66] and where hereditary property and hereditary honours have drained the privileged few of their humanity and turned them into 'artificial monster[s]'.[67] 'If the poor are in distress', she writes, the rich 'will make some benevolent exertions.'[68] They will attend to the 'distribution of alms', and will offer 'compassion' and do those less fortunate 'a favour'.[69] But they will refuse to recognise rights. The rights of men are 'grating sounds that set their teeth on edge;

61. Although Wollstonecraft follows Burke in using the plural formulation 'the rights of men', she uses it interchangeably with the formulation 'the rights of humanity', and it seems that she intends to speak of rights that belong to humanity in general. See Mary Wollstonecraft, *A Vindication of the Rights of Men*, in Sylvana Tomaselli (ed.), *Mary Wollstonecraft: A Vindication of the Rights of Men and A Vindication of the Rights of Woman* (Cambridge: Cambridge University Press, 1995), 1, 5, 9.
62. Ibid, 8.
63. Ibid, 11. See also 9.
64. Ibid, 5, 12–13.
65. Ibid, 7.
66. Ibid, 23.
67. Ibid, 9, 8.
68. Ibid, 55.
69. Ibid, 9, 6, 55.

the impertinent enquiry of philosophic meddling innovation'.[70] At the same time, the rich will condemn every attempt to divert wealth from its current 'narrow channel' out into 'the sea' where it can 'water all the land'.[71]

Wollstonecraft tells Burke: 'You should have hinted [to your French correspondent] that property in England is much more secure than liberty.'[72] Or rather, Burke should have hinted that security of property *is* what passes for liberty in England. 'Security of property!' she exclaims. 'Behold, in a few words, the definition of English liberty.' To which she immediately adds: 'But softly — it is only the property of the rich that is secure; the man who lives by the sweat of his brow has no asylum from oppression.'[73] Yet in her estimation, the sole 'security of property that nature authorizes and reason sanctions is, the right a man has to enjoy the acquisitions which his talents and industry have acquired; and to bequeath them to whom he chooses'.[74] As an example of the working man's oppression, Wollstonecraft cites the English game laws. In force since feudal times, these laws underwrote the aristocratic privilege of hunting animals for sport by imposing heavy penalties for the unauthorised killing of game. 'In this land of liberty', she asks, 'what is to secure the property of the poor farmer when his noble landlord chooses to plant a decoy field [to lure game birds] near his little property? Game devour the fruit of his labour; but fines and imprisonment await him if he dare to kill any — or lift up his hand to interrupt the pleasure of his lord.'[75]

Part of Wollstonecraft's response to Burke concerns the language he uses to make his arguments. This she characterises as the twisting and evasive 'idiom of politeness', against which she states her own view that 'truth . . . has ever appeared to me the essence of the sublime; and . . . simplicity the only criterion of the beautiful'.[76] The sublime and beautiful were central categories of an aesthetic theory which Burke had elaborated several decades earlier, but he had understood the two concepts rather differently.[77] In *A Philosophical Enquiry into the Origin of our Ideas of the Sublime and Beautiful,*

70. Ibid, 55.
71. Ibid, 51.
72. Ibid, 14.
73. Ibid, 13.
74. Ibid, 23–24.
75. Ibid, 16.
76. Ibid, 5.
77. Edmund Burke (David Womersley, ed.), *A Philosophical Enquiry into the Origin of our Ideas of the Sublime and Beautiful and Other Pre-Revolutionary Writings* (London: Penguin Books, 1998), first published in 1757.

he argues that the essence of the sublime is terror, or the sense of awe and danger that he takes to be experienced in the face of objects that are vast, powerful, or obscure. In contrast, the beautiful is to be identified with joy, or the love and tenderness that he takes to be kindled by the presence of objects that are small, delicate and vulnerable.[78] In the course of her discussion, Wollstonecraft returns to this distinction in order to challenge it from another angle. She shows how Burke's theory carries with it a gender politics that perpetuates the subordination of women inasmuch as it seeks to convince women (and men) that 'littleness and weakness are the very essence of beauty'. In effect, it teaches that God commanded women 'not to cultivate the moral virtues that might chance to excite respect', for those are 'within the rigid pale of manly morals'. The implicit message is 'that Nature, by making women little, smooth, delicate, fair creatures, never designed that they should exercise their reason to acquire the virtues that produce opposite, if not contradictory, feelings'.[79]

Gender politics were, of course, the central preoccupation of *A Vindication of the Rights of Woman*, which appeared a little over a year after *A Vindication of the Rights of Men*. Taking up and developing Wollstonecraft's points about the sublime and beautiful, the second *Vindication* highlights the real effects of that ideological formation. As she sees it, women's 'manners' — their mode of behaviour, speech and interaction — are rendered 'factitious' and 'corrupt', and their powers of reason stunted.[80] To correct this situation, Wollstonecraft argues that what is needed is a nothing less than 'revolution in female manners', and in successive chapters she outlines a range of proposals for realising such a revolution through developments in the domains of education, parenting, and social mores.[81] While Wollstonecraft articulates her concerns in terms of manners and indeed morals, the title of her pamphlet already makes clear that her moralism is rooted in advocacy for the 'rights of woman', to use again her phrase. She '[contends] for the rights of woman', and wishes the pamphlet to be read as a treatise on 'female rights and manners'.[82]

78. See ibid, esp. 86–97.
79. Mary Wollstonecraft, *A Vindication of the Rights of Men*, in Sylvana Tomaselli (ed.), *Mary Wollstonecraft: A Vindication of the Rights of Men and A Vindication of the Rights of Woman* (Cambridge: Cambridge University Press, 1995), 1, 47 (emphasis omitted).
80. Mary Wollstonecraft, *A Vindication of the Rights of Woman*, in Sylvana Tomaselli (ed.), *Mary Wollstonecraft: A Vindication of the Rights of Men and A Vindication of the Rights of Woman* (Cambridge: Cambridge University Press, 1995), 65, 68.
81. Ibid, 73 et seq.
82. Ibid, 68, 74.

For [i]f the abstract rights of man will bear discussion and explanation, those of woman, by a parity of reasoning, will not shrink from the same test'. The fact that 'a different opinion prevails in this country' is only due to the very arguments that are used to 'justify the oppression of woman — prescription'.[83]

For Wollstonecraft, the denial to women of 'civil and political rights' contributes to the underdevelopment of their powers of reason, insofar as it confines women to the domestic sphere. '[I]mmured in their families', they are condemned to '[grope] in the dark', lacking the enlightenment that would come from participation in public affairs. In her account, this applies no less to wealthy women than to poor women. For '[d]estructive . . . as riches and inherited honours are to the human character, women are more debased and cramped, if possible, by them, than men, because men may still, in some degree, unfold their faculities by becoming soldiers and statesmen'.[84] Women thus join unpropertied men in revealing the truth that the 'whole system of representation is now, in this country, only a convenient handle for despotism', and Wollstonecraft states her intention to pursue at a future time the idea that her sex ought to have representatives in Parliament 'instead of being arbitrarily governed without having any direct share allowed them in the deliberations of government'.[85] '[T]he world is almost, literally speaking, a den of sharpers or oppressors', she writes. 'There must be more equality established in society, or morality will never gain ground.' Yet 'this virtuous equality will not rest firmly even when founded on a rock, [while] one half of mankind be chained to its bottom by fate'.[86]

'I will advocate the rights of man'

If Wollstonecraft's *A Vindication of the Rights of Men* was the earliest riposte to Burke, Paine's *Rights of Man* was by a very large margin the most influential. Published in two parts in March 1791 and February 1792, it was read and discussed in cities, towns and villages around the country. The authorities did

83. Ibid, 68–69.
84. Ibid, 233.
85. Ibid, 237.
86. Ibid, 230.

their best to prevent its success. After Paine arranged for the whole work to be printed in a cheap edition that would be affordable to ordinary working people, the pamphlet's sale was proscribed, its publisher prosecuted for seditious libel, and Paine charged with the same offence. Harassed as well by government-backed loyalist groups, he left for Paris in September 1792. He was tried and convicted *in absentia* in December 1792, never to return again to England. A spate of 'Paine burnings' — demonstrations by government-backed loyalist groups in which Paine was ceremonially burned in effigy — began in November 1792 and did not end until well into 1793.[87] During those months and for some time thereafter, Paine and his pamphlet were alternately denounced and celebrated in inscriptions on mugs, jugs, teapots, kerchiefs, plaques, and tokens and in poems, songs and toasts.[88] They were also copiously satirised.

In another of James Gillray's etchings, entitled *Tom Paine's Nightly Pest*, Paine is depicted as a hack writer asleep in a miserable garret (fig. 5).[89] Lying on a bed of straw, he wears a tattered shirt and red nightcap with the tricolore cockade of the French revolutionaries pinned to it, and has only his coat to keep him warm. Notebooks scattered around inform us of the absurdities on which he has been working. One reads *The Rights of Farthing Candles proving their Equality with the Sun & Moon and the necessity of a Reform in the Planetary System*; another, partly obscured by a passing rat, *The Golden Age, or The Age of Equalizing the Property of Princes and Pikemen*. To one side, an elaborate diorama shows the consequences of this work. There is a tribunal of three judges, a charge sheet with accusations of 'Libels, Scurrilities, Falsehood, Perjuries, Rebellions' etc., a plea in mitigation that cites 'Ignorance, Poverty, Envy', a catalogue of punishments listing 'Corporal Pain, Contempt, Detestation, Extinction from Society', the scales of justice, and a gallows. At the sleeping figure's window playing the revolutionaries' song *Ça ira* on a fiddle is a bizarre demonic creature — the fiend or 'pest' that evidently inspires him.[90]

87. See Frank O'Gorman, 'The Paine Burnings of 1792–1793', *Past and Present* 193(1) (2006) 111.
88. For an informative and wonderfully illustrated catalogue of some of the objects, see David Bindman, *The Shadow of the Guillotine: Britain and the French Revolution* (London: British Museum, 1989).
89. Gillray made many Paine-themed cartoons. See also, e.g., *The Rights of Man;–or–Tommy Paine, the little American taylor, taking the measure of the crown, for a new pair of Revolution-breeches* (London: Hannah Humphrey, 1791), available at: https://www.britishmuseum.org/research/collection_online/collection_object_details.aspx?objectId=1477187&partId=1.
90. See further David Bindman, *The Shadow of the Guillotine: Britain and the French Revolution* (London: British Museum, 1989), 108–09.

Figure 5 *Tom Paine's Nightly Pest*, published by Hannah Humphrey in 1792 (hand-coloured etching), Gillray, James (1757-1815) / Courtesy of the Warden and Scholars of New College, Oxford / Bridgeman Images

Rights of Man continues and extends a theme which Paine had already adumbrated in his important intervention in the American Revolution, *Common Sense*, published in January 1776. That work set the colonists' cause against the backdrop of a deeply flawed English constitution, with its 'two ancient tyrannies' of the king and the peers, and its fanciful assumption that those tyrannies could be checked merely by mixing them with 'some new republican materials'.[91] His later response to Burke's *Reflections* was an opportunity to take these ideas, along with the insights gained from his more recent engagement with the revolution in France, back to the country of his birth. *Part I* of the text begins by framing Burke's argument in terms of a privileging of the dead — the weight of history, tradition, and precedent — over the current generations — the living. Paine writes that he, contrarily, contends

91. Thomas Paine, *Common Sense*, in Bruce Kuklick (ed.), *Paine: Political Writings* (Cambridge: Cambridge University Press, 2000), 1, 6.

'for the right of the living . . . against . . . the manuscript-assumed authority of the dead'.[92]

Parsing this right, he affirms the various entitlements regarding self-government highlighted by Price — the right of the people to choose their own governors, hold those governors to account for misconduct, and frame government for themselves. In Burke's analysis, if ever the English people possessed such rights, they had been renounced in the Glorious Revolution for the sake of stabilising hereditary monarchy, but Paine contends that it was simply not possible for those who drew up the 1688–9 settlement to bind their posterity in that way. 'It is the living and not the dead that are to be accommodated', he avers.[93] Paine then goes on to identify the idea that no generation has the 'right of dictating the mode by which the world should be governed forever' with the rights of man.[94] By the rights of man, he explains that he means the natural or 'original inherent' rights of man, as distinct from the civil rights conferred by the state and law.[95]

Like Price and Wollstonecraft, Paine holds that natural rights are God-given rights — those conferred at the 'time when man came from the hand of his maker'.[96] Civil rights are 'those which appertain to man in right of his being a member of society'. As he analyses them, the two are connected in that civil rights have as their foundation natural rights, and exist to provide 'security and protection' for them.[97] Inasmuch as Burke sees only hereditary rights, and attaches importance only to hereditary succession, Paine proposes that Burke fails to understand this. On the one hand, he treats natural rights as though they were civil rights, ignoring the 'divine' principle of the 'equal rights of man' according to which every generation has an equal right of self-government to those preceding it 'by the same rule that every individual is born equal in rights with his contemporary'.[98] On the other hand, he treats civil arrangements as though they were natural phenomena. Burke 'talks about what he calls an hereditary crown, as if it were some production of nature; or as if, like time, it had power to operate not only independently

92. Thomas Paine, *Rights of Man, Part I*, in Bruce Kuklick (ed.), *Paine: Political Writings* (Cambridge: Cambridge University Press, 2000), 57, 64 (emphasis omitted).
93. Ibid, 63, 64.
94. Ibid, 84.
95. Thomas Paine, *Rights of Man, Part II*, in Bruce Kuklick (ed.), *Paine: Political Writings* (Cambridge: Cambridge University Press, 2000), 155, 172.
96. Thomas Paine, *Rights of Man, Part I*, in Bruce Kuklick (ed.), *Paine: Political Writings* (Cambridge: Cambridge University Press, 2000), 57, 84.
97. Ibid, 86.
98. Ibid, 85.

but in spite of man'.[99] Yet the reality is quite the reverse; inherited privilege is 'a thing of imagination'.[100]

In *Part II* of *Rights of Man*, Paine contrasts the 'old system' of hereditary government with the 'new system' of representative government adopted in America and in the course of establishment in France.[101] On his account, the old system is the 'most irregular and imperfect of all the systems of government'. It is 'inadequate', 'irrational', tyrannical, war-prone, and 'ridiculous'.[102] The majesty of the monarchy is just a joke. 'I compare it [the monarchy] to something kept behind a curtain', Paine writes, 'about which there is a great deal of bustle and fuss, and a wonderful air of seeming solemnity; but when, by any accident, the curtain happens to be open and the company see what it is, they burst into laughter'.[103] Whereas the old system of hereditary government is an 'assumption of power' and an 'imposition on mankind', the new system of representative government is a 'delegation of power for the common benefit of society'.[104] The new system takes 'nature, reason, and experience for its guide', and gives effect to the 'republican' idea of government that makes the '*res-publica* or . . . public good . . .its whole and sole object'.[105]

In the new system, government is founded 'on the indefeasible . . . rights of man', and '[e]very man is a proprietor in government'.[106] Indeed, while the new system is 'new' inasmuch as it does not conform either to classical typology or to traditional practice, from another perspective it is 'the most ancient in principle of all [the forms of government] that have existed, being founded on the original inherent rights of man'.[107] Turning Burke's preoccupation against him, Paine proposes that the real question of inheritance is 'whether man shall inherit his rights, and universal civilization take place'.[108] For '[w]hen in countries that are called civilized, we see age going to the work-house, and youth to the gallows, something must be wrong in the system of government'. All may look well, but 'there lies hidden from the eye

99. Ibid, 132–33.
100. Ibid, 133.
101. Thomas Paine, *Rights of Man, Part II*, in Bruce Kuklick (ed.), *Paine: Political Writings* (Cambridge: Cambridge University Press, 2000), 155, 171.
102. Ibid, 172, 173.
103. Ibid, 181.
104. Ibid, 171, 172.
105. Ibid, 175, 178.
106. Ibid, 164 (emphasis omitted), 183.
107. Ibid, 172.
108. Ibid, 212.

of common observation, a mass of wretchedness that has scarcely any other chance than to expire in poverty or infamy'.[109]

Paine had an awareness of this from his earliest youth. Born in the town of Thetford in Norfolk, his family's house stood facing Gallows Hill, so-called because it was where convicted criminals were brought for execution. Hangings had been taking place on Gallows Hill after the annual Lent assizes since medieval times, but the number of capital offences increased exponentially in Paine's century, and most of the new capital offences were property-related. As E. P. Thompson relates in *Whigs and Hunters*, the passage of the Black Act in 1723 — creating a whole range of capital offences to protect private property — 'signalled the onset of [a] flood tide of eighteenth-century retributive justice'.[110] Thereafter it became 'a matter of course that the legislature should, in every session, attach the penalty of death to new descriptions of offence', and the point was soon reached where property was 'trenched around on every side by capital statutes'.[111]

'Why is it', Paine asks, 'that scarcely any are executed but the poor? The fact is a proof, among other things, of a wretchedness in their condition.'[112] Using an image that would have put his readers in mind of the introduction of toll charges on public highways, he characterises English society as a 'wilderness of turnpike gates' that thwarted the lives of ordinary people at every turn.[113] And while some people were becoming wretchedly poor, others were becoming extravagantly rich. In the area where Paine lived, the Duke of Grafton, owner of an estate with a circumference of sixty-five kilometres, fell into that tiny category of super-rich. Through a system of patronage, the Grafton family controlled local affairs and Parliamentary representation alike. Their seat was Euston Hall in the village of Euston, about five kilometres from Thetford. A substantial project of remodelling initiated in the 1730s turned the house and grounds into one of the finest Palladian mansions with one of the finest landscape parks in England.[114] Burke called the House

109. Ibid, 212–13.
110. E.P. Thompson, *Whigs and Hunters* (London: Allen Lane, 1975), 23. The Act created multiple new capital offences designed to protect enclosed land and Crown forests against trespass by people asserting customary rights. The main target of the legislation was the Waltham Blacks, so-called because they 'blacked' their faces for disguise.
111. Ibid, 21.
112. Thomas Paine, *Rights of Man, Part II*, in Bruce Kuklick (ed.), *Paine: Political Writings* (Cambridge: Cambridge University Press, 2000), 155, 213.
113. Thomas Paine, *Rights of Man, Part I*, in Bruce Kuklick (ed.), *Paine: Political Writings* (Cambridge: Cambridge University Press, 2000), 57, 86.
114. See John Keane, *Tom Paine: A Political Life* (London: Bloomsbury, 1995), 13–14. See further chap. 9 below.

of Peers 'the great ground and pillar of security to the landed interest',[115] but Paine observes that, were that 'pillar to sink into the earth, the same landed property would continue, and the same plowing, sowing, and reaping would go on'.[116] For such people are 'not the farmers who work the land . . . [they] are the mere consumers of the rent'. To him, the Duke of Grafton and his ilk are to be compared to 'drones . . . who neither collect the honey nor form the hive, but exist only for lazy enjoyment'.[117]

Like Price, Wollstonecraft and many others, Paine attributes the deepening poverty of those who actually produced the wealth of the nation to causes that included the continuing role in social and political life of this 'Norman' aristocracy, its complicity in the lavishing of public resources on kings and their vainglorious wars, primogeniture and similar vestiges of feudal law, a corrupt system of Parliamentary representation, and a scheme of taxation that compelled the poor to 'support the fraud that oppresses them' and disproportionately burdened them to boot.[118] Faced with this situation, Paine announces: 'I will advocate the Rights of Man.'[119] The institution in England of the new system of representative government was clearly his primary demand, but with that came advocacy for the reform of inheritance laws to eliminate primogeniture, and for the reform of taxation laws to replace the existing regressive arrangements with a scheme of progressive taxation. Paine also put forward proposals to replace the system of poor relief with a new system of social welfare.

Explaining the thinking behind this, he remarks that '[c]ivil government does not consist in executions; but in making [appropriate] provision for the instruction of youth, and the support of age',[120] and a considerable portion of *Rights of Man, Part II* is devoted to calculations showing how unnecessary expenditure might be reduced to enable such provision. Under Paine's scheme, there would be payments to families with young children, an old-age pension, grants for the education of children, financial assistance to women who have just given birth, and subventions for newly married couples. Paine suggests that his innovative plan would simultaneously provide for the poor and lay a basis for civil peace. Civil peace would follow because, through the implementation of his scheme, the 'poor, as well as the rich, will [become]

115. Edmund Burke, *An Appeal from the New to the Old Whigs* (London: J. Dodsley, 3rd ed., 1791), 86.
116. Thomas Paine, *Rights of Man, Part II*, in Bruce Kuklick (ed.), *Paine: Political Writings* (Cambridge: Cambridge University Press, 2000), 155, 220.
117. Ibid.
118. Ibid, 213.
119. Ibid.
120. Ibid.

interested in the support of government, and the cause and apprehension of riots and tumults will cease'.[121] At the same time, and reinforcing this, he proposes that it is part of the new system of government that disagreement leads to debate, rather than to civil strife. In contradistinction to the 'savage custom' of the old system, in which political controversies are resolved by the sword, '[d]iscussion and the general will' become the arbiters.[122]

One aspect of the establishment of representative government, then, is to break the elite monopoly of deliberation over public affairs. I have already referred to the fact that Paine had his pamphlet printed in a cheap edition so that everyone could read it or have it read to them. He also purported to write in a way that would be clear and accessible, taking 'popular truth [and] principle' as his guide and avoiding the artifice that, like Wollstonecraft, he held to be the hallmark of Burke's prose.[123] As Paine reads it, *Reflections* is like a 'dramatic performance' that may divert and entertain, but never enlightens.[124] Lampooning the comment in *Reflections* about the French revolutionaries' setting up in the air that which should remain on the ground, he maintains that Burke has himself 'mounted in the air like a balloon, to draw the eyes of the multitude from the ground they stand upon'.[125]

Contrasted opinions

That lastmentioned passage from *Rights of Man* is featured in an etching attributed to Frederick George Byron (fig. 6). Entitled *Contrasted Opinions of Paine's Pamphlet*, the cartoon depicts a series of prominent individuals, including Pitt and Burke, reading and reacting to Paine's *Rights of Man (Part I)*. Pitt is shown clapping himself on the forehead as though struck by a sudden headache, while Burke thrusts his fist above his head and opens his mouth wide, the better to shout. Above each figure is a quotation from Paine's text, together with words that reveal the reader's thoughts. In Burke's case, the quotation is Paine's suggestion that Burke has mounted in the air like a balloon, and Burke is thinking, 'If ever I read such an infernal book, damn me!'

121. Ibid, 240.
122. Ibid, 262.
123. Thomas Paine, *Rights of Man, Part I*, in Bruce Kuklick (ed.), *Paine: Political Writings* (Cambridge: Cambridge University Press, 2000), 57, 127.
124. Ibid, 79.
125. Ibid, 93.

Published in May 1791, Byron's etching is an early memento of the controversy about the significance of the French Revolution for England which we have begun to examine in this chapter. We have seen that for Burke, as for Pitt, the rights of man are a destructive and delusory doctrine that holds the revolutionaries of France in its thrall, and threatens likewise to foment revolution in England. The only rights which men and women have are their 'civil rights', the rights they have by virtue of living in civil society, the rights they may justifiably claim under the constitution of the country in which they live. For Price, Wollstonecraft and Paine, such a view elides the natural rights held purely by virtue of humanity. To reduce the rights of man to civil rights in the manner of Burke is to allow governing arrangements put in place by long-dead generations to prevail over the rights of the living.

Figure 6 Byron, Frederick George, *Contrasted Opinions of Paine's Pamphlet* 1791 © Fitzwilliam Museum, Cambridge

In particular, these authors emphasise the rights of the living to control the political community of which they are members — their right to choose government, to hold government to account, and to frame government on the basis that political authority derives from the people and always depends on their consent. Popular sovereignty is the main sense of the rights of man that emerges in the work we have considered here, and Wollstonecraft raises the possibility that that may include women. Beyond that, our advocates for the rights of man also articulate a series of concerns to do with the conditions in which popular sovereignty would be realised, at least in England. All three deplore the persistence of feudal forms of inherited privilege, and especially primogeniture. Price further highlights the way enclosure is changing the circumstances of poorer people for the worse in almost every respect. Wollstonecraft comments that security of the property of the rich has become the definition of English liberty. Paine observes that there lies hidden from the eye of polite society a mass of wretchedness that has scarcely any other chance than to expire in poverty or infamy. And not to forget that the war of words was also a war of images, Gillray satirises Paine's ideas about the equal rights of man, and in doing so, prompts reflection on whether it is really those ideas that are absurd or instead the inequalities to which they are addressed.

Writing about this period of English history in *The Making of the English Working Class*, E. P. Thompson recalls that the demand of the governed for a form of government which does not derive from conquest and inherited power 'had, of course, been voiced before'.[126] 'To read the controversies between reformers and authority, and between different reforming groups, in the 1790s', he writes, 'is to see the Putney Debates come to life once again'. Rainborough's '"poorest he"' in England', Sexby's 'man with a "birthright", becomes the *Rights of Man'*, while Ireton's fear that universal manhood suffrage will destroy property and 'take away all by that' returns as Burke's 'threat of the "swinish multitude"'.[127] Equally, the question is posed afresh of where the challenge will lead. In one contemporary's words, '[i]f Mr Paine should be able to rouze up the lower classes, their interference will probably be marked by wild work, and all we now possess, whether in private property or public liberty, will be at the mercy of a lawless and furious rabble'.[128] 'It is the old debate continued', Thompson declares. 'The same aspirations, fears and tensions are there: but they arise in a new context, with new language and arguments, and a changed balance of forces.'[129]

We get a clue to the character of that new context from a certain motif which has been threaded through our discussion in this chapter. It first appeared with Pitt's attack on the 'monstrous doctrine of the rights of man'. Then we noted how, for Burke too, the rights of man are a 'monstrous fiction' and the basis of a 'monstrous tragic-comic scene' in France, led by a 'monstrous medley of all conditions, tongues and nations' engaged in deforming public measures 'into monsters'. In response, Paine countered that it was Burke's analysis that was 'marvellous and monstrous'. Paine also praised the French

126. E. P. Thompson, *The Making of the English Working Class* (New York: Vintage, 1966), 22.
127. Ibid, 23. On the Putney Debates, see chap. 4 above and the references there cited.
128. Christopher Wyvill, *Political Papers, Vol. V* (York: W. Blanchard, 1804), 381–82, quoted in E. P. Thompson, *The Making of the English Working Class* (New York: Vintage, 1966), 24.
129. E. P. Thompson, *The Making of the English Working Class* (New York: Vintage, 1966), 24.

for their moves to '[e]xterminate the monster aristocracy', and wrote of the British aristocracy as 'still a monster'.[130] Along similar lines, Wollstonecraft maintained that the hereditary system turned the privileged few into 'artificial monsters', and that the 'demon of property' had ever been at hand to encroach on the sacred rights of man. Gillray portrayed Burke as a monstrous apparition arriving to terrify Price, and Paine as taking inspiration from a 'pest' or fiend that comes to his window at night. And nor did the monstering end there.[131]

Historians of late eighteenth-century English thought explain that monstrosity was a central category in aesthetic judgement of the period. At a time of industrialisation and revolution, monsters channelled fears and gave shape to uncertainties and threats. Fred Botting writes that '[i]n political texts of the 1790s like Burke's *Reflections* the construction of revolutionary excesses as a terrifying monster served to define the threat and thus contain and legitimate its exclusion'.[132] The terror was designed to 'purge [readers'] minds of any radical ideas', so that the 'evil in France and in radical writings is expelled from the shores of England'.[133] Mark Neocleous traces 'the idiom of monstrosity . . . to the new processes of industrial society then emerging', and to the new social formations and new collective forces that seemed to arise with them. Through monsters, Burke and others expressed a 'generalized fear of what we would now call mass action'.[134]

But, of course, the quintessential early-industrial work of Gothic literature was not Burke's *Reflections* or any of the other political pamphlets on which we have touched. It was the work of fiction by Wollstonecraft's daughter with William Godwin, Mary Shelley — *Frankenstein*, published in 1818.[135] *Frankenstein* has been widely read as reflecting the turbulence of the French revolutionary decade. In a vast interpretive literature, Shelley's themes are related to fears of revolutionary violence breaking out in England, but also to anxieties about the effects of industrialisation and enclosure, and to the idea

130. Thomas Paine, *Rights of Man, Part I*, in Bruce Kuklick (ed.), *Paine: Political Writings* (Cambridge: Cambridge University Press, 2000), 57, 99.
131. E.g. Paine also denounced the 'monstrous' practice of hereditary succession. See ibid, 64.
132. Fred Botting, *Gothic* (London: Routledge, 1996), 7. See also David McNally, *Monsters of the Market* (Leiden: Brill, 2011), chap. 1.
133. Fred Botting, *Gothic* (London: Routledge, 1996), 87.
134. Mark Neocleous, 'The Monstrous Multitude: Edmund Burke's Political Teratology', *Contemporary Political Theory* 3 (2004) 70, 82, 78. See also William Musgrave, '"That Monstrous Fiction": Radical Agency and Aesthetic Ideology in Burke', *Studies in Romanticism* 36 (1997) 3.
135. Mary Shelley, *Frankenstein* (London: Penguin, rev. ed., 2003).

of capitalism as a system that (for better or worse, according to one's perspective) generates the means of its own destruction.[136]

Towards the beginning of the novel, the Creature tells of how, abandoned by his creator, he takes refuge in a hovel adjacent to the cottage of a poor rural family. By observing the family unseen at night, he acquires language. At one point, the son of the family is reading aloud from a well-known radical text of the time, Volney's *Ruins of Empire*.[137] Listening to this, the Creature says, 'the strange system of human society was explained to me'. He goes on: 'I heard of the division of property, of immense wealth and squalid poverty . . . I learned that the possessions most esteemed [in human society] were high and unsullied descent united with riches.' Finally, '[I discovered that] a man might be respected with only one of these advantages; but without either he was considered, except in very rare instances, a vagabond and a slave, doomed to waste his powers for the profits of the chosen few!'[138]

The division of property; immense wealth and squalid poverty; privilege linked to aristocratic descent, and both in turn linked to the accumulation of riches; a system that condemns the many to sell their labour-power for the profit of the few, with vagabondage the only alternative to permanent wage-slavery — Shelley reminds us here that, if the Revolution controversy was a contrast of opinions about government and the locus of sovereignty, it was grounded in social realities that were not simply a matter of opinion. As we will investigate further in the chapters to follow, the 'strange system' of economy and society was also at stake.

136. See, e.g., Johanna Smith (ed.), *Frankenstein: Mary Shelley* (London: Macmillan, 1992).
137. Constantin François (de Chasseboeuf, comte de) Volney (James Marshall, trans. and ed.), *The Ruins, or a Survey of the Revolutions of Empires* (London: Thomas Tegg, 1823).
138. Mary Shelley, *Frankenstein* (London: Penguin, rev. ed., 2003), 122–23.

6

In the Shadow of Dearth

Fire at the Albion Mills

On 2 March 1791 a fire broke out at the Albion Flour Mills in London.[1] Opened in 1786, the mills were the city's first great factory. They stood on Blackfriars Road near the southern end of Blackfriars Bridge, and had steam-powered engines designed by James Watt that one contemporary dubbed the 'most powerful machines in the world'.[2] With twenty pairs of 150 horsepower millstones, the factory could grind an astonishing ten bushels[3] of wheat per hour. No wind- or water-powered mill would ever be able to compete with that. Indeed, by the end of 1790, several nearby wind-driven undertakings had already closed.

The fire at the Albion Mills started in the early morning, in dry, windy conditions, and at a time when the Thames was at low tide. Though the insurer's fire brigade came quickly to the scene, the low level of the river meant that the firefighters struggled to fill their hoses. It seems that they were also distracted by the crowd that had gathered to watch the blaze. According to contemporary reports, the firefighters broke off in the middle of their operation to douse scuffling onlookers. In the end, the building was completely destroyed — the one-time wonder reduced to a burnt-out shell, with spoiled wheat smouldering at its base. It remained in that state for some years until it was finally demolished in 1809 and replaced with

1. The account that follows draws principally on 'The Burning of the Albion Mills', available at www.alphabetthreat.co.uk/pasttense/albionmills.html. See also 'Albion Mill', available at www.vauxhallcivicsociety.org.uk/history/albion-mill/.
2. Eramus Darwin. See 'The Burning of the Albion Mills', available at www.alphabetthreat.co.uk/pasttense/albionmills.html.
3. c. 300 kilograms.

A False Tree of Liberty. Susan Marks, Oxford University Press (2019). © Susan Marks.
DOI: 10.1093/oso/9780199675456.003.0006

housing. The engraver and poet William Blake lived a little way to the west at Lambeth, and it is believed that the charred ruin may have served as the inspiration for the 'dark satanic Mills' of which he writes in the preface to *Milton*.[4]

What caused the fire was never definitively determined. The Albion's manager, along with the man who supervised the construction and erection of the engines, thought the initial spark came from a machine that had been insufficiently greased, but an alternative and widely circulating theory was arson. Perhaps the local millers, or the local millworkers, or both, fearing for their futures, took matters into their own hands and set the place alight. Certainly, Blackfriars, along with adjacent Southwark, is known to have been an area with a long tradition of popular rebelliousness. And while machine-breaking became an organised movement only in later years and other regions, the capital was no stranger to direct action in that form.[5] The Spitalfields silkweavers had been wrecking machine looms ever since those looms were first introduced in the early seventeenth century. They did so over three days in August 1675, and again during a particularly bitter struggle waged during the 1760s.[6] Machine looms had also been smashed at silk mills in Lewisham,[7] while at Limehouse a mechanical sawmill that put 500 sawyers out of work was burnt down in 1768.[8]

In some cases, this early machine-breaking was a tactic used by workers against their employers — the practice Eric Hobsbawm called 'collective bargaining by riot'.[9] In other cases, workers acted in alliance with their own or other small-scale employers. Either way, their objection was not so much to machinery *per se* as to the social costs of mechanisation, and to the erosion of traditional forms of workplace regulation that provided protection against such costs. For the men and women affected, technological change combined

4. See Graham Gibberd, *On Lambeth Marsh: The South Bank and Waterloo* (London: Jane Gibberd, 1992), 155. Blake composed the preface in 1804. See William Blake, *Milton: A Poem in Two Books*, Plate I (i), Preface, in David Erdman (ed.), *The Complete Poetry and Prose of William Blake* (New York: Anchor, rev. ed., 1988), 95.
5. See Michael Berlin, '"Broken all in pieces": Artisans and the Regulation of Workmanship in Early Modern London', in Geoffrey Crossick (ed.), *The Artisan and the European Town* (Brookfield, VT: Ashgate, 1997), 75, 84–86.
6. See Eric Hobsbawm, *Labouring Men* (London: Weidenfeld & Nicolson, 1964), 11, and, for a detailed account, Isaac Ashley, 'Bold Defiance: the Spitalfields Silk Weavers: London's Luddites?' (2012), available at www.past-tense.org.uk.
7. See Isaac Ashley, 'Bold Defiance: the Spitalfields Silk Weavers: London's Luddites?' (2012), available at www.past-tense.org.uk.
8. See George Rudé, *Wilkes and Liberty* (Oxford: Clarendon Press, 1962), 93–94.
9. Eric Hobsbawm, *Labouring Men* (London: Weidenfeld & Nicolson, 1964), 7.

with a new ideology of *laissez faire* to threaten a perfect storm of impoverishment and degradation.[10]

If indeed the fire at the Albion Mills was an instance of deliberate machine-breaking, those responsible evidently had the support of the assembled crowd, who are said to have made no moves to help save the factory and, on the contrary, to have cheered on its demise. One of the many ballads inspired by the events tells of how 'very few did sorrow show / That the Albion Mills were burnt so low'. It goes on: 'Says one they had it in their power, / For to reduce the price of flour, / Instead of letting the bread raise / But now the Mills are all on blaze.' And the final verse concludes with a prayer that 'God [may] bless us one and all, / And send the price of bread may fall.'[11]

These lines remind us that there was also another aspect to the popular distress. After a half-century of mostly affordable food, the second half of the eighteenth century saw persistently high and generally rising prices for bread and other foodstuffs. In particular, spikes in the price of bread led to widespread rioting in 1756–7, 1766–7, 1773, 1782 — and again, after the fire at the Albion Mills, in 1795–6 and 1800–1.[12] From the growing of grain to its consumption as loaves, bread passed through many hands including farmers, merchants, millers, carters and bakers, and popular ire was turned on all of them.[13] Rioters intercepted grain in transit, took supplies from granaries and mills, attacked profiteering merchants' homes, and protested against bakers who missold bread that had been adulterated by the admixture of inferior grains. In E. P. Thompson's well-known thesis, they did so on the basis of a belief that they were 'defending traditional rights or customs', and were 'supported by the wider consensus of the community'.[14]

'The moral economy of the poor' is Thompson's term for the set of assumptions and expectations about norms, obligations and propriety in social and especially economic relations that underpinned that belief. 'An outrage to

10. See further below. On pre-Luddite machine-breaking, see Adrian Randall, *Before the Luddites: Custom, Community and Machinery in the English Woollen Industry, 1776–1809* (Cambridge: Cambridge University Press, 1991), esp. chap. 5.
11. 'The Albion Mills on Fire' (1791), BL1876.e.20.(1.), available at www.bl.uk/collection-items/broadside-albion-mills-on-fire. It seems that, in August 1789, a letter was sent to the Lord Mayor of London warning that the Albion Mills would be burned down 'unless you regulate the price of Bread & c.'. Regarding that letter, see David Worrall, 'Blake and 1790s Plebeian Culture', in Steve Clark and David Worrall (eds.), *Blake in the Nineties* (London: Macmillan, 1999), 194, 199.
12. See E. P. Thompson, *Customs in Common* (Pontypool: Merlin Press, 1991), 189. (A slightly different chronology appears in John Bohstedt, *The Politics of Provisions: Food Riots, Moral Economy, and Market Transition in England, c. 1550–1850* (Farnham: Ashgate, 2010).)
13. See Walter Stern, 'The Bread Crisis in Britain, 1795–96', *Economica* 31 (122) (1964) 168, 174.
14. E. P. Thompson, *Customs in Common* (Pontypool: Merlin Press, 1991), 188.

these moral assumptions', he writes, 'quite as much as actual deprivation, was the usual occasion for direct action'.[15] In a previous chapter we touched on early modern English approaches to food distribution, especially in times of dearth.[16] We noted that, during the late sixteenth and early seventeenth centuries, the Book of Orders laid down directions for preventing profiteering when there were food shortages, and for ensuring that as much grain as possible reached the market and at prices affordable to the poor. By the last quarter of the eighteenth century, little of this law was left. The most conspicuous element of it — the statutory prohibition on forestalling, regrating, and engrossing — was repealed in 1772.[17] But while the legal framework associated with the old system had been largely dismantled, Thompson's point is that it endured in popular memory, and so too did the customary rights it was supposed to have protected.

His evidence for this is that food rioters demanded food at affordable prices as a matter not of charity, but of entitlement. They protested that it was wrong for some people to derive profit from the desperation of others; that however scarce food may be, it should be priced so that the basic necessities of life always remained available to everyone. Further to that, they asserted that the burden of dearth could not be allowed to fall wholly or disproportionately on the poor; a reduced harvest had to be shared out fairly. Finally, they insisted that it was the right, and indeed the duty, of the people to defend these principles if the state would not. The often heard cry of 'we'd rather be hanged than starved!' signals the repressive violence which was the authorities' response to that last claim. Those taking part in food riots, including peaceful moral-economic protest, were among the victims of the flood-tide of eighteenth-century retributive justice to which reference was made in the previous chapter. Many of them were executed. Thus, Thompson observes that, at a time when the state was aligning itself ever more closely with commercial interests, and when the more or less transparent and regulated market was giving way to the invisible hand, the market-place became 'as much an arena of class war as the factory and mine [would become] in the industrial revolution'.[18]

15. Ibid.
16. See chap. 3 above.
17. There is some evidence that these remained offences for a time at common law, however. See further below.
18. E. P. Thompson, *Customs in Common* (Pontypool: Merlin Press, 1991), 239.

Continuing our discussion of the Revolution controversy, this chapter considers how these developments informed thinking about the rights of man. Our focus will mostly be on texts composed after the initial flurry of publications that were our subject-matter in the preceding chapter. The start of this period is marked by the outbreak of war with revolutionary France in 1793, but of more immediate importance for the writings which will preoccupy us here is the severe food crisis that took place in 1795–6. Historical research has demonstrated a massive spike in the average price of wheat between April 1795 and September 1796, with mortality rates rising markedly in 1795. As always, the causes of the crisis were complex and contested. Certainly harvests were bad. The 1794 yield was one-fifth below the ten-year average, while the 1795 yield was worse still, due to sharp frost and floods throughout the sowing season.[19] At the same time, the war was relevant, inasmuch as the exigencies of troop provisioning and the disruption of grain imports from continental Europe exacerbated the effects of harvest failure.[20] As prices soared while wages remained static, food rioting spread on a scale not previously known. One of the most serious riots actually involved soldiers. In April 1795, a group of armed militiamen stationed in Sussex seized all the flour and other provisions they could find in two nearby towns.[21]

These food-related disturbances also intersected with the new political demands of the age, as is illustrated by an event that occurred on 29 October 1795.[22] The king was on his way to open Parliament. As his coach left St James's Palace and turned into the Mall, it encountered a hostile crowd hissing and hooting, and shouting 'Down with George!', 'No king!', 'No George!', 'Bread, bread!', 'No famine!', 'No War!', 'No Pitt!'. The coach was pelted with mud, and stones were thrown at it, cracking the panes of glass in one or two of its windows. Then, at a certain moment, something struck the glass in the door of the coach, and made a small hole in it. The projectile might have been a marble or, again, a stone, but George III believed it was a bullet, and on arrival at the House of Lords, he famously announced to the Lord Chancellor,

19. See Walter Stern, 'The Bread Crisis in Britain 1795–6', *Economica* 31 (122) (1964) 168, 168–70 and 174.
20. See Roger Wells, *Wretched Faces: Famine in Wartime England 1793–1801* (Gloucester: Alan Sutton, 1988).
21. See Walter Stern, 'The Bread Crisis in Britain 1795–6', *Economica* 31 (122) (1964) 168, 172.
22. See Adrian Randall, *Riotous Assemblies: Popular Protest in Hanoverian England* (Oxford: Oxford University Press, 2006), 225 et seq.

Lord Loughborough, 'My Lord, I have been shot at!'[23] Thompson describes how a hawker who had been selling copies of *Rights of Man* at the demonstration was 'taken into custody, [then] rescued, and chaired [held aloft on the shoulders of members of the crowd] in triumph'. In another detail, also mentioned by Thompson, some members of the crowd 'brandished small loaves on sticks decorated with black crepe' — 'mourning loaves' in the traditional symbology of famine.[24]

Often mentioned as a pivotal event of this period insofar as its aftermath was a phase of heightened anti-Jacobin repression, the 'attack on the king's coach' appears, then, to have been at once a political rally — a 'republican attack', as Gillray called it in an etching made shortly afterwards (fig. 7) — and a food riot. So too it appears that, if the country's leading pamphleteers came

Figure 7 *The Republican attack*. James Gillray 1795. Art Collection 2 / Alamy Stock Photo

23. See John Barrell, *Imagining the King's Death: Figurative Treason, Fantasies of Regicide 1793–1796* (Oxford: Oxford University Press, 2000), 554–57. See also E. P. Thompson, *The Making of the English Working Class* (New York: Vintage, 1966), 144.
24. E. P. Thompson, *The Making of the English Working Class* (New York: Vintage, 1966), 144.

into dispute over popular sovereignty and republican government, fraught issues of subsistence soon impinged.

Two approaches to dearth

In a moment we will look at contributions by Burke and Paine, along with writing by the dissident political leader John Thelwall and by the author of conservative popular fiction Hannah More. But first let us notice a little more about the subsistence crisis of this time, and especially its significance for trends in theory and practice. Broadly speaking, contemporaries approached the problem of dearth in ways that led in two quite distinct directions. One direction, already touched upon, is elucidated by Thompson in his work on the moral economy, and by others building on his investigations. For Thompson, the very phrase 'food riot' is questionable to the extent that it misrepresents food-related disturbances as 'rebellions of the belly'. In fact, he writes, far from being a purely instinctive or spasmodic reaction to hunger or fear of hunger, '[t]he food riot in eighteenth-century England was a highly complex form of direct popular action, disciplined and with clear objectives'.[25]

Of course, high prices and hunger or fear of hunger supplied the trigger, but these 'grievances operated within a popular consensus as to what were legitimate and what were illegitimate practices in marketing, milling, baking, etc'.[26] In turn, that popular consensus was 'grounded upon a consistent traditional view of social norms and obligations, of the proper economic functions of several parties within the community, which, taken together, can be said to constitute the moral economy of the poor'.[27] Illegitimacy in this context had mostly to do with effect on the availability, quality and price of provisions. In Thompson's account, the fire at the Albion Mills should be understood as an instance of action against illegitimate market practices affecting the sale of flour.[28]

25. E. P. Thompson, *Customs in Common* (Pontypool: Merlin Press, 1991), 186, 188. In contrast, John Bohstedt maintains in a later study that the food-related disturbances of this time were manifestations of the 'law of necessity', with acute hunger the key driver. See John Bohstedt, *The Politics of Provisions: Food Riots, Moral Economy, and Market Transition in England, c. 1550–1850* (Farnham: Ashgate, 2010), 9 and passim.
26. E. P. Thompson, *Customs in Common* (Pontypool: Merlin Press, 1991), 188.
27. Ibid.
28. See ibid, 221.

As described in this seminal work, the moral economy of the eighteenth-century poor was quite specific in its operation. '[I]t is this miller, this dealer, those farmers hoarding grain, who provoke indignation and action.'[29] Yet behind that specificity, Thompson shows that popular perceptions of what was legitimate and what was not were animated and informed by more general principles. The 'consistent traditional view of social norms and obligations' had as its corollary 'general notions of rights' that referenced the old order of market supervision and consumer protection.[30] Partly codified in earlier centuries, this was always also customary in character. In brief, the idea was that selling should take place transparently, on an open competitive market; that arrangements should be structured so as to give priority to local people, and to enable the poor to satisfy their needs in advance of purchases by business customers; that careful regulation, backed up by penalties for non-compliance, was necessary to prevent harmful advantage or gain in trade; and that purveyors of provisions, and especially millers and bakers (remembering that the staple of the English diet had long been, and still remained, bread), were to be regarded as working not for profit, but to supply the community, their work remunerated by a fair allowance.

It seems that these principles were not simply normative, but rather described, more or less, an operative regime of food distribution. By the eighteenth century, however, Thompson observes that the model 'was drifting apart from reality'.[31] Outside the main cereal-growing districts, urban populations could not have been supplied without the activity of intermediaries of various kinds. A national market was being created, in which the assize of bread — once a powerful institution for controlling bread production and distribution in the interests of consumers — had lost much of its significance,[32] and the historic offences of 'regrating, forestalling and engrossing' no longer made sense. As Thompson reads the evidence, this was widely recognised at the time. But if the authorities were able to forget the earlier regulatory system in years of good harvests and moderate prices, they had no such chance when famine loomed. Popular direct action served as an abrupt reminder of 'the proper economic functions of several parties within the community' (to use his formulation, quoted above) and what each was expected to do.

29. Ibid, 212.
30. Ibid, 188, 212.
31. Ibid, 199.
32. Walter Stern, 'The Bread Crisis in Britain, 1795–96', *Economica* 31 (122) (1964) 168, 185, fn 2.

Thus Thompson proposes that the old model continued to have 'an ideal existence, and . . . a fragmentary real existence', disclosed by the poor when they intercepted grain in transit, raided a granary, or forced a baker to sell at the 'just price', and by the authorities when they took steps to deal with the cause of that unrest.[33] For while official action took many forms, sometimes it too referenced the norms of market regulation and consumer protection. As already mentioned, the statutory prohibition on forestalling, regrating, and engrossing was repealed in 1772, but the corresponding common law offences appear to have persisted for some time, and Thompson reports prosecutions for forestalling in 1795, and then again during the later subsistence crisis of 1800–1.[34] He also cites instances of landowners and local magistrates trying to control prices without recourse to legal processes, simply by persuasion or 'giving a nod and a wink to the crowd'.[35]

Yet the primary actor in this story of moral-economic theory and practice is not the rich and powerful, but the poor. Thompson wants to capture the seeming oxymoron of a 'rebellious traditional culture'[36] — a culture that invoked tradition to legitimate revolt, and that fought abjection by defending custom and attempting to reorient change. If later studies have questioned the extent to which a market model that was, after all, paternalistic in spirit did, and could, serve the poor,[37] it is noteworthy that Thompson writes of a partly invented tradition. In his account, the eighteenth-century moral economy was an artefact of its own time. It was a 'selective reconstruction' of the earlier paternalist order, taking 'all those features which most favoured the poor', and decidedly departing insofar as 'the popular ethic sanctioned direct action by the crowd, whereas the values . . . underpinning the paternalist model emphatically did not'.[38] It was 'moral' in that it had things to say about social norms, justice, rights and obligations. At the same time, it was an 'economy' and hence also political in that those things bore on the means of sustaining life and their contested distribution among different groups in society.

33. E. P. Thompson, *Customs in Common* (Pontypool: Merlin Press, 1991), 200.
34. Ibid. John Bohstedt also reports on successful prosecutions for engrossing and regrating in 1800; see John Bohstedt, *The Politics of Provisions: Food Riots, Moral Economy, and Market Transition in England, c. 1550–1850* (Farnham: Ashgate, 2010), 172.
35. E. P. Thompson, *Customs in Common* (Pontypool: Merlin Press, 1991), 292.
36. Ibid, 9 (emphasis omitted).
37. See, e.g., John Bohstedt, *The Politics of Provisions: Food Riots, Moral Economy, and Market Transition in England, c. 1550–1850* (Farnham: Ashgate, 2010), 14 and passim.
38. E. P. Thompson, *Customs in Common* (Pontypool: Merlin Press, 1991), 212.

The moral economy, then, names one sort of approach to the problem of dearth. The other, also already touched upon, is *laissez-faire* or the new 'political economy'. That too is discussed by Thompson in his work on customs in common. Indeed, as he explains, his point is to contrast the moral economy with 'the new political economy of the free market in grain, associated above all' with Adam Smith's *Inquiry into the Nature and Causes of the Wealth of Nations*, and to show how, in times of high prices and hardship, the former provided a basis for popular direct action.[39] Smith's text appeared in March 1776, a few years after an earlier episode of food rioting that had taken place in 1773 and a decade after the food riots of 1766–7. Of course, taken as a whole, the *Wealth of Nations* provided no simple endorsement of *laissez-faire*. However, the particular section that is relevant here is the less nuanced 'Digression concerning the Corn Trade and Corn Laws' (the so-called 'Digression on Dearth'), which comes at the end of the chapter on bounties in *Book IV*.[40] Thompson dubs the 'Digression' 'the most lucid expression in English of the standpoint of the new political economy upon market relations in subsistence foodstuffs',[41] and in subsequent work on Smith, Emma Rothschild describes how the text was rediscovered, or at any rate, given new prominence, in the circumstances of the mid-1790s.[42]

The main argument of the 'Digression' is that the best way of palliating the effect of dearth and preventing it from developing into full-blown famine is for the authorities to leave the market alone. Certainly, price rises during periods of scarcity mean greater profit for those who have grain to sell. But it is in years of scarcity that grain traders need to make their principal profit, offsetting the losses they inevitably sustain at other times due to the perishable nature of the commodity and to the occurrence of unforeseen price fluctuations. More importantly, higher prices also mean reduced consumption, which is essential if stocks are to last until the next season. Smith explains that, while the interests of grain traders and the population in general may seem at first sight opposed, in fact they are precisely aligned, and never more so than when the harvest is bad. For it is in the interest of traders to raise the price of grain as high as the scarcity of the season requires, but no higher. If they raise

39. Ibid, 260–61.
40. Adam Smith (Andrew Skinner, ed.), *The Wealth of Nations Books IV–V* (London: Penguin, 1999), 102.
41. E. P. Thompson, *Customs in Common* (Pontypool: Merlin Press, 1991), 276.
42. Emma Rothschild, *Economic Sentiments: Adam Smith, Condorcet, and the Enlightenment* (Cambridge, MA: Harvard University Press, 2001), 61 et seq.

the price too high, consumption is discouraged so much that existing supplies will last too long, and existing stock will eventually have to be sold at a much lower price than would have been the case a few months earlier. If they keep the price too low, consumption is discouraged so little that existing supplies will not last long enough, and dearth risks turning into famine; at the same time, a portion of the profit which might have been made will be forfeited.

In this way, writes Smith, and '[w]ithout intending the interest of the people, [the trader] is necessarily led, by a regard to his own interest', to serve the common good. Like the prudent master of a vessel who foresees that food supplies will soon run short and puts his crew on reduced rations, the trader helps to stave off famine and to moderate the hardships of dearth by '[putting] everybody more or less, but particularly the inferior ranks of people, upon thrift and good management'.[43] Insofar as those inferior ranks may resist this, and demand or themselves take action to control prices, Smith comments that they misunderstand the nature of dearth. What is involved is a simple matter of deficient food production, the result of seasonal perturbations. To be sure, war may sometimes be a factor, but the free market is not part of the problem. Instead, it is the solution. Or rather, it is a means — the only effective and hence proper means — of mitigating a state of affairs, the impact of which can be lessened, but never wholly eliminated. As for full-blown famine, Smith offers that it has 'never arisen from any other cause but the violence of government attempting, by improper means, to remedy the inconveniences of a dearth'.[44] Thus Smith advises that the 'unlimited, unrestrained freedom of the corn trade . . . is the only effectual preventative of the miseries of a famine ... [and] the best palliative of the inconveniences of a dearth'.[45]

It follows from this that governments should not take measures which inhibit that trade or constrain those who take part in it. To do so is to yield to irrational popular 'prejudices' for the sake of short-term civil peace.[46] For in Smith's judgement, famously, the consensus that underpinned food-related disturbances, like the prohibition of forestalling, regrating and engrossing to which they partly appealed, was to be 'compared to the popular terrors and suspicions of witchcraft'.[47] Thompson writes that '[i]t should not be necessary

43. Adam Smith (Andrew Skinner, ed.), *The Wealth of Nations, Books IV–V* (London: Penguin, 1999), 103, 102.
44. Ibid, 105.
45. Ibid, 106.
46. Ibid, 119.
47. Ibid, 113.

to argue that the model of a natural and self-adjusting economy, working providentially for the best good of all, is as much a superstition as the notions which upheld the paternalist model'.[48] As an example of how this was evident at the time, he refers to a calculation made in 1796 by the agricultural analyst Arthur Young (about whom more in the next chapter), putting the crop deficiency at less than 25 per cent, the price increase at 81 per cent, and the expected annual profit for the grain trade at £20m over the year.[49] Nonetheless, the idea of a free market in which the pursuit of individual self-interest would generate systematic societal advantage was a superstition that was rapidly gaining ground. According to Thompson, there was wide acceptance of the need for a more free-flowing national grain trade. The question was how to deal with hardship, and on that, he proposes that Smith's 'Digression' was acquiring 'oracular authority'.[50] For their part, the food riots of 1795 were 'a last desperate effort' to reimpose elements of the old model of provisioning in the face of advancing market liberalisation.[51]

The jurisdiction of mercy

The conflict between the moral economy of the poor and the new political economy was played out, as we have seen, on the terrain of provisioning. But provisioning was not the only issue at this time of dearth. In particular, attention also turned to social protection and wages. On 6 May 1795 the Berkshire Court of Quarter Sessions held a special meeting at the Pelican Inn in Speenhamland — today part of the city of Newbury — to discuss the deepening subsistence crisis. What could be done to alleviate the distress being experienced by the poor and to prevent the recurrence or escalation of the preceding months' food riots? The magistrates were especially concerned about the situation of waged workers — rural agricultural labourers, whose wages no longer enabled them to buy enough food to sustain themselves and their families. People without any paid employment could rely on (albeit hardly lavish) parish relief of various sorts, but waged workers fell through the cracks.

48. E. P. Thompson, *Customs in Common* (Pontypool: Merlin Press, 1991), 203.
49. See ibid, 205.
50. Ibid, 279.
51. E. P. Thompson, *The Making of the English Working Class* (New York: Vintage, 1966), 67.

There is evidence that the magistrates' initial intention had been to set higher wage rates, but in the event they came up with a different scheme.[52] This was a system of wage supplementation or aid-in-wages tied to the price of bread. Wages would be topped up from parish funds (and hence indirectly by employers as landowning rate-payers), so that workers would receive a sufficient guaranteed income every week. A sliding scale was laid down, according to which the guaranteed income would increase as the cost of a gallon loaf went up. The size of a family was also factored in, so that larger families would receive correspondingly larger payments. The 'Speenhamland system', as it was to become known, gained considerable traction, and was subsequently adopted in many parts of southern England. In Karl Polanyi's widely quoted gloss, it 'introduced no less a social and economic innovation than the *"right to live"*'.[53]

Historians continue to debate the effects of the Speenhamland system, but one undisputed consequence was to keep wages low. If the magistrates had planned to do something about raising wages, they instituted a system that, on the contrary, allowed employers to go on paying wages at below-subsistence levels, secure in the knowledge that the parishes would step in and meet workers' income needs. Might not the right to live entail instead the right to a living wage? That it did was the premise of an initiative some months later by the brewery owner and Member of Parliament, Samuel Whitbread. On 9 December 1795 Whitbread presented to Parliament a bill that would have provided the basis for a minimum wage.[54] Still valid Tudor legislation — the Statute of Artificers of 1563 — established a framework for setting maximum wages for particular kinds of work, and his idea was to extend that framework to encompass also annual assessments of minimum pay. The bill met with overwhelming opposition, and did not pass.

Speaking against it, Prime Minister William Pitt acknowledged that the 'present situation of the labouring poor in this country, was certainly not such as could be wished'; '[t]hat class had of late been exposed to hardships which [everyone] concurred in lamenting, and were equally actuated by a desire to remove'.[55] The question was how to remove those hardships, and specifically,

52. See J. L. and Barbara Hammond, *The Village Labourer, 1760–1832* (Stroud: Alan Sutton, 1987), 161–62.
53. Karl Polanyi, *The Great Transformation* (Boston: Beacon Press, 1944), 78 (emphasis added).
54. See *The Parliamentary History of England from the Earliest Period to the Year 1803, Vol. XXXII* (London: Hansard, 1818), 700.
55. Ibid, 705.

whether this was best accomplished by regulating the price of labour, or 'by the unassisted operation of principles'.[56] By 'the unassisted operation of principles', Pitt made clear that he meant the unlimited, unrestrained freedom of trade, that is to say, the approach outlined by Smith in the 'Digression on Dearth'. Pitt took that approach to state a rule of general application, and in the circumstances he saw no justification for making an exception in the matter of wages.

In introducing his bill, Whitbread also drew on Smithian ideas. He said that he 'felt as much as any man how greatly it was to be desired that there should be no legislative interference in matters of this nature'.[57] He identified with the belief 'that the price of labour, like every other commodity, should be left to find its own level'.[58] But he maintained, as Smith himself ordinarily held, that 'till that level be found', regulation was needed.[59] A great 'disproportion' had developed 'between the price of labour, and the price of living',[60] and the 'pressure [on labourers] had become almost too grievous to be endured'.[61] Whitbread explained that it was to this evil that his bill was directed. It was 'his wish to . . . enable the husbandman, who dedicated his days to incessant toil, to feed, to clothe, and to lodge his family with some degree of comfort'. He wanted to 'exempt the youth of this country from the necessity of . . . flocking to great towns for subsistence', and to 'put it in the power of him who ploughed and sowed and threshed the corn, to taste of the fruits of his industry, by giving him a right to a part of the produce of his labour'.[62]

Underscoring that last point, one of the few others who spoke in favour of the bill declared that 'he would rather have the labourer enjoy the honest fruits of his industry, than be obliged to receive his due as an eleemosynary [i.e. charitable] gift'.[63] Pitt would have none of it. Whitbread and his friends 'should look to the instances where interference had shackled industry',[64] and if they were worried about youth flocking to towns, they would do well to take note of 'how much could be done by the industry of children and the advantages of early employing them in such branches of manufactures as they

56. Ibid, 706.
57. Ibid, 703.
58. Ibid.
59. Ibid, 714.
60. These were Pitt's words. See ibid, 707.
61. Ibid, 703.
62. Ibid, 704.
63. Ibid, 712.
64. Ibid, 707.

are capable to execute'.[65] '[T]rade, industry and barter [were] always . . . impeded by regulations which violated their natural operation, and deranged their proper effect.'[66]

I mentioned Rothschild's account of the rediscovery, or at any rate, new prominence, of the 'Digression' in the mid-1790s. For her, this debate on Whitbread's bill serves as a striking illustration of what she characterises as a 'conflict between two different "Smiths"'.[67] She argues that 'Whitbread's Smith is in many respects closer to the "real" Smith, or to the real *Wealth of Nations*'.[68] 'Pitt's Smith', on the other hand, is the Smith of the 'Digression', and points to the way that short passage was being read at this time and used as a prescription for *laissez-faire* — and not only in the market for corn, but also in the market more generally, including the market for labour. How did Pitt arrive at this 'Smith'? According to Thompson, Pitt read 'the Digression' in the 1780s, and 'became wholly converted'.[69] By the time Whitbread's bill was presented in December 1795, however, 'Pitt's Smith' had also received important reinforcement from another text. In November of that year, Edmund Burke sent Pitt a memorandum setting out his views on the policy implications of the subsistence crisis. The memorandum was published posthumously in 1800, under the title *Thoughts and Details on Scarcity*.[70]

More than two decades earlier, when himself a Member of Parliament, Burke had been a vocal advocate for the repeal of the statutory prohibitions on forestalling, regrating and engrossing. That was during the build-up to the food crisis of 1773. He now put forward a case for the adoption of a broad set of anti-regulatory doctrines, framed against the backdrop of the moral-economic demands of the mid-1790s, as also against the backdrop of the Speenhamland system and of calls like that shortly to be heard in Parliament for statutory measures to raise agricultural wages. The text opens with the declaration that '[o]f all things, an indiscreet tampering with the trade of provisions is the most dangerous, and it is always the worst in the time when men are most disposed to it; — that is, in the time of scarcity'. Burke remarks on the baneful influence in that regard of 'a multitude of ill-founded popular prejudices'.[71] Then, after a few further words on the subject

65. Ibid, 710.
66. Ibid, 707.
67. Emma Rothschild, *Economic Sentiments* (Cambridge, MA: Harvard University Press, 2001), 63.
68. Ibid.
69. E. P. Thompson, *Customs in Common* (Pontypool: Merlin Press, 1991), 276.
70. Edmund Burke, *Thoughts and Details on Scarcity* (London: Rivington, 1800).
71. Ibid, 1.

of provisions, his focus quickly shifts to labour, and in particular to the question of below-subsistence wages.

Do the authorities have a responsibility to ensure that wages remain in proportion to prices? No, he writes, wages are the outcome of contracts between labourers and their employers, and '[w]hen a contract is making, it is a matter of discretion and of interest between the parties', and only the parties.[72] What if the wages contracted for are not, or no longer, sufficient to provide the necessities of life? 'Labour is a commodity, like every other', Burke explains.[73] Because of this, it is, and must remain, 'subject to all the laws and principles of trade, and not to regulations foreign to them'. Under the laws and principles of trade, the sole relevant criterion is the relation between supply and demand. 'If the goods at market are beyond the demand, they fall in their value; if below it, they rise.' He goes on: 'The impossibility of the subsistence of a man, who carries his labour to a market, is totally beside the question ... The only question is, what is it [the labour] worth to the buyer?'[74] How then is starvation to be prevented when dearth comes and wages fall short? Burke's answer is that those affected pass into 'the jurisdiction of mercy'. '[C]harity to the poor is a direct and obligatory duty upon all Christians . . . [though] the manner, mode, time, choice of objects, and proportion, are left to private discretion.'[75] Certainly, he affirms, the solution does not lie in 'breaking the laws of commerce, which are the laws of nature, and consequently the laws of God'.[76]

Like Smith, Burke considers that these laws work in a way that, as he puts it, 'obliges men, whether they will or not, in pursuing their own selfish interests, to connect the general good with their own individual success'. It is 'the farmer's interest that his men should thrive', just as it is in the interest of labourers 'that the farmer should have a full incoming profit' so that he can see to their thriving.[77] While seasonal perturbations sometimes entail hardship, the farmer must be 'permitted, and even expected, to look to all possible profit . . . [and] to turn . . . scarcity to the best advantage he can'.[78] In Burke's portrayal, this does not make the agricultural employer akin to a prudent shipmaster who puts his crew on reduced rations, as Smith proposes,

72. Ibid, 8.
73. Ibid, 6
74. Ibid, 13.
75. Ibid, 18.
76. Ibid, 32.
77. Ibid, 11.
78. Ibid, 20.

for the employer is simply the counter-party in a contract of employment, to which questions of subsistence are irrelevant. But it does reflect the providential ordinances of commerce. As for those whose subsistence is at stake, Burke writes that 'patience, labour, sobriety, frugality, and religion, should be recommended to them'.[79]

I have recalled that *Thoughts and Details on Scarcity* was written as a memorandum for Pitt, and was not made available to the wider world until 1800. In the meantime, its message about patience, labour, sobriety, frugality and religion was disseminated by others, and perhaps none more energetically than Hannah More. Unlike Burke, More wrote for a popular audience, and she did so through mostly literary modes of composition, rather than pamphlets. A playwright, poet and prolific writer of fiction, she was especially known for her moral tales, today read as vehicles for promoting habits of docility, piety, humility and industriousness among ordinary people.[80] Her influence was all the greater as she addressed, in part, women — both poor women and women of greater means or, at any rate, higher social status. She laid particular emphasis on 'good household management', or what would later be called 'home economics'. *The Cottage Cook, or Mrs Jones's Cheap Dishes* showed women 'ways of doing much good with little money', dispensing such 'Friendly Hints' as that '[t]he difference between eating bread new and stale, is one loaf in five'.[81] The hints are provided by a female character of the 'middle rank', who explains that she is engaged in the 'manufacture . . . [of] an excellent staple commodity', namely, the making of 'good wives for working men',[82] and the author has been understood as identifying with that project herself.[83] It was a project of patriarchical subordination, but also, and linked to that, an attempt to put a stop to enforcement of the moral economy, and enrol the poor in the new political economy.[84]

79. Ibid, 4.
80. See further Anne Stott, *Hannah More: the First Victorian* (New York: Oxford University Press, 2003).
81. Hannah More, *The Cottage Cook, or Mrs Jones's Cheap Dishes* (London: J Marshall, 1797), 16.
82. See ibid, 13.
83. See Mona Scheuermann, *In Praise of Poverty* (Lexington: University of Kentucky Press, 2002), 137.
84. On the role of women in food riots, see E. P. Thompson, *Customs in Common* (Pontypool: Merlin Press, 1991), 305 et seq., and John Bohstedt, 'The Myth of the Feminine Food Riot: Women as Proto-Citizens in English Community Politics, 1790–1810', in Harriet Applewhite and Darline Levy (eds.), *Women and Politics in the Age of Democratic Revolution* (Ann Arbor: University of Michigan Press, 1990), 21.

More's earliest significant text, appearing in 1792, was a contribution to the effort to curb the popular influence of Paine's *Rights of Man*. *Village Politics* takes the form of a dialogue between Jack Anvil, a blacksmith, and Tom Hod, a mason, in which sensible Jack sets straight naive Paine-inclining Tom.[85] As the story builds to its conclusion, Jack declares:

> 'Tom! I have got the use of my limbs, of my liberty, of the laws, and of my bible. The two first I take to be my *natural* rights; the two last my *civil* and *religious*; these, I take it, are the *true Rights of Man*, and all the rest is nothing but nonsense, and madness, and wickedness.'[86]

More continued to write against Paine; a later story culminates in a scene in which his alter ego in her work ('Mr Fantom') repents on his deathbed, and orders his books to be publicly burned.[87] At the same time, her best known work pursued other themes. *The Shepherd of Salisbury Plain*, published in 1795, tells the story of Mr Johnson, 'a very worthy charitable gentleman', who is out riding one day when he comes across a (nameless) poor shepherd.[88] What is immediately noticeable to Mr Johnson is how neatly mended and patched the shepherd's clothes are. Mr Johnson takes that as evidence that the shepherd has a 'notable' wife, 'worthy of encouragement'. The two fall into conversation, and the gentleman learns of the dreadful hardships of his interlocutor's life, though also of the latter's unfailing cheerfulness and gratitude for the little he has. The notable wife is ill due to having to work too soon after childbirth, and the family live in a tiny hovel, with no wood for the fire and, in any case, not much to cook, but the poor man has no complaints. He explains, 'I get my shilling a-day, and most of my children will soon be able to earn something; for we have only three under five years old'. By the end of their encounter, Mr Johnson is convinced that 'a laborious life is a happy one', and is 'more disposed to envy . . . the shepherd' than 'to pity' him.[89]

This fantasy of popular contentment in the face of exploitation and deprivation pervades much of More's writing. However, in another text from that same dearth year, she set it aside and portrayed instead the actuality of popular discontent and unrest. *The Riot; Or Half a Loaf is better than no Bread* is

85. Hannah More, *Village Politics* (York: G. Walker, 1793). Like the initial text published by Rivington in 1792, this publication appeared under the authorship of 'Will Chip: A Country Carpenter'.
86. Ibid, 13 (emphasis in original).
87. Hannah More, *The Death of Mr Fantom*, in *Cheap Repository Tracts: Suited to the Present Times* (London: F. C. & J. Rivington, 1819), 96–99.
88. Hannah More, *The Shepherd of Salisbury Plain*, in Hannah More et al, *Cheap Repository Tracts: Entertaining, Moral, and Religious, Vol. 1* (London: J. Marshall, 1795), 9.
89. Ibid, 11, 19, 29.

a dialogue in verse that again features Jack Anvil and Tom Hod.[90] Tom is now inciting his friends to join him in a food riot, and Jack steps in to make him see the foolishness of his plans.[91] Sure we are hungry, says Jack, but '[w]hat a whimsey to think we shall mend our spare diet / By breeding disturbance, by murder and riot!' High food prices are the inevitable result of food shortages, which are in turn the result of bad harvests. The authorities cannot be expected to do anything, since, of course, no-one can 'help a bad season'. Direct action in the market is mindless and unhelpful. Thus, Jack advises that he and Tom should 'patiently wait and the prices will fall'. In the meantime, '[t]he Gentlefolks . . . will afford us supplies; / They'll subscribe [i.e. make donations to charitable subscriptions]' — but only if 'we're . . . quiet'.[92] 'So', Jack tells Tom, and Tom ultimately accepts his advice and follows his lead, 'I'll work the whole day, and on Sundays I'll seek / At church how to bear all the wants of the week'.[93]

Very evidently, More concurred with Burke there is no right to live, just as she concurred with him that there is no right of popular sovereignty. Instead there is the 'jurisdiction of mercy', and there are the 'true rights of man', understood as the right to 'use limbs' (or, in later language, 'sell labour-power') and uphold the 'liberty, laws and bible' of the established order.

The right to live

If these authors lined up to make those claims, what was the position of their shared antagonist and principal opponent in the Revolution controversy, Thomas Paine? In departing from them on the rights of man, did he also depart in asserting the right to live? Already in the previous chapter, we touched on some indications that he did. As we saw, Paine lamented the 'mass of wretchedness that [lies hidden from the eye of common observation and] has scarcely any other chance than to expire in poverty or infamy', and in *Rights of Man, Part II* he outlined a solution, in the shape of a new system of public welfare backed up by progressive taxation.[94] He argued that these

90. Hannah More, *The Riot; Or, Half a Loaf is Better than No Bread* (London: J. Marshall, 1795).
91. Ibid.
92. Ibid.
93. Ibid.
94. Thomas Paine, *Rights of Man, Part II*, in Bruce Kuklick (ed.), *Paine: Political Writings* (Cambridge: Cambridge University Press, 2000), 155, 212–13.

reforms transcended politics. In his words, the question is not 'whether this or that party shall be in or out, or Whig or Tory, or high or low shall . . . prevail'; it is 'whether man shall inherit his rights, and universal civilization take place'.[95]

Paine went on to urge further redistributive interventions. In one of the last publications to appear under his name, *Agrarian Justice*, he put forward a proposal for an inheritance tax on landed property.[96] However, the arguments he advanced to justify this proposal made clear that he had by then come to understand the situation a little differently from the way he had seen it earlier. While no less convinced than he was at the time he wrote *Rights of Man* that England's troubles were caused by its hereditary government, iniquitous tax system, and deficient arrangements for poor relief, to say nothing of its feudal succession practice, he now maintained that part of the problem was 'civilization' itself. Paine's usage of this term was informed by the widely accepted 'four stages' theory of human history, according to which the progress of humankind is a passage from hunting to shepherding, then settled agriculture, and finally 'commercial society' (or, to use again later language, capitalism), as the highest stage of economic and social development.[97] 'Civilization' was, of course, the antithesis of 'barbarism', but it also denoted the process of advancing beyond the more 'primitive' stages associated with the 'state of nature' or 'natural state' of human existence, as well as the terminus of that process.

Agrarian Justice was published in 1797. From the preface we learn that Paine wrote the text during the subsistence crisis of 1795–6, when the mass of wretchedness to which he had referred previously was not so hidden from the eye of common observation, and when the growing disparity between rich and poor was likewise plain to see.[98] His starting-point is the idea that '[c]ivilization . . . or that which is so called, has operated in two ways: to make one part of society more affluent, and the other more wretched, than would

95. Ibid, 212.
96. Thomas Paine, *Agrarian Justice*, in Bruce Kuklick (ed.), *Paine: Political Writings* (Cambridge: Cambridge University Press, 2000), 319. For further details, see below.
97. See, e.g., Adam Smith (R. L. Meek, D. D. Raphael and P. G. Stein, eds.), *Lectures on Jurisprudence* (Oxford: Oxford University Press, 1978), 14.
98. Paine also says in the preface that he decided to see to the publication of *Agrarian Justice* after reading a sermon by Richard Watson, Bishop of Llandaff, entitled 'The Wisdom and Goodness of God, in having made both Rich and Poor'. Watson's sermon is appended to a book in which he denounces Paine's *The Age of Reason*, published in 1794. Paine says he will respond on that later; for now, *Agrarian Justice* will answer the bishop on the issue of how 'rich' and 'poor' were 'made'. Watson claims God made the world that way, but Paine believes the maker is instead 'civilization'. See Thomas Paine, *Agrarian Justice*, in Bruce Kuklick (ed.), *Paine: Political Writings* (Cambridge: Cambridge University Press, 2000) 219, 323.

have been the lot of either in a natural state'.[99] Yet he presumes that there can be no returning to the natural state, and nor should there be, for in that condition humanity is 'without those advantages which flow from agriculture, arts, science and manufactures'. Instead, the 'thing . . . now to be done is to remedy the evils and preserve the benefits that have arisen to society' in the passage to 'civilization'.[100]

Before going further, Paine sets out three principles upon which, in his view, any practical proposals for achieving this should be based. The first principle is that no-one should be worse off 'after a state of civilization commences . . . than if he had been born before that period'.[101] The second is that everyone is born with a legitimate claim on what Paine calls 'natural property' or 'that which comes to us from the Creator of the universe' ('earth, air, water').[102] Whereas 'artificial or acquired property' belongs to whoever made or now possesses it, natural property is 'the common property of the human race'.[103] A difficulty of this is that, under conditions of 'civilization', it is impossible to disentangle these analytically distinct forms of property. The 'improvement made by cultivation' cannot be separated from 'the earth itself' on which that improvement is wrought. Nonetheless, 'it is the value of the improvement, only, and not the earth itself, that is individual property'.[104]

From these two principles Paine deduces a third, which is that every owner of landed property 'owes to the community a *ground-rent* . . . for the land which he holds' — a ground-rent, that is to say, like the ground-rent paid under the terms of a lease by the owner of a building to the owner of the land upon which the building stands.[105] How is payment of this ground-rent to be organised? Paine proposes that 10 per cent of the value of landed property should be deducted from the heritable estate of deceased landowners, and the revenue raised should be brought together as a fund to be used for the support of the rest of the population. He is at pains to stress that what is at issue here is not benevolence, but justice — 'it is a right, not a charity, that I am pleading for'. The 'landed monopoly . . . has dispossessed more than half the

99. Thomas Paine, *Agrarian Justice*, in Bruce Kuklick (ed.), *Paine: Political Writings* (Cambridge: Cambridge University Press, 2000), 319, 324.
100. Ibid.
101. Ibid, 324–25.
102. Ibid, 320.
103. Ibid, 325.
104. Ibid, 325.
105. Ibid, 325. If his usage of the word is unorthodox, Paine simply says: 'I know of no better term to express the idea'.

inhabitants of every nation of their natural inheritance, without providing for them, as it ought to have been done, an indemnification for that loss, and has thereby created a species of poverty and wretchedness that did not exist before'. That said, the fault 'is not in the present possessors' of land. Rather, the 'fault is in the system'; 'it has stolen imperceptibly upon the world, aided afterwards by the agrarian law of the sword'.[106]

Regarding the means of remedying the ill-effects of this, Paine remarks that '[t]here are, in every country, some magnificent charities established by individuals' which give relief to households in need. Yet individuals can do 'but little' when the nature and extent of the problem are considered. An individual 'may satisfy his conscience, but . . . [i]t is only by organizing civilization upon such principles as to act like a system of pulleys, that the whole weight of misery can be removed'. Besides, and *pace* Burke, 'it ought not to be left to the choice of detached individuals whether they will do justice or not'.[107] As Paine describes it, the proposed national fund that is formed out of deductions from the estates of landed proprietors will benefit the poor by providing them with insurance against destitution in old age. But equally it will benefit the rich, in that it will turn property-owning into a 'national blessing', and will remove the dangerous 'antipathies' of those who, on his account, have lost the 'awe' and 'reverence' with which they formerly regarded affluence.[108] He explains: 'when it shall be seen that the prosperity of [the] fund depends on the prosperity of individuals; when the more riches a man acquires, the better it shall be for the general mass; it is then that antipathies will cease, and property be placed on the permanent basis of national interest and protection'.[109]

Paine's scheme of inheritance tax only applied to landed property. He did not put forward any claim that would encompass personal ('artificial or acquired') property, though towards the end of *Agrarian Justice* he does observe that 'it is as impossible for an individual to acquire personal property without the aid of society, as it is for him to make land originally'. Wealth depends on the labour of others, and Paine considers that, even if in this context there is no right to 'indemnification', it is not improper to expect that a part of what is owned should be given 'back again to society from whence the whole came'.[110] This is all the more the case given that, as he affirms, 'the

106. Ibid, 326–27.
107. Ibid, 332.
108. Ibid, 334–35.
109. Ibid, 335–36.
110. Ibid, 334–35 (emphasis omitted).

accumulation of personal property is, in many instances, the effect of paying too little for the labor that produced it'.[111]

Writing at around the same time, John Thelwall agreed that too little was being paid for labour. For him, however, Paine's point about justice being at issue, rather than simply benevolence, also applied to wage rates. Thelwall was another well-known proponent of the rights of man. One of the founders and leaders of the radical working people's association, the London Corresponding Society, he was a talented orator, and was especially famous for the lectures he delivered at meetings of the Society. I have referred to several etchings by the political satirist James Gillray. In one of Gillray's most celebrated works, Thelwall is shown addressing a huge open-air meeting of the London Corresponding Society that took place at Copenhagen Fields in Islington on 12 November 1795 (fig. 8) . Standing on a high platform, he leans forward, raises his right arm, and clenches his fist in a gesture of powerful declamation. The crowd looks up at him, attentive and thoughtful. A number of others are also making speeches elsewhere in the fields, but those speakers

Figure 8 *Copenhagen House* published by H. Humphrey, 1795 (print), Gillray, James (1757-1815) / London Metropolitan Archives, City of London / Bridgeman Images

111. Ibid, 335.

look much less reputable and, with smaller audiences too, they only cast into relief the compelling intensity of his address. Underneath the image, Gillray inscribes Thelwall's words: 'I tell you, Citizens, we mean to new-dress the Constitution, and turn it, and set a new Nap upon it.'[112]

Thelwall's ideas about constitutional reform and other current topics were laid out both in his lectures and in writings of various kinds. A three-volume collection of the lectures, said by him to be based on the work of a shorthand note-taker whose draft he corrected, was published in 1795–6 under the title *The Tribune*. 'The dearness [i.e. high cost] and scarcity of provisions', and the causes of that situation, emerge as a key theme of his lectures during those years. On the issue of causation, he highlights in particular the role of the economically debilitating war with France, a venture he repeatedly denounces.[113] At the same time, he observes that it is the 'inevitable consequence' of high prices and 'the want of a proportionate increase in the wages paid to the industrious poor' that the latter will lack basic necessities.[114] The previous quarter-century had been characterised by a 'growth of wealth, commerce and prosperity', yet the 'lower orders of the people have [not] been benefited'.[115] To the contrary, starvation threatened them, while their 'opulent oppressors' enjoyed more 'luxuries and extravagance' than ever.[116]

In a lecture delivered on 29 April 1795, Thelwall says that he does 'not at present decide' the question of '[w]hether the proper remedy is to remove the causes of the extravagant price of provisions, or to raise the wages of labour, or whether both ought in some degree to be done'.[117] However, he is clear that popular direct action in the market for provisions is not the answer. As he sees it, the 'miller, the baker, and the butcher, against whom [the people's] violence is directed, are as much oppressed as themselves'. The country's rulers are quite happy to sacrifice such figures 'to the ignorant indignation of the people, provided thereby they avert the dreaded calamity of calm enquiry'.[118] For enquiry would reveal that they — the governing few — are themselves the real villains, insofar as they think 'no man has rights who was not wrapped

112. The cartoon perhaps betrays the admiration, or at least ambivalence, of a cartoonist whose work was regularly carried in the loyalist press.
113. John Thelwall, *The Tribune*, in Gregory Claeys (ed.), *The Politics of English Jacobinism: Writings of John Thelwall* (Pennsylvania: Pennsylvania State University Press, 1995), 65, 138, 153.
114. Ibid, 167.
115. Ibid, 147.
116. Ibid, 167.
117. Ibid, 146.
118. Ibid, 153.

in a swaddling band of [aristocratic] ermine'.[119] In other words, the source to which current problems need ultimately to be traced is the existence of a political system that excludes the unpropertied.

Thelwall's most important publication, *The Rights of Nature, against the Usurpations of Establishments*, appeared in December 1796.[120] A response to Burke's *Letters on a Regicide Peace* (in which Burke argues that there should be no appeasement with France),[121] it ranges across much the same territory as the lectures, with the difference that Thelwall now 'decides' on the question of wages. Prefacing his main argument on this, the text contains near the beginning a striking claim, of a kind of that will become very familiar in the next century. 'The fact is', he declares, 'that the hideous accumulation of capital in a few hands, like all diseases not absolutely mortal, carries, in its own enormity, the seeds of cure.' According to him, the reason is that whatever 'presses men together' — by which he means whatever puts people into contact with one another, as when they are all working under a single roof — is conducive to the spread among them of ideas, and, in turn, to the promotion of liberty. In practical terms, 'every large workshop and manufactory [i.e. factory] is a sort of political society, which no act of parliament can silence, and no magistrate disperse'.[122] If Thelwall deprecated collective action in the market for provisions, these passages plainly indicate that, in circumstances of growing industrialisation, he envisioned a much more promising future for collective action in the labour market.

Later in the text, he takes up the issue of pay rates. His discussion begins with a similar story of dispossession to the one narrated by Paine. In Thelwall's telling, however, the crucial outcome is the social division between proprietors and labourers. He considers that this was a natural and necessary result of progress beyond the primitive state of society, but holds that it laid the foundation of 'what may be called the Tyranny of Property: that is to say — the power and disposition of the wealthy few, to oppress and plunder the indigent and unprotected many'.[123] As Thelwall has it, '[a]t first . . . this unhappy

119. Ibid.
120. John Thelwall, *The Rights of Nature, against the Usurpations of Establishments*, in Gregory Claeys (ed.), *The Politics of English Jacobinism: Writings of John Thelwall* (Pennsylvania: Pennsylvania State University Press, 1995), 389.
121. Edmund Burke, *Two Letters Addressed to a Member of the Present Parliament, on the Proposals for Peace with the Regicide Directory of France* (London: Rivington, 1796).
122. John Thelwall, *The Rights of Nature, against the Usurpations of Establishments*, in Gregory Claeys (ed.), *The Politics of English Jacobinism: Writings of John Thelwall* (Pennsylvania: Pennsylvania State University Press, 1995), 389, 400.
123. Ibid, 475 (emphasis omitted).

distinction would not be productive of any serious oppression'. Contracts were 'comparatively fair, and grounded in mutual advantage: the workman deriving a full subsistence from his labour; and the employer (himself a labourer also) deriving but little more'.[124] But that did not last. Eventually '[t]he whole condition of the universe' would be transformed by agriculture, and the advantages of this new state of affairs would be monopolised by the proprietors, leaving for the multitude, thanks to whose labour the transformation was effected, 'only a dark vicissitude of woes'.[125] There would then emerge a strange, 'inverted' social order, in which the country's laws do not restrain individual accumulation, but instead encourage and even enforce it, and in which the labourer, the real producer of wealth, can be paid wages that are 'totally insufficient for the decent and comfortable subsistence of himself and family'.[126] And whereas expediency, as a governing principle, properly refers 'not to the individual, but to the whole society', the country's rulers would uphold the 'expediency of individual interest', which 'is the expediency of the swindler, and the housebreaker'.[127]

Like Paine, Thelwall is quite explicit in connecting his analysis to rights. 'We have heard much of the Rights of Property, and the Rights of Nations', he writes, adding parenthetically: 'Of the Rights of Man, also, we have heard some things, well worthy of serious consideration.' He continues: 'Much also we have heard of the Rights of the Peerage, the Rights of Parliaments, and the Rights of the Crown.' Then, finally: 'let us, for once, enquire a little into the Rights of Labourers'.[128] What are they, and on what basis are they claimed? Thelwall highlights three bases for asserting the rights of labourers. To begin with, 'Nature . . . (through that organ of reason that dwells in every breast)' informs us that '[s]ociety is responsible . . . for an equivalent for that which society has taken away'. The 'common bounties of nature' may have largely been alienated, but there remains an inalienable right to the satisfaction of human needs and to the enjoyment of rational faculties and affective relationships.[129] So does the employer reject nature's design? Does he say '*I agreed with you for so much; and I pay you what I agreed!*'? According to Thelwall, '[a]n unjust agreement, extorted by the power of an oppressor,

124. Ibid.
125. Ibid.
126. Ibid, 476.
127. Ibid, 475.
128. Ibid, 476 (emphasis omitted).
129. Ibid (emphasis omitted).

is morally, and politically, void.' Yet, 'in a variety of instances', that is the character of agreements between proprietors and labourers. 'The territorial monopolist dictates the terms upon which he will condescend to employ the disenfranchised labourer', and if the latter demurs about the price, the response is *'Fellow! there are many labourers and few employers. If you do not choose to drudge through the whole day for half a meal, go home to your family, and starve there altogether[; if you] will not work for half a loaf, there are others that will.'*[130]

Against that background, a second basis for asserting the rights of labourers arises from the fact that, as Thelwall proposes, there exists concurrently another compact 'implied in the very distinction [between] labourer and employer'. Its terms are determined not by the power of the one and the wretchedness of the other, but rather 'by the reason of the thing, and the rules of moral justice'. And what the reason of the thing and the rules of moral justice 'call upon us to appreciate' is 'the comparative value of capital and of labour'. The former 'could *never* be productive' without the latter; conversely, 'in the present state of society' the latter 'cannot have the means of production' without the former. Approaching the evaluation of both sides fairly and impartially, the analyst will conclude that 'the labourer has a right to a share of the produce, not merely equal to his support, but, proportionate to the profits of the employer'.[131]

A third basis for asserting the rights of labourers further confirms this by reference to the 'principles upon which all civil association rests'. In establishing society, humankind does not aim to make the many 'more wretched' and the few 'better accommodated'; it aims at 'a common, not . . . a particular, advantage'.[132] Society is a project of increasing 'the comforts and abundance of all', and in the distribution of those comforts and that abundance, the 'accident of birth' has no place. Accordingly, the labourer, just as much as the proprietor, has a 'right (as his share of the benefit) to maintain himself, and a family, in decency and plenty', and to enable his children, 'if they should have the virtue and the talent, to improve their condition, and mount to their intellectual level — though it should be from the lowest to the very highest station of society'.[133]

130. Ibid, 477.
131. Ibid (emphasis in original).
132. Ibid.
133. Ibid, 478 (emphasis omitted).

Was Jerusalem builded here?

John Walter writes of how, over many centuries of English history, dearth served as an important arena in which rights, duties and responsibilities were renegotiated between the propertied and the poor.[134] We have seen that that continued into the mid-1790s. In the shadow of high food prices and hunger or fear of hunger, men and women of mostly low social rank asserted their entitlement to have provisions at a price they could afford. The many food riots of the period constituted their effort to enforce a model of fair and carefully regulated market activity which, since Thompson's pioneering study, has been known as the *moral economy*.

In part at least, this was a response to the rising influence of another, very different model of market activity. Under that model, far from being carefully regulated, markets should be 'free'. The new *political economy* found a major point of reference and source of inspiration in Smith's 'Digression on Dearth' in *Book IV* of the *Wealth of Nations*. Even so, Smith's legacy remained contentious, with some, like Pitt in the debate over Whitbread's minimum wage bill, emphasising the arguments of the 'Digression on Dearth', and others, like Whitbread himself, adopting a more moderate stance that was seemingly informed by a broader reading of the *Wealth of Nations* and related works.

Whitbread's bill did not pass, but the Speenhamland system of aid-in-wages was a momentous new departure. In Polanyi's phrase, it gave official recognition to the idea that everyone has the *right to live*. Examining the work of four influential protagonists in the Revolution controversy, we have seen that Burke and More repudiated that idea, while Paine and Thelwall espoused it. To Burke, the moral economy was just a manifestation of ill-founded popular prejudices, like the popular terrors and suspicions of witchcraft of which Smith had written earlier. Prices, wages, and the extent to which they stand in proportion to one another, are matters for the laws of commerce, which are the laws of nature and the laws of God. As for dearth, More reminded her readers that no-one can help the seasons. The way to deal with privation

134. John Walter, 'The Social Economy of Dearth in Early Modern England', in John Walter and Roger Schofield (eds.), *Famine, Disease and the Social Order in Early Modern Society* (Cambridge: Cambridge University Press, 1989), 75, 127, cited in E. P. Thompson, *Customs in Common* (Pontypool: Merlin Press, 1991), 301.

is by working harder, improving household management, seeking solace in religion, and relying on the munificence of private charity.

Paine, in contrast, commented that it ought not to be left to the discretion of private individuals whether they will do justice or not. Poverty is a systemic problem arising from dispossession of the poor by the rich, who therefore owe to the community a compensatory ground-rent on which the poor have a legitimate claim as the basis of social protection. Thelwall reflected on the strange inverted social order that encouraged exploitation and accumulation, rather than restraining them, and that upheld the expediency of individual interest, which he characterised as the expediency of the swindler and the housebreaker. Those whose livelihood depended on wage-labour had the right to a living wage. More than that, he argued that they had the right to a share of the produce of their labour proportionate to their employer's profit.

A prominent theme of Paine's *Rights of Man*, highlighted in the previous chapter, is the *rights of the living*, as against the manuscript-assumed authority of the dead. Here we have seen that, among the rights of the living, Paine affirmed the *right to live*. The belief that there is a right to live was implicit as well in the moral economy of the poor. Yet Paine was no advocate for a rebellious traditional culture. Indeed, in *Agrarian Justice* he writes as if that culture was simply antipathetic, rather than rebellious and traditional. Far from championing the customary demands of the poor, he appeals to the enlightened self-interest of the rich, and looks forward to the day when property will be placed on the permanent basis of national interest and protection.

In Thompson's overall assessment, Paine 'did not challenge the property-rights of the rich, nor the doctrines of *laissez faire*'. His proposals for social welfare and progressive taxation — anticipating as they do later, more far-reaching schemes of property redistribution — rested on a world-view according to which '[i]n political society every man must have equal rights as a citizen [but] in economic society he must naturally remain employer or employed, and the State should not interfere with the capital of the one or the wages of the other'.[135] Thelwall, like Whitbread, differed in thinking that the state should interfere to regulate wages. But he too postulated a natural and necessary division between employer and employed. He too assumed that the equal rights of citizens were to be realised within the existing structure

135. E. P. Thompson, *The Making of the English Working Class* (New York: Vintage, 1966), 96.

of economic life. And when it came to food riots, he tended to agree with Burke that direct action in the market for provisions was rooted in popular prejudice or ignorance.

It seems that the 1790s were 'both the climax and the terminus of the riot tradition' in England.[136] The country's marketplaces would soon be free in the double sense that they would become liberated both from official regulation and from moral-economic crowd action.[137] Aid-in-wages would likewise disappear.[138] According to Polanyi, its disappearance should not be lamented inasmuch as, however valuable in preventing starvation during the years of dearth, over the longer term the Speenhamland system only exacerbated the immiseration of working people. By making the poor dependent on parish support, it pauperised them and left them destitute when, eventually, that support declined. Thus, he argues, the magistrates' well-intentioned initiative was ultimately counter-productive; 'the "right to live" proved a death trap'.[139] What were needed, in Polanyi's account, were not grants in aid of wages, but wages; 'the wage system had to be made universal in the interest [not only of capitalists but] . . . of the wage earners themselves'.[140]

Yet, as Peter Linebaugh observes, the association of '"wages" and "rights of man"' also had its lethal aspect. For the universalisation of the wage system had as its corollary the proscription of livelihoods that depended on unwaged labour and non-market resources. The 'monetary [extraction] of human labour as wages presupposed criminalizing customary appropriation'.[141] And if the law now signalled that there was to be no living outside the market, we noted in the previous chapter that the method not infrequently used to drive that point home was death by hanging.[142] On one side, then, was the death trap of the right to live; on the other side, the death sentence

136. See E. P. Thompson, *Customs in Common* (Pontypool: Merlin Press, 1991), 292. For Thompson, '[t]hese years of the eighteenth century were . . . a watershed in marketing constituencies and practices, mid-way between locally-supplied markets where consumers and farmers, magistrates and dealers, all knew something of each other, might come face to face with each other, and could "negotiate" prices, even by "riot"; and the more impersonal relations of the large urban markets which farmers rarely visited, supplied by dealers who purchased in distant markets' (292). To say this is not, of course, to imply that no further food-related protest activity occurred.
137. John Bohstedt, *The Politics of Provisions: Food Riots, Moral Economy, and Market Transition in England, c. 1550–1850* (Farnham: Ashgate, 2010), 4.
138. The Speenhamland system was abolished by the Poor Law Amendment Act 1834.
139. Karl Polanyi, *The Great Transformation* (Boston: Beacon Press, 1957), 78.
140. Ibid, 78–79.
141. Peter Linebaugh, *The London Hanged* (London: Verso, 2006), 439, 440.
142. See chap. 5 above.

pronounced against non-proletarianised labour and reliance on the resources of the commons. Near the beginning of this chapter, I mentioned Blake's *Milton,* in which the question is posed of whether 'Jerusalem [was] builded here, / Among these dark Satanic Mills'.[143] In another text of the same year, Blake provides a kind of answer: 'All the Arts of Life they change into the Arts of Death in Albion.'[144]

143. William Blake, *Milton: A Poem in Two Books*, Plate I (i), Preface, in David Erdman (ed.), *The Complete Poetry and Prose of William Blake* (New York: Anchor, rev. ed., 1988), 95.
144. William Blake, *Jerusalem: The Emanation of the Giant Albion*, Chapter 3, Plate 65, in David Erdman (ed.), *The Complete Poetry and Prose of William Blake* (New York: Anchor, rev. ed., 1988), 216. (In Blake's mythological universe, Albion — the mythical founder of Great Britain, and the poetic name sometimes given to the country — is the primeval man whose fall and division are described in Blake's prophetic books, *The Four Zoas*. See David Erdman (ed.), *The Complete Poetry and Prose of William Blake* (New York: Anchor, rev. ed., 1988), 300.)

7

Improvement and the Real Rights of Man

Ill fares the land

First published in May 1770, Oliver Goldsmith's poem *The Deserted Village* tells of the destruction of an English village it calls Auburn.[1] Auburn's demise begins when a rich landowner buys up all the village land — '[o]ne only master grasps the whole domain'. This landowner then builds for himself a palatial house, surrounded by a fashionable ornamental park and hunting ground, and in the process the inhabitants of the village are forced to leave their homes. The details are not spelled out, but whatever happens, its upshot is that a 'man of wealth and pride / Takes up a space that many poor supplied'. A once thriving community is displaced in order that he may have '[s]pace for his lake, his park's extended bounds, / Space for his horses, equipage, and hounds'.

Identifying the depopulation of Auburn with the larger history of rural depopulation in England, the poem invites reflection on the consequences of this development. 'A time there was, ere England's griefs began, / When every rood of ground maintained its man.' But 'now times are altered', and everywhere the scene is one of baneful contradiction. '[S]plendours rise', yet the nation is 'verging to decline'. The 'rich man's joys encrease', while the dispossessed peasant 'sinks', 'scourged by famine from the smiling land'. The countryside is 'a garden, and a grave'. And if the poor man accepts exile and

1. Oliver Goldsmith, *The Deserted Village, A Poem* (London: W. Griffin, 1770).

A False Tree of Liberty. Susan Marks, Oxford University Press (2019). © Susan Marks.
DOI: 10.1093/oso/9780199675456.003.0007

makes for the city, '[w]hat waits him there? / To see profusion that he must not share'. In this context, anyone disposed to applaud the changes affecting agrarian society is urged to think again. For, as we read, '[i]ll fares the land, to hastening ills a prey, / Where wealth accumulates, and men decay'.

The Deserted Village was heard in its time as a condemnation of Parliamentary enclosure. Earlier chapters of this book have dwelled at some length on the phenomenon of enclosure and on condemnations of it in the sixteenth and seventeenth centuries.[2] The movement known to scholars of English history as Parliamentary enclosure began in the second half of the eighteenth century. The epithet 'Parliamentary' is used because statutory enactment became an important method of accomplishing enclosure in this period. For Goldsmith and his contemporaries, the proliferation of great houses set within huge private parks, which was another feature of their century, was inextricably linked to enclosure inasmuch as the enclosure of land subject to rights of common constituted an essential precondition to the realisation of such building and landscaping projects. A key aspect of the criticism levelled at enclosure was that these extravagant symbols of post-feudal wealth and power caused rural dislocation and immiseration.

This chapter probes the relation between the rights of man as debated in 1790s England, on the one hand, and Parliamentary enclosure and other distinctive features of eighteenth-century English agrarian transformation, on the other. If Goldsmith has provided a point of departure, it needs to be stated immediately that he would have had little truck with the rights of man had he lived long enough to see them proclaimed by the revolutionaries in France and their supporters in England. (He died in 1774.) *The Deserted Village* makes clear that his concern was, at root, a concern about the decline of the established order, with its traditional relationships, hierarchies, and patterns of responsibility and dependence. In contrast, the writers whose work will preoccupy us here eschewed Goldsmith's nostalgia. So did they also eschew his opposition to enclosure? What was their judgement on the issue, posed starkly in his poem, of 'how wide the limits stand / Between a splendid and a happy land'?

2. See chaps. 2 and 3 above.

The line between proprietor and labourer

Before taking up that work, we need to spend a little longer clarifying the context. For whereas Thomas More wrote of men being devoured by sheep, the eighteenth-century enclosure movement was quite different.[3] By that time sheep farming had lost the place in the English economy it once occupied, and the point was no longer to convert arable land into sheep pasture. Very often it was instead to turn pastures into arable land. More generally, though, the point of enclosure at this time was to develop large country estates, and incorporate within them all kinds of land — open fields, common pastures, and all the other, more marginal areas of uncultivated land that formed the manorial 'waste' (woodlands, moors, marshes, bogs, heaths, downs, fens, etc.) — for use as arable or mixed farmland. The Parliamentary procedure that became important in the mid-eighteenth century also differed from the earlier mechanisms for accomplishing enclosure in that it made enclosure easier to impose in the face of local opposition. To be sure, enclosure by agreement — the main pre-existing method — could be the outcome of highly coercive negotiations.[4] However, Parliamentary enclosure strengthened the capacity of wealthier members of a community to force the issue, as the principle was quickly established that it sufficed for enclosure to go forward if those with claims representing a preponderance — generally four-fifths — of the land in question consented.

Within the history of enclosure in England, Parliamentary enclosure has particular significance because it more or less completed the long process of 'land reform' that had been underway since the later fifteenth and sixteenth centuries. Between 1750 and 1830 almost all the unenclosed land still remaining in the country — one-fifth, or by some reckonings closer to a quarter, of the total English land mass — was brought into private ownership, thanks to the passage of some 5000 Inclosure Acts.[5] With a few exceptions, these Acts were local laws, initiated by petition and applying only to the area

3. See chap. 2 above and the references there cited.
4. Historical scholarship emphasises that, despite the rise of Parliamentary enclosure, a significant proportion of enclosures continued to be effected by agreement. See, e.g., Tom Williamson and Liz Bellamy, *Property and Landscape: A Social History of Land Ownership and the English Countryside* (London: George Philip, 1987), 105.
5. See Michael Turner, *Enclosures in Britain 1750–1830* (London: Macmillan Press, 1984), esp. 21; and John Chapman, 'The Extent and Nature of Parliamentary Enclosure', *Agricultural History Review* 35 (1987) 25, 28.

in which the petitioners claimed an interest. Inclosure Acts declared void all pre-existing rights, privileges and obligations, and appointed enclosure commissioners to determine how the specified land should be allocated among the various claimants. Enclosure commissioners also determined the course of new roads, bridleways and footpaths to be established following enclosure, and approved schemes of land reclamation and conversion, such as fen drainage. The outcome of the process was an enclosure award, which was placed on public record with a local clerk of the peace or other state official. Whilst this ultimate phase of enclosure affected different regions to very different extents and in very different ways, the impact on rural topography was in some regions profound. Straight roads are among the most conspicuous and widespread topographical legacies of Parliamentary enclosure.

The primary instigators and beneficiaries of Parliamentary enclosure were landlords and wealthy tenant farmers. As in earlier periods of enclosure, landlords benefited because enclosed land commanded a higher rent than unenclosed land, and because enclosure nullified existing leases and authorised the raising of rents. If such rent rises could occur, that was due to the fact that enclosure provided correspondingly valuable benefits to tenant farmers with money to spend on the various practical innovations — advances in crop rotation, plough design and selective breeding, along with schemes of land reclamation and, in the second half of the eighteenth century, canal construction — that led farm revenues to increase exponentially. During the era of Parliamentary enclosure, a greater proportion of common pastures and wastes were enclosed than in any previous era, though overall the bulk of the land enclosed remained open-field land.[6] The enclosure of common pastures and wastes meant that land could be repurposed for intensive agricultural use that was not previously available for it. The enclosure of open-field land made it possible to consolidate holdings, and often provided opportunities for enlarging holdings as well by buying out neighbours. Whatever the nature of the land, enclosure created the conditions for developing agricultural businesses and investing in new agricultural methods, technologies and infrastructure without regard to the rights of commoners. In doing so, and crucially, it also helped to supply the workforce needed to reap the rewards from this, as can be seen if we now turn to consider how Parliamentary enclosure affected other members of agrarian society.

6. See Michael Turner, *Enclosures in Britain 1750–1830* (London: Macmillan Press, 1984), esp. 21.

To ask how Parliamentary enclosure affected ordinary men and women is to ask about the consequences for them of extinguishing extant rights of common. In the case of people who worked their own farms (whether as tenants or owner-occupiers) and also the inhabitants of some rural dwellings (millhouses, farmhouses, inns, etc.), rights of common were legally demonstrable entitlements conferred under the customary system of land tenure. In the case of landless labourers, many rural artisans and tradespeople, and dependent villagers such as elderly people and widows, they were informal rights, based on accepted use. Informal rights of common went unrecognised in enclosure procedures; the holders of them had no standing and were dispossessed without compensation. Commoners who could prove their entitlements were in a better position in that they received compensation, generally in the form of land. However, the cost of taking part in enclosure procedures for the purpose of proving entitlements was high, compensatory allocations of land were often small and of poor quality, and there was the additional expense of erecting fences within a defined period. In consequence, many of those affected did not deem it worthwhile to assert their rights. Or if they did, they could not carry on long with the land allocated to them, and soon sold it. Concurrently, post-enclosure rent rises led to the eviction of less affluent tenant farmers from rented holdings, and incentivised the sale of farms belonging to small-scale owner-occupiers faced with competitive pressures to implement the latest innovations in agricultural practice they could not afford.

It was in the nature of commoners' rights that they varied from place to place and according to local circumstance. Broadly speaking, though, and as already discussed in an earlier chapter, rights of common were entitlements to graze animals and to collect fuel, food, building supplies, and materials for making everyday items such as baskets and brooms.[7] Some historians have maintained that, in the era of Parliamentary enclosure, the value of these entitlements was quite marginal. Writing in 1953, John Chambers put forward the assessment — often quoted in subsequent literature — that, by the mid-eighteenth century, rights of common had become nothing more than a 'thin and squalid curtain' separating England's 'growing army of labourers' from 'utter proletarianization'.[8] In contrast, much later scholarship takes a

7. See chap. 2 above.
8. John Chambers, 'Enclosure and Labour Supply in the Industrial Revolution', *Economic History Review* 5(3) (1953) 319, 336.

more positive view of the enduring efficacy of rights of common as bulwarks against wage dependence. The point is underlined that, while a majority of rural families were already in receipt of wages at the start of the movement for Parliamentary enclosure, many were not, and of those who were, few were entirely dependent on wages. Most families relied on a combination of wage income and income and resources derived from commons-based self-employment.

This self-employment typically engaged all members of a household to some degree, but where there was wage income, the predominant pattern was that men worked mainly to earn it and women undertook the bulk of the commons-based labour. Jane Humphries argues that low estimations of the value of commoners' rights proceed from 'ahistoric stereotypes of male breadwinners and appurtenant wives and children' that elide the extent to which women (often with their children) contributed to family subsistence through the exercise of rights of common.[9] Gleaning after the harvest is the activity perhaps most closely associated with female commons-based labour,[10] but throughout the year women often assumed responsibility for collecting wood or other fuel as well. So too they engaged in cowkeeping, market gardening, foraging, handicraft production, and other cottage industries, both to provision the family and as a means of generating income.

By eliminating the possibilities for work of that sort, enclosure and related developments increased the dependence of families on wages and wage-earners, and turned semi-proletarianised households into wholly proletarianised ones. In the process, the elimination of those possibilities altered the position of rural women, now a deskilled agricultural workforce available for, and frequently limited to, such low-paid, seasonal activities as weeding, stone-picking, haymaking and helping out at calving time.[11] Deborah Valenze highlights how the extinguishment of customary rights enlisted misogynistic attitudes to legitimate the values of the new system of private landowning. 'Women could be construed as typically stubborn, intractable, or simply ignorant', their subsistence work on the commons and wastes denigrated, belittled, or simply denied. Similarly, households headed by women (whether

9. Jane Humphries, 'Enclosures, Common Rights, and Women: The Proletarianization of Families in the Late Eighteenth and Early Nineteenth Centuries', *Journal of Economic History* 50(1) (1990) 17, 18.
10. Gleaning was a common law right, abolished in *Steel v Houghton* (1788) 1 H Bl 51.
11. See further Keith Snell, *Annals of the Labouring Poor: Social Change and Agrarian England 1660–1900* (Cambridge: Cambridge University Press, 1987), 156.

widowed, abandoned, or unmarried, and generally with children), which made up a considerable proportion of those most reliant on the resources of commons and wastes, could be held up as epitomes of the idle poor.[12]

Janette Neeson reports that, like earlier phases of enclosure, Parliamentary enclosure met with considerable resistance, including initially resistance within Parliament and in other establishment circles. In the last decade of the eighteenth century, however, defence of the commons at the upper echelons of society largely evaporated.[13] How did that happen? In Neeson's account, enclosers and their allies won the argument by changing its terms. On the one hand, they reframed debate about the legitimacy of extinguishing rights of common such that the issue was no longer individual self-interest (the greed of landlords, the cupidity of newly rich tenant farmers, the arrogance and venality of lawyers, surveyors and estate managers, and so on), but the 'national interest' and 'what sort of society best served that interest'.[14] On the other hand, they captured the ground of national interest, identifying it with a society made up of property-owners and wage-labourers, and with the reconstitution to that end of rural communities as cohorts of wage-labourers. Viewed in this light, 'proletarianization, instead of damning enclosure and the disappearance of common right, justified' them.[15]

It was a striking reversal. That the end of common right meant the end of life outside wage-labour relations traditionally belonged to the argument against it. Defenders of the commons pointed to the way enclosure cut off access to supplies and sources of income, and destroyed commoners' relative independence. They objected that the loss of land, use-rights and possibilities for self-employment made rural dwellers into wholly wage-dependent labourers at the beck and call of farmers (or, in the case of unemployed and unemployable rural dwellers, into wholly relief-dependent paupers). Critics of the commons now conceded this, but maintained that the creation of a disciplined proletariat was not a bad thing. Rather, it was a very good thing, and indeed the key to national prosperity and progress. 'However beautiful it may be in theory to raise the lower orders to a situation of comparative independence', one contemporary authority opined, the line 'between the proprietor

12. Deborah Valenze, *The First Industrial Woman* (Oxford: Oxford University Press, 1995), 35 (and chap. 2 passim).
13. J. M. Neeson, *Commoners: Common Right, Enclosure and Social Change in England, 1700–1820* (Cambridge: Cambridge University Press, 1993), 46 et seq.
14. Ibid, 43 (emphasis omitted).
15. Ibid, 27.

and the labourer' must be firmly drawn. Without it, 'neither agriculture nor commerce can flourish'.[16] The problem, as expressed by another, was that, '[i]n sauntering after his cattle, [the commoner] acquires a habit of indolence'. 'Day labour becomes disgusting' to him, and the aversion only 'increases by indulgence'.[17] Yet a third remarked that 'if by converting the little farmers into a body of men who must work for others, more labour is produced, it is an advantage which the nation should wish for: the compulsion will be that of honest industry to provide for a family'.[18]

These writers and others like them had a word for this vision of national advantage and honest industry, a word that was ultimately perhaps their most powerful rhetorical weapon: *improvement*. Though deployed to similar effect in previous centuries, the concept of improvement came into its own in the eighteenth century as the ideology of agrarian capitalism. To improve was, first and foremost, to establish the conditions of profitable husbandry. It meant enlarging farms and enhancing the productivity of land through the use of advanced farming practices and investment in technological innovations. It meant promoting agricultural science, along with the development of new, more 'businesslike' approaches to land management. It meant securing a ready supply of labour to carry out the work of commercial agriculture by proletarianising the poor. It meant insisting on the sanctity of private property and disparaging common lands as terrains of idleness, destitution and crime. And, as the basis and necessary implication of all that, it meant enclosing land still subject to rights of common. (Indeed, the words 'enclosure' and 'improvement' were often used interchangeably.)[19]

At the same time, improvement also had another connotation, on which we touched at the beginning of this chapter. At least in the eighteenth century, it was coterminous with the fashion for building big houses in elaborate grounds that served as visual displays of the wealth amassed through improvement in the first sense. Sarah Wilmot explains that 'an elision was effectively made between landed estate improvement and economic, social, cultural and moral improvement'. Just as estate improvement was identified

16. Thomas Rudge, quoted in J. M. Neeson, *Commoners: Common Right, Enclosure and Social Change in England, 1700–1820* (Cambridge: Cambridge University Press, 1993), 30.
17. John Billingsley, quoted in Keith Snell, *Annals of the Labouring Poor: Social Change and Agrarian England 1660–1900* (Cambridge: Cambridge University Press, 1987), 172.
18. John Arbuthnot, quoted in Keith Snell, *Annals of the Labouring Poor: Social Change and Agrarian England 1660–1900* (Cambridge: Cambridge University Press, 1987), 173.
19. On improvement and its relation to empire, see Richard Drayton, *Nature's Government: Science, Imperial Britain and the 'Improvement' of the World* (New Haven: Yale University Press, 2000).

with furthering the national economic interest, and a well organised farm was identified with social and moral amelioration in rural life, so too the aesthetic embellishment of a country seat was identified with the elevation of cultural standards, 'the "improvement" of public taste'.[20] The 'stately homes' that are today tourist attractions, wedding venues, and, insofar as they remain in private ownership, trophy purchases for celebrities and magnates, date mostly from this period (even if they, of course, evolved into their current form through successive renovations carried out at various times). With their grand facades, sweeping carriageways and gracious parklands, they 'improve' the English countryside in a way which is not difficult to understand.

Lest we become lost in the admiration, however, Raymond Williams has some instructive suggestions. Discussing the legacy of that 'extraordinary phase of extension, rebuilding and enlarging, which occurred in the eighteenth century', he suggests that the visitor 'stand at any point and look at that land. Look at what those fields, those streams, those woods even today produce.' He goes on: 'Think it through as labour.' Call to mind an ordinary farm, and recollect what working people are able to bring into being 'in the ordinary scale of human achievement'. Note how these imposing buildings 'break the scale', and do so 'by an act of will [that corresponds to their] real and systematic exploitation of others'. See now the 'visible stamping of power', the 'social disproportion which was meant to impress and overawe'.[21] To stand before one of these edifices, Williams writes, 'is to know what many generations of countrymen bitterly learned and were consciously taught: that these were the families, this [was] the shape of the society'.[22] It is also to be aware that, as he observes, '[m]uch of the real profit of a more modern agriculture went not into productive investment but into that explicit social declaration . . . of an established and commanding class power'.[23]

A distinctive feature of improvement in this second sense was that it created a spatial separation between landowners and the population at large. Tom Williamson and Liz Bellamy explain that, whereas the manorial hall of medieval times was, in important respects, a centre of communal life, from the sixteenth century landed elites gradually isolated themselves from the local community and, more generally, from the everyday world of agricultural

20. Sarah Wilmot, *'The Business of Improvement': Agriculture and Scientific Culture in Britain c. 1700–c. 1870* (Historical Geography Research Series, No. 24, November 1990), 40.
21. Raymond Williams, *The Country and the City* (Nottingham: Spokesman, 2011), 105–06.
22. Ibid, 106.
23. Ibid.

activity and rural work.[24] This development reached its apogee in the eighteenth century, with the setting of great houses in 'landscape parks'. To create a landscape park, it was first necessary to enclose the land. Such a project normally also involved the redirection of roads and footpaths and the removal of cottages and barns. On a number of occasions, whole villages were 'cleared'. Part of the background to Goldsmith's *The Deserted Village* may be that the poet witnessed an instance of this during travels around Oxfordshire in 1760. In that year the first Earl Harcourt had the village of Nuneham Courtenay demolished and relocated to enable the construction of his new seat, Nuneham House.[25]

Landscape parks made manifest the capacity of their owners to shape their environment, and to have laid out for them sites of 'pleasing prospects', to use a phrase highlighted by Williams.[26] A pleasing prospect was at once a commanding view and a scene that could be judged 'a triumph of "unspoiled" nature'.[27] Working to commissions by Whig landowners who associated formal gardens with absolutist Europe, William Kent, Lancelot 'Capability' Brown and Humphry Repton developed an 'informal' style for the design of landscape parks that privileged 'natural-looking' arrangements. At the end of the century, Uvedale Price and Richard Payne Knight criticised that style as still too ordered and artificial, and initiated a practice of the 'picturesque', in which the accent was on creating landscape parks with elements of irregularity, roughness, wildness and decay.[28] Approaches evolved to reincorporate into the terrain a degree of agricultural life — a few labourers' cottages, a distant barn, a glimpse over working fields. Fundamentally, however, and whatever their design, landscape parks 'improved' land by largely effacing the signs of rural production and the people engaged in it.[29]

24. Tom Williamson and Liz Bellamy, *Property and Landscape: A Social History of Land Ownership and the English Countryside* (London: George Philip, 1987), 116 et seq.
25. See Mavis Batey, 'Nuneham Courtenay: an Oxfordshire 18th-century Deserted Village', *Oxoniensia* 33 (1968) 108.
26. Raymond Williams, *The Country and the City* (Nottingham: Spokesman, 2011), 120.
27. Ibid, 125. Of course, 'pleasing prospects' had a double meaning which also evoked the idea of expected economic and social advantage.
28. See Stephen Copley and Peter Garside, 'Introduction', in Stephen Copley and Peter Garside, (eds.), *The Politics of the Picturesque: Literature, Landscape and Aesthetics Since 1770* (Cambridge: Cambridge University Press, 1994), 1.
29. See further Raymond Williams, *The Country and the City* (Nottingham: Spokesman, 2011), 124–25.

Fixing the felicity of the poor

We are now in a position to consider in more detail arguments put forward by some writers of the period. It will be instructive to begin with the author and agriculturalist Arthur Young. In the last quarter of the eighteenth century, Young was England's best known commentator on rural affairs and the person perhaps most closely associated with the agenda of Parliamentary enclosure. He established and edited the influential agricultural almanac, *Annals of Agriculture*, and served as long-term Secretary of the Board of Agriculture, a pro-enclosure lobby group with strong links to government. He conducted agricultural experiments at his farm in Hertfordshire, and played a leading role in the promotion of agricultural science and businesslike land management. He was also at the forefront of 'political arithmetic' — the new science of compiling and analysing economic and demographic data.[30]

In connection with that latter work, Young undertook during the 1760s a series of journeys around England and Wales to collect information about conditions in the countryside. A prominent theme of the publications that resulted was the benefits of enclosure. His most acclaimed text, *Political Arithmetic*, characterises those benefits in terms of job creation and heightened consumption.[31] Where open fields are enclosed, he writes, 'the landlord doubles his income, which enables him to employ so many more manufacturers and artisans'. Likewise, 'the farmer increases his income, by means of which he also does the same'. These gains are then enlarged still further where manorial waste is converted into farmland, and that is 'not to speak of the great numbers of men that in enclosed counties are constantly employed in winter in hedging and ditching'.[32]

In the late 1780s Young began a fresh series of investigative journeys, this time in France. The last of those visits coincided with the fall of the Bastille, and upon returning to England, he entered the Revolution controversy with a pamphlet on the French Revolution viewed from his perspective as a

30. Regarding Richard Price's engagement with this new science, see chap. 5 above.
31. Arthur Young, *Political Arithmetic: Containing Observations on the Present State of Great Britain; and the Principles of her Policy in the Encouragement of Agriculture* (London: W Nicoll, 1774).
32. On the lastmentioned aspect, see Nicholas Blomley, 'Making Private Property: Enclosure, Common Right and the Work of Hedges', *Rural History* 18(1) (2007) 1, 11 (observing that supporters of enclosure argued that the poor 'could be usefully employed in diking, hedging and fencing the new enclosures . . . The poor, in other words, dispossessed through enclosure, could be enrolled in further hedging themselves out.')

champion of the landed interest and an advocate for enclosure. Published in 1792, *A Plain and Earnest Address to Britons* provides an account of what Young witnessed and learned subsequently about the ascendancy, as he perceived it, of the propertyless mob in France, and of what the consequences would be were something similar to come to pass in England.[33] 'The watchword, from one end of France to the other', he reports, 'is equality.' And 'what do they mean by equality? The word is absurd if it attaches not to property.' For 'there can be no equality while one man is rich and another poor'.[34] To be sure, the French *Declaration of the Rights of Man and the Citizen* includes among the rights recognised the 'right to property'. But such 'trees of goodly appearance' must be judged by the actual 'fruit they have produced'. And far from enshrining security of property, the Declaration has in fact been a 'signal of plunder'.[35] As Young interprets it, the French Revolution is a 'trial at arms' to determine 'whether those that have *nothing* [will successfully] seize and possess the property of those who have *something*' — a trial 'which can never end but in the equal and universal ruin of all'.[36]

Like Edmund Burke and Hannah More, Young regarded Thomas Paine as seeking to bring that ruin to England. *A Plain and Earnest Address to Britons* opens with the assertion that *Rights of Man* enunciates nothing other than 'a steady and deliberate plan to sap and undermine the happiness and prosperity of Great Britain'.[37] In Young's estimation, '[t]here is in this country a spirit of attention to the labouring part of the community far beyond what is the case in any other kingdom of the world'. The English peasantry are 'the happiest upon the face of the earth'. But, he cautions, 'adieu to every thing like peace and pleasure, if once the levelling principles of Mr Paine become the object of their desire'.[38] Developing this line of thought in a later pamphlet, Young remarks that '[e]quality is a romantic phantom of the imagination'. 'Every where, while the world endures, the rich will be purchasers of the labour of the poor. To be forced to labour for life, may appear, speculatively considered, to be a moral evil', but it is 'an evil no more to be banished from

33. Arthur Young, *A Plain and Earnest Address to Britons, Especially Farmers, on the Interesting State of Public Affairs in Great Britain and France* (London: Allin and Ridge, 1792). See also Arthur Young, *The Example of France: A Warning to Britain* (London: W. Richardson, 1794), where some of the same passages are repeated.
34. Arthur Young, *A Plain and Earnest Address to Britons, Especially Farmers, on the Interesting State of Public Affairs in Great Britain and France* (London: Allin and Ridge, 1792), 5.
35. Ibid, 9.
36. Ibid, 4 (emphasis in original, but some emphasis also omitted).
37. Ibid, 3.
38. Ibid, 10.

political communities than sickness or death'. It can only 'be rendered as light as is compatible with human affairs, and as easy to the lowest classes as the distinction between wealth and poverty admits'. And so, he writes, it has been in England, where '[c]ompared with the poor of all other countries', the poor live in conditions of 'ease and comfort', and they 'would in every event remain quiet and contented, were it not the interest of persons in higher stations to take the kind trouble of convincing them that they are unhappy'.[39]

What lends particular interest to these passages is that Young's complacency did not last. On further investigation, and after the onset of yet another subsistence crisis in 1800–1, it seems that he became not at all sure that the English poor really were so happy and so well-off.[40] In 1801 he reported in *Annals of Agriculture* on a tour he had made of various parts of the country during the previous year. There is a tally headed 'Effect of Enclosures on the Poor', with entries for different places. Whilst in a few cases he records that commoners were 'well treated', in the great majority he records that they were 'injured', 'suffered', 'suffered greatly', or that '[t]hose of property benefited, all who hired were ruined'.[41] In doing so, Young still judges that, at least in areas kept in tillage, enclosure has brought 'a considerable increase of employment truly valuable to the poor'.[42] Nonetheless, his overall assessment is that 'by nineteen enclosure bills in twenty [the poor] are injured, in some [cases] grossly injured',[43] and he warns of the 'ruin fast coming on' to the nation due to the 'misery of the poor'.[44] The injury which particularly exercised him was the loss of the capacity to keep a cow. Commoners lost this when they were deprived of access to land of sufficient size and quality not just for grazing, but also for producing feed that would enable them to sustain an animal during the winter months. But he also deplored their loss of the capacity to produce subsistence crops and collect fuel. Very evidently, it was now clear to him that the commoners of his country did not (as he had earlier

39. Arthur Young, *An Enquiry into the State of the Public Mind Amongst the Lower Classes: and on the Means of Turning it to the Welfare of the State* (1798), 6.
40. On Young's 'apostasy', see J. M. Neeson, *Commoners: Common Right, Enclosure and Social Change in England, 1700–1820* (Cambridge: Cambridge University Press, 1993), 8, 47 et seq.
41. Arthur Young, 'An Inquiry into the Propriety of Applying Wastes to the Better Maintenance and Support of the Poor', *Annals of Agriculture* 36 (1801) 497, 513–15.
42. Ibid, 515.
43. Ibid, 538.
44. Matilda Betham-Edwards (ed.), *The Autobiography of Arthur Young* (London: Smith, Elder & Co., 1898), 351, quoted in J. M. Neeson, *Commoners: Common Right, Enclosure and Social Change in England, 1700–1820* (Cambridge: Cambridge University Press, 1993), 48.

claimed about the French third estate) 'have nothing' — or rather, they did not have nothing until enclosure took away their land and rights.

Despite this, Young never resiled from his support for Parliamentary enclosure, and nor did he ever call for it to be halted. As he saw it, the injuries being caused to commoners were 'by no means *necessarily* connected with the measure of enclosing'.[45] They occurred only because, in passing Inclosure Acts, Parliament failed adequately to attend to the 'rights and interests of the poor'.[46] The creation of rights of private property could be structured in such a way as not to harm, and on the contrary to benefit, the poor. It was just a matter of changing the terms on which enclosures took place so as to give commoners such rights too. Parliament '[must give] property to the poor', he argued. With property of their own, they will be protected during periods of dearth from price rises 'so utterly ruinous to [those who] are without land'.[47] To that end, he developed a proposal for granting to the poor allotments of land, mostly from areas of manorial waste, as part of the process of enclosure.

A number of variants of this scheme appear in his writings, but the general idea was to build on the existing practice of enclosure commissioners relating to compensatory allocations of land. He envisioned expanding that practice to encompass families who could not prove their entitlements, and also providing larger allocations, so that cow-keeping and other subsistence activities would remain sustainable.[48] Young elaborated his proposals at a time when Parliament was debating general enclosure legislation designed to facilitate the enclosure process. The Inclosure Consolidation Act 1801 that was the outcome of these debates provided standardised conditions and other boilerplate for use in local Inclosure Acts. Explaining his position, Young said that there was no-one in England 'more urgent' than he was for Parliamentary enclosure and for its facilitation by means of general enclosure legislation, 'but I contend that the felicity of the poor should be fixed by means of enclosure'.[49]

45. Arthur Young, 'An Inquiry into the Propriety of Applying Wastes to the Better Maintenance and Support of the Poor', *Annals of Agriculture* 36 (1801) 497, 515 (emphasis in original).
46. Ibid, 517.
47. Ibid, 510, 511.
48. See, e.g., Arthur Young, *The Question of Scarcity Plainly Stated, and Remedies Considered* (London: B. McMillan, 1800), and Arthur Young, 'An Inquiry into the Propriety of Applying Wastes to the Better Maintenance and Support of the Poor', *Annals of Agriculture* 36 (1801) 497.
49. Arthur Young, 'An Inquiry into the Propriety of Applying Wastes to the Better Maintenance and Support of the Poor', *Annals of Agriculture* 36 (1801) 497, 539.

If we turn from Young to other contemporaries, it can be seen that he was not alone in advancing that contention. Already in 1781, the Scottish classical scholar and philosopher William Ogilvie argued in his *Essay on the Right to Property in Land* that the institution of landed property could, and should, be made 'beneficial to all ranks of men'. Prevailing practices of enclosure 'locked up' land by reserving the right of property to the wealthy few.[50] Instead, the right of property in land ought to be available to all: 'every individual who would [choose] it, should be the proprietor of a field'. Conversely, and here he emphasised a point that was not part of Young's plan, 'every field should be cultivated by its proprietor'.[51]

To put that into practice, Ogilvie developed a proposal for what he called a 'progressive agrarian law' — so-called, he explained, because it governed the distribution of land like the ancient Roman agrarian laws, but differed in that it operated continuously, rather than episodically, so as to achieve progressively a situation in which all agricultural land was the private property of owner-occupiers. Under the scheme, everyone who was not already a landowner would have the right, upon reaching the age of twenty-one, to be allotted land of up to forty acres in perpetuity, for the purpose of cultivation and residence. Magistrates would be appointed to document allotments, fix ground rents, and determine compensatory payments where pre-existing landholders were affected, and arbitrators would be appointed in the event of disputes. People acquiring landed property in this way would have the right to transmit it to their heirs and to sell it, but if they sold their land to someone who did not reside on it, one-tenth of the price would be collected publicly as a tax.[52]

Young's belief that enclosure caused harm as currently configured, but could be made to work for the poor was also shared by writers whose views otherwise sharply diverged from his own. In particular, it was shared by some prominent advocates of the rights of man. In an earlier chapter, we noted Mary Wollstonecraft's remark that the 'demon of property has ever been at hand to encroach on the sacred rights of men, and to fence round with awful pomp laws that war with justice'.[53] As that passage suggests, inherited property

50. William Ogilvie, *An Essay on the Right of Property in Land; its present Establishment by the Municipal Laws of Europe and the Regulations by which it might be rendered more beneficial to the lower Ranks of Mankind* (London: J. Walter, 1781), 42.
51. Ibid, 33.
52. See ibid, 141 et seq.
53. Mary Wollstonecraft, *A Vindication of the Rights of Men*, in Sylvana Tomaselli (ed.), *Mary Wollstonecraft: A Vindication of the Rights of Men and A Vindication of the Rights of Woman* (Cambridge: Cambridge University Press, 1995), 1, 7. See chap. 5 above.

and privilege and the law of primogeniture which underpinned them were, for her, themselves forms of enclosure; Parliamentary enclosure belonged to a much longer history of 'encroaching' and 'fencing'. In the current phase, the poor were being shut out in the name of improvement, obligated to 'respect that property of which they cannot partake'. The 'rich man builds a house, art and taste give it the highest finish. His gardens are planted, and trees grow to recreate the fancy of the planter . . . Every thing on the estate is cherished but man.' Is England to become a country of 'awful contrast' between 'stately palace' and 'pestiferous hovel'?[54]

What 'if, instead of sweeping pleasure-grounds, obelisks, temples, and elegant cottages', estates were scattered with 'decent farms', Wollstonecraft wonders. Why cannot 'large estates be divided into small farms? Why are huge forests still allowed to stretch out with idle pomp? . . . Why does the brown waste meet the traveller's view when men want [lack] work?' Having posed these questions, she immediately answers them with the observation that, of course, 'commons cannot be enclosed without acts of parliament to increase the property of the rich'.[55] Whereas once those working the land would be 'watched over with fatherly solicitude' by the man 'whose duty and pleasure it was to guard their happiness', now the poor have no shield from 'rapacity', and land monopoly has become the rule.[56] 'This sight I have seen', she goes on: 'the cow that supported the children grazed near the hut, and the cheerful poultry were fed by the chubby babes'. If Parliamentary enclosure can permit the propertied to 'blast all these prospects', then for Wollstonecraft it is reasonable and just for the 'industrious peasant' to 'steal a farm from the heath' — the shared waste land — and gain rights of property in that farm too.[57]

John Thelwall similarly decried the 'infernal spirit of monopoly', which he took to be a 'cruel and wasteful demon' that had 'rendered poverty, want, and distress the portion of the mass of the people of this country', and produced destitution in the midst of abundance.[58] In the previous chapter we reviewed his arguments about extortion in the labour market, and about the right of workers to wages proportionate to the profits of their employers. Alongside those arguments addressed to monopoly with respect to the economic

54. Ibid, 58–60 (emphasis omitted).
55. Ibid, 60 (emphasis omitted).
56. Ibid, 59.
57. Ibid, 61.
58. John Thelwall, *The Tribune*, in Gregory Claeys (ed.), *The Politics of English Jacobinism: Writings of John Thelwall* (Pennsylvania: Pennsylvania State University Press, 1995), 65, 69.

surplus, he also raised the issue of monopoly with respect to landholding, and mooted the possibility of restructuring enclosure so as to benefit the poor.

In the text of a lecture delivered on 1 May 1795, Thelwall remarks that 'it has been said, and I am much inclined to agree . . ., that the inclosures which have taken place in this country, have been a great calamity'.[59] As he characterises the system, rich men obtain the passage of Acts of Parliament in order to commit 'highway robbery' against poor commoners, depriving them of their rightful inheritance. The rich men then '[talk] of the security of property', and get the government to silence anyone disposed to '[enquire] into the right by which these robberies have been committed'.[60] Yet, he insists, things need not be this way. If carried out 'upon a fair and honest principle', enclosure could be 'productive of the greatest advantages'.[61] The enclosure and development of remaining tracts of uncultivated waste could be undertaken to provide daily necessities for the common people.[62] Like Wollstonecraft, Thelwall does not go further into this, though to support his case, he refers to information about the scope and potential of England's waste lands which he took from a report of the Board of Agriculture.[63]

Whatever their other differences, Young, Ogilvie, Wollstonecraft and Thelwall were united, then, in the belief that enclosure did not currently serve the poor, but that it could be reoriented to do so. More generally, they were united in the belief that private property was a cause of poverty, but also the basis of potential solutions. Paine held to that idea too. To be sure, he and Young clashed over issues of constitutional reform and the rights of man. He also disagreed with Ogilvie about the concept of agrarian law, which he considered not at all serviceable in modern times.[64] But he shared these writers' concern that improvement was producing poverty at the same time as it produced wealth. Equally, he shared their conviction that this situation was remediable by adjustments to current arrangements. In doing so, he stressed

59. Ibid, 176–77.
60. Ibid, 180.
61. Ibid, 177.
62. Ibid, 180.
63. *Report of the Committee, Appointed by the Board of Agriculture, to Take into Consideration the State of Waste Lands and Common Fields in this Kingdom* (1795). See John Thelwall, *The Tribune*, in Gregory Claeys (ed.), *The Politics of English Jacobinism: Writing of John Thelwall* (Pennsylvania: Pennsylvania State University Press, 1995), 65, 175.
64. In *Agrarian Justice* Paine explains that his title has been chosen 'to distinguish it from *Agrarian Law*', for 'nothing could be more unjust than agrarian law in a country improved by cultivation'. See Thomas Paine, *Agrarian Justice*, in Bruce Kuklick (ed.), *Paine: Political Writings* (Cambridge: Cambridge University Press, 2000), 319, 326.

the need to respect 'the right of the possessor to the part which is his'.[65] As he explained in introducing the proposed scheme of inheritance tax which was the centrepiece of *Agrarian Justice*, 'I care not how affluent some may be, provided that none be miserable in consequence of it'.[66]

This was a notable viewpoint. However, not everyone who saw the need for change went along with it, and in the remaining part of this chapter we consider the work of someone who was distinctly less sanguine about the possibility for affluence and misery to be decoupled in the way Paine supposed, and less confident as well that solutions to the problem of poverty could be found without disturbance to the property rights of the rich and to the system of private landholding they had inaugurated.

Striking at the root

Thomas Spence was born into a poor family in Newcastle upon Tyne. His father was a netmaker and sometime shoemaker and hardware seller, and his mother kept a stall at which she sold stockings. He lived in the city until he was in his late twenties, initially apprenticed to his father and then working as a schoolteacher. While engaged in that latter occupation, he devised a new phonetic alphabet for the English language, which he published in 1775.[67] Spence hoped by this means to make learning to read and write easier, especially for those who lacked access to formal schooling and were thus reliant on self-education, as he had himself been. Using language borrowed from the history of struggles against enclosure, he characterised illiteracy as a 'fence', and his alphabet as a contribution to 'throwing it down'.[68]

In the same year, Spence became a member of the newly founded Philosophical Society of Newcastle. The Society was one of many such groups established around that time for rational debate among the minor gentry, 'middling' classes, and, to a lesser extent, literate poor like him.[69] Under its

65. Thomas Paine, *Agrarian Justice*, in Bruce Kuklick (ed.), *Paine: Political Writings* (Cambridge: Cambridge University Press, 2000), 319, 326.
66. Ibid, 332.
67. Thomas Spence, *The Grand Repository of the English Language* (Newcastle: T. Saint, 1775).
68. See Thomas Spence, *The Real Reading Made Easy* (Newcastle: T. Saint, 1782): 'Then little book if thou this Fence throw'st down / And learning renderest common, twill work thy great renown.' Spence's dictionary was also designed to make the English language easier for foreigners to acquire.
69. See further Kathleen Wilson, *The Sense of the People: Politics, Culture and Imperialism in England, 1715–1785* (Cambridge: Cambridge University Press, 1995), esp. 67–68.

rules, members took turns to read papers on topics of mutual interest. Spence's turn arrived on 8 November 1775. After delivering his paper, he had copies of it printed, which he then sold on the streets of Newcastle at a low price.[70] For this breach of decorum, though perhaps also for reasons not unconnected to his argument, Spence was expelled from the Newcastle Philosophical Society.

The title of Spence's lecture was *Property in Land Every One's Right*.[71] He announces at the beginning that his subject will be '[t]he important question . . . whether mankind, in society, reap all the advantages from their natural and equal rights of property in land and liberty, which in that state they possibly may, and ought to expect'. In discussing this, he starts with the idea — which he takes to be generally accepted — that the 'country of any people, in a native state, is properly their common'. Thus, all the inhabitants may jointly enjoy the advantages of their country 'without having their right [to do so] called in question by any, not even by the most selfish and corrupted'. Yet, he goes on, some say that it is just and reasonable for a people to sell or give away their country, that is to say their common, to whomever they wish, to be held by the acquirers and their heirs and successors forever. To this his reply is that, if the people's posterity 'require no grosser materials to live and move upon than air', then certainly, there can be no objection. But if their posterity require more than air, as all human beings patently do, then they do not have the right to sell or give away common lands and other resources upon which everyone depends. 'For a right to deprive any thing of the means of living, supposes a right to deprive it of life', and that right one generation or group of inhabitants cannot justifiably claim over others.

Turning from philosophy to history, Spence reflects on the misappropriation, alienation and exclusion that have in fact characterised the history of a country such as his own. In his account, land was initially misappropriated by a few, who quickly 'fell into a habit of thinking, or which is the same thing, to the rest of mankind, of acting as if the earth was made for or by them, and did not scruple to call it their own property, which they might dispose of without

70. Though long absent from the historical archive, a copy of the publication was found in 2005. On the redisovery of the text, see Alastair Bonnett, 'The Other Rights of Man: the Revolutionary Plan of Thomas Spence', *History Today* 57(9) (2007) 42.

71. Thomas Spence, *Property in Land Every One's Right: A Lecture Delivered at the Philosophical Society, Newcastle upon Tyne*, 8 November 1775. See further Alastair Bonnett, 'Thomas Spence, *Property in Land Every One's Right* (1775)', *Labour History Review* 74 (2009) 134. The quotations that follow are taken from Spence's later reissue of the lecture, Thomas Spence, 'The Real Rights of Man', *Pig's Meat* 3 (1795) 220, reprinted in H.T. Dickinson, *The Political Works of Thomas Spence* (Newcastle upon Tyne: Avero, 1982), 1. On the lecture's reissue, see below.

regard to any other living creature'. They and their heirs and successors then continued in that manner, to the point where 'no-one could claim a right to so much as a blade of grass, or a nut, or an acorn, or a fish or a fowl, or any natural production whatever, though to save his life, without the permission of the pretended proprietor', and 'all things, men as well as other creatures who lived, were obliged to owe their lives to some or other's property'. In this way people became strangers even in the locality of their birth, inasmuch as they could only live where they were 'by the permission of the pretender to the property thereof: which permission is, for the most part, paid extravagantly for'. Given these 'hard conditions' upon which unpropertied people have access to the 'common gifts of nature', Spence concludes that the answer to his original question is that mankind in society is far from reaping all the advantages from their natural and equal rights in land and liberty which they may and ought to expect.

What can be done about this situation? The remainder (and bulk) of the paper was devoted to outlining a proposal by which, parish (small local community) by parish, the people might act to 'take their long-lost rights into possession'. Specifically, his idea was that 'all men who are inhabitants'[72] of each parish would meet on an appointed day to form themselves into a corporate entity. They would then declare all the land within the parish, along with everything appertaining to it, to be the property of this corporate entity, which would have 'as ample power to let, repair or alter all or any part thereof as a Lord of the manor enjoys over his lands, houses, etc.', with the crucial exception that it would have no power of alienation. That is to say, the land could never be sold, but would remain the property of the corporate entity in perpetuity, the inhabitants now paying rent to the parish, rather than to a landlord. These rental revenues would be used to defray local public expenditures (including poor relief), and to contribute to national public expenditures, and moneys left over would be paid back to the inhabitants of the parish in equal shares. The corporate entity would be controlled by all its members, acting in plenary meeting or committees by majority vote and secret ballot; to secure a particular course of action, it would only be necessary 'to make it appear in the best light possible by speaking or writing'. Given that everyone would take part in decision-making, Spence considers it likely that

72. It is unclear whether Spence intends this to include women. His later writings indicate that he may do so; see esp. Thomas Spence, *The Rights of Infants* (London: T. Spence, 1796), 3, reprinted in H. T. Dickinson, *The Political Works of Thomas Spence* (Newcastle upon Tyne: Avero, 1982), 46, 48 et seq.

parish land would be let 'in very small farms, which makes employment for a greater number of hands, and makes more victualling of all kinds be raised'. Finally, he predicts that, once 'this empire of right and reason' is established, other nations will be encouraged to follow the example, 'and thus the whole earth shall at last be happy, and live like brethren'.

Spence was twenty-five when he delivered his lecture to the Newcastle Philosophical Society, and he continued to advocate for this proposal, which he referred to as his 'plan' and often in the third person as 'Spence's Plan', throughout the rest of his (relatively long) life. After the French Revolution began, he republished the lecture with minor changes under the title *Rights of Man*, and, again in 1793, under the title *The Real Rights of Man*, and also reformulated its main ideas under other titles in subsequent years.[73] By that time, of course, Paine's work had appeared. Spence summarised his response to Paine's *Rights of Man* in a text published in 1795 that took the form of dialogue between a naive Young Man and a wise Old Man:

> *Young Man*: I hear there is another RIGHTS OF MAN by Spence, that goes farther than Paine's.
> *Old Man*: Yet it goes no farther than it ought.
> *Young Man*: I understand it suffers *no* private Property in Land, but gives it all to the Parishes.
> *Old Man*: In so doing it does right, the earth was not made for Individuals.

The dialogue goes on:

> *Young Man*: But most people believe that it would be unjust to deprive Landed Men of their Property, as many of them have purchased their Estates.
> *Old Man*: Landed Property always was originally acquired, either by conquest or encroachment on the common Property of Mankind . . . [B]uying stolen Goods is as bad as stealing.[74]

To Spence, Paine's focus on political revolution, even with the introduction of a scheme of public welfare and social insurance, was inadequate. What was needed was a *social* revolution that could challenge the basis on which political power arose and was maintained:

73. See Thomas Spence, 'The Real Rights of Man', *Pig's Meat* 3 (1795) 220, reprinted in H. T. Dickinson, *The Political Works of Thomas Spence* (Newcastle upon Tyne: Avero, 1982), 1.
74. Thomas Spence, *The End of Oppression* (London: T. Spence, 1795), 3, 4–5, reprinted in H. T. Dickinson, *The Political Works of Thomas Spence* (Newcastle upon Tyne: Avero, 1982), 34–35.

> *Young Man*: It is amazing that Paine and other Democrats should level all their Artillery at Kings, without striking like Spence at [the] root of every abuse and of every grievance.[75]

And the root of every abuse and every grievance, in his analysis, was private property in land. 'What does it signify whether the Form of a Government be Monarchical or Republican while Estates can be acquired?', he later wrote.[76] To 'allow the justice of private property in land' is to 'justify every thing the landed interest do, both in their own estates and in the Government, for the country is theirs'. That which Paine and others 'call oppression, is only [landed proprietors] acting consistently with their interest'.[77] Until action is taken to 'destroy not only personal and hereditary Lordship, but [also its efficient] cause' in land-owning, farm enlargement, and enclosure, the rights of man will remain illusory.[78] '[L]ike the rainbow, [they will] always recede from us as we advance.'[79] It followed for Spence that adjustments to the system of Parliamentary enclosure, however well-intentioned, would only serve to assure the persistence of oppression. The same applied to Paine's proposal in *Agrarian Justice* for an inheritance tax on landed property, and to Thelwall's proposal regarding wage rates.

After *Agrarian Justice* appeared, Spence expressed gladness that Paine 'at last' acknowledged that God gave the earth to mankind in common. He said he was happy about this because Paine's 'celebrity will procure him many readers, and greatly add both to the investigation of this great fundamental truth, and of such philosophical superstructures as may be built on the same'.[80] Regarding the proposal which Paine elaborated from that premise, however, Spence considered it no more satisfactory than anything Paine had propounded in his *Rights of Man*. In lieu of the people's 'just pretensions to the soil of our birth', Paine encouraged acceptance of 'poor, beggarly stipends'.[81]

75. Thomas Spence, *The End of Oppression* (London: T. Spence, 1795), 5, reprinted in H.T. Dickinson, *The Political Works of Thomas Spence* (Newcastle upon Tyne: Avero, 1982), 34, 35.
76. Thomas Spence, *The Restorer of Society to its Natural State in a series of letters to a fellow citizen* (London: J. Smith, 1801), Preface, reprinted in H. T. Dickinson, *The Political Works of Thomas Spence* (Newcastle upon Tyne: Avero, 1982), 69, 71.
77. Thomas Spence, *The Meridian Sun of Liberty* (London: T. Spence, 1796), 4, reprinted in G. I. Gallop (ed.), *Pig's Meat: Selected Writings* (Nottingham: Spokesman, 1982), 107, 109.
78. Thomas Spence, *The Restorer of Society to its Natural State in a series of letters to a fellow citizen* (London: J. Smith, 1801), Letter 1, reprinted in H. T. Dickinson, *The Political Works of Thomas Spence* (Newcastle upon Tyne: Avero, 1982), 69, 74.
79. Thomas Spence, *The Meridian Sun of Liberty* (London: T. Spence, 1796), 3, reprinted in G. I. Gallop (ed.), *Pig's Meat: Selected Writings* (Nottingham: Spokesman, 1982), 107, 108–09.
80. Thomas Spence, *The Rights of Infants* (London: T. Spence, 1796), 3, reprinted in H.T. Dickinson, *The Political Works of Thomas Spence* (Newcastle upon Tyne: Avero, 1982), 46, 47.
81. Ibid.

Why was only 10 per cent of the value of landed property to be redistributed?[82] Spence writes that, according to Paine, the land 'has so improved in the hands of private proprietors as to be of ten times the value it was of in its natural state'. 'But', Spence goes on, 'may we not ask who improved the land? Did the proprietors alone work and toil at this improvement? And did we labourers and our forefathers stand . . . idle spectators of so much public-spirited industry? I suppose not.'[83]

To bring out more fully what is at stake, Spence sets out in tabular form the various points of disparity between his plan (which he identifies with the 'end of oppression') and Paine's scheme of agrarian justice. Whereas Paine's scheme is consistent with non-democratic government and the perpetuation of social relations that promote arrogance on one side and deference on the other, and whereas he invites the people to 'sell their birth-right for a mess of porridge', under Spence's plan 'government must of necessity be democratic', a 'spirit of independence' develops that is 'tempered by the presence and check of equally independent fellow-citizens', and the people 'receive, without deduction, the whole produce of their common inheritance'.[84] From this perspective, Thelwall's focus on wage rates was likewise inadequate insofar as it presupposed the wage dependence of the poor. In contrast, and *pace* also Young with his claim that compulsory wage-labour could no more be banished than sickness or death, Spence insists that there is nothing natural or inevitable about the demise of commons-based self-employment.

Rather, this is an historical process, under which '[p]roprietors . . . first exclude [the poor] from a share in the soil, [so] that want may compel them to sell their labour for daily bread'.[85] 'Thus destitute', the multitude are driven to 'cities and towns to get employment in trade and manufactures'.[86] Then 'our Taskmasters because we talk of Liberty, take Care to manage Matters so that we shall be closely employed, and instead of working only six days a Week, we are obliged to work at the rate of eight or nine, and yet can hardly subsist. And still the cry is, work — work — ye are idle.' '[We], God help us; have

82. See chap. 6 above.
83. Thomas Spence, *The Rights of Infants* (London: T. Spence, 1796), 15, reprinted in H.T. Dickinson, *The Political Works of Thomas Spence* (Newcastle upon Tyne: Avero, 1982), 46, 53.
84. Thomas Spence, *The Rights of Infants* (London: T. Spence, 1796), Appendix, 11, reprinted in G.I. Gallop (ed.), *Pig's Meat: Selected Writings* (Nottingham: Spokesman, 1982), 123–24.
85. Thomas Spence, *The Rights of Infants* (London: T. Spence, 1796), 15–16, reprinted in H.T. Dickinson, *The Political Works of Thomas Spence* (Newcastle upon Tyne: Avero, 1982), 46, 53.
86. Thomas Spence, 'A Dream', in *Spence's Songs, Part 3* (London: Seale and Bates, 1807), reprinted in H.T. Dickinson, *The Political Works of Thomas Spence* (Newcastle upon Tyne: Avero, 1982), 118, 119.

fallen under the power of the hardest set of Masters that ever existed', Spence writes. Not content to '[s]wallow up every species of common property',[87] 'these People of Property [require that] all Bounds must be thrown down and every thing must be vendable . . . [so that] the cursed Spirit of Traffic pervades every Thing'. It is no wonder, he suggests, that the call is heard for free trade in land, provisions and 'like great Babylon, even in "Slaves and the Souls of Men"'. 'I begin with prohibiting all Commerce in Land', he explains, because 'that is the Root of all the other Branches of injurious Trade'.[88] Once land is decommodified and placed under collective co-ownership, the people will become their 'own masters and landlords'. 'Trade', including the market in labour, 'will then be genuine, unforced and natural'. No-one will enter employment in trade and manufacturing 'but those who can live well by [it], because tillage would . . . be open to all'.[89]

Spence's belief in the importance of tillage remaining open to all was formed despite, or perhaps in some measure because of, living his whole life in two cities. Regarding his time in Newcastle upon Tyne, he later highlighted as an especially formative episode a dispute that arose in 1771, while he was in his early twenties, over the attempted enclosure of Newcastle Town Moor.[90] The Town Moor was a large area of common land over which those with the status of 'freemen' (or 'burgesses') of the city had grazing and other rights. The freemen were so-called because their medieval ancestors had been 'free' in the sense that they had not been bound to the land as serfs or villeins, but nor had they been landowning nobles. In December 1771 the city's municipal authorities ('Common Council') enclosed and purported to let part of the Town Moor. The freemen protested and re-entered the land, prompting the lessee, with the support of the Common Council, to initiate proceedings for trespass. In a judgment delivered on 10 August 1773, the court affirmed the rights of the freemen. It was held that the land could be leased, but that such lease would be subject to a scheme of management that involved the freemen and protected their rights, as set out in legislation which the

87. Thomas Spence, *The Restorer of Society to its Natural State in a series of letters to a fellow citizen* (London: J. Smith, 1801), 18, reprinted in H.T. Dickinson, *The Political Works of Thomas Spence* (Newcastle upon Tyne: Avero, 1982), 69, 72–73.
88. Thomas Spence, *The Restorer of Society to its Natural State in a series of letters to a fellow citizen* (London: J. Smith, 1801), 19, 16, reprinted in H.T. Dickinson, *The Political Works of Thomas Spence* (Newcastle upon Tyne: Avero, 1982), 69, 71.
89. Thomas Spence, 'A Dream', in *Spence's Songs, Part 3* (London: Seale and Bates, 1807), reprinted in H.T. Dickinson, *The Political Works of Thomas Spence* (Newcastle upon Tyne: Avero, 1982), 118, 119.
90. On this, see further chap. 10 below.

Common Council was to arrange to have enacted. The judgment was celebrated as a victory for the unpropertied, and it is reported that signet rings were presented to the freemen's representatives in the litigation bearing the inscription '*vox populi vox dei*'.[91] Several decades afterwards, Spence wrote that he 'took a Lesson from this Affair which I shall never forget'. Landholding must be under collective, local control, for '[i]t is impossible . . . for a Poor Man to enjoy equal Rights in Society with Men of overgrown consolidated Estates'.[92]

At some point in the late 1780s, Spence left Newcastle and moved to London. There he kept a stall in Chancery Lane, and later a shop not far away at 8 Little Turnstile (which he called 'The Hive of Liberty'), and finally a series of premises or pitches in and around Oxford Street, at which he sold radical books.[93] Amongst his offerings in December 1792 was Paine's *Rights of Man, Part II*, a fact which is known because Spence was arrested in that month for selling it (though he suggests that the arrest may actually have been the result of confusion between Paine's text and his own lecture republished under the same title).[94] Spence also operated as a publisher, both of his own compositions and of works by others, leading to further arrests for seditious libel and, on one occasion, treason, and to several periods of imprisonment. Between 1793 and 1795 he put out a periodical which, in ironic homage to Burke's contemptuous reference to the 'swinish multitude' in *Reflections on the Revolution in France*,[95] he entitled *Pig's Meat*.

Many of the works by Spence quoted above were published in *Pig's Meat*, along with excerpts from writings by other contemporary authors and earlier texts.[96] All too aware of the dangers of publication under a repressive regime, Spence did not limit himself to printed material, but disseminated his thought

91. The voice of the people is the voice of God. A detailed account of the Newcastle Town Moor affair is given in P.M. Ashraf, *The Life and Times of Thomas Spence* (Newcastle upon Tyne: Frank Graham, 1983), 29–32. See also the website of the Freemen of Newcastle: www.freemenofnewcastle.org.
92. Thomas Spence, *The Restorer of Society to its Natural State in a series of letters to a fellow citizen* (London: J. Smith, 1801), 27 fn 5, reprinted in G. I. Gallop (ed.), *Pig's Meat: Selected Writings* (Nottingham: Spokesman, 1982), 127, 163.
93. Spence moved his shop initially to 9 Oxford Street, and also had a street pitch on Oxford Street. His subsequent addresses were given as: 3 Great Castle Street; 15 Princes Street, Soho; 29 Castle Street; and 71 Castle Street. See P. M. Ashraf, *The Life and Times of Thomas Spence* (Newcastle upon Tyne: Frank Graham, 1983), 73, 83–84.
94. See Thomas Spence, *The Case of Thomas Spence* (London: T. Spence 1792), esp. 5, reprinted in H. T. Dickinson, *The Political Works of Thomas Spence* (Newcastle upon Tyne: Avero, 1982), 15, 16.
95. Edmund Burke, *Reflections on the Revolution in France* (London: Penguin, 1968), 173. See further chap. 5 above.
96. On the contents of *Pig's Meat*, see further chap. 8 below.

in an inventive variety of formats. He chalked graffiti on pavements and walls, devised toasts and songs for use at tavern gatherings (which he organised), had slogans stamped onto coins, and struck tokens with original legends and designs. Token collection was a popular pursuit in later eighteenth- and early nineteenth-century England, and for a time the sale of tokens seems to have provided Spence with his main source of income.[97] It is said that two of his favourite tokens were buried with him, one showing a meridian sun with the words 'Spence's Plan', the other depicting a cat with the legend 'I among slaves enjoy my freedom' (fig. 9a).[98]

Figure 9a Thomas Spence, *cat token*, 1796.

97. On Spence's tokens and coins, see R. H. Thompson, 'The Dies of Thomas Spence (1750–1814)', *British Numismatic Journal* 38 (1969) 126, and Mathew Crowther, 'Mo Money Mo Problems — Radical political satire and the satirical coinage of Thomas Spence' (2013), available at: https://theprintshopwindow.wordpress.com/2013/09/30/mo-money-mo-problems-radical-political-satire-and-the-satirical-coinage-of-thomas-spence/. See also David Bindman, *The Shadow of the Guillotine: Britain and the French Revolution* (London: British Museum, 1989), 56–57, 198–203.
98. See Mathew Crowther, 'Mo Money Mo Problems — Radical political satire and the satirical coinage of Thomas Spence' (2013), available at: https://theprintshopwindow.wordpress.com/2013/09/30/mo-money-mo-problems-radical-political-satire-and-the-satirical-coinage-of-thomas-spence/.

Most favourable to existence

Another of Spence's tokens should be mentioned here because it carries a line from the poem quoted at the beginning of this chapter — 'Only one master grasps the whole domain' — around a desolate scene of ruined cottages and dead trees (fig. 9b).[99] An excerpt from *The Deserted Village* is also reprinted near the beginning of the first volume of *Pig's Meat*, under the title 'A Lamentation for the Oppressed'.[100] Whatever the perspective of Goldsmith, Spence evidently read the poem not as an exercise in nostalgia, but as a piece of radical literature which resonated with his ideas about oppression and how to end it.[101] We have seen that, in his assessment, oppression was not simply a political problem. Attention needed to be directed to the socio-economic

Figure 9b Thomas Spence, *token*, 1795. © The Trustees of the British Museum. All rights reserved

99. See David Bindman, *The Shadow of the Guillotine: Britain and the French Revolution* (London: British Museum, 1989), 199, 201.
100. 'A Lamentation for the Oppressed: from *The Deserted Village*', *Pig's Meat* 1 (1794) 32–36.
101. On this, see John Barrell, *The Dark Side of the Landscape: The Rural Poor in English Painting 1730–1840* (Cambridge: Cambridge University Press, 1980), 82.

conditions in which it arose and was sustained. And for him, the key to those conditions in his own country was private ownership of land. From the initial seizure of land down to Parliamentary enclosure and the emergence of a speculative land market, land had been misappropriated by a few who had fallen into the habit of thinking, or at any rate acting as if, the earth had been made for them, and now the cursed spirit of traffic was pervading everything. If 'the people wish to have the government in their own hands', Spence declares, 'they must begin first, by taking the land into their own hands'.[102]

As we have also seen in this chapter, Young — the enclosers' friend — came to agree with Spence that ruin was fast coming on to the nation due to the miseries being inflicted by Parliamentary enclosure. Equally, Ogilvie condemned Parliamentary enclosure as a mechanism that locked up land for the wealthy few, Wollstonecraft deprecated it for taking away sources of subsistence and blasting the prospects of poor, and Thelwall pronounced it a great calamity which perpetrated highway robbery against commoners. To these writers, the remedy for the ill-effects of Parliamentary enclosure was more or better Parliamentary enclosure. By that, they generally intended that allotments of some sort should be allocated from the manorial waste, so that the poor would have property of their own. In the version put forward by Ogilvie, all agricultural land would be worked by its proprietor. Paine's prescription for agrarian justice differed, inasmuch as he did not propose inclusion of the poor in the system of private landownership. But the inheritance tax and other redistributive measures he envisaged similarly worked within that system, and were framed in terms that emphasised the importance of respecting the rights of possessors to the part which was theirs.

Spence instead advanced a plan for socialising ownership of land by vesting it in local communities (the parishes). In a commentary on the plan written in 1793, he notes that, compared to him, Paine 'acts more cautiously, and does not hurt the feelings of any gentleman that is unconnected with government, and so, of course, may retain their good will, notwithstanding all the lengths he goes'.[103] But, to Spence's mind, there exists a 'superfluity of concern . . . for the richest'.[104] The 'piercing grievance' of the poor requires attention, and his

102. 'A Further Account of Spensonia', *Pig's Meat 2* (1794) 215, reprinted in H.T. Dickinson, *The Political Works of Thomas Spence* (Newcastle upon Tyne: Avero, 1982), 27, 32.

103. 'An Interesting Conversation, between a Gentleman and the Author, on the Subject of the foregoing Lecture', *Pig's Meat* 3 (1795) 229, 238, reprinted in G. I. Gallop (ed.), *Pig's Meat: Selected Writings* (Nottingham: Spokesman, 1982), 67, 74.

104. Thomas Spence, *The Restorer of Society to its Natural State in a series of letters to a fellow citizen* (London: J. Smith, 1801), Letter 9, reprinted in H.T. Dickinson, *The Political Works of Thomas Spence* (Newcastle upon Tyne: Avero, 1982), 69, 84.

proposals stem from an effort to elucidate and address its 'cause'.[105] Explaining this further, Spence recalls in a number of writings the deprivation he had himself experienced in his youth, and his parents' struggle to provide for the family, despite their unremitting labour and extreme frugality. He says that he 'could not help imputing all our Privations and Hardships, to the bad System of the World'.[106] Had this system been voluntarily adopted, or had the people been 'compelled into it' for the benefit of those who ruled them? Upon investigation of that question, he reports that 'I could observe nothing like the effects of a social compact'. He adds that it was realisations such as this that stirred him 'to lay before the world a plan of society, so consonant to the Rights of Man' that people everywhere would wish to be members of it.[107]

In previous chapters I have highlighted the identification of the rights of man with the rights of the living and the right to live. It transpired that in the 1790s and early 1800s the right to live, understood as aid-in-wages, became a death trap. So too, I recalled, the death penalty was not infrequently the fate of those who continued to assert the right to a livelihood derived in whole or in part from the commons. But if for the leading English Jacobins the ascendancy of a property-based model of the human relationship to land was an established fact, our discussion in this chapter has pointed to another analysis.[108] Spence's plan did not propose a return to the customary arrangements of former times, but it did evoke something of the older rights-based model of the human relationship to land, carried forward in new form. To campaign for allotments, wages and welfare whilst levelling all one's artillery at kings was, he believed, to miss the point that the basis for a decent life was not secure without the right to some measure of non-market-based access to the means of subsistence. 'The question . . . is no longer about which form of Government is most favourable to liberty', he wrote, nor about which set of measures is most favourable to civil peace (because it can best remediate

105. 'An Interesting Conversation, between a Gentleman and the Author, on the Subject of the foregoing Lecture', *Pig's Meat* 3 (1795) 229, 239, reprinted in G. I. Gallop (ed.), *Pig's Meat: Selected Writings* (Nottingham: Spokesman, 1982), 67, 74.
106. Thomas Spence, *The Important Trial of Thomas Spence* (London: A. Seale, 2nd ed., 1803), 56, reprinted in H. T. Dickinson, *The Political Works of Thomas Spence* (Newcastle upon Tyne: Avero, 1982), 92, 94.
107. 'An Interesting Conversation, between a Gentleman and the Author, on the Subject of the foregoing Lecture', *Pig's Meat* 3 (1795) 229, 239, reprinted in G. I. Gallop (ed.), *Pig's Meat: Selected Writings* (Nottingham: Spokesman, 1982), 67, 75.
108. On the distinction between a property-based and rights-based model of the human relationship to land, see chap. 4 above, citing James Holstun, *Ehud's Dagger: Class Struggle in the English Revolution* (London: Verso, 2000), 378.

the damaging effects of economic arrangements on the proletarianised poor). Rather, it is about 'which system of society is most favourable to existence'.[109]

Spence's counter-vision of the right to live puts him in company with writers stretching back many centuries, for whom the turn from rights to property likewise presented itself as a social-systemic issue implicating existence. We have touched on some of them in this book — Robert Crowley's poor man from the country who does not know 'which way to turn so as to live';[110] the common folk of Kett's Rebellion who are 'almost killed with labour';[111] the participants in the Midland Rising who are being 'pined to death';[112] the anonymous Levellers with their warning to rich men who 'live off other mens labours' that God will punish them for their oppressions;[113] the Digger Robert Coster's declaration that 'a Livelihood [is] . . . the right . . . of every man';[114] Gerrard Winstanley's demand for 'Foundation-Freedom' and access to the earth for all.[115] In the work of these and other writers, convergent themes of exploitation, life-sapping wage-labour and the right to a(n adequate and dignified) livelihood had as their context the extinguishment of rights of common and the rise of compulsory market-dependence. For Christopher Hill, Spence's plan for communal ownership and local democracy was a secularised version of Winstanley's dream of heaven on earth.[116] '[L]et the common-People . . . say the earth is ours, not mine', [117] Spence also urged, but now as a claim that this was the meaning of the real rights of man.

109. Thomas Spence, *The Restorer of Society to its Natural State in a series of letters to a fellow citizen* (London: J. Smith, 1801), Letter 14, reprinted in H.T. Dickinson, *The Political Works of Thomas Spence* (Newcastle upon Tyne: Avero, 1982), 69, 92.
110. See chap. 2 above.
111. See chap. 3 above.
112. See chap. 3 above.
113. See chap. 4 above.
114. See chap. 4 above.
115. See chap. 4 above.
116. See Christopher Hill, *Puritanism and Revolution* (London: Secker and Warburg, 1958), 53. On the comparison between Spence and the Diggers of the English Civil War, see also Iain McCalman, *Radical Underworld: Prophets, Revolutionaries and Pornographers in London, 1795–1840* (Cambridge: Cambridge University Press, 1988), 64; and William Stafford, *Socialism, Radicalism and Nostalgia: Social Criticism in Britain, 1775–1830* (Cambridge: Cambridge University Press, 1987), 102.
117. Gerrard Winstanley, *The New Law of Righteousnes*, in Thomas Corns, Ann Hughes and David Loewenstein (eds.), *The Complete Works of Gerrard Winstanley, Vol. I* (Oxford: Oxford University Press, 2009), 472, 518. See chap. 4 above.

8

Does Nature Confer Rights?

A perplexing paradox

For the philosopher Hannah Arendt, the French Declaration of the Rights of Man and the Citizen of 1789 marked 'a turning point in history'.[1] Whereas previously life chances had been a matter of God's command or the customs of history, from that time on it became necessary to reckon with the idea that certain rights were the natural endowment of every human being. The rights of man delivered a challenge to the claims of divine revelation and historical privilege that would alter the terms of moral and political debate irrevocably. As Arendt told the story in *Origins of Totalitarianism*, this momentous development brought with it, however, a perplexing paradox. For if the rights of man belonged to *all* human beings purely by virtue of being human, then the mode of government of a state and the particularities of personal status were irrelevant to these rights. Yet if *any* human being was to be able to claim the rights of man, then a specifically self-governing polity and membership of that polity were crucial. Absent those conditions, the institutional guarantees needed to protect the rights of man would be lacking — or, at any rate, inoperative for the claimants concerned. It followed that self-government and citizenship were at once irrelevant and crucial to the natural rights of man.

Arendt's famous argument, standardly related by later scholars to her personal experience as a Jewish refugee from Nazi Germany, was that the significance of all this only became fully apparent in the mid-twentieth century. Or rather, the significance of citizenship (as distinct from self-government) only became fully apparent then. The 'completely organized' state of the world meant that, for the first time in history, large numbers of people were forced

1. Hannah Arendt, *Origins of Totalitarianism* (Orlando, FL: Harcourt, 1968), 290.

A False Tree of Liberty. Susan Marks, Oxford University Press (2019). © Susan Marks.
DOI: 10.1093/oso/9780199675456.003.0008

to flee their homes without having the possibility of establishing a new home somewhere else. Such people were left with no 'place in the world'[2] — a predicament which Arendt identified not just with persecution and the violation of specific human rights, but more generally, with a loss of the status of right-holder that is the concomitant of political association. In her resonant phrase, these stateless were deprived of the very 'right to have rights'.[3] To her mind, this was tantamount to an expulsion from humanity, or reduction to 'mere existence',[4] and she observed that in Nazi Germany denationalisation had been a prelude to genocide. The major conclusion she invited her readers to draw was that, to guarantee human freedom, dignity and indeed life, what are needed are not so much human rights as the rights which come from, and allow for, membership of a political community, that is to say, citizenship.

Reflecting on that conclusion, and returning to the French Declaration of the Rights of Man and the Citizen, Arendt proposed that twentieth-century history seemingly provided 'an ironical, bitter, and belated confirmation' of Edmund Burke's arguments against the rights of man in *Reflections on the Revolution in France*.[5] According to Burke, she recalled, 'it was much wiser to rely on an "entailed inheritance" of rights which one transmits to one's children like life itself, and to claim one's rights as the "rights of an Englishman" rather than the inalienable rights of man'. And again, 'the rights which we enjoy spring "from within the nation", so that neither natural law, nor divine command, nor any concept of mankind . . . are needed as a source of law'.[6] For Arendt, the plight of people deprived by statelessness of a political community showed that indeed the rights that matter are the rights of co-nationals, the time-honoured rights transmitted from one generation to the next as collective patrimony. Inasmuch as the preceding two centuries had seen a turn towards natural, and later human, rights, she believed that it was necessary to reconsider our commitment to nature and humanity as the basis of rights, and acknowledge with Burke that our real entitlements are the products of history — the history of nations and their traditions, customs and laws.

Does nature confer rights, or only history? Is it better to rely on the rights of an Englishman, or on the inalienable rights of man? Do the rights we enjoy spring from within the nation, or are natural law, divine command

2. Ibid, 293.
3. Ibid, 296.
4. Ibid, 301.
5. Ibid, 299.
6. Ibid.

or some 'concept of mankind' needed, or to be credited, as a source of law? This chapter takes Arendt's retrospective validation of Burke as a starting-point for probing more extensively than hitherto the interrelation in the Revolution controversy of nature, history and rights. On the one hand, the chapter gathers together something of the range of different perspectives on rights as natural endowments and the gap (or instead compatibility) between that idea and rights as historical products. On the other hand, it also examines how protagonists in the controversy approached the question of the history of the rights of man. What narrative did advocates for the rights of man relate about this concept's history, and what did, and does, that signal about the scope and significance of the rights themselves? In particular, we will consider the implications of representing the rights of man as a largely novel discovery or departure of these authors' own time, without connection to the popular struggles and discourses that were our subject in earlier chapters of this book.

Nature, place and circumstance

It will be valuable to begin by recalling Burke's position in a little more detail, before passing to Paine and other contemporaries. The general view laid out in *Reflections* is that natural rights are abstractions from the reality of circumstances, and as such, a poor basis for political judgement, action and claim. Thus, Burke explains that it is 'circumstances' which lend principles their 'distinguishing colour, and discriminating effect'. '[S]tripped of every relation', and existing only in 'the nakedness and solitude of metaphysical abstraction', the natural rights of man are nothing more than empty speculation.[7] As Arendt highlights, and as already noted in chapter 5, *Reflections* counterposes to these artefacts of a 'theoretic science' the 'practical wisdom' of entailed inheritance.[8]

Addressing the case of England, Burke writes that 'it has been the uniform policy of our constitution to claim and assert our liberties, as an entailed inheritance derived to us from our forefathers, and to be transmitted to our posterity'.[9] Such liberties are 'an estate specially belonging to the people of this kingdom without any reference whatever to any other more general

7. Edmund Burke, *Reflections on the Revolution in France* (London: Penguin, 1968), 90.
8. Ibid, 118.
9. Ibid, 119 (emphasis omitted).

or prior right',[10] and defended 'not on abstract principles "as the rights of men", but as the rights of Englishmen'.[11] Burke considers that this 'idea of a liberal descent inspires us with a sense of habitual native dignity'. Liberty becomes a 'noble freedom'. Fortified by the material practice of its 'ensigns armorial', 'gallery of portraits', 'monumental inscriptions', and 'records, evidences and titles', it takes on a 'pedigree and illustrating ancestors'.[12] The intended corollary is that natural rights are not conducive to habitual native dignity. In Burke's account, the revolutionaries in France have 'rudely torn off [a]ll the decent drapery of life'. Thanks to their tawdry and corrosive ideology of the natural rights of man, '[a]ll the pleasing illusions, which made power gentle, and obedience liberal, which harmonized the different shades of life, and . . . incorporated into politics the sentiments which beautify and soften private society, are to be dissolved'.[13]

Burke warns that '[w]hen antient opinions and rules of life are taken away, the loss cannot possibly be estimated'. Were this to happen in England, he writes, 'we [would] have no compass to govern us'.[14] As these statements indicate, that loss of any compass is linked to what Burke takes to be the 'levelling' effect of natural rights. These 'French builders, clearing away as mere rubbish whatever they found, [tried], like their ornamental gardeners, [to form] every thing into an exact level'. Yet 'in politics, the most fallacious of all things [is] geometrical demonstration'.[15] After referring his readers to some passages from Tacitus's *Annals*, Burke remarks that the framers of the Declaration of the Rights of Man and the Citizen might have learned from the lawmakers of antiquity that government '[has] to do with men', and is best informed by the study of 'human nature' and 'the circumstances of civil life'. Little can be accomplished 'with no better apparatus than the metaphysics of an undergraduate, and the mathematics and arithmetic of an exciseman'.[16]

Thomas Paine was an exciseman before he became an author and revolutionary.[17] Richard Price, whose sermon in praise of the rights of man served as the point of departure for the Burke's reflections, was a clergyman, and Burke suggests that he (Price) should probably have stuck to religion. 'Politics

10. Ibid.
11. Ibid, 118.
12. Ibid, 121.
13. Ibid, 171.
14. Ibid, 172.
15. Ibid, 285–86.
16. Ibid, 299.
17. See John Keane, *Tom Paine: A Political Life* (London: Bloomsbury, 1995), 52 et seq.

and the pulpit are terms that have little agreement', Burke writes, and the 'cause of civil liberty and civil government gains as little as that of religion by this confusion of duties'.[18] But for Paine and Price, it is instead Burke who confuses. Natural rights are not simply speculative or theoretical; they are real entitlements that are as much part of the order of nature as humankind itself. In Paine's telling, the 'error of those [like Burke] who reason by precedents drawn from antiquity . . . is that they do not go far enough into antiquity. They do not go the whole way.'[19] '[I]f we proceed on', he writes, 'we shall at last come out right: we shall come to the time when man came from the hand of his maker . . .' For the 'origin of man' is also 'the origin of his rights'.[20] The rights of man belong with the work of God in populating the earth, and it is only in the 'false systems of government, and false theology' championed by the likes of Burke — which Paine denounces as part of a 'general wreck of superstition' in his 1794 work *Age of Reason* — that things are made to appear otherwise.[21]

Paine agrees with Burke that 'place and circumstance' matter.[22] However, when it comes to England, he firmly refutes the suggestion that entailed inheritance or some notion of liberal descent can, or does, conduce to habitual native dignity. To the contrary, the dignity of the English consists, he maintains, in asserting their natural rights so as to overcome a legacy that remains rooted in 'dark and slavish times'.[23] Of a similar mind, John Thelwall characterises the inherited institutions of the English as 'insulting mausoleums of buried rights'.[24] This line of argument would have been heard by readers of the period as a reference to the long held belief that the English constitution and the institutions associated with it were a yoke that oppressed the English people and deprived them of their liberty. That is to say, it would have been heard as a reference to the trope of the Norman Yoke, touched on in earlier chapters.[25] Indeed, the two authors were quite explicit about this, writing

18. Edmund Burke, *Reflections on the Revolution in France* (London: Penguin, 1968), 94.
19. Thomas Paine, *Rights of Man, Part I*, in Bruce Kuklick (ed.), *Paine: Political Writings* (Cambridge: Cambridge University Press, 2000), 57, 83–84.
20. Ibid, 84.
21. Thomas Paine, *The Age of Reason, Part I*, in Bruce Kuklick (ed.), *Paine: Political Writings* (Cambridge: Cambridge University Press, 2000), 265, 267.
22. Thomas Paine, *Rights of Man, Part I*, in Bruce Kuklick (ed.), *Paine: Political Writings* (Cambridge: Cambridge University Press, 2000), 57, 132.
23. Thomas Paine, *Common Sense*, in Bruce Kuklick (ed.), *Paine: Political Writings* (Cambridge: Cambridge University Press, 2000) 1, 5.
24. John Thelwall, *The Rights of Nature, against the Usurpations of Establishments*, in Gregory Claeys (ed.), *The Politics of English Jacobinism: Writings of John Thelwall* (Pennsylvania: Pennsylvania State University Press, 1995), 389, 398.
25. See chaps. 4 and 5 above.

of the 'band of Norman robbers' who seized land and 'held the country in progressive links of slavery',[26] and whose leader 'contrived', once his power was established, 'to lose the name of robber in that of monarch'.[27] Paine adds that the contrivance did not succeed in obliterating the 'hatred which the Norman invasion and tyranny began'. 'Though not a courtier will talk of the curfew-bell [the bell that was the signal in medieval England for people to cover their fires and go to bed, said to have been mandated by William I as a measure to prevent assembly and hence revolt], not a village in England has forgotten it.'[28]

Mary Wollstonecraft likewise writes of the violence and ignominy of Burke's cherished constitution, and of its foundation on the 'lawless power of an ambitious individual' and his mostly disreputable successors.[29] What Burke calls the decent drapery of life is better understood, she proposes, as 'a graceful veil [thrown over] vices that degrade humanity'.[30] Yet there can be no abrogating the natural rights of man, which are received 'not from [our] forefathers, but, from God'.[31] Reason reveals this, and, in so doing, holds out the prospect of a dignified life for all. It is in that context that Wollstonecraft raises the question of the dignity of women in a system of patriarchal power that treats them 'as if they were in a state of perpetual childhood, unable to stand alone'.[32] In her analysis, the illusions which are so pleasing to Burke insofar as they make power gentle and obedience liberal, and incorporate into politics the sentiments that beautify and soften private society, form part of an oppressive ideology which associates beauty with weakness and keeps women from fully developing as rational beings.[33] The consequence is to debase private society, and shut women out of public society. At the same time, it remains the case that the 'man who lives by the sweat of his brow has no asylum from oppression'. A rich man's home is his castle, but 'when was the

26. John Thelwall, *The Tribune*, in Gregory Claeys (ed.), *The Politics of English Jacobinism: Writings of John Thelwall* (Pennsylvania: Pennsylvania State University Press, 1995), 65, 302 (emphasis omitted).
27. Thomas Paine, *Rights of Man, Part II,* in Bruce Kuklick (ed.), *Paine: Political Writings* (Cambridge: Cambridge University Press, 2000), 155, 170.
28. Ibid.
29. Mary Wollstonecraft, *A Vindication of the Rights of Men*, in Sylvana Tomaselli (ed.), *Mary Wollstonecraft: A Vindication of the Rights of Men and A Vindication of the Rights of Woman* (Cambridge: Cambridge University Press), 1, 9.
30. Ibid, 14.
31. Ibid, 13.
32. Mary Wollstonecraft, *A Vindication of the Rights of Woman*, in Sylvana Tomaselli (ed.), *Mary Wollstonecraft: A Vindication of the Rights of Men and A Vindication of the Rights of Woman* (Cambridge: Cambridge University Press), 65, 176.
33. On this, see further chap. 5 above and the references cited there.

castle of the poor sacred?'[34] Pleasing illusions these may be, then, only from the perspective of those whose power and authority — as property-owners and as men — they prop up.

Another author who contributed to the argument for natural rights was George Dyer. Dyer was a poet, literary scholar, and political commentator, and a prominent figure within the London reform movement of the early 1790s. In 1789 he wrote a pamphlet entitled *An Inquiry into the Nature of Subscription to the Thirty-Nine Articles*.[35] The 'thirty-nine articles' were the articles of faith in the teachings of the Church of England, to which the holders of various kinds of office, benefit and status were obliged by law to subscribe, and Dyer's text was one of many by religious dissenters — he identified initially as a Baptist and later (like Price) as a Unitarian — arguing that the subscription law should be repealed.[36] In making his case, Dyer poses the question 'how far is the establishment of Subscription consistent with the natural rights of mankind?' He says that by natural rights he means 'those, with which I am invested by the Author of my existence'.[37] Natural rights are the 'original rights, of which no one [can be justly deprived]' — 'the rights of men', of which governments are, or should be, the guardians.[38] 'Is it asked', he goes on, 'what those rights are?' His answer is this: 'Survey the soil where you received your origin. On that soil grow your rights.'[39] If you were born in Britain, your natural rights 'grow in Britain: and each individual, according to our different ages, and stations in society, should in justice reap them'.[40] The refinements, advantages, and possibilities for thought, expression and belief that are available to some should, in principle, be available to all.

Dyer's conclusion is, of course, that the establishment of Subscription is not consistent with the natural rights of mankind. 'There is a Being who created us; he has commanded us to worship him', and it then 'becomes the leading duty of life, and one of our most important natural rights, to consult

34. Mary Wollstonecraft, *A Vindication of the Rights of Men*, in Sylvana Tomaselli (ed.), *Mary Wollstonecraft: A Vindication of the Rights of Men and A Vindication of the Rights of Woman* (Cambridge: Cambridge University Press), 1, 13.
35. George Dyer, *An Inquiry into the Nature of Subscription to the Thirty Nine Articles* (London: Joseph Johnson, 1792).
36. Dyer was particularly exercised by the conditioning of admission to universities upon subscription to the thirty-nine articles. See Nicholas Roe, 'Dyer, George (1755–1841)', in *Oxford Dictionary of National Biography* (Oxford: Oxford University Press, 2004).
37. George Dyer, *An Inquiry into the Nature of Subscription to the Thirty Nine Articles* (London: Joseph Johnson, 1792), 6.
38. Ibid, 7.
39. Ibid.
40. Ibid, 9.

that revelation, and to choose our religion.' 'These and others like them, I call natural rights', he reaffirms. 'They are claims, arising out of our present situation, our mutual relation, and our common equality. They are therefore just claims', and '[w]hoever attempts to violate them encroaches on our common privileges, and supports the cause of tyranny'.[41] In a later passage, Dyer states that he has taken his definition of natural rights from 'nature', rather than from books, and is aware that, to some, it will not be reckoned accurate. To 'political writers', natural rights are 'those, which men possess, before they enter into a state of society', and partly '[resign] when they advance to civil society'. But he declares that he feels no inclination to correct himself, as '[w]hatever degree of liberty be resigned, [men] resign in common, and whatever benefits be enjoyed, should be enjoyed in common'. Just laws, which serve the public interest, are characterised by a tendency to restore in some measure the natural equality that was the original condition of humankind. Laws that instead 'ordain exclusive privileges' involve 'oppression', and cause injury to 'some individuals'.[42] More than that, such laws 'destroy the notion of a birthright; a natural, or birthright, being a common right'.[43]

On Dyer's account, then, natural rights come from the author of existence *and also* from the soil where we received our origin. Claims invoking them arise out of our present situation and mutual relations *and also* out of the common equality that was our original condition. If for Burke the natural rights of man are nothing more than empty abstractions, and for Paine, Thelwall, and Wollstonecraft liberal descent consigns the English to an insulting mausoleum of buried rights, for Dyer, it seems, nativist and rationalist justifications happily coexist.[44] Is Dyer an exception among his contemporaries? Certainly Paine leaves no doubt about his belief that the rights of man belong to the order of nature. Yet recall that, even as he derives from them precepts 'as universal as truth and the existence of man',[45] he appeals to a distinctively English narrative of national subjugation. Thelwall commends 'the simple plans of reason, and of nature',[46] and argues that, as

41. Ibid, 9–10.
42. Ibid, 16.
43. Ibid, 25.
44. On this, see Anne Janowitz, *Lyric and Labour in the Romantic Tradition* (Cambridge: Cambridge University Press, 1998), 51.
45. Thomas Paine, *Rights of Man, Part I*, in Bruce Kuklick (ed.), *Paine: Political Writings* (Cambridge: Cambridge University Press, 2000), 57, 151.
46. John Thelwall, *The Rights of Nature, against the Usurpations of Establishments*, in Gregory Claeys (ed.), *The Politics of English Jacobinism: Writings of John Thelwall* (Pennsylvania: Pennsylvania State University Press, 1995), 389, 435.

man was created with certain 'wants and faculties', so God also 'dictated the rights by the means'.[47] In making that argument, he too invites his audience not to forget that 'since the overthrow of our Saxon institutions, the sun of Liberty [has] never shone'.[48] He too looks forward to a full 'restoration of the ancient rights of Englishmen'.[49] Modern scholars like Arendt assume a categorical separation of arguments based on nature and arguments based on history. But while these eighteenth-century authors laid their emphasis in varying ways, it seems that they saw no need to choose between those two modes of justification. The rights of man were at once natural endowments and the long-lost heritage of a nation.

A new study in this world

In a world still comfortable with such analytical amalgams, Thomas Spence was among the most comfortable of all. His writing brings together a profusion of registers, discourses, and modes of argumentation — nativist and rationalist, secular and religious, utopian, republican, and millenarian, to mention just a few. Thus, Spence characterises his plan for the deprivatisation of land[50] as a project of restoring enjoyment of the 'natural and equal rights of property in land and liberty' which belonged to human beings 'in a state of nature'.[51] By that means, he proposes, there will be brought into being an 'empire of right and reason'.[52] In one of his early works, entitled *A Supplement to the History of Robinson Crusoe*, Spence adds a new episode to Defoe's celebrated work, in which the plan is implemented on the island to 'universal Joy'.[53] He also invents his own ideal society called 'Spensonia',[54] and composes a generic

47. Ibid, 457.
48. John Thelwall, *The Tribune*, in Gregory Claeys (ed.), *The Politics of English Jacobinism: Writings of John Thelwall* (Pennsylvania: Pennsylvania State University Press, 1995), 65, 302.
49. Ibid, 303 (emphasis omitted).
50. See chap. 7 above.
51. Thomas Spence, 'The Real Rights of Man: A Lecture Read at the Philosophical Society in Newcastle, on the 8th November, 1775', *Pig's Meat* 3 (1795) 220–21, reprinted in H.T. Dickinson, *The Political Works of Thomas Spence* (Newcastle upon Tyne: Avero, 1982), 1.
52. Thomas Spence, 'The Real Rights of Man: A Lecture Read at the Philosophical Society in Newcastle, on the 8th November, 1775', *Pig's Meat* 3 (1795) 220, 229, reprinted in H. T. Dickinson, *The Political Works of Thomas Spence* (Newcastle upon Tyne: Avero, 1982), 1, 5.
53. Thomas Spence, *A Supplement to the History of Robinson Crusoe, Being the History of Crusonia, or Robinson Crusoe's Island* (Newcastle: T. Saint, 2nd ed., 1782), 20, reprinted in H.T. Dickinson, *The Political Works of Thomas Spence* (Newcastle upon Tyne: Avero, 1982), 5, 10.
54. See Thomas Spence, *Description of Spensonia* (London: T. Spence, 1795) and 'A Further Account of Spensonia', *Pig's Meat* 2 (1794) 207, reprinted in H.T. Dickinson, *The Political Works of Thomas Spence* (Newcastle upon Tyne: Avero, 1982), 25, 27.

'Constitution' for that and other places. This begins by reciting the people's conviction that 'Forgetfulness of, and Contempt for, the natural Rights of Man, are the only causes of the crimes and misfortunes of the World'.[55] The constitution goes on to proclaim that 'Government is instituted to secure to man the enjoyment of his natural and imprescriptible rights', among them the right to 'property in the earth, and its natural productions'. In other articles it is stated that 'laws . . . can never proscribe natural rights', and that 'Sovereignty resides in the people' and '[n]o proportion of the people can exercise the power of the whole'.[56]

Spence also writes of his plan's realisation as the fulfilment of the biblical 'jubilee', foretold in the Book of Leviticus of the Hebrew Bible.[57] In the Levitican teaching, the jubilee is a special year during which the beneficence of God becomes especially manifest. A sabbath year that follows seven sabbaths of years, it is supposed to arrive every fiftieth year. A trumpet sounds, and liberty is proclaimed throughout the land. Debts are forgiven, prisoners and slaves are freed, and the land is repossessed by its original owners. The commandment in Leviticus that 'each of you shall return to his possession' is especially important to Spence.[58] He highlights the related teaching that, whatever the transactions of human beings, the land always belongs ultimately to God, so that no sale can be regarded as definitive. As it is said, 'The land shall not be sold for ever: For the land is mine; for ye are strangers and sojourners with me.'[59] He also calls attention to a passage from the Book of Isaiah that would have had very particular resonance for those living through a period of rapidly advancing farm enlargement and near-complete enclosure. The passage reads: 'Wo unto them that join house to house, that lay field to field, till there be no place, that they may be placed alone in the midst of the earth.'[60] Spence tells his readers that God has been 'belied by designing priests, colleagued with overbearing knaves' who have falsely made it seem divinely ordained that 'some few shall have the lordship and disposal of the

55. Thomas Spence, *The Constitution of Spensonia* (London: T. Spence, 1803), reprinted in H. T. Dickinson, *The Political Works of Thomas Spence* (Newcastle upon Tyne: Avero, 1982) 58.

56. Ibid, 58–61.

57. E.g. 'An Interesting Conversation, between a Gentleman and the Author, on the Subject of the foregoing Lecture', *Pig's Meat* 3 (1795) 229, 231, 233, reprinted in G. I. Gallop (ed.), *Pig's Meat: Selected Writings* (Nottingham: Spokesman, 1982), 67, 68, 70. See also 'From Spence's Rights of Man', *Pig's Meat* 1 (1794) 42–43.

58. *Leviticus* 25:13.

59. 'Lessons for Monopolizers of Land, Lesson I', *Pig's Meat* 1 (1794) 87, 88, quoting Leviticus 25:23 (emphasis omitted).

60. 'Lessons for Monopolizers of Land, Lesson II', *Pig's Meat* 1 (1794) 89, quoting Isaiah 5:8. For invocations of this same passage in the context of the Midland Rising of 1607, see chap. 3 above.

earth, whilst the far greater part must be reduced to supplicate to become their tributaries and vassals'.[61]

Alongside these portrayals, Spence presents his land plan as an effort to redress historic dispossession. In this regard, he joins the chorus against '[t]hat conquering blade, who did us invade / Ev'n William the Norman by name'.[62] As noted previously, however, the Norman Yoke was not a single or uniform set of ideas and claims, and Spence's version of it appears to have differed somewhat from that of Paine and the others. In Paine's account, as we saw above, what remains etched in the memory of every English village is the curfew bell — a symbol of political repression or, at any rate, paranoid despotism. In Spence's account, the Norman Yoke stands additionally, and more fundamentally, for a loss of control of land. As he has it, not only the country's monarch, but its entire landowning class has contrived to lose the name of robber in some respectable moniker (to adapt Paine's phrase), and none more cunningly than those who in his own century set up, and gained title through, the system of Parliamentary enclosure. There may also be another difference. For while Spence holds firmly to the natural freedom and equality of all humankind, it is not clear that he subscribes to the view that this state of affairs, or something like it, existed in pre-Norman England. Certainly, his version of the Norman Yoke is at best mixed when it comes to the earlier Saxons, whom he brackets with 'all the other civilizers of mankind', including the Normans and their successors the English, who have invaded lands and reduced the 'great body of the people to a state of dependence and vassalage'.[63]

Whatever the antiquity of this 'very uncivil way of civilizing the world',[64] the main point for Spence is that the future can, and should, be different. Deprivation of land and rights by 'force' and 'sophistry' is not inevitable; another form of civilized life is possible that instead recognises the great body of the people as the true and rightful 'Lord of the Manor, from generation to generation'.[65] Of course, the idea of the rights of man as a project for bringing about change was something Spence shared with Paine and other authors,

61. 'A Further Account of Spensonia', *Pig's Meat* 2 (1794) 207, 206, reprinted in H.T. Dickinson, *The Political Works of Thomas Spence* (Newcastle upon Tyne: Avero, 1982) 27, 28.
62. 'The Downfall of Feudal Tyranny, Severely felt by the Moderns, under the System of Landlord and Tenant', *Pig's Meat* 3 (1795) 250.
63. Thomas Spence, *The Reign of Felicity* (London: T. Spence, 1796), 4, 6, reprinted in H.T. Dickinson, *The Political Works of Thomas Spence* (Newcastle upon Tyne: Avero, 1982), 41, 42.
64. Ibid, 5, reprinted in H. T. Dickinson, *The Political Works of Thomas Spence* (Newcastle upon Tyne: Avero, 1982), 41, 42.
65. Ibid, 8 (emphasis omitted), reprinted in H. T. Dickinson, *The Political Works of Thomas Spence* (Newcastle upon Tyne: Avero, 1982), 41, 43.

whose ambition to alter the course charted by the forces of conservatism and reaction was very much on the surface of their writings. Where ways parted was over the project itself. That manifestly encompassed divergence as to what should be. At the same time, the disparities regarding the Norman Yoke already confirm that it also encompassed divergence as to what once was. To explore further these authors' respective orientations to the past, let us now take up the question of how advocates for the rights of man situated their concept within history. What antecedents did they cite, what time-frames did they emphasise, what people, processes and events made up their narratives of revolution and reform?

We will return presently to Spence, but first it will be instructive to revisit Price and his sermon delivered at the Old Jewry Meeting-house in London on 4 November 1789. It will be recalled that the occasion for the sermon was a commemoration of England's 'Glorious Revolution' just over a century earlier.[66] Price leads the congregation in giving thanks to God for 'our deliverance at the Revolution from the dangers of popery and arbitrary power'.[67] Then, after rehearsing the standard story of how, '[b]y a bloodless victory, the fetters which despotism had long been preparing for us were broken', etc.,[68] he advises that '[o]ur gratitude, if genuine, will be accompanied with endeavours to . . . improve the happiness with which the Revolution has blest us'.[69] For 'though the Revolution was a great work, it was by no means a perfect work'.[70]

As indicated in an earlier chapter, the imperfections which Price has principally in mind are that the protection of religious freedom remains inadequate, and that participation in Parliament continues to be a privilege enjoyed by the property-owning few.[71] He maintains that in both respects the British constitution fails to conform to the principles upon which — he claims or perhaps pretends — the Glorious Revolution was founded, and he exhorts those assembled to act without further delay to realise those principles. As things stand, according to him, the country's constitution is 'excellent chiefly in form and theory'.[72] In order for it to become excellent also in substance and practice, it is necessary to '[supply] what [the settlement of 1688]

66. See further chap. 5 above.
67. Richard Price, *A Discourse on the Love of Our Country* (London: T. Cadell, 3rd ed., 1790), 2.
68. Ibid, 31–32.
69. Ibid, 33–34.
70. Ibid, 35. Quoted in chap. 5 above.
71. See chap. 5 above.
72. Richard Price, *A Discourse on the Love of Our Country* (London: T. Cadell, 3rd ed., 1790), 39.

left deficient'.[73] The sermon concludes with reference to the revolutions in America and latterly France, and to the consequential 'favourableness of the present times to all exertions in the cause of public liberty' and the rights of man.[74] Price's message, then, was that to assert the rights of man was to fulfil the principles of the Glorious Revolution of 1688, and to carry out the business it started but left incomplete.

When Burke countered shortly afterwards that there were no principles of the kind for which Price contended, since, whatever natural rights the people may have had to religious freedom and self-government, Parliament renounced on their behalf in the settlement with William and Mary, Paine in turn came back with a distinctive reprise of Price's theme. The 'marvellous and monstrous' idea upon which Burke based his argument, Paine writes in *Rights of Man*, was that rights died with the men who renounced them.[75] As to which Paine's comment is: 'The English Parliament of 1688 did a certain thing which for themselves and their constituents they had a right to do, and which appeared right should be done.' But no parliament, no generation, possesses the power of 'commanding forever how the world shall be governed, or who shall govern it'. Rights are for the living, not the dead, and the 'vanity and presumption of governing beyond the grave is the most ridiculous and insolent of all tyrannies'.[76] Paine suggests that it is 'somewhat extraordinary that the offense for which James II was expelled . . . should be reacted [that is to say, re-enacted and replicated] under another shape and form by the parliament that expelled him'. For 'certain it is that the right which that [1688] parliament set up . . . over the persons and freedom of posterity forever, was of the same tyrannical, unfounded kind which James attempted to set up over the parliament and the nation, and for which he was expelled'.[77]

Explaining that homology, Paine affirms that the principle of the equal rights of man entails not only that there may be no absolute monarchy of the kind for which he took James II to have been deposed, but also that there may be no irrevocable Parliamentary settlement. For just as 'every individual is born equal in rights with his contemporary', so 'every generation is equal in rights to the generations which preceded it'. Paine says that this is

73. Ibid, 42.
74. Ibid, 48–49.
75. Thomas Paine, *Rights of Man, Part I*, in Bruce Kuklick (ed.), *Paine: Political Writings* (Cambridge: Cambridge University Press, 2000), 57, 62.
76. Ibid, 63.
77. Ibid, 65 (emphasis omitted).

recognised in 'every traditionary account, whether from the lettered or unlettered world', whatever the differences over particulars. All agree that humankind is 'of one degree, and consequently that all men are born equal and with equal natural rights, in the same manner as if posterity had been continued by creation instead of generation, the latter being only the mode by which the former is carried forward'.[78]

If the Parliament of 1688 failed to recognise this, that 'shows that the rights of man were but imperfectly understood' in the Glorious Revolution.[79] A better understanding had emerged since then, and Paine commends to his readers an address by the Marquis de la Fayette (the American 'Lafayette') presenting a draft of the French Declaration of the Rights of Man and the Citizen to the French national assembly in July 1789. 'Call to mind the sentiments which nature has engraved in the heart of every citizen, and which take a new force when they are solemnly recognized by all', he reports the Marquis to have declared; 'for a nation to love liberty, it is sufficient that she knows it; and to be free, it is sufficient that she wills it'.[80] To Paine, this statement exemplifies the inspiring ethos of 'a revolution generated in the rational contemplation of the rights of man'.[81]

One might summarise Paine's position by noting that he argues, first, that the rights of man have a history which goes back to the creation of the world, and the error of those who reason like Burke is that they do not go far enough back into antiquity; second, that these rights align with the rights which once belonged to Englishmen but no longer do so due to the Norman Yoke; and third, that the rights of man were imperfectly understood in the Glorious Revolution, and to gain an adequate understanding of them, attention needs to be redirected to the more favourable and illuminating present times. For generation is only the mode by which creation is carried forward, and the 'divine principles of the equal rights of man'[82] exist for, and are reflected in events involving, those currently alive. Thus, we read in the preface to *Agrarian Justice* that the 'rights of man are a new study in this world',[83] having already

78. Ibid, 85 (emphasis omitted).
79. Ibid, 65.
80. Marquis de la Fayette, quoted in Thomas Paine, *Rights of Man, Part I*, in Bruce Kuklick (ed.), *Paine: Political Writings* (Cambridge: Cambridge University Press, 2000), 57, 67.
81. Thomas Paine, *Rights of Man, Part I*, in Bruce Kuklick (ed.), *Paine: Political Writings* (Cambridge: Cambridge University Press, 2000), 57, 70.
82. Ibid, 85.
83. Thomas Paine, *Agrarian Justice*, in Bruce Kuklick (ed.), *Paine: Political Writings* (Cambridge: Cambridge University Press, 2000), 319, 320.

read in the earlier *Rights of Man* that the Marquis de la Fayette is among their most insightful and inspiring students.

If we return now to Spence, the claim will again be heard that rights are for the living and not the dead. He agreed with Paine and Price that no-one should have the power to command forever how the world is to be governed. However, on the novelty of the study of the rights of man, he did not concur. It was precisely part of his project to assemble a dissident canon that would demonstrate the strong and deep roots of what he believed to be the real rights of man within the history of revelation and thought. In short, he wanted to show that the rights of man were an old study in the world. *Pig's Meat* was especially notable in this respect. According to Anne Janowitz, the journal set 'a precedent for organising and inventing a cultural tradition, laying claim to texts from the past, and juxtaposing them in such a way as to generate new meanings which fasten these texts to the social and political claims being made by the unenfranchised and the labouring poor'.[84]

This is the rights of man!

Pig's Meat was, for a time, Spence's vehicle for publishing works of his own composition, but in addition it anthologised works said to have been 'collected by the poor man's advocate, in the course of his reading for more than twenty years'. The texts were chosen for their value in providing 'lessons for [those whom Burke had denigrated as] the swinish multitude'. More specifically, Spence's intention, advertised on the journal's title page, was to 'promote among the Labouring Part of Mankind proper Ideas of their Situation, of their Importance, and of their Rights', and 'convince them That their forlorn Condition has not been entirely overlooked and forgotten, nor their just Cause unpleaded, neither by their Maker nor by the best and most enlightened of Men in all Ages'.[85] These proper ideas came in many forms. There were verses from the scriptures, excerpts from political tracts and from sermons, treatises and reviews, along with stories, poems and songs.

Spence did not provide commentary or annotations, but he did use headings and typography to frame the works he reprinted, and to place emphasis

84. Anne Janowitz, *Lyric and Labour in the Romantic Tradition* (Cambridge: Cambridge University Press, 1998), 76.
85. *Pig's Meat* 1 (1794) 1.

on particular aspects. For example, the passages from the Book of Leviticus and the Book of Isaiah mentioned above appear under the heading 'Lessons for Monopolizers of Land', with key words and phrases capitalised.[86] We have already noted that *Pig's Meat* contained excerpts from Goldsmith's *The Deserted Village*.[87] Alongside those, it contained excerpts from other works by Goldsmith, and from works by Price, Dyer, Paine,[88] and such other contemporary authors as William Godwin, Joseph Priestley, Joel Barlow, Richard Lee, William Frend, Charles Pigott, James Murray, and Thomas Cooper. Excerpts from Montesquieu's *Persian Letters* and Volney's *Ruins of Empires* were included in translation.

Among works by thinkers from previous ages, *Pig's Meat* gave prominence to publications from the 1650s by two authors: James Harrington's *The Commonwealth of Oceana* (1656), *The Prerogative of Popular Government* (1657), and other works, and William Sprigg's *A Modest Plea for an Equal Commonwealth against Monarchy* (1659). From Harrington, Spence took, in particular, passages that gave expression to the republican theorist's ideas about the relationship between power and land — his belief that power follows the ownership of land, and that public welfare depends on achieving the right balance of landowning. In one of Spence's excerpts, Harrington writes: 'if the whole people be landlords, or hold the land so divided among them, that no one man or number of men within the compass of the few, or aristocracy over-balance them, it is a commonwealth',[89] and an 'equal and well ordered commonwealth' is the 'highest earthly felicity that a people can ask, or God can give'.[90] Harrington goes on to discuss alterations in the balance of landowning, using the language of 'natural revolution' and 'violent revolution' to refer to the different modes by which structural change affecting property and government may occur.[91]

86. See *Pig's Meat* 1 (1794) 87.
87. See chap. 7 above.
88. In the case of Paine, the excerpts were in a book review reproduced in *Pig's Meat* of *Rights of Man, Part II*. See 'Strictures on the Second Part of Paine's Rights of Man, with Copious Extracts', *Pig's Meat* 2 (1794) 223.
89. 'Whether the Balance of Dominion in Land be the Natural Cause of Empire?', *Pig's Meat* 1 (1794) 114, 116–17. (Although Spence refers to *Oceana* as the source of this, the passage comes from *The Prerogative of Popular Government*, in which Harrington responded to critics of *The Commonwealth of Oceana*. For a similar statement in *The Commonwealth of Oceana*, see James Harrington (J. G. A. Pocock ed.), *The Commonwealth of Oceana* and *A System of Politics* (Cambridge: Cambridge University Press, 1992), 12.)
90. 'General Political Aphorisms or Maxims', *Pig's Meat* 1 (1794) 96, 98.
91. 'Whether the Balance of Dominion in Land be the Natural Cause of Empire?', *Pig's Meat* 1 (1794) 114, 117. (Again, Spence refers to *Oceana* as the source of this, but the passage comes from

Sprigg also held to the doctrine of the 'balance of lands', and Spence excerpts passages from *A Modest Plea* in which the author writes of the 'raging passion' for farm engrossment that was taking the country in quite the opposite direction from the one Harrington identified with a well ordered commonwealth. Landowning was being concentrated in ever fewer hands, to the point where there would soon remain 'nothing for either [the rich] to purchase, or us to sell, but ourselves to be their slaves'.[92] The 'great disputes and sharp controversies' about constitutional arrangements that loomed so large in public life were 'not worth a bullrush; for the case is the same, whether Lords or not Lords, when as the great landlords in each country, shall be constantly chosen by their tenants, to be our legislators'.[93] In another excerpt, Sprigg wonders at the idea that establishing a commonwealth or republic 'requires no more [than] inserting, *the keepers of the liberties*, instead of the name *king*, and that then the work is finished, without any farther trouble or alteration, as may seem to be of opinion'.[94]

But these Interregnum works by Harrington and Sprigg were not Spence's only forays into the history of political thought. Among other and, in his time more famous, texts, he reprinted, under the heading 'A Lesson for All Men', this sentence from John Locke's *Second Treatise of Government* (1689), chap.V: 'Whether we consider natural reason, which tells us, that men, being once born, have a right to their preservation, and consequently to meat and drink, and such other things as nature affords for their subsistence: Or revelation . . . it is very clear, that God . . . has given the earth to the children of men, given it to mankind in common.'[95] Also appearing in *Pig's Meat* were a number of texts by Jonathan Swift, himself no dissident, but a popular and suggestive satirist nonetheless. In one passage taken from *Gulliver's Travels* (1726), the voyager relates the story of how, in a certain place, he 'had the curiosity to enquire . . . by what method great numbers had procured to themselves high titles of honour, and prodigious estates'. He continues: 'I confined my enquiry to a very modern period . . . [during which I] discovered such a scene

The Prerogative of Popular Government.) On this aspect of Harrington's work, see Neil Davidson, *How Revolutionary Were the Bourgeois Revolutions?* (Chicago: Haymarket Books, 2012), 24 et seq.

92. 'Of an Agrarian; Or, Division of Land', *Pig's Meat* 3 (1795) 62, 63, quoting William Sprigg, *A Modest Plea, for an Equal Commonwealth, Against Monarchy* (London: Giles Calvert, 1659).
93. Ibid.
94. 'Of the Hereditary Nobility', *Pig's Meat* 2 (1794) 83, 91 (emphasis omitted), quoting William Sprigg, *A Modest Plea, for an Equal Commonwealth, Against Monarchy* (London: Giles Calvert, 1659).
95. 'A Lesson for All Men', *Pig's Meat* 1 (1794) 42 (emphasis omitted). The quoted text is reprinted in John Locke (Peter Laslett, ed.), *Two Treatises of Government* (Cambridge: Cambridge University Press, 1988), 285–86.

of infamy, that I cannot reflect upon it without some seriousness. Perjury, oppression, subornation, [and] fraud . . . were among the most excuseable arts [that were involved, and this] inclined me a little to abate of that profound veneration which I am naturally apt to pay to persons of high rank.'[96]

If for Price and Paine, the rights of man are a matter of supplying what the settlement of 1688 left deficient, it seems, then, that Spence perceived the challenge rather differently. As represented in *Pig's Meat*, the project of the rights of man carries forward into the present a longer history of efforts to bring out, and insist upon, the social basis of freedom and self-government. In the light of writings by Harrington and Sprigg, Spence invites us to see that it is not enough simply to replace a monarchy with some attractively styled republican institutions and think that then the job is done. Nor, *pace* the Marquis de la Fayette, for a nation to love liberty, is it enough simply that the nation knows it, and for a nation to be free, is it enough that the nation wills it. Social conditions — especially those to do with the ownership of land, as the means for sustaining life — affect political outcomes, and a raging passion for farm engrossment thwarts national emancipation.

From Swift's tale, we may take the thought that those who own great estates and hold high office carry all the dignity due to criminals, and perjury, oppression, subordination and fraud are only the least of their heinous crimes (which also encompass, according to Spence, murder and specifically infanticide).[97] As for Locke, Spence made a speech when on trial for seditious libel in 1801 which he subsequently wrote up and published. Protesting his innocence, he explained that many 'eminent Works as well as the Bible' had contributed to strengthening his confidence in the rightness and justice of his ideas. He then quoted the sentence from Locke's *Second Treatise of Government* which he had earlier reprinted in *Pig's Meat* ('Whether we consider natural Reason . . . Or Revelation . . . it is very clear that God . . . has given the Earth . . . to the Children of Men . . . to Mankind in Common'), and declared to the jury: 'This, Gentlemen, is the Rights of Man!'[98]

96. 'An Unpleasant Lesson for the Pigs' Betters', *Pig's Meat* 1 (1794) 86–87. The quoted text is reprinted in Jonathan Swift, *Gulliver's Travels, into Several Remote Nations of the World* (London: J. Walker, 1819), 215–16.

97. See Thomas Spence, *The Rights of Infants* (London: T. Spence, 1796), 7, reprinted in H. T. Dickinson, *The Political Works of Thomas Spence* (Newcastle upon Tyne: Avero, 1982), 48, 50.

98. Thomas Spence, *The Important Trial of Thomas Spence* (London: A. Seale, 2nd ed., 1803), 59–60, reprinted in H.T. Dickinson, *The Political Works of Thomas Spence* (Newcastle upon Tyne: Avero, 1982), 92, 95, 97. The same passage is also quoted in 'An Interesting Conversation, between a Gentleman and the Author, on the Subject of the Foregoing Lecture', *Pig's Meat* 3 (1795) 229, 232, reprinted in G. I. Gallop (ed.), *Pig's Meat: Selected Writings* (Nottingham: Spokesman, 1982), 67, 69.

Olive Rudkin advises that Spence probably misunderstood Locke. 'It would seem', she writes in an early study of Spence's work, that he had either read only extracts, or had read books such as Locke's 'without fully understanding their meaning, and had fastened upon odd passages which he had detached from their proper context'.[99] There can be no denying that Spence lifted the passages he excerpted for *Pig's Meat* out of their wider context. In the case of the *Second Treatise*, he reproduced only the single opening sentence of the chapter on property. There was no reference to the dual purpose Locke announced of refuting the claim that God gave the earth to kings, and explaining the emergence of private property out of that which had been bestowed on mankind in common. Also passed over was the explanation Locke provided in the rest of the chapter for how the original community of property had become individuated — how private right arose out of labour or the hire of labour, how God gave the world to the industrious and rational, and for 'improvement', rather than 'waste', and how, thanks to the invention of money, men could fairly appropriate more than they needed or could use. Yet however well or badly Spence knew or comprehended Locke's text, and whatever the bearing of these omitted sections on the passage he did include, his brief excerpt lent important authority to the idea that the problem of property belonged at the centre of debates about the rights of man, and that the starting-point for analysis of the problem of property was common ownership of the earth.

It needs to be said that writings by Locke lent authority to a wide variety of arguments in the Revolution controversy, most of them premised on the legitimacy and inviolability of the regime of private landowning which Spence used the great philosopher to help put into question. Bringing together the controversy's two leading adversaries, E. P. Thompson writes that '[i]n the 1790s the ambiguities of Locke seem to fall into two halves: one Burke, the other Paine'. By that, he says he means that '[w]here Burke assumes government and examines its operation in the light of experience and tradition, Paine speaks for the governed, and assumes that the authority of [existing] government derives from conquest and inherited power in a class-divided society'.[100] Thompson also has another way of putting into historical perspective these two halves of Locke, on which we touched in an earlier chapter. He

99. Olive Rudkin, *Thomas Spence and His Connections* (London: George Allen & Unwin, 1927), 18–19.
100. E. P. Thompson, *The Making of the English Working Class* (New York: Vintage, 1966), 92.

likens the arguments of Burke and Paine to those advanced by the Grandees and Levellers in the Putney Debates of 1647, just as, for Christopher Hill, the work of Spence should be compared to that of the Winstanley and the Diggers.[101] Regarding Spence, Iain McCalman likewise highlights the affinity with Winstanley's views about 'a greedy few appropriating private property from God's common storehouse'. In his account, even the dispute over the enclosure of Newcastle Town Moor 'was redolent of Digger agitations'.[102]

McCalman places Spence within the wider radical underworld of 1790s London, and describes the tavern meetings that were the setting for much of its members' interaction. With their toasts, songs and debates that refused deference and skewered symbols of authority and respectability, McCalman suggests that the meetings had at times the atmosphere of Ranter gatherings from the same Civil War decade which saw the emergence of the Levellers and Diggers.[103] He also describes the distinctive fusion of enlightenment rationalism, materialist scepticism and millenarian religion that characterised these radicals' thought, again connecting it with antinomian thinking of the previous century, in which 'God [was equated] with Reason, and Reason with the law of the universe'. Thus, '[s]ome "mechanic preachers" [that is, lay preachers who were also working people] prepared the ground' for plebeian thinkers of the late eighteenth century to argue that the Age of Reason announced by secular philosophers was the Millennium promised by God.[104] It may be speculated that Spence's dissident canon would have included work by at least some such figures had he had the opportunity to learn of them — but he did not.[105] Timothy Morton and Nigel Smith tell the story of how, in the late 1810s and early 1820s, Percy Shelley wanted to write a play about the

101. See chaps. 5 and 7 above.
102. Iain McCalman, *Radical Underworld: Prophets, Revolutionaries and Pornographers in London, 1795–1840* (Cambridge: Cambridge University Press, 1988), 64. On the Newcastle Town Moor 'affair', see chap. 7 above.
103. Iain McCalman, *Radical Underworld: Prophets, Revolutionaries and Pornographers in London, 1795–1840* (Cambridge: Cambridge University Press, 1988), 121.
104. Ibid, 65–66. Regarding mechanic preachers, see Christopher Hill, *The World Turned Upside Down* (London: Penguin, 1975), chap. 14.
105. Eduard Bernstein is generally credited with the 'rediscovery' of the Levellers and Diggers. See Eduard Bernstein (H. J. Stenning, trans.), *Cromwell and Communism: Socialism and Democracy in the Great English Revolution* (London: Frank Cass, rev. ed., 1963), first published in 1895 as *Sozialismus und Demokratie in der grossen Englischen Revolution*. Though not widely cited, Leveller writings were previously available and known in England. See F. K. Donnelly, 'Levellerism in Eighteenth and Early Nineteenth-Century Britain', *Albion* 20(2) (1988) 261. Detailed knowledge of Winstanley and the Diggers mostly dates from David Petegorsky, *Left-Wing Democracy in the English Civil War: A Study of the Social Philosophy of Gerrard Winstanley* (London: Victor Gollancz, 1940).

English Civil War, and arranged to have a box of materials on the period sent to him. In the event, the box went down in a shipwreck, and *Charles I* never got written.[106] For Morton and Smith this is something of an allegory of the transmission of information about the English Revolution in the two centuries that followed it.[107]

If the memory of the Levellers and Diggers had temporarily sunk, or at any rate faded, the *language* of levelling was, however, highly conspicuous during the long eighteenth century. The emergence of the term 'levelling' has been located in this book in the activities of those who, from the late fifteenth century onwards, levelled hedges and other barriers put up by enclosers.[108] We have seen that the participants of the Midland Rising of 1607 called themselves 'levellers'.[109] In the conflicts of the mid-seventeenth century, the label was deployed by royalists as a slur — and heard as such by most of those to whom it was applied. A manifesto issued by John Lilburne and the other Leveller leaders during their imprisonment in 1649 denied that anyone had the right to 'level mens Estates, destroy Propriety, or make all things Common'.[110] The small group of Diggers who laid claim to the title of 'True Levellers' did not seek to level estates, destroy property, or make everything common, but they did believe that God had made the earth to be a common treasury for all, and that ordinary people had a right to sustain themselves from its use.[111] Returning to the succeeding century, it is notable that the main semi-official loyalist organisation of the 1790s was called the Association for Protecting Liberty and Property against Republicans and Levellers.[112]

Blair Worden explains that, by this time, the terms 'leveller' and 'levelling' had lost their meaning as denotations of particular people or activities.

106. Fragmentary material for the play survives. See Steven Jones, '"Choose Reform or Civil War": Shelley, the English Revolution and the Problem of Succession', *The Wordsworth Circle* 25(3) (1994) 149.

107. See Timothy Morton and Nigel Smith, 'Introduction', in Timothy Morton and Nigel Smith (eds.), *Radicalism in British Literary Culture 1650–1830* (Cambridge: Cambridge University Press, 2002), 1, 6.

108. See chap. 2 above.

109. See chap. 3 above.

110. See John Lilburne, William Walwyn, Thomas Prince and Richard Overton, *An Agreement of the Free People of England*, 1 May 1649 (London: Gyles Calvert, 1649), 7.

111. See chap. 4 above.

112. E. P. Thompson highlights this as an implicit connection with the Civil War Levellers. See *The Making of the English Working Class* (New York: Vintage, 1966), 23–24. *Cf* Blair Worden writes that the organisation's founder John Reeve 'evidently did not have the civil-war Levellers in mind'. See Blair Worden, 'The Levellers in History and Memory', in Michael Mendle (ed.), *The Putney Debates of 1647: the Army, the Levellers and the English State* (Cambridge: Cambridge University Press, 2001), 256, 270.

Instead, they referred to a particular 'principle or proclivity', namely, 'an impulse towards parity, whether constitutional or social or economic or some indeterminate mixture of the three'.[113] According to him, these words' circulation was wider, and more strongly discrediting, in the final decade of the eighteenth century than at any other moment since the mid-seventeenth century. In the Revolution controversy there was also the added twist or historical irony that levelling took on the connotation of being something alien to English tradition. Thus, Burke warned of the influence of the 'Levellers of France' in England,[114] and, as we have seen, attacked those 'French builders' who, 'like their ornamental gardeners, [tried to form] every thing into an exact level'.[115] Paine countered that France had not 'levelled', it had 'exalted'.[116] Ridding itself of the childishness of aristocratic titles and so forth, it had raised itself up to full maturity. Himself faced with persistent charges of levelling, Paine disclaimed and, again, deflected the label. In *Rights of Man* he writes: 'We have heard the rights of man called a leveling system; but the only system to which the word leveling is truly applicable is the hereditary monarchical system.' How so? Because it 'is a system of mental leveling. It indiscriminately admits every species of character to the same authority. Vice and virtue, ignorance and wisdom, in short, every quality, good or bad, is put on the same level.'[117]

While Paine was plainly stretching the concept here, the fact of turning it onto his opponents in this way was a significant rhetorical move. In disavowing levelling ambitions, reformists and reformist organisations drew a distinction between efforts to achieve equality of wealth and possessions, which they identified with levelling, and efforts to achieve equality of rights, which was how they characterised their own project. In 1794 the Sheffield Society for Constitutional Information challenged their 'most virulent enemies to prove, that they have ever held any other doctrine other than that

113. Blair Worden, 'The Levellers in History and Memory', in Michael Mendle (ed.), *The Putney Debates of 1647: the Army, the Levellers and the English State* (Cambridge: Cambridge University Press, 2001), 256, 267.
114. Edmund Burke, *Letter to a Noble Lord*, quoted in Blair Worden, 'The Levellers in History and Memory', in Michael Mendle (ed.), *The Putney Debates of 1647: the Army, the Levellers and the English State* (Cambridge: Cambridge University Press, 2001), 256, 271.
115. See fn 15 of this chapter above.
116. Thomas Paine, *Rights of Man, Part I*, in Bruce Kuklick (ed.), *Paine: Political Writings* (Cambridge: Cambridge University Press, 2000), 57, 97.
117. Thomas Paine, *Rights of Man, Part II*, in Bruce Kuklick (ed.), *Paine: Political Writings* (Cambridge: Cambridge University Press, 2000), 155, 173 (emphasis omitted).

of an Equality of Rights', and rejected the alternative 'idea of equalizing Property, [as] too futile to deserve a serious answer'.[118] Thompson reports that, as early as 1793, the minutes of the London Corresponding Society record a motion calling for the expulsion of persons propagating levelling principles, in this sense of principles that carried implications for the ownership of property.[119] Thelwall, who was a co-founder and leader of the London group, wrote that 'Philosophy and Humanity forbid the propagation of [the] levelling doctrine'.[120]

Around the same time, however, George Dyer — he of the text on subscription to the thirty-nine articles of faith — made a striking observation, which appeared in a pamphlet entitled *The Complaints of the Poor People of England*.[121] Dyer was commenting on proposals to reform Parliament so as to achieve fair and equal representation of the adult male population. He set out the benefits this would bring, and then stated the 'great objection': '[r]eformers are levellers'.[122] He seems to have had in mind such worries as that the salaries of bishops would be reduced to those of rectors, and that sinecures and pensions would be abolished. Dyer thought these concerns could largely be allayed, but what is more significant is his assumption that reformers were necessarily levellers. If that was a problem for others, it was not so for Spence, who took the rare step of owning the 'leveller' label. In a letter dated 18 October 1800, he writes that one might well 'wonder why none of the modern Champions for the Rights of Man, should take Notice of my Scheme in their Books and Harangues, though . . . I [did not] conceal

118. Sheffield Constitutional Society, *An Appeal to Britons* (June 1794), quoted in F. K. Donnelly, 'Levellerism in Eighteenth and Early Nineteenth-Century Britain', *Albion* 20(2) (1988) 261, 266. See also *An Explanation of the Word Equality* (1793), quoted in Jon Mee, *Print, Publicity, and Popular Radicalism in the 1790s: the Laurel of Liberty* (Cambridge: Cambridge University Press, 2016), 88.

119. E. P. Thompson, *The Making of the English Working Class* (New York: Vintage, 1966), 138. See also Saree Makdisi, *Blake and the Impossible History of the 1790s* (Chicago: University of Chicago Press, 2nd ed., 2003), esp. 295 (reporting that the London Corresponding Society consistently denounced levelling).

120. John Thelwall, *The Rights of Nature, against the Usurpations of Establishments*, in Gregory Claeys (ed.), *The Politics of English Jacobinism: Writings of John Thelwall* (Pennsylvania: Pennsylvania State University Press, 1995), 389, 472. It may be noted in passing that Thelwall was familiar with some aspects of the career of the Leveller leader John Lilburne, whom he admired and with whom he identified. On this, see Peter Kitson, '"Sages and patriots that being dead do yet speak to us": Readings of the English Revolution in the Late Eighteenth Century', in James Holstun (ed.), *Pamphlet Wars: Prose in the English Revolution* (London: Frank Cass, 1992), 205, 217–20.

121. George Dyer, *The Complaints of the Poor People of England* (London: J. Ridgway, 2nd ed., 1793).

122. Ibid, 92. On this, see F. K. Donnelly, 'Levellerism in Eighteenth and Early Nineteenth-Century Britain', *Albion* 20(2) (1988) 261, 267.

my Ideas under a bushel'. Spence says that it is because he has put forward a 'levelling Constitution', which 'makes no partial Distinction of its children into happy Elect and rejected Reprobates', and admits all — men, women and children, the 'Eloquent' and the 'Dumb', the able-bodied as well as the disabled — 'to an equal Participation of the Rights of Nature'.[123] In this, he explains elsewhere, he only follows God, who 'himself is a very notorious leveller'.[124]

Not without great examples

At the beginning of this chapter, we recalled the crucial significance attached by Hannah Arendt to membership of a political community. To her, the predicament of stateless people in the mid-twentieth century showed that national citizenship was what mattered, not human rights. Human freedom, dignity and even survival depended not on the endowments of nature, but on the legacies of history, and she took this as ironical, bitter and belated confirmation of Burke's animadversions against the idea of the natural rights of man. The irony which Arendt seems to have had in mind was that Burke did not himself endorse inclusive citizenship, instead opposing what was later to become 'liberal democracy' and the forms of citizenship associated with it. Yet the confirmation was also ironic for the additional reason that Burke took the history out of social and political analysis, instead representing contested historical products as though they were fixed and eternal essences. Of Paine, Christopher Hill wrote that he was wrong to '[brush] history aside to rest his claims on natural right'. 'The state of nature gives the right answers', Hill proposed, 'because it is peopled with abstractions'.[125] The same applied to Burke's history, which elided the concrete realities of class-divided society and what Spence called the 'piercing grievance' of the poor.[126] It too gave the right answers because

123. Thomas Spence, *The Restorer of Society to its Natural State in a series of letters to a fellow citizen* (London: J. Smith, 1801), Letter 12, reprinted in H.T. Dickinson, *The Political Works of Thomas Spence* (Newcastle upon Tyne: Avero, 1982), 88.

124. 'An Interesting Conversation, between a Gentleman and the Author, on the Subject of the Foregoing Lecture', *Pig's Meat* 3 (1795) 229, 231, reprinted in G.I. Gallop (ed.), *Pig's Meat: Selected Writings* (Nottingham: Spokesman, 1982), 67, 69.

125. Christopher Hill, *Puritanism and Revolution* (London: Secker and Warburg, 1958), 116.

126. See chap. 7 above.

it portrayed a world without conflict, a world in which property relations, social hierarchies and legitimating ideologies were not problems, but elementary facts.

It is well known that, long before Arendt wrote *Origins of Totalitarianism*, Karl Marx similarly called into question the claims being made under the banner of natural rights, though on the very different basis of a materialist account of history. In *On the Jewish Question,* published in 1843, he observes that the '*droits de l'homme*, the rights of man, human rights, *as such* are different from the *droits du citoyen*, from the rights of the citizen'. 'Who is the *homme* who differs from the citizen?'[127] Marx argues that he is the member of bourgeois society, his specificity hidden behind a veneer of generality, universality and timelessness. Under the French Declaration of the Rights of Man and the Citizen, the freedom of this person is the freedom to do everything that does not harm another. So, says Marx, the 'human right of freedom is not based on the connection of man with man, but much more on the separation of man from man'. As enclosure separates human beings from land, so the Declaration protects a form of freedom that presupposes and preserves the individual 'enclosed within himself'. 'The limit within which everyone can operate in a way not harmful to others is determined by law, like the boundary between two [enclosed] fields is determined by the fencepost'. Thus, the right of private property is the 'right to enjoy and dispose of one's wealth arbitrarily . . . without relation to other men', while equality is the equal right of every human being to be considered 'a self-based monad'.[128] Marx sums up his argument with the remark that '[n]one of the so-called human rights then goes beyond the egoistic man . . . withdrawn into his private interests and his private will'.[129]

The phrase 'so-called human rights' is worth pausing over. In criticising the rights of man as part of the ideology of capitalism, Marx seemingly leaves open the possibility of another, more authentic account of the rights of man that is conducive to truly human emancipation. Whatever affinities such an account would have or not have with Spence's 'real rights of man' (of which Marx appears to have been unaware, though he does mention

127. Karl Marx, *On the Jewish Question*, in Joseph O'Malley (trans. and ed.), *Marx: Early Political Writings* (Cambridge: Cambridge University Press, 1994), 28, 44.
128. Ibid, 45.
129. Ibid, 46.

Spence in passing in one text),[130] we may be certain that its frame of reference would be quite different. As we have seen, Spence worked in an older radical idiom that was not yet committed to the absolutism of enlightenment rationality. The real rights of man were, for him, rights that belonged to human beings in a state of nature, rights which expressed his countrymen's historic loss of control of land, and rights associated with the fulfilment of the Levitican jubilee or promise of the millennium. They were all those things at once. Spence himself calls attention to this non-exclusivity or relativity of discourses in a publication based on a speech made in his defence when on trial in 1801. Describing his intellectual development, he says: 'I found . . . as I proceeded that the Hopes of a future blessed State arising from pure Justice, [were] congenial to the Ideas of all Men. For religious People look for such a State under the Notion of a Millenium, Philosophers in an Age of Reason, and Poets in a future Golden Age.'[131]

For Spence, moreover, this congeniality also extended into past, inasmuch as the study of the natural rights of man had a history that could itself be studied. For Paine, as we have seen, the rights of man were a new topic, taken up for the sake of completing England's Glorious Revolution of 1688. Spence had very little to say about the Glorious Revolution, perhaps sharing the assessment articulated almost a century after him and Paine by Friedrich Engels that it was a 'comparatively puny event'.[132] More recent research into the history of that period has yielded an array of different analyses and evaluations, but in the eighteenth century, there can be no doubt that, as Perry Anderson has it, the Glorious Revolution was the official creation myth of England's new, or at any rate newly stable, order. In Anderson's words, '[b]y a classic process of psychological suppression, the Civil War was forgotten and its decorous epilogue, the Glorious Revolution of 1688, became the official radiant myth of creation in the collective memory' of the capitalist landowners and bourgeoisie who increasingly made up the country's propertied class.[133]

130. Alastair Bonnett, *Left in the Past: Radicalism and the Politics of Nostalgia* (New York: Continuum, 2010), 68.
131. Thomas Spence, *The Important Trial of Thomas Spence* (London: A. Seale, 2nd ed., 1803), 57, reprinted in H.T. Dickinson, *The Political Works of Thomas Spence* (Newcastle upon Tyne: Avero, 1982), 92, 95.
132. Friedrich Engels (Edward Aveling, trans.), *Socialism: Utopian and Scientific* (New York: New York Labor News Company, 1901), Introduction, xxv.
133. Perry Anderson, 'Origins of the Present Crisis', *New Left Review* I-23 (1964) 26, 30–31.

Spence said that he studied 'not without great Examples',[134] but the examples that interested him related instead to the collective memory of the dispossessed and despised multitude — the myths, stories, teachings, and claims about rights, humanity, and the earth as the inheritance of all mankind in common.

134. Thomas Spence, *The Important Trial of Thomas Spence* (London: A. Seale, 2nd ed., 1803), 65, reprinted in H.T. Dickinson, *The Political Works of Thomas Spence* (Newcastle upon Tyne: Avero, 1982), 92, 101.

9

Trees and Liberty

Boston's sacred elm

One evening in November 1792 a group of people met at the Bear Inn in Bath and raised their glasses in a toast to liberty and equality. Specifically, what they said was: 'May the tree of liberty flourish in every part of the globe, and every human being partake of its fruit!'[1] Why the *tree of liberty*? Within what frame of reference did it seem right to these opponents of ruling power and privilege to express their hopes through *that* image (of which we know because the toast was written down and reported to the authorities by a government spy in the company's midst)?

The tree of liberty is generally traced to the American Revolution, and in particular to events that took place in Boston in 1765. On 14 August of that year a crowd gathered to protest against the passage in the British Parliament of the Stamp Act.[2] Addressed to the colonies of British America, the Act imposed a tax on printed material. Such material had to be embossed with a revenue stamp before it could be legally circulated. For those burdened, this was taxation without representation, all the more tyrannical insofar as it was also a form of censorship. The focus of the protesters' ire was the man responsible for implementing the tax in Massachusetts, Andrew Oliver. Their message to Oliver was not subtle. Assembled under a large elm tree at the corner of the present Essex and Washington Streets, the colonists hanged him in effigy from one branch of the tree, while from another branch they dangled a British

1. See David Worrall, 'Blake and 1790s Plebeian Radical Culture', in Steve Clark and David Worrall (eds.), *Blake in the Nineties* (London: Macmillan, 1999), 194, 207.
2. See Arthur Schlesinger, 'Liberty Tree: a Genealogy', *New England Quarterly* 25(1) (1952) 435. See also Alfred Young, *Liberty Tree: Ordinary People and the American Revolution* (New York: New York University Press, 2006).

A False Tree of Liberty. Susan Marks, Oxford University Press (2019). © Susan Marks.
DOI: 10.1093/oso/9780199675456.003.0009

cavalry jackboot, out of which there emerged the Devil with a scroll marked 'Stamp Act' in its hand. Oliver resigned a few days later. The next month, at a small ceremony on 11 September, a copper plate was nailed to the tree's trunk bearing the inscription 'The Tree of Liberty'.

And so it was that this previously nameless elm became, in the months and years that followed, a symbol of the revolutionary cause and the site of many important events associated with it. Or, as Oliver's brother, the Massachusetts Bay chief justice Peter Oliver, had it, it became 'an idol for the Mob to worship' and a place where they could inflict the 'Tree ordeal' on those whom they regarded as 'State delinquents'.[3] (Oliver presumably refers here to incidents of tarring and feathering beneath the tree, such as that depicted in the well-known print attributed to Philip Dawe (fig. 10), but he may also have had in mind his brother's being summoned to the tree on 17 December 1765 and forced to take a solemn oath never again to accept an office in which he would play a part in putting the Stamp Act into effect.)[4] Felled by British soldiers and loyalists in 1775 and ostentatiously cut up for firewood, Boston's 'sacred elm' encouraged the designation of liberty trees as rallying-points in other cities and towns. Sometimes another elm was used, sometimes a buttonwood, oak, or tulip tree, and sometimes, as in New York, a pine mast or flagstaff.[5]

Passing from the American Revolution to the French Revolution, the *arbre de la liberté* had immense significance in that context too, with trees planted to serve as living symbols of the new order.[6] According to the Abbé Grégoire, the first French liberty tree was planted in the village of Saint-Gaudent in Vienne in May 1790. Norbert Pressac, the parish priest, had a sapling oak uprooted from the seigneurial forest and planted in the village square. He then 'made a speech on the benefits of the revolution and of liberty', and exhorted his parishioners to see to the flourishing of the tree, which he identified with those benefits.[7] Similar tree-planting ceremonies were held during the early

3. Douglass Adair and John Schutz, *Peter Oliver's Origin & Progress of the American Rebellion: A Tory View* (San Marino, CA: Huntington Library, 1961), 54.
4. See Arthur Schlesinger, 'Liberty Tree: a Genealogy', *New England Quarterly* 25(1) (1952) 435, 440.
5. See ibid, 441.
6. In the later years of the Revolution, this was made obligatory for each commune. See Andrée Corvol, 'The Transformation of a Political Symbol: Tree Festivals in France from the Eighteenth to the Twentieth Centuries', *French History* 4(4) (1990) 455, 476. On the connection between the American and French practice, see David Harden, 'Liberty Caps and Liberty Trees', *Past and Present* 146 (1995), 66, 80 et seq.
7. Henri Grégoire, *Essai historique et patriotique sur les arbres de la liberté* (Paris: Desenne, Bleuet, Firmin Didot, 1793–4), 21–22.

Figure 10 Philip Dawe, *The Bostonians Paying the Excise-Man, or Tarring & Feathering*, 1774, Pictorial Press Ltd / Alamy Stock Photo

1790s in villages, towns, and cities throughout the country. Grégoire claims that by 1794 there were more than 60,000 liberty trees in France.[8] While he advised the planting of oaks on account of their strength, longevity, and great height and girth,[9] there is evidence that poplars were also favoured, inasmuch as their Latin name — *populus* — was a homonym for 'the people'. Decorated

8. Ibid, 23.
9. Ibid, 26–28.

with flowers, ribbons, Phrygian caps, tricoloured flags, and message-bearing cards, liberty trees were the scene of dancing and a centrepiece of Jacobin spectacles.[10]

At the same time, they were emblems of solidarity with the French Revolution and its wider goals outside France. In England, liberty tree-planting ceremonies were held at numerous locations, until the practice was outlawed as part of the Pittite 'reign of alarm'.[11] As we have seen, toasts were raised to the tree of liberty, and it was celebrated as well in poems and songs.[12] It appeared in etchings,[13] and on commemorative objects such as tokens and countermarked coins.[14] In the mid-1790s Richard ('Citizen') Lee kept a shop in London called the 'Tree of Liberty', at which he sold radical literature.[15] Yet if all this connected English republicans with the revolutionary project in France and, before that, America, it also connected them with an English political tradition in which *trees* had long enjoyed a striking prominence. The famous attentive reader will have remarked that that has been reflected in this book. From Edmund Dudley's early sixteenth-century 'Tree of Commonwealth' onwards, trees have featured repeatedly in our discussion, both as metaphors and in the material form of forests, wood supplies and enclosure hedges. This chapter brings that arboreal preoccupation into focus, and with it the complex and contested interrelation of trees, liberty and the rights of man.

10. See Reay Tannahill (ed.), *Paris in the Revolution* (London: Folio Society, 1966), quoted in William Ruddick, 'Liberty Trees and Loyal Oaks: Emblematic Presences in some English Poems of the French Revolutionary Period', in Alison Yarrington and Kelvin Everest (eds.), *Reflections of Revolution: Images of Romanticism* (London: Routledge, 1993), 59, 60.
11. See Kenneth Johnston, *Unusual Suspects: Pitt's Reign of Alarm and the Lost Generation of the 1790s* (Oxford: Oxford University Press, 2013). On liberty tree-planting in England, see William Ruddick, 'Liberty Trees and Loyal Oaks: Emblematic Presences in some English Poems of the French Revolutionary Period', in Alison Yarrington and Kelvin Everest (eds.), *Reflections of Revolution: Images of Romanticism* (London: Routledge, 1993), 59, 60.
12. See also the entry in Charles Pigott's satirical *Political Dictionary*: '*Tree of Liberty–Habitat* where kings are not, and where priests are not.' Charles Pigott, *A Political Dictionary* (London: D.I. Eaton, 1795), 154.
13. By no means all of these were celebratory; see further below.
14. E.g. a token designed by Thomas Spence, depicting the tree of liberty as a maypole topped by the severed head of William Pitt, around which four men dance. See David Bindman, *The Shadow of the Guillotine: Britain and the French Revolution* (London: British Museum, 1989), 200 (fig. p) and 202 ('Tree of Liberty').
15. See Jane Douglas, 'Citizen Lee and the Tree of Liberty', *Factotum* No. 7 (December 1979), 8. Opened in 1795, the shop (later renamed the 'British Tree of Liberty') only survived for around a year, and even then Lee had to move it to different premises several times. It could be found at 2 St Ann's Court, Dean Street; then at 47 Haymarket; 98 Berwick Street; and 444 Strand.

Sweet days of freedom

How are we to understand the symbolic power of the tree of liberty? Historians tell us that it was an appropriation of the tree-related rituals that had long been associated with the coming of spring, and especially those involving the maypole.[16] Contemporaries, including the Abbé Grégoire, appear likewise to have understood it in that way.[17] It was no accident that, by his report, the original French liberty tree-planting occurred in the month of May. The poet Samuel Taylor Coleridge went so far as to argue that, at least where England was concerned, the maypole *was* the tree of liberty. For him, the revelries around the maypole, led in medieval tradition by a May king and queen, epitomised the experience of freedom. As he explains:

> Each village, in the absence of the Baron at the assembly of the nation, enjoyed a kind of Saturnalia. The vassals met upon the common green around the May-pole, where they elected a village lord, or king, as he was called, who chose his queen. He wore an oaken, and she a hawthorn wreath, and together they gave laws to the rustic sports during these sweet days of freedom. The MAY-POLE, then, is the *English Tree of Liberty*! Are there many yet standing?[18]

Writing in 1796, Coleridge highlights with his question at the end of that passage the unfreedom occasioned by the Pitt Government's recently intensified repression, including, perhaps, its prohibition of liberty trees.

But, of course, the linkage of trees and liberty is by no means exhausted by the maypole. Another longstanding trope concerns the idea of forests as settings for freedom.[19] In the legend of Robin Hood, the hero and his band

16. See, e.g., Arthur Schlesinger, 'Liberty Tree: a Genealogy', *New England Quarterly* 25(1) (1952) 435, 436, and Stephen Daniels, 'The Political Iconography of Woodland in Later Georgian England', in Denis Cosgrove and Stephen Daniels (eds.), *The Iconography of Landscape* (Cambridge: Cambridge University Press, 1988), 43, 57. A link is also suggested with the ancient Roman practice of displaying poles topped by Phrygian caps (these being a type of cap worn by emancipated slaves) as symbols of liberation from tyrannical rule. Certainly, poles and trees appear to have been used more or less interchangeably by the American colonists, and in France the Phrygian cap was a frequent decoration for liberty trees.
17. Henri Grégoire, *Essai historique et patriotique sur les arbres de la liberté* (Paris: Desenne, Bleuet, Firmin Didot, 1793–4), 19 et seq.
18. Samuel Taylor Coleridge (S. Coleridge, ed.), *Essays on his Own Times*, Vol. 1 (London: Pickering, 1850), 137 (emphasis in original).
19. I use the term forest in its modern sense. Contemporaries distinguished between 'forests', which were subject to forest law and had their origins in land requisitioned by the Normans for use as hunting grounds, and 'woods', which belonged to the manorial waste.

have escaped an unjust system of law to live in Sherwood Forest.[20] According to local lore, the oak tree — known as the 'Major Oak' — under which they slept still survives. The earliest Robin Hood ballads are believed to date from the fourteenth or perhaps thirteenth century.[21] Inasmuch as this was a period in which peasants and artisans were experiencing increasing hardship at the hands of ever-more demanding lords, the ballads have been understood as giving voice to the desire for justice and for a life free from exploitation and domination. They may also hint at the attenuation of the possibilities for lawful protest. As fears of popular rebellion led officials in many places to impose restrictions on public assembly, protest is imagined as moving away from towns and villages and into the relatively ungovernable zone of the forest.[22]

Forests are likewise places of escape, or, at any rate, of suspension of the normal laws of society and nature, in many of Shakespeare's plays. The Forest of Arden to which the exiles repair in *As You Like It*, the enchanted forest outside Athens in *A Midsummer Night's Dream*, and the strangely mobile Birnam Wood in *Macbeth* are only a few examples.[23] If the medieval association of forests with ungovernability still persisted in post-feudal times, the realities of enclosure invested it with new significance. Forests were among the areas in which a dispossessed peasant might just be able to eke out a living. Poaching game was frequently part of that, for while forest law protected game, which was supposed to be reserved for the royal hunt, enforcement remained patchy. Parochial control of forest populations was similarly weak, as was those populations' integration into the relations of clientage that were an important part of the disciplinary control exercised in many areas. Not yet fully colonised by the ruling powers, forests supported a form of life in which the practices and institutions of authority impinged less than virtually anywhere else, and forest communities became known for their independent spirit, distinctive

20. The earliest versions of the story refer not to Sherwood Forest, but rather to Barnsdale Forest in South Yorkshire. See Stephen Knight, *Robin Hood: A Mythic Biography* (Ithaca, NY: Cornell University Press, 2003), 13.
21. The earliest extant reference to Robin Hood appears in William Langland's late fourteenth-century *The Vision of Piers the Plowman*, though that reference is to a figure who was already familiar. See further Rodney Hilton, 'The Origins of Robin Hood', *Past and Present* 14 (1958) 30, 31.
22. On this aspect, see Richard Tardif, 'The "Mistery" of Robin Hood: a New Social Context for the Texts', in Stephen Knight and Soumyen Mukherjee (eds.), *Words and Worlds: Studies in the Social Role of Verbal Cultures* (Sydney: Sydney Association for Studies in Society and Culture, 1983), 130, 138.
23. See further Anne Barton, *The Shakespearean Forest* (Cambridge: Cambridge University Press, 2017).

culture, and religious nonconformity.[24] Deriving your subsistence from the forest after enclosure, or from other uncultivated land that formed part of the manorial waste, meant refusing to join the ranks of full-time wage-labourers and making as your home a terrain that was practically, and often also quite literally, on the borderlands of organised society.[25] The other side of that independence and liminality was the idea which we have encountered in earlier chapters that unenclosed forests and wastes were to be decried as breeding grounds for lawlessness, insubordination and crime.

No wood, no kingdom

In this book, as already recalled, the first reference to trees was to Edmund Dudley's 'Tree of Commonwealth'.[26] Laying out what he takes to be the proper structure of society and the moral principles upon which public welfare depends, Dudley likens the commonwealth — the realm and the collective interest of all its subjects — to a great tree. Its roots are the Christian faith, the fair administration of justice, honest dealing, social concord, and peace with other realms. Its fruits are honour, prosperity, tranquillity, and 'good example'. And the 'perilous cores' of those fruits, which permanently threaten the latter's enjoyment if not kept in check, are 'unreasonable elation', 'vain delectation', 'lewd enterprise' and 'glorification'. Thus, Dudley uses the imagery of the tree to suggest a political order that has firm and deep foundations, and that will flourish, provided the various groups which form its component parts do their duty and remain steadfast, according to their station. His metaphor patently trades on familiarity with the story of the Tree of Knowledge of Good and Evil in the Hebrew Bible. As in the Book of Genesis, expulsion from paradise is presented as a choice, with right conduct in the face of inevitable temptations as the key determinant.

At the same time, there was also a more local aspect of the context for Dudley's metaphor, which has to do with the importance of trees in the

24. See Robert Malcolmson, '"A Set of Ungovernable People": the Kingswood Colliers in the Eighteenth Century', in John Brewer and John Styles (eds.), *An Ungovernable People: The English and their Law in the Seventeenth and Eighteenth Centuries* (New Brunswick, NJ: Rutgers University Press, 1980), 85, 86.
25. See Carl Griffin, 'Protest Practice and (Tree) Cultures of Conflict: Understanding the Spaces of "Tree Maiming" in Eighteenth- and Early Nineteenth-Century England', *Transactions of the Institute of British Geographers* 33(1) (2007) 91, 97.
26. See chap. 2 above.

culture and economy of early modern England. While the early Christians had put a stop to the worship of 'sacred groves', evidence abounds that trees remained objects of quasi-religious veneration.[27] Branches were carried in May celebrations, an ancient yew stood in most churchyards, and parishioners gathered under 'gospel oaks' to hear readings of the scriptures. When it came to the annual parish perambulation, trees were typically the principal landmarks used to verify a community's territorial boundaries. Particular trees that were extraordinary in some way — whether due to their age, size, or shape, or to an association with historic events or prominent individuals — were often named, and were a source of considerable communal pride.

Conditioning this attitude to trees was the pivotal significance of wood in everyday and national life. Silviculturists draw a distinction between, on the one hand, 'timber' (large pieces of wood produced by allowing trees to grow to a reasonable size, and then felling and processing them) and, on the other hand, smaller pieces of wood that can be lopped or gathered from living trees. Timber, of course, was used in the construction and repair of buildings, as of farm equipment, carriages, boats, ships and other sailing vessels, bridges, wharves, windmills, and (mostly in the eighteenth century) canals. But when Dudley lived and for a long time thereafter, nothing happened without smaller pieces of wood, which (along with wood derivatives such as charcoal) were the main source of fuel. Brushwood and wood harvested from coppiced or pollarded trees also had a myriad of other household, craft and agricultural uses, while the bark of certain trees was employed in tanning.[28] As the agricultural writer Arthur Standish put it in 1611, 'no wood, no Kingdome'.[29]

One consequence of that state of affairs was considerable anxiety over security of supply. This briefly surfaces in another of the texts we have discussed, More's *Utopia*. Alluding to the constraints imposed by transport infrastructure, and to the difficulty and expense of getting timber and wood from places where it is in ready supply to places where it is in high demand, More has Raphael Hythloday tell of how the Utopians devised an ingenious plan of woodland management. In Utopia, he says, 'you can see a forest which they tore up by the roots with their own hands and moved to another site'. Hythloday explains that '[t]hey did this not so much for the sake of better growth but to make transport easier, by having wood closer to the sea, the

27. See Keith Thomas, *Man and the Natural World* (London: Penguin, 1984), 212 et seq.
28. See further Tom Williamson, Gerry Barnes and Toby Pillatt, *Trees in England* (Hatfield: University of Hertfordshire Press, 2017).
29. Arthur Standish, *The Commons Complaint* (London: William Stansby, 1611), 2.

rivers, or the cities themselves'. 'For grain is easier than wood to carry by land over a long distance', as he aptly observes.[30]

Standish's own approach to better woodland management centred on a less fantastical (though similarly unrealised) scheme of nation-wide tree-planting. His perspective on the issues came from living through the Midland Rising of 1607 and subsequently visiting the areas affected.[31] To his mind, a major part of what had caused the uprising was the destruction of woodlands and the resulting high price of wood in regions like the Midlands where woodlands were already relatively sparse. The 'desperate tree of want' was the problem, he declared, referring both to the hardships of the poor and, by implicit chiasmus, to the want (or lack) of trees,[32] and only a 'generall planting of wood' could solve that problem.[33]

Mobilised to an argument about the preservation of the established order, which then drew on this association with prudential public policy, Dudley's Tree of Commonwealth contrasts markedly with the Major Oak of the ungovernable forest. So too it contrasts with yet another of this book's trees, Kett's Tree of Reformation.[34] According to the chroniclers of the 1549 rebellion which Kett led, it was agreed at an early stage by those camped on Mousehold Heath that 'a place should be appointed, where judgements might bee exercised, as in a judiciall hall'. 'Whereupon', the chronicler Holinshed writes, 'they found a great old oke, where the said Ket, and the other governors or deputies might sit and place themselves, to heare and determine such quareling matters as came in question . . . This oke they named the tree of reformation.'[35]

The later chronicler Neville describes the tree as having 'great spred boughes', which the campmen 'laid over with raftes and balkes acrosse' and covered with 'a roofe [made of] boords'.[36] An outdoor court, but also the

30. Thomas More, *Utopia*, in George Logan and Robert Adams (eds.), *Thomas More: Utopia* (Cambridge: Cambridge University Press, rev. ed., 2002), 1, 75. My attention was directed to this passage by Vin Nardizzi, *Wooden Os: Shakespeare's Theatres and England's Trees* (Toronto: University of Toronto Press, 2013), 3–4 and passim.
31. On the Midland Rising, see chap. 3 above and the references there cited.
32. Arthur Standish, *The Commons Complaint* (London: William Stansby, 1611), Preface to the Reader, page B.
33. Arthur Standish, *New Directions of Experience to the Commons Complaint* (London: N. Okes, 1613), 4.
34. On Kett's rebellion, see chap. 3 above and the references there cited.
35. Raphael Holinshed, *Holinshed's Chronicles of England, Scotlande, and Irelande, Vol. 3* (London: John Harrison, 1577), 967.
36. Alexander Neville (Rich Wood trans.), *Norfolke Furies, and their Foyle under Kett* (London: Casson, 1623), sigC3v.

seat of a governing council and a platform or pulpit from which speeches were delivered, the Tree of Reformation was the site of, and a metonym for, the self-governing institutions of Norfolk's rebellious commoners. Norwich gentlemen got stripped of their fine clothing and forced to hide among the trees of Thorpe Wood,[37] while under this oak — for a time — the possibility came to light of an alternative, popular authority. That the contemporary keyword 'reformation' was used was significant inasmuch as, in its received sense, it denoted a process of change initiated by the powerful and realised without disturbance to established hierarchies.[38]

Kett's Rebellion began with the 'throwing down' of enclosures. Enclosure did not always involve the putting in place of physical boundaries, but it often did, and in most places those boundaries were hedges — 'dead' hedges constructed from interwoven branches (i.e. fences), or living ('quick') hedges made of growing trees. Trees, then, played a major part in the production of private property. Enclosers set them to work to help make possession exclusive.[39] And since the corollary of that was to dispossess commoners of their rights, trees also entered the story at the other end, so to speak, for among the rights of which commoners were dispossessed through processes of enclosure were rights of access to woodlands and wood. In the mid-seventeenth century the Digger leader Gerrard Winstanley used arboreal language to deliver a warning that the oppression of the poor had not ended with the execution of Charles I and the establishment of a republic in England. Signalling the dual character of trees as both 'objects of cultivation, and the site of a battle for rights',[40] he affirmed that oppression was 'a great tree still'. With 'many branches and great roots', it 'keeps off the sun of freedome from the poor Commons still'.[41]

A Declaration issued by Winstanley and forty-four others announced the Diggers' intention 'to take both Common Land and Common woods to

37. See James Holstun, 'Utopia Pre-Empted: Kett's Rebellion, Commoning, and the Hysterical Sublime', *Historical Materialism* 16 (2008) 3, 10.
38. See Andy Wood, *The 1549 Rebellions and the Making of Early Modern England* (Cambridge: Cambridge University Press, 2007), 144.
39. See Nicholas Blomley, 'Making Private Property: Enclosure, Common Right and the Work of Hedges', *Rural History* 18(1) (2007) 1.
40. James Holstun, 'Rational Hunger: Gerrard Winstanley's Hortus Inconclusus', in James Holstun (ed.), *Pamphlet Wars: Prose in the English Revolution* (Portland, OR: Frank Cass, 1992), 158, 192.
41. Gerrard Winstanley, *A New-yeers Gift*, in Thomas Corns, Ann Hughes and David Loewenstein (eds.), *The Complete Works of Gerrard Winstanley, Vol. II* (Oxford: Oxford University Press, 2009), 107, 112.

be a livelihood for us'.[42] Enclosers were cutting down trees on commons and wastes, and selling the timber for their own private enrichment, and the Diggers were resolved to be 'cheated no longer'. They would 'Dig and Plough up the Commons, and waste Lands', and would themselves 'lay hold upon, and as we stand in need, . . . cut and fell, and . . . make the best advantage we can of the Woods and Trees, that grow upon the Commons', using those 'Woods and Trees' in part as a means 'to provide us [and our poor Brethren] bread to eat, till the Fruit of our labors in the Earth bring forth increase'. In the name of 'all the poor oppressed people of England, and the whole world', the Diggers objurgated the self-seeking 'wood-mongers', and asserted their determination to 'plant', and also reclaim, 'the pleasant fruit trees of freedom'. For '[m]oney shall not any longer . . . be the great god, that hedges in some, and hedges out others'.

After the Restoration, the fight to control and, as the Diggers put it, 'make the best advantage' of England's trees moved decisively in favour of the wood-mongers, whose attention now turned to the development of a new, 'scientific' approach to woodland management. Among the many works advancing and fostering that interest was John Evelyn's *Sylva*.[43] Initially published in 1664 and reissued posthumously in several editions between 1776 and the early nineteenth century, *Sylva* was the very first text to appear under the imprimatur of the Royal Society. It originated in a paper prepared by Evelyn and collaborators in response to a request by the Commissioner of the Navy for advice on how best to secure stocks of naval timber. Standish had been largely focused on energy security, but by the later seventeenth century the use of coal was becoming more widespread, and for Evelyn the key issue was timber production. There was concern that the country's reserves of timber had become seriously depleted due to factors that included wood-consuming industrial processes (notably, the production of iron and glass), land clearance for agricultural 'improvement', and lax administration of royal forests. Evelyn's response was to renew Standish's call for a general plantation and provide detailed instruction on how to achieve success in commercial

42. *A Declaration from the Poor Oppressed People of England* (Digger Manifesto No. 2), 1649. The succeeding quotations in this paragraph also come from this (unpaginated) text. On the Diggers, see chap. 4 above and the references there cited.
43. John Evelyn, *Sylva, or a Discourse of Forest-Trees, and the Propagation of Timber in His Majesties Dominions* (London: Jo. Martyn and Ja. Allestry, 1664). It is now believed that, although Evelyn's role in this work was central, *Sylva* originated in a collective project. See Beryl Hartley, 'Exploring and Communicating Knowledge of Trees in the Early Royal Society', *Notes and Records of the Royal Society* 64 (2010) 229, 230.

forestry, reframing what was at stake in terms of a happy alignment of patriotic duty with money-making opportunity. Timber, and especially oak, he wrote, is the 'only support of that Navigation which makes us fear'd abroad, and flourish at Home', and improving gentlemen who are also 'good Patriots' will do well to reflect on that.[44]

Albion's fatal tree[45]

Historical research has shown that the concern about timber depletion was somewhat exaggerated, but it resonated with those to whom *Sylva* and other similar works were addressed, and the century that followed indeed saw a 'Great Replanting', only partially offset by ongoing land clearance.[46] As discussed in chapter 7, this period also saw the rise of landscape parks, with designers artfully arranging trees to provide 'pleasing prospects' from palatial houses. Both commercial tree-planting and decorative landscaping served as tokens of confidence in the future, and to that extent, earnests of the permanence of England's Glorious Revolution.[47] What then of the mass of unpropertied men and women whose revolution it was not, and for whom Evelyn and his peers did not write?

While the trend towards coal was consolidated in the eighteenth century, so that wood ceased to be the primary industrial fuel, and also ceased to be the primary domestic fuel in the households of the rich, poor people continued to depend on burning wood. Under forest law, commoners had the right to take both dead wood lying on the ground ('lops and tops') and 'snapwood', by which was meant whatever could be snapped off a tree by hand or pulled down with a hook fixed to the end of a pole ('by hook or by crook'). This was the 'common of estovers', and it was fiercely defended when enclosure turned custom into crime. Wood theft is said to have been the most prevalent offence against private property at this time.[48] Commoners also engaged in

44. John Evelyn, *Sylva, or a Discourse of Forest-Trees, and the Propagation of Timber in His Majesties Dominions* (London: Jo. Martyn and Ja. Allestry, 1664), 112.
45. Douglas Hay et al., *Albion's Fatal Tree: Crime and Society in Eighteenth-Century England* (London: Verso, 2nd ed., 2011).
46. See Tom Williamson, 'The Management of Trees and Woods in Eighteenth-Century England', in Laura Auricchio, Elizabeth Heckendorn Cook and Giulia Pacini (eds.), *Invaluable Trees: Cultures of Nature, 1660–1830* (Oxford: Voltaire Foundation, 2012), 221, esp. 223–25.
47. See ibid, 226.
48. See Bob Bushaway, *By Rite: Custom, Ceremony and Community in England 1770–1880* (London: Junction Books, 1982), 208.

hostile 'wood maiming' — the cutting down of newly planted trees in gentry enclosures.[49] Evelyn advocated severe punishments for wood-stealing and attacks on young trees,[50] though perhaps even he did not fully anticipate the 1723 Black Act, by which it was made a capital offence to 'cut down or otherwise destroy any trees planted in any avenue, or growing in any garden, orchard or plantation, for ornament, shelter or profit'.[51]

Prompted by that harbinger of the sanguinary criminal code of eighteenth-century England, let us notice a final tree — *the* final one, the 'tree' that ended human life. Execution has, of course, a long and varied association with trees, but in the time and place we investigate here, the tree was a euphemism for the gallows, which were fabricated out of timber and in their simplest form emulated the shape of a trunk and bough.[52] In Blake's poem *Jerusalem*, the 'hanging tree' is the 'fatal tree' under which 'Albion slept'.[53] As recalled in an earlier chapter, Blake lived in London, where, two centuries earlier, a novel form of gallows had been erected at Tyburn near the present site of Marble Arch at the intersection of Edgware Road, Bayswater Road and Oxford Street (formerly called Tyburn Road). The 'Tyburn tree' or 'triple tree' consisted of three posts of three or four metres high connected by crossbeams at the top.[54] What made it novel was that it could be used to hang multiple prisoners at once. In the eighteenth century the Tyburn tree was not used to execute more people than in former centuries, but it was used to execute a higher proportion of people for small property offences.[55] At Tyburn, as at the country's other gallows, 'each hanging repeated the lesson "Respect Private Property"'.[56]

49. On this, see Carl Griffin, 'Protest Practice and (Tree) Cultures of Conflict: Understanding the Spaces of "Tree Maiming" in Eighteenth- and Early Nineteenth-Century England', *Transactions of the Institute of British Geographers* 33(1) (2007) 91.
50. John Evelyn, *Sylva, or a Discourse of Forest-Trees, and the Propagation of Timber in His Majesties Dominions* (London: Jo. Martyn and Ja. Allestry, 1664), 108.
51. That said, in the passage just referenced Evelyn likened wood-stealing to horse-stealing, which was punishable by death. For the text of the Black Act, see E. P. Thompson, *Whigs and Hunters* (London: Allen Lane, 1975), Appendix 1: the Black Act; this provision appears at 271.
52. See further Vic Gatrell, *The Hanging Tree: Execution and the English People 1770–1868* (Oxford: Oxford University Press, 1994).
53. 'Where Albion slept beneath the Fatal Tree, / And the Druid's golden Knife,/Rioted in human gore, / In Offerings of Human Life.' See William Blake, *Jerusalem: The Emanation of the Giant Albion*, Plate 27, in David Erdman (ed.), *The Complete Poetry and Prose of William Blake* (New York: Anchor, rev. ed., 1988), 172 (and the reference in the same poem to Tyburn's fatal Tree [Plate 12, 155]).
54. See further Peter Linebaugh, 'The Tyburn Riot against the Surgeons', in Douglas Hay et al. (eds.), *Albion's Fatal Tree* (London: Verso, rev. ed., 2011), 65, 66.
55. See Peter Linebaugh, *The London Hanged* (London: Verso, 2006), 50–51.
56. Ibid, xxii.

The last hanging at Tyburn took place on 3 November 1783, after which executions were carried out on a scaffold outside Newgate Prison. It seems that local residents and businesses in the newly fashionable area to the north of Oxford Street near Edgware Road lobbied for the move.[57] At the same time, the hanging of multiple prisoners at once met with growing disapproval. Edmund Burke was among those who spoke against it. Mass hangings dissipated and weakened the effect of execution on the labouring classes, he maintained. To ensure that the law retained its capacity to instil reverence and terror, a more judicious approach to the death penalty was needed.[58] Burke's argument helped to bring about the demise of the Tyburn tree. Yet his arboreal interests by no means ended there — and nor do ours. If we now take up the story in the decade that followed the French Revolution, it will appear that he and others were parties to a lively exchange about trees which encompassed many issues, aspects and species, but perhaps especially the liberty tree.

Under the British oak

As a point of entry, we can take a well-known passage from *Reflections*, in which Burke offers that, from the vantage-point of the 'French gentleman' to whom his text is purportedly a letter, it may appear that views such as those expressed by Richard Price reflect widely held opinions in England.[59] But nothing could be further from the truth.

> Because half a dozen grasshoppers under a fern make the field ring with their importunate chink, whilst thousands of great cattle, reposed beneath the shadow of the British oak, chew the cud and are silent, pray do not imagine that those who make the noise are the only inhabitants of the field; that, of course, they are many in number; or that, after all, they are other than the little shrivelled, meagre, hopping, though loud and troublesome insects of the hour.[60]

57. See Vic Gatrell, *The Hanging Tree: Execution and the English People 1770–1868* (Oxford: Oxford University Press, 1994), 602.
58. Burke's views were framed in relation to the aftermath of the Gordon Riots of 1780. See Edmund Burke, 'Some Thoughts on the Approaching Executions 10 July 1780', in Warren Elofson and John Woods (eds.), *The Writings and Speeches of Edmund Burke, Vol. 3* (Oxford: Oxford University Press, 1996), 611.
59. On Richard Price, see chap. 5 above.
60. Edmund Burke, *Reflections on the Revolution in France* (London: Penguin, 1968), 181.

What makes this passage notable is less Burke's withering condescension towards those in England who are disposed to welcome the French Revolution than the imagery through which that condescension is expressed. Burke analogises the state to one of the large landed estates that increasingly dominated his country's rural landscape.[61] In this estate, he invites us to think of the silent majority of the British people as sturdy cattle, chewing the cud contentedly beneath the protective shade of an old oak, and of Price and his ilk as so many tiny grasshoppers, hopping about and disturbing the peace, but ultimately insignificant.

The symbolism of the oak would have been lost on none of Burke's readers. Most obviously, it evoked the royal oak — the oak at Boscobel Wood in which Charles II is said to have hidden in 1651 to escape the Roundheads after the Battle of Worcester. On the Restoration of the monarchy in 1660, Parliament declared 'Royal Oak Day' (also known as 'Oak Apple Day') a public holiday to commemorate the event, and it remained a public holiday until the mid-nineteenth century.[62] Linked to that association, but also predating it, the oak was a familiar symbol of national strength, manly character, and constitutional stability. As recalled above, oak was used in the construction of boats and ships, and although by the late eighteenth century considerable quantities of that and other kinds of shipbuilding timber were imported, British oak — and especially its hardest central part ('heart') — remained the favoured material for the frames of warships.[63] In 1759 the actor, playwright and theatre manager David Garrick wrote the lyrics for a song called *Hearts of Oak* ('Hearts of oak are our ships, jolly tars are our men, / We always are ready, / Steady, boys, steady, / We'll fight and we'll conquer again and again') that became an anthem of the Royal Navy.[64]

When a great man died, it was common for the funeral eulogy to describe him as a 'spreading oak'.[65] The oak is a slow-growing, deciduous tree, with

61. See Stephen Daniels, 'The Political Iconography of Woodland in Later Georgian England', in Denis Cosgrove and Stephen Daniels (eds.), *The Iconography of Landscape* (Cambridge: Cambridge University Press, 1988), 43, 45.
62. See further http://calendarcustoms.com/articles/oak-apple-day/ and http://www.woodlandtrust.presscentre.com/News-Releases/Royal-Oak-Day-returns-to-England-7cb.aspx. Regarding Oak Apple Day in the present, see Roger Deakin, *Wildwood: A Journey Through Trees* (London: Penguin, 2008), 85–94.
63. See Miles Hadfield, *Landscape with Trees* (London: Country Life, 1967), 110.
64. See http://ballads.bodleian.ox.ac.uk/static/images/sheets/20000/18025.gif. 'Tar' is a word for 'sailor', thought perhaps to come from 'tarpaulin'.
65. See Keith Thomas, *Man and the Natural World* (London: Penguin, 1984), 218.

the potential for remarkable longevity. Keith Thomas reports that, in the late eighteenth century, the Greendale Oak at Welbeck in Nottinghamshire was over 700 years old, while Salcey Forest in Northamptonshire had an oak tree said to have been in existence for 1500 years.[66] In 1670 a forestry expert claimed that some living oaks in England dated from before the Flood, while a few went back to Creation.[67] Against that backdrop, Burke is suggesting as well the idea of the organic constitution and its long history and steady, patient rhythm of change.[68] As he puts it in another passage in *Reflections*, '[o]ur political system' moves through a cyclical pattern of 'decay, fall, renovation, and progression'.[69] 'We compensate, we reconcile, we balance', and by that means we achieve a 'well-sustained progress'. To bring about reform while also preserving the 'useful parts' of existing establishments, 'time is required'. 'A process of this kind is slow', he repeats. 'It is not fit for an assembly [such as the French] which glories in performing in a few months the work of ages.'[70]

But what is perhaps most important of all in Burke's image is the 'shadow' of the oak. The French may have proclaimed themselves citizens, but Burke's grazing cattle enjoy a shade which puts one firmly in mind of subjects under the benevolent care and protection of the state. In this regard, the aristocracy had a particular role in his view. Writing to the Duke of Richmond in 1772, Burke hailed his noble addressee with the words: 'You people of great families and hereditary Trusts and fortunes . . . if you are what you ought to be are the great Oaks that shade a Country and perpetuate your benefits from Generation to Generation.' Burke went on to say that the immediate power of a particular peer was 'not so much of moment but if their conduct and example hands down their principles to their successors; then their houses become the publick repositories and offices of Record for the constitution'.[71] Then they become the country's leaders and provide stable, virtuous government.

66. Ibid, 217.
67. John Smith, quoted in Keith Thomas, *Man and the Natural World* (London: Penguin, 1984), 217.
68. See Tim Fulford, 'Cowper, Wordsworth, Clare: The Politics of Trees', *John Clare Society Journal* 14 (1995) 47.
69. See chap. 5 above for a more extensive quotation from this passage. Edmund Burke, *Reflections on the Revolution in France* (London: Penguin, 1968), 120.
70. Edmund Burke, *Reflections on the Revolution in France* (London: Penguin, 1968), 281, 280.
71. Edmund Burke, Letter to the Duke of Richmond, 15 November 1772, reprinted in H. C. Mansfield (ed.), *Selected Letters of Edmund Burke* (Chicago: University of Chicago Press, 1984), 179, 184.

There is another feature we should notice here, which has to do with the quality of the light in Burke's oak-shaded field. It would be a soft, dappled light, a refracted light, far removed from the enlightening glare and levelling drive of the new political environment in France. Thus, in a study of the political iconography of woodland in later Georgian England, Stephen Daniels observes that Burke 'constructed a politics of landscape which counterposed the chiaroscuro of maturely wooded English parkland to the clarity and brilliance of "experimental" landscapes like the "geometrical constitution" of revolutionary France'.[72] As against France's 'new conquering empire of light and reason', Burke depicted an English constitution that 'harmonized the different shades of life', beautified and softened relations in 'private society', and 'made power gentle, and obedience liberal'.[73]

These various points of contrast are well captured in a pair of painted engravings of the period (fig. 11).[74] The two engravings look at first glance quite similar; each depicts a similarly sized oak tree against the backdrop of a light sky. On closer inspection, however, that superficial resemblance only serves to cast in relief some very sharp disparities. One tree, captioned 'A Foreign Tree', is assigned the mock Latin genus 'Subitarius' (from the Latin *subitus,* meaning 'sudden' or 'rash'). This oak looks sick; its branches are sparse, and at the top is a skull in a cloud of black smoke. Labels appear at the foot of the tree, as well as along each branch: 'Confusion', 'Infidelity', 'Misery'. A snake marked 'Imaginary Rights of Man' curls around the trunk, and in the background are scenes of fighting and a guillotine. The other tree, captioned 'British Tree of True Liberty', is assigned the mock Latin genus 'Stabilissimus' (from the superlative of the Latin *stabilis*, meaning 'stable'). This one is clearly flourishing; its leaves are abundant, and rays of sunshine radiate from the top. Again there are labels, but this time they read: 'Happiness', 'Religion',

72. Stephen Daniels, 'The Political Iconography of Woodland in Later Georgian England', in Denis Cosgrove and Stephen Daniels (eds.), *The Iconography of Landscape* (Cambridge: Cambridge University Press, 1988), 43, 46.

73. Edmund Burke, *Reflections on the Revolution in France* (London: Penguin, 1968), 171. On this, see chap. 8 above.

74. I have been unable to discover the artist. For a variation on the same theme, see Gillray's 'The Tree of Liberty — with the Devil Tempting John Bull', available at: http://commons.wikimedia.org/wiki/File:Tree_of_liberty.jpg.

'Prosperity'. In the background is a delightful scene with ships at sea, a village around a church, and people walking in well-tended countryside. For Burke, it seems, this British oak — which bears no decorations, features in no spectacles, and is the site of no ceremonies — is indeed the true tree of liberty.

Figure 11a *A foreign tree*, subitarius Engraving, Musée de la Révolution française. Inv. MRF 1988.72.2, © Coll. Musée de la Révolution française / Domaine de Vizille

Figure 11b *British tree of true Liberty*, stabilissimus Engraving, Musée de la Révolution française. Inv. MRF 1988.72.1, © Coll. Musée de la Révolution française / Domaine de Vizille

Fair budding branch

I mentioned earlier Coleridge and his 'political appropriation of the symbolism of the maypole', as one scholar terms it.[75] Coleridge's poem *The Raven*, composed in 1798, is also of interest in our present context inasmuch

75. Essaka Joshua, *The Romantics and the May Day Tradition* (Aldershot: Ashgate, 2007), 64.

as it opens by bringing into the mind's eye, like Burke's text, an oak tree in a field under which animals feed. Only now the oak is decidedly old, the animals are swine crunching mast ('Underneath an old oak tree / There was of swine a huge company . . .'), and when a high wind begins to blow, the tree can no longer provide shelter, and the animals need to move away. In doing so, they leave behind a single acorn. A raven picks up the acorn ('Next came a raven, that liked not such folly: / He belonged, they did say, to the witch Melancholy!'), and buries it. Years pass, and one day the raven returns with his mate to find that the acorn has grown into a tall oak. The pair build a nest in the tree, and young arrive. But soon a woodman comes, and the tree is felled, killing the young and causing their mother to die of a broken heart. The dead tree is cut up for timber which is then used to make a ship. On its first voyage, however, and still within sight of the land, the ship encounters a massive storm, and is sunk. As the wreck goes down, the raven flies round and round overhead, cawing with mad pleasure ('Right glad was the Raven and off he went fleet . . . / They had taken his all, and revenge it was sweet').[76]

In later life the poet abjured his dissident beliefs,[77] but in 1794 he developed, together with Robert Southey, a scheme for a community without private property, to be governed according to a principle the two men called 'pantisocracy' — everyone's government.[78] In 1795 he delivered a lecture in which he spoke the absurdity of treating equality as a matter of equality of rights, and not equality of condition (as if it is enough that a poor man 'should possess the same Right to an Hovel which [rich men] claim to a Palace').[79] The lecture was part of a series reportedly arranged to raise money for the pantisocracy scheme. In another lecture in the series, Coleridge expatiates on the multiplying anti-sedition laws, high-profile treason trials and repeated suspensions of *habeas corpus* that were the Pitt government's response to British Jacobinism. After warning his audience that 'we have been impelled by dark and terrifying Generalities to sacrifice the personal Security of ourselves and perhaps of our posterity', he expresses what he takes to be the current reality

76. *The Raven*, in Samuel Taylor Coleridge (William Keach, ed.), *The Complete Poems* (London: Penguin, 1997), 131.
77. See, e.g., Samuel Taylor Coleridge, Letter to George Coleridge dated c. 10 March 1798, in Earl Leslie Griggs, *Collected Letters of Samuel Taylor Coleridge, Vol. I: 1785–1800* (Oxford: Clarendon Press, 1956), 394, esp. 397 ('I have snapped my squeaking baby-trumpet of Sedition & the fragments lie scattered in the lumber-room of Penitence').
78. The scheme was never implemented.
79. Samuel Taylor Coleridge, *Conciones ad Populum, or Address to the People* (1795), 32, available at archive.org/details/concionesadpopuloocole.

in terms that again involve a tree.[80] The witch Melancholy of his gothic fable about the raven again appears, though now as the tree itself, a 'melancholy memorial of conquered Freedom'.

> The august and lofty Tree, which while it rose above the palace of the Monarch, sheltered the distant dwelling of the Cottager, stripped of its boughs, now stands the melancholy memorial of conquered Freedom. — We can only water its roots with our tears, or look forward with anxious eye to the distant Springtide, when it shall branch forth anew![81]

As Coleridge portrays it, the tree that 'rose above the palace of the Monarch' now stood stripped and diminished. But was that the problem — or was the problem rather, or in addition, that the 'palace of the Monarch' still stood? In previous chapters of this book, we have seen that, for Thomas Paine, Pitt's repression was not the *cause* of a political malfunction. It was a *symptom* of something deeper. The real issue was the outdated British constitution, preserving as it did the hereditary power and privilege of the monarchy and aristocracy. Paine grew up, as has also been noted, in the shadow of the powerful Duke of Grafton.[82] The Grafton family lived at Euston Hall, on an estate inherited by the first Duke of Grafton in the late seventeenth century. Around Euston Hall was an exceptionally large and magnificent landscape park. The original park and gardens had been laid out shortly before the estate came into the possession of the first Duke by the author of *Sylva*, John Evelyn.

Between 1730 and 1748 the park was altered and expanded according to a plan by the famous architect and pioneer of English landscape design, William Kent. Part of the project included razing and re-siting the village of Euston, a course of action said to have been undertaken to improve the view from the second Duke's bedroom.[83] Paine left Thetford in the 1750s, but between 1767 and 1783 the park was further developed and expanded for the third Duke of Grafton by Lancelot 'Capability' Brown. The agricultural writer Arthur Young visited the Grafton estate in the late 1760s as part of his tour around rural England, commenting in his published diary that the park and plantations were 'very expensive and sketched with great taste'.[84] It will

80. Ibid, 51.
81. Ibid.
82. See chap. 5 above.
83. See John Keane, *Tom Paine: A Political Life* (London: Bloomsbury, 1995), 13.
84. Arthur Young, *A Six Weeks Tour, Through the Southern Counties of England and Wales* (London, 1769), 50, quoted in John Keane, *Tom Paine: A Political Life* (London: Bloomsbury, 1995), 10.

be recalled from an earlier chapter that, after 1789, Young wrote with alarm about the 'plunder' of landed estates across the Channel. The right to property in the French Declaration of the Rights of Man and the Citizen was a '[tree] of goodly appearance', but it needed to be judged by the actual 'fruit [it had] produced'.[85]

If Paine and the young Coleridge can be bracketed together for some purposes, the older man was emphatically not a poet. Commentators often emphasise the plain, accessible style of Paine's writing, and in *Rights of Man* he emphasises this himself, claiming to eschew Burke's 'gay and flowery' language for straightforward prose that tells things as they are, and can be understood by all.[86] At the very end of *Rights of Man*, however, the author allows himself a rare extended metaphor, albeit one that remains consistent with his communicative style in appealing to ordinary experience. He asks his readers to imagine him in the middle of (an English) February, leaving his desk to head out for a bracing countryside walk:

> Were I to take a turn into the country, the trees would present a leafless, winterly appearance. As people are apt to pluck twigs as they walk along, I perhaps might do the same, and by chance might observe that a *single bud* on that twig had begun to swell. I should reason very unnaturally, or rather not reason at all, to suppose *this* was the *only bud* in England which had this appearance.[87]

If one bud appears on a twig, this is a sure sign that spring is on the way, and that buds will soon be appearing on trees everywhere. He goes on:

> [T]hough the vegetable sleep will continue longer on some trees and plants than on others, and though some of them may not *blossom* for two or three years, all will be in leaf in the summer, except those which are *rotten*.[88]

And finally, in case there is still doubt, Paine makes known that he speaks of seasonal change for the sake of delivering a message about political change. Far from being 'distant', Coleridge's 'Springtide' of renewed freedom is very near at hand:

> What pace the political summer may keep with the natural, no human foresight can determine. It is, however, not difficult to perceive that the spring is begun.[89]

85. See chap. 7 above.
86. Thomas Paine, *Rights of Man, Part I*, in Bruce Kuklick (ed.), *Paine: Political Writings* (Cambridge: Cambridge University Press, 2000), 57, 70.
87. Thomas Paine, *Rights of Man, Part II*, in Bruce Kuklick (ed.), *Paine: Political Writings* (Cambridge: Cambridge University Press, 2000), 155, 262.
88. Ibid, 262–63.
89. Ibid, 263.

Paine's 'turn' into the country has been read as the trope, or linguistic turn, that he hopes will help to turn a country, make a revolution.[90] It is also a trope that returns us to Burke's oak-shaded field and turns it around. What has happened to that serene scene? Coleridge had swine crunching mast under an oak that could not provide shelter against the wind and seems to have been too old for a woodman to bother cutting down for timber. In Paine's text, the contented 'silence' and 'repose' of Burke's 'thousands of great cattle' becomes a 'vegetable sleep' from which the natural world is now beginning to awake. The political spring is coming, and all the trees will soon be in leaf, 'except those which are rotten'.

We may suspect that Paine considers Burke's oak to be that latter category. Indeed, Paine seems to confirm this in an earlier passage of *Rights of Man*. The context is a discussion of the storming of the Bastille. Paine notes that Burke is greatly preoccupied by certain outrages committed by the revolutionaries: a number of people were murdered, and their heads carried around the city on spikes. Paine then writes: 'Let us therefore examine how men came by the idea of punishing in this manner. They learn it from the governments they live under.' Sanguinary punishment instructs men 'how to punish when power falls into their hands'. Adapting the well-known verse from the gospel of St Matthew about the 'tree which bringeth not forth good fruit', he concludes: 'Lay then the axe to the root, and teach governments humanity.'[91]

Although accused by his conservative detractors of 'levelling', we have seen that Paine vehemently disclaimed the label.[92] With his tongue only slightly in his cheek, he argued that the real 'levellers' were those who supported the persistence of a monarchical system which indiscriminately admitted to rulership whoever (wise or stupid, virtuous or vicious) inherited a noble title. Following E. P. Thompson, we might observe that Paine's main quarrel was not with the system of property relations *per se*, and nor was it with new breed of commercially minded tenant farmers and urban manufacturers. It was with the 'great landed aristocracy . . . where the hereditary principle involved

90. See Tom Furniss, 'Rhetoric in Revolution: the Role of Language in Paine's Critique of Burke', in Keith Hanley and Raman Selden (eds.), *Revolution and English Romanticism: Politics and Rhetoric* (London: Palgrave Macmillan, 1991), 23, 42.
91. Thomas Paine, *Rights of Man, Part I*, in Bruce Kuklick (ed.), *Paine: Political Writings* (Cambridge: Cambridge University Press, 2000), 57, 77–78. Matthew, 3:10: 'And now also the axe is laid unto the root of the trees: therefore every tree which bringeth not forth good fruit is hewn down, and cast into the fire.'
92. See chap. 8 above.

in . . . primogeniture gave him offence'.[93] So when Paine writes of the political spring, he is writing of new growth made possible by the uprooting of the old regime of privilege and property—'Old England'.

This is already suggested in one of his earliest texts, the lyrics of a song entitled *Liberty Tree*, written in 1775 for a magazine Paine edited when he first arrived in Philadelphia. The song describes a mock myth-of-origin that has the Goddess of Liberty descending from the heavens to bring the future tree of liberty to America:

> In a chariot of light from the regions of day,
> The Goddess of Liberty came:
> Ten thousand celestials directed the way,
> And hither conducted the dame.
> A fair budding branch from the gardens above,
> Where millions with millions agree,
> She brought in her hand, as a pledge of her love,
> And the plant she named LIBERTY TREE.[94]

Almost two decades later, *Rights of Man* bids us follow the course of that 'fair budding branch' (or, as it would then appear, 'twig'), via France, to England.

A false tree of liberty

In his 1801 pamphlet *The Restorer of Society to its Natural State*,[95] Thomas Spence tells the story of an encounter he once had with a forester in a wood near Hexham, about forty kilometres east of where Spence came from in Newcastle upon Tyne. He was alone gathering nuts when the forester put his head through the bushes, and asked what he (Spence) was doing there. 'I answered gathering nuts.' '[G]athering nuts! said he, and dare you say so?' 'Yes, said I, why not? Would you question a monkey, or a squirrel, about such a business?' Spence then asked: 'But who are you . . . that thus take

93. E. P. Thompson, *The Making of the English Working Class* (London: Vintage, 1966), 96.
94. Thomas Paine, *Liberty Tree* (1775), available at: http://bartleby.com/338/2.html.
95. Thomas Spence, *The Restorer of Society to its Natural State in a series of letters to a fellow citizen* (London: J. Smith, 1801), reprinted in H. T. Dickinson, *The Political Works of Thomas Spence* (Newcastle upon Tyne: Avero, 1982), 69. The text takes the form of fourteen letters dated between 19 July and 27 December 1800, together with an introductory text dated 5 February 1801. Spence was tried and imprisoned for the publication of this pamphlet. See further chaps. 7 and 8 above.

upon you to interrupt me?' To which the forester replied: 'I'll let you know that . . . when I lay you fast for trespassing here.' Spence pretended not to understand. 'But how can I trespass here where no man ever planted or cultivated, for these nuts are the spontaneous gifts of nature ordained alike for the sustenance of man and beast that choose to gather them, and therefore they are common.' No, said the forester, 'this wood is no common. It belongs to the Duke of Portland.' 'Oh! My service to the Duke . . .', Spence rejoined in mock-obeisance, before reminding the official that 'nature knows no more of him than of me. Therefore, as in nature's storehouse, the rule is "First come, first served," so the Duke of Portland must look sharp if he wants any nuts.' It was a joke, of course. '[I]n the name of seriousness, continued I, must not one's privileges be very great in a country where we dare not pluck a hazel nut? Is this an Englishman's birthright?'[96]

Spence explains that he relates this story in order to 'show how far we are cut off from the rights of nature'.[97] As hunting grounds, forests and woodlands had been patrolled on behalf of kings and lords since medieval times, and in part Spence is alluding to the framework of forest, game and related laws which, though amended over the centuries, continued to mandate that. In part too, however, he is alluding to the post-medieval phenomenon of enclosure. The span of Spence's life — from 1750 to 1814 — coincided with the rise and eventual peak of Parliamentary enclosure, itself the final phase of the long process of extinguishing rights of common and placing landholding in England under a regime of exclusive possession.[98] Rights of common took many different forms, and applied differently to different categories of commoners. But while some commoners worked the land in open fields and grazed animals on common pasture, everyone could expect to take food, fuel and materials from the manorial waste. Like Spence, the early nineteenth-century poet John Clare writes of going out nutting.[99] In particular, hazelnuts and chestnuts were collected for sale in towns and cities.[100] The extinguishment of common rights deprived commoners of the

96. Thomas Spence, *The Restorer of Society to its Natural State in a series of letters to a fellow citizen* (London: J. Smith, 1801), Postscript to Letter 5, reprinted in H.T. Dickinson, *The Political Works of Thomas Spence* (Newcastle upon Tyne: Avero, 1982), 69, 79.
97. Ibid.
98. On this, see further chap. 7 above.
99. John Clare (Eric Robinson and David Powell, eds.), *Major Works* (Oxford: Oxford University Press, 2004), 131 (*Nutting*).
100. See J. M. Neeson, *Commoners: Common Right, Enclosure and Social Change in England, 1700–1820* (Cambridge: Cambridge University Press, 1993), 169.

possibility of supplementing their incomes in such a way, just as it deprived them of the possibility of meeting their own needs other than by purchasing commodities on the market. From the evidence mentioned above of the prevalence in this period of wood theft, [101] it may be inferred that this proved especially disastrous when it came to fuel.[102]

Perhaps more than any other writer, Clare expressed the experience of enclosure and improvement as loss, captivity and disaster, and he often did so using language that referenced trees. *The Village Minstrel* evokes a peasant commoner's 'anguish' when 'curst improvement 'gan his fields inclose'. 'O greens and fields and trees, farewell, farewell! / His heart-wrung pains, his unavailing woes / No words can utter and no tongue can tell, / When ploughs destroyed the green, when groves of willows fell.' Yet the calamity was not just personal; it was also national. 'O England, boasted land of liberty . . . / Like emigrating bird thy freedom's flown.' And again, 'Enclosure came and all your glories fell: / E'en the old oak that crowned yon rifled dell.'[103] *The Moors* reprises the line, but with a more vivid sense that this was the outcome of class war: 'Enclosure came and trampled on the grave / Of labour's rights and left the poor a slave.' The paths which had served and sustained ordinary people were now 'stopped', and everywhere '[a] board sticks up to notice "no road here"'.[104] In *The Fallen Elm* (to touch on one final poem), we read of the cant that was used to justify all this. The eponymous beloved tree 'owned a language by which hearts are stirred / Deeper than by a feeling clothed in words'. But to 'self-interest', it offended the language of efficiency and productivity. So '[w]ith axe at root he felled thee to the ground / And barked of freedom. O I hate the sound!'[105]

Tim Fulford writes that, in Clare's poetry, the 'rightful possessor of the land' is the poet, son of poor farm labourers, and those like him, whose relationship with the trees around, underneath, and from which they lived was 'far closer and more complex' than that of commercially-minded landowners and the landscape architects they engaged to create their parks. To Fulford, the poems 'suggest that freedom lies elsewhere than in the language and the actions of

101. See Bob Bushaway, *By Rite: Custom, Ceremony and Community in England 1700–1880* (London: Junction Books, 1982), 208.
102. For commoners with grazing rights, the loss of the capacity to keep a cow was believed by some contemporaries to have been another extremely significant loss. See chap. 6 above.
103. John Clare (Jonathan Bate, ed.), *Selected Poems* (London: Faber and Faber, 2003), 31, 35, 37.
104. Ibid, 89, 91.
105. Ibid, 141, 142.

those who claim to uphold the nation's liberty'.[106] Spence plainly agreed that the land belonged to the people, and as we have seen, he devised a plan by which the people's lost rights to it might be retaken into possession, parish by parish.[107] Along similar lines to Clare, though from the different perspective of a city-dweller and activist,[108] Spence argued that this was a matter of reaping the advantages from the natural and equal rights in land and liberty which humankind could, or should, expect. To what notion of liberty did he advert?

It is said that, as a young man in Newcastle upon Tyne, Spence moved in the same circle as Joseph Ritson.[109] Ritson is significant as the editor of *Robin Hood*, the first major collection of poems, songs and ballads about the folk hero, published in 1795.[110] In introducing the work, Ritson writes of Robin Hood's 'spirit of freedom and independence, which has endeared him to the common people, whose cause he maintained, . . . and [which] in spite of the malicious endeavours of pitiful monks, . . . will render his name immortal'.[111] However, it was not the sylvan liberty of Robin Hood that Spence advocated for. The great modern scholar of social banditry, Eric Hobsbawm, characterises Robin Hood as the archetype of the 'noble robber'. The noble robber is a 'champion' of the common people, a 'righter of wrongs', and a 'bringer of justice'. He 'takes from the rich to give to the poor', and is 'admired, helped and supported by his people'. He fights with the local gentry and clergy (or other oppressors), whom he despises. Notably, though, he is 'not the enemy of the king' (or other ruler), who, in his eyes, always remains 'the fount of justice'. In Hobsbawm's portrayal, Robin Hood thus stands for something 'comparatively modest'; he wants 'fair dealing in a society of oppression . . . He does not seek to establish a society of freedom and equality . . . He is an individual who refuses to bend his back, that is all.'[112]

It is evident from our discussion in previous chapters that Spence's vision had little to do with this. He certainly believed that poor people should not

106. Tim Fulford, 'Cowper, Wordsworth, Clare: The Politics of Trees', *John Clare Society Journal* 14 (1995) 47, 50.
107. See chap. 7 above.
108. Regarding Clare's background and politics, see Hugh Haughton et al. (eds.), *John Clare in Context* (Cambridge: Cambridge University Press, 1994), esp. John Lucas, 'Clare's politics', 148.
109. See Marilyn Butler (ed.), *Burke, Paine, Godwin, and the Revolution Controversy* (Cambridge: Cambridge University Press, 1984), 203.
110. Joseph Ritson (ed.), *Robin Hood: A Collection of All the Ancient Poems, Songs, and Ballads, Now Extant, Relative to that celebrated English Outlaw* (London: C. Stocking, 1823).
111. Ibid, xii–xiii.
112. Eric Hobsbawm, *Bandits* (London: Abacus, 2001), 47–48, 60, 61.

bend their backs. His nutting story is a brief essay in non-deference. Yet the point for him was not that wrongs needed righting here and there, and still less was it that emancipation came with escape from society to the greenwood, or with the transitory diversions of the May games (a related phenomenon insofar as the traditions apparently often included dressing up as Robin Hood and his band of outlaws, and re-enacting tales from the ballads).[113] What then of the republican liberty espoused by Paine? Two years after *Rights of Man* announced that the political 'spring is begun', Spence similarly compared the beneficent effects of implementing his land plan to a 'benign and sudden Spring . . . after a long and severe Winter'. But he pointedly said that it would not be 'a barren Revolution of mere unproductive Rights, such as many contend for, nor yet a glut of sudden and temporary Wealth as if acquired by conquest'. Rather it would be 'a continual flow of permanent Wealth established by a System of Truth and Justice'.[114]

The next year Spence developed that line of thought in an intriguing format. *A Fragment of an Ancient Prophecy* foretells a future in which 'certain philosophers of great abilities' will arise to set up the tree of liberty and proclaim the rights of man. The 'prophecy' goes like this:

> And during the propagation of the true system certain philosophers shall arise of great abilities who shall erect a false Tree of Liberty composed of heterogeneous materials . . . part liberty, and part tyranny, capable of shedding the influence of liberty and independence only on the wealthy, the shadow scarcely falling on the poor . . . Nevertheless, they [those philosophers] shall so far animate the people with the display of their specious, but partial Rights of Man, that the multitude shall arise and great convulsions shall be in many countries, and kingdoms and principalities, and hierarchies and governments shall be overthrown, but oppression shall still remain.[115]

For Paine, liberation became possible once the old, residually feudal regime of privilege and property had been uprooted. For Spence, in contrast, what needed to be uprooted was the (relatively) *new* regime of privilege and property as well — the post-feudal regime that had advanced through enclosure, and that was now, and more generally, the programme Clare called 'curst improvement'. Anything less was a 'barren revolution of mere unproductive rights'. Anything less would be 'capable of shedding the influence of liberty

113. See Rodney Hilton, 'The Origins of Robin Hood', *Past and Present* 14 (1958) 30, 31.
114. Thomas Spence, *The End of Oppression* (London: T. Spence, 1795), 9, reprinted in H. T. Dickinson, *The Political Works of Thomas Spence* (Newcastle upon Tyne: Avero, 1982), 34, 37.
115. Thomas Spence, *A Fragment of An Ancient Prophecy* (London: T. Spence, 1796), 3–4, reprinted in H.T. Dickinson, *The Political Works of Thomas Spence* (Newcastle upon Tyne: Avero, 1982), 45.

and independence only on the wealthy, the shadow scarcely falling on the poor'. Anything less conduced to a future in which 'great convulsions shall be in many countries, and kingdoms and principalities, and hierarchies and governments shall be overthrown, but oppression shall still remain'. Anything less deceived the people by erecting a 'false Tree of Liberty'.

Three liberty trees

If, as Stephen Daniels writes, '[t]rees and woodland have proved as rich a symbolic resource as a material one', it is no surprise that those two dimensions of their value are, or have been, connected.[116] Introducing a study of trees in history and culture, Laura Auricchio and collaborators observe that, by virtue of their ubiquity throughout the world, their usefulness in so many dimensions of life, their 'often superhuman sizes and their uncommon longevity, trees . . . have long been central objects of human thought and action'.[117] In part as a way of drawing together something of the threads of the preceding chapters, this chapter has reviewed (some aspects of) the relation between trees and liberty in the thought and action of early sixteenth- to late eighteenth-century England. We began at the Bear Inn in Bath, where in 1792 a toast was raised to the tree of liberty. However, when we then traced the fortunes of the tree of liberty in that period, we found that there was not a singular liberty tree; instead, there were three of them.

The first was Burke's British oak, the 'British Tree of True Liberty'. This belonged with a vision of constitutional stability, and with an understanding of the people as subjects under the beneficent care and protection of the monarchy, aristocracy, and Church. The poet William Wordsworth depicted Burke as himself an oak: 'I see him, old, but vigorous in age, — / Stand, like an Oak whose stag-horn branches start / Out of its leafy brow . . . / Exploding upstart Theory.'[118] The second tree of liberty was that of one of the upstart theorists, Thomas Paine. Paine's 'fair budding branch' belonged with a desire to put an end to hereditary succession, and to establish government on the basis of popular sovereignty and republican citizenship. The third tree of

116. Stephen Daniels, 'The Political Iconography of Woodland in Later Georgian England', in Denis Cosgrove and Stephen Daniels (eds.), *The Iconography of Landscape* (Cambridge: Cambridge University Press, 1988), 43.
117. Laura Auricchio, Elizabeth Heckendorn Cook and Giulia Pacini, 'Introduction: Invaluable Trees', in Laura Auricchio, Elizabeth Heckendorn Cook and Giulia Pacini (eds.), *Invaluable Trees: Cultures of Nature, 1660–1830* (Oxford: Voltaire Foundation, 2012), 1.
118. William Wordsworth (J. Wordsworth, ed.), *The Prelude* (London: Penguin, 1995), Book VII, 281.

liberty (albeit not one to which anybody would be likely to raise a toast) was Spence's 'false Tree of Liberty'. This belonged with attention to the roots of unfreedom in patterns of social organisation, and especially the organisation of access to land, and to the very many ways in which what is called freedom may be 'composed of heterogeneous materials, part liberty and part tyranny'.

Spence's tree differs from the other two in the obvious sense that it expresses a critical judgement, rather than an affirmative claim. His concern was not the true tree of liberty, but the false one. The 'true' trees (or tree parts) that featured in the work of Burke and Paine trade on the familiar distinction between nature, on the one hand, and culture, on the other, and on the association of the former with the pristine, unaffected, authentic condition of the world — the condition of the world as it 'originally' was, or, in some sense, is 'meant' to be. Thus, Burke used the imagery of the oak to naturalise hereditary succession and denaturalise the rights of man (rights are 'an inheritance from our forefathers'). In countering Burke, Paine did the reverse; he used the imagery of the budding branch to denaturalise hereditary succession (the monarchy is just 'a thing of the imagination') and naturalise the rights of man. Spence used the imagery of the *false* tree to challenge Paine's naturalised republican form of the rights of man as 'specious' and 'partial'.

What made Paine's naturalised republican form of the rights of man specious and partial to Spence was in no small measure a function of its relation to actual trees. The symbolism of the tree of liberty belied realities — the creation of private landscape parks, the clearing of woodland wastes, the development of commercial forestry on large landed estates, and the criminalisation of wood collection by local commoners under conditions of comprehensive enclosure — that did not tend to everyone's advantage. Returning momentarily to a different time and place, we might recall the ambiguity of the elm that once stood at the corner of the present Essex and Washington Streets in Boston — a liberty tree, but also a symbolic gallows or execution 'tree'. Paine would point out that, when power falls into their hands, 'men learn how to punish from the governments they live under'. But if it was the *ancien régime* in France that taught the revolutionaries there to carry severed heads on spikes, the American colonists took their lesson from the criminal law of early- and mid-eighteenth-century England — a law marked by, and adapted to, the system of private property, generalised wage-labour, and capital accumulation which was then and there taking shape.

10

Afterword

Bread helmet man

On 3 February 2011 a protester was photographed at a demonstration in Sanaa, Yemen, with two baguettes and a flatbread taped to his head (fig. 12). He became known as 'bread helmet man', and the image turned into an internet meme. The story behind the photograph was that 20,000 people had taken to the streets of Sanaa that day,[1] in an uprising against the country's government which culminated the following year with the toppling of Ali Abdullah Saleh's long-term rule.

Linked to the wider Arab Spring of 2010–12, the Yemeni revolution saw the expression of discontent on a variety of mutually reinforcing grounds. But as this individual's headgear clearly announced, one aspect of what was going wrong had to do with food. Factors including US subsidies for corn-to-ethanol conversion and heightened speculation on food commodity markets had set the scene for a spike in the cost of staple foods in 2007–8, leading to violence in many countries, and now, three years on, another steep rise in global food prices was underway. Yemen was especially vulnerable to the effects of this because it relies heavily on imported grain, and is among the poorest countries in the Arab world. Much of its population spends a large

1. See 'Yemen protests: 20,000 call for President Saleh to go', BBC News, 3 February 2011, available at https://www.bbc.com/news/world-middle-east-12353479.

A False Tree of Liberty. Susan Marks, Oxford University Press (2019). © Susan Marks.
DOI: 10.1093/oso/9780199675456.003.0010

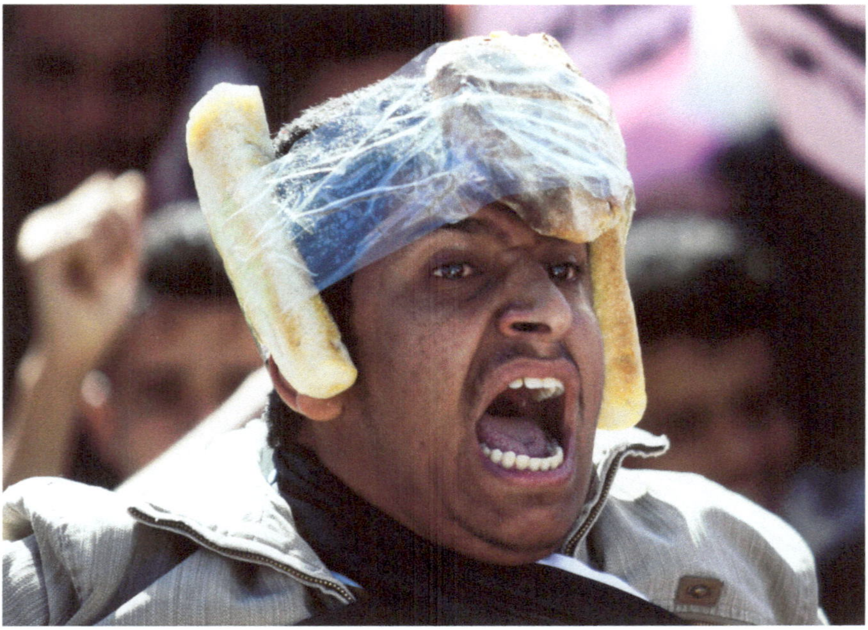

Figure 12 REUTERS, *An opposition supporter with pieces of bread taped onto his head shouts slogans during anti-government protest in Sanaa* 3 February 2011

proportion of household income on food, with few social safety nets or other measures in place to provide protection when prices increase.[2]

Twenty-first-century Yemen is a long way from eighteenth-century England, but this photograph and this story came into my mind when, some years later, I learned of the 'mourning loaves' that had been brandished at the king's coach in London on 29 October 1795.[3] Of course, the context of the distress experienced in 1790s London was quite different, but there and then too, people with little money and less social insurance who were obliged to buy their food on the market expressed anger at the failure of the authorities to control spiralling prices. And there and then too, they did so using a cultural symbol that functioned synedochically to represent not just sustenance, but also human dignity, well-being, life.[4]

2. See further Andreas Gros et al., 'Conflict in Yemen: From Ethnic Fighting to Food Riots', in Philip Vos Fellman et al. (eds.), *Conflict and Complexity: Countering Terrorism, Insurgency, Ethnic and Regional Violence* (New York: Springer, 2015), 269.
3. On this, see chap. 6 above and the references there cited.
4. It is often mentioned in writing about 'food riots' in the Middle East that, in Egyptian Arabic, the word for 'bread', *aish,* also means 'life'. See, e.g., Rami Zurayk, 'Use your loaf: why food prices were crucial in the Arab spring', *The Guardian*, 17 July 2011, available at: https://www.theguardian.com/lifeandstyle/2011/jul/17/bread-food-arab-spring.

The reappearance (for that is how it seemed) of mourning loaves as a Yemeni bread helmet led me to wonder about other things I had written about in this book. What had become of the places? What was now made of the people? Long gone though those people were, what still reverberated of their arguments, controversies and complaints? To what extent, and in what ways, were their issues also our issues? The focus of the study presented in the preceding chapters is the past, but in these final pages I want to add just a few words about the present. True to the spirit of the early twenty-first century, I begin with a list.

Six very short stories

Albion Mills: History repeated itself when, on 27 November 2013, the Albion Flour Mill in Brisbane, Australia, was destroyed by fire.[5] Completed in 1931, the mill was built for the Gillespie Brothers whose father George had come to Australia from Scotland and established a successful grain products business in Melbourne. The three brothers George, John and Robert had set up business as flour millers in Sydney, and become known for 'Anchor flour'. Their new Brisbane mill, designed by the architectural practice of Francis Hall, cost them £60,000. It stood five storeys tall, and had all the most modern equipment. Operating continuously in three shifts a day, it was later enlarged and its capacity almost doubled.[6]

Over the decades, the mill changed hands several times. In 1999 it was bought by Pat O'Brien and Ron Plant. Speaking to a journalist from Brisbane's *Courier Mail* in July 2005, Mr O'Brien said that he and Mr Plant had been approached a number of times to sell the mill, but their 'response was always we would be milling flour here forever'. However, the *Courier Mail* went on to report that '[a]fter discussions with the council and the [Queensland] State Government, [the owners] had recognised the land could play a prominent role in the renewal of the area', which was close to the city centre with lots of new developments and good transport links. As Mr O'Brien explained,

5. On the fire that destroyed the Albion Mills in London in 1791, see chap. 6 above.
6. See Myles Sinnamon, 'The Albion Flour Mill, Scottish Links and Another Era', John Oxley Library (State Library of Queensland) Blog, available at: http://blogs.slq.qld.gov.au/jol/2013/12/05/the-albion-flour-mill-scottish-links-and-another-era/.

milling flour 'was probably an inefficient use of the site', and the mill building 'would be great converted to apartments, with its high ceilings and timber'.[7]

In October 2005, the Albion flour mill was sold to FKP Property Group. The appropriately named Matthew Miller of FKP Queensland said that the Group intended to turn the site into an 'urban lifestyle hub', comprising apartments, offices, restaurants, cafes and shops set within the refurbished mill and two new towers.[8] By 2013 marketing was underway, but then the fire broke out and the sales and display suite was completely gutted, while the mill itself was so badly damaged that it had to be demolished. The Queensland Fire and Rescue Service said they suspected arson. According to a spokesperson, there was 'no power actually going into the old mill', which had become derelict, so the fire was 'very unlikely [to have] started all by itself'. Based on information from security guards, police were reported to be looking for a youth wearing a dark baseball cap, dark shirt and dark trousers, and a man with extensive tattoos on his neck and arms, wearing a white shirt.[9]

At a champagne reception held just over four years after the fire, Twin Ocean Corporation celebrated the completion of the redevelopment project's first stage, a 164-apartment mixed-use building named 'The Hudson', boasting a residents' pool deck, gym and barbecue facilities, and twenty-four hour concierge service. All of the ground-floor retail spaces had by then already been leased, and most of the apartments had likewise been sold.[10] The remaining apartments appear to have proved harder to sell. In June 2017 the *Courier Mail* reported that 'bank lending restrictions and a changing market' were leading developers in the city to 'slash prices and offer lucrative incentives to secure sales'. Twin Ocean Corporation was believed to have reduced the price of apartments in The Hudson by as much as 25 per cent, with one buyer saying 'There's no way I could have purchased in that building at the prices they were originally asking. It was way out of my reach.'[11]

Diggers: If you are interested in the Digger movement of the English Civil War, [12] there is a trail you can follow that takes you to locations in

7. See Michelle Hele, 'Historic Albion landmark for sale', *The Courier Mail* (Australia), 29 July 2005.
8. See Michelle Hele, 'Old mill to blend with inner-city houses', *The Courier Mail* (Australia), 7 October 2005.
9. See Marissa Calligeros, 'Historic Albion flour mill destroyed by fire', *The Brisbane Times*, 27 November 2013.
10. See Belinda Seeney, 'The Hudson launch', *The Courier Mail* (Australia), 18 December 2016, and Belinda Clinton, 'Views add to appeal', *The Courier Mail* (Australia), 7 January 2017.
11. See Elizabeth Tilley, 'Cranes gone from skyline', *The Courier Mail* (Australia), 18 June 2017.
12. On the Diggers, see chaps. 4 and 9 above and the references there cited.

the county of Surrey associated with the Diggers.[13] The trail was designed by the Elmbridge Diggers Heritage Group, and encompasses five sites around the towns of Weybridge and Walton-on-Thames, spread over a distance of approximately thirty kilometres. Historical information is provided about each site, along with general information about the Diggers. It is explained that the movement's name 'comes from the practice of digging and manuring the "waste" and common land, which was what they did both to grow food and to show that everybody had a right to enjoy the Earth and its fruits'. Regarding the movement's legacy, it is stated that '[t]he brutality of their opponents meant that [the Diggers] did not survive for long, but their writings and ideas continue to inspire people throughout the world'.[14]

The third site on the trail is St George's Hill. Today St George's Hill in Weybridge is ranked among the ten most expensive places to live in the United Kingdom. In the early twentieth century it was turned into a private residential estate with leafy streets, big houses and leisure facilities (golf course, tennis courts), and since then it has become well known as an out-of-London neighbourhood for the rich and famous. But St George's Hill is also the place where, on 1 April 1649, the Diggers first broke ground, and from which they issued their most famous manifesto, *The True Levellers Standard Advanced*. They were not able to remain there long, and by August of that year, the group had resettled at Little Heath in Cobham—the fifth site on the trail.

Again facing hostility and in need of moral and material support, the Little Heath Diggers sent emissaries to other Digger communities which, in the meantime, had been established. It is known that four of the emissaries reached Wellingborough in the East Midlands county of Northamptonshire, where they were arrested. A letter, believed to have been written by Gerrard Winstanley, was taken from them on their arrest and still survives.[15] Since 2011 the Wellingborough Diggers have been celebrated at an annual festival, with music, speakers and a short commemorative service. Attendees at the 2018 Wellingborough Diggers' Festival were asked to remember Winstanley's

13. Surrey Diggers Trail, available at https://www.diggerstrail.org.uk/.
14. 'The Diggers', Surrey Diggers Trail, https://www.diggerstrail.org.uk/the-diggers/.
15. See *A Letter Taken at Wellingborough*, in Thomas Corns, Ann Hughes and David Loewenstein (eds.), *The Complete Works of Gerrard Winstanley, Vol. II* (Oxford: Oxford University Press, 2009), 430. The letter states that its bearers are Thomas Heaydon and Adam Knight, 'who can relate by word of mouth more largely the condition of the Diggers and their work' (432). The names of the remaining two arrested emissaries are not currently known.

letter by bringing 'one item of non perishable goods . . . which will be collected and distributed to the local foodbank'.[16]

Another Diggers' Festival was also launched in 2011, at Wigan in north-west England. Now part of Greater Manchester, Wigan is Winstanley's birthplace. You can view a clip of a film, *Winstanley*, made in 1975 about the eponymous Wiganer on the website of the Wigan Diggers' Festival.[17] The website commends the film, albeit with some regret at leading actor Miles Halliwell's posh Southern accent.[18] In a newspaper report about the festival, one of the organisers highlights as a key influence on the Digger leader's thought the success of Wigan clay and coal miners at protecting their livelihoods by establishing their right to dig on common land. But if Winstanley's views need be related to the Lancashire context in which he was raised, the organiser echoes the Elmbridge Diggers Heritage Group in proposing that those views are 'as relevant today as they were in 1649, particularly given the economic situation'.[19]

Newcastle Town Moor: Thanks to its Town Moor, Newcastle upon Tyne has around 1000 acres or 400 hectares of open space stretching out from the city centre.[20] The area is mostly treeless and, rather than being laid out as parkland, it takes the form of a grassy expanse traversed by a number of paths and roads (fig. 13). A distinctive feature of Newcastle Town Moor is that cows graze there. Under the provisions of the Newcastle upon Tyne Town Moor Act 1988, a maximum of 800 cows can be grazed on the Moor by those with the status of 'freemen' of the city.[21] 'Freedom' of the city of Newcastle is a centuries-old hereditary status passed by existing freemen to their children, and is occasionally bestowed on an honorary basis as well to eminent individuals or groups associated with the city.[22]

The 1988 Act replaced earlier legislation, beginning with the Newcastle upon Tyne Town Moor Act 1774. The 1774 Act was adopted following a

16. Eighth Wellingborough Diggers' Festival and Fringe Programme, https://jonathanhornett.wordpress.com/2018/02/13/8th-wellingborough-diggers-festival-and-fringe-programme/.
17. *Winstanley*, Dirs. Kevin Brownlow and Andrew Mollo, United Kingdom (1975), based on the 1961 novel *Comrade Jacob* by David Caute. See http://www.bfi.org.uk/blu-rays-dvds/winstanley.
18. See https://wigandiggersfestival.org/about/.
19. Bernadette Hyland, 'Wigan stakes its claim to be the home of Socialism', *The Guardian*, 31 August 2012.
20. This total actually comprises several moors: the Town Moor, together with Nuns Moor, Hunters Moor, Dukes Moor, Little Moor, Castle Leazes, and a number of other areas.
21. Newcastle upon Tyne Town Moor Act 1988, esp. section 10.
22. See https://www.newcastle.gov.uk/your-council-and-democracy/councillors-and-democracy/lord-mayor/freemen.

Figure 13 *New path after autumn shower, Newcastle Town Moor*, October 2004. Jacky Longstaff

dispute in which the local authorities purported to enclose and let part of the Moor without consulting the freemen.[23] The freemen had customary grazing rights with respect to this land, which they sought to defend by entering and taking possession of the area. The lessee, a man named Joshua Hopper, then sued them for trespass, and the 1774 Act records the outcome of that litigation — a scheme of management which allowed for the land to be leased, but also protected the freemen's right to graze cattle on the land in perpetuity. Under the current management scheme, the Moor is placed under the dual control of the City Council and the freemen.

23. On the Town Moor dispute and its significance in the work of Thomas Spence, see chap. 7 above.

Newcastle Town Moor is famous as the site of an annual fun fair called 'the Hoppings' that claims to be Europe's largest travelling fun fair. A large annual fair has taken place on the Moor almost continuously since 1882, when the Newcastle upon Tyne Temperance Association organised a fair as part of an attempt to draw patrons away from the drinking, gambling, and card-sharping at nearby Gosforth Park racecourse. Horseracing previously took place on the Moor, as did rabbit coursing, running races, and cricket and football matches.[24] The area continues to be used by sporting clubs, and is the venue for several annual fun runs. It is also the venue for one of the UK's largest LGBT Pride events, Newcastle Pride.

There are allotments on the Moor, where local residents grow vegetables, fruit and flowers, and the ecosystem is reported to support an exceptional array of species of birds for an urban environment, along with bats, squirrels, hedgehogs, badgers and toads.[25] In 2008 an exhibition was held in Newcastle of photographs of the Town Moor taken by photographer Jacky Longstaff.[26] Interviewed for the BBC, Ms Longstaff says, 'I think most people just cross [the Moor] or run on it, and you never see kids playing on it or using it for a picnic.' As she describes it, the Moor 'is quite a bleak and stark space . . . but . . . it can also be beautiful'. She believes 'it should be celebrated that there's this big green space that will hopefully not be built on'.[27]

Paine: No doubt there are, and have been, many Thomas Paines in the world, but if you search that name on Google, you get results in the multi-millions and it is possible to scroll down for a very long time without reaching a result that does not relate to the eighteenth-century writer and revolutionary (either because it is about him, or because it borrows his identity for a Twitter handle, etc.). Websites differ in the works with which they most closely associate him. For example, Goodreads refers to Paine as 'the author of *Common Sense*',[28] while the American Humanist Association highlights *The Age of Reason*.[29] The statue of Paine which

24. See 'Newcastle Town Moor', National Fairground and Circus Archive, available at: https://www.sheffield.ac.uk/nfca/researchandarticles/newcastlefair.
25. See SPACE for Gosforth, *Why is the Town Moor Special?* (2016), available at: http://spaceforgosforth.com/blue-house-environmental-impact-assessment/.
26. See Jacky Longstaff, *Room: Photographs and Essays from the Town Moor, Newcastle upon Tyne* (Stockport: Dewi Lewis, 2008).
27. BBC Tyne, 'Focus on the Town Moor', 27 August 2008, available at: http://www.bbc.co.uk/tyne/content/articles/2008/08/27/town_moor_feature.shtml.
28. See, e.g., https://www.goodreads.com/author/show/57639.Thomas_Paine.
29. See, e.g., https://thehumanist.com/magazine/july-august-2009/commentary/thomas-paine-1737-1809.

stands in Thetford, where he was born, shows a spirited man wearing a wig and frock coat with a pen in one hand and *Rights of Man* in the other.

Barack Obama quoted a line from Paine's *American Crisis* essay of 23 December 1776 at the end of his first inaugural address in January 2009: 'Let it be told to the future world . . . that in the depth of winter, when nothing but hope and virtue could survive . . . that the city and the country, alarmed at one common danger, came forth to meet [it].'[30] The three sentences with which that same text opens were quoted by Franklin D. Roosevelt in a fireside chat to the American people after the attack on Pearl Harbour in February 1942: 'These are the times that try men's souls . . .' In reciting the passage, Roosevelt noted that 'George Washington ordered that these great words . . . be read to the men of every regiment in the Continental Army'.[31]

Paine was also quoted by Ronald Reagan in his speech accepting the presidential nomination at the Republican National Convention in July 1980: 'We have it in our power to begin the world over again.'[32] The sentence comes from *Common Sense*, which US radio and television host Glenn Beck more recently referenced in his 2009 book, *Glenn Beck's Common Sense: the Case against an Out-of-Control Government, Inspired by Thomas Paine.*[33] Responding to the book in *Jacobin* magazine, Sean Monahan argues that the neoconservative misreads Paine, who 'was a consistent advocate of a strong federal government', as well as being 'a sharp critic of economic inequality . . . and class society'.[34] 2009 was the bicentennial of Paine's death, and in another Paine-related work published that year — a new edition of *Rights of Man* and *Common Sense* put out by Verso — Peter Linebaugh locates Paine within 'a long English anti-capitalist tradition'.[35]

30. Barack Obama, *First Inaugural Address* (20 January 2009), available at: https://en.wikisource.org/wiki/Barack_Obama%27s_First_Inaugural_Address. See Thomas Paine, *The Crisis, Number 1*, in Bruce Kuklick (ed.), *Paine: Political Writings* (Cambridge: Cambridge University Press, 2000), 47, 54.
31. Franklin D. Roosevelt, *Fireside Chat* (23 February 1942), available at: http://www.presidency.ucsb.edu/ws/index.php?pid=16224. See Thomas Paine, *The Crisis, Number 1*, in Bruce Kuklick (ed.), *Paine: Political Writings* (Cambridge: Cambridge University Press, 2000), 47, 49.
32. Ronald Reagan, *Address Accepting the Presidential Nomination at the Republican National Convention in Detroit* (17 July 1980), available at: https://www.presidency.ucsb.edu/documents/address-accepting-the-presidential-nomination-the-republican-national-convention-detroit. See Thomas Paine, *Common Sense*, in Bruce Kuklick (ed.), *Paine: Political Writings* (Cambridge: Cambridge University Press, 2000), 1, 44.
33. Glenn Beck, *Glenn Beck's Common Sense: the Case Against an Out-of-Control Government, Inspired by Thomas Paine* (New York: Mercury Radio Arts/Threshold, 2009).
34. Sean Monahan, 'Reading Paine from the Left', *Jacobin* (2015), available at https://www.jacobinmag.com/2015/03/thomas-paine-american-revolution-common-sense/.
35. Peter Linebaugh, 'Introduction', in Jessica Kimpell (ed.), *Peter Linebaugh presents Thomas Paine: Rights of Man, Common Sense and Agrarian Justice* (London: Verso, 2009), vii, ix.

Lines from Paine's works frequently appear in lists of favourite quotations. At the same time, the US-based Thomas Paine National Historical Association maintains a list of statements that have been wrongly attributed to him. These include: 'The government that governs best governs least'; 'The duty of a patriot is to protect his country from its government'; and 'Arms discourage and keep the invader and plunderer in awe, and preserve order in the world as well as property . . . Horrid mischief would ensue were the law-abiding deprived of the use of them.'[36] In a 'biography' of *Rights of Man* written for a series on 'books that changed the world', Christopher Hitchens comments on this history of quotation and misquotation, appropriation and misascription. It 'is a very particular kind of flattery', Hitchens suggests, which 'promotes Paine's work to that exalted company shared by the Bible and the works of Shakespeare'.[37]

Shakespeare: First performed in 1973, Edward Bond's play *Bingo* dramatises the involvement of William Shakespeare in a dispute which arose near the end of his life over the enclosure of land at Welcombe in the parish of Stratford-upon-Avon.[38] In 1602 Shakespeare bought a tract of open-field land at Welcombe, and three years later he also bought an interest in some tithes there.[39] After the Midland Rising,[40] the main local freeholder, William Combe, decided to enclose the open fields at Welcombe, and in 1614 steps to that end were initiated on his behalf. The enclosure was successfully fought in the courts by the parish council, which got an injunction to stop it, but Combe went ahead regardless, evicting the villagers with threats, beatings and other forms of harassment. Since its depopulation at that time, the village of Welcombe has disappeared without trace.[41]

The historical record is patchy on the question of Shakespeare's attitude to Combe's scheme of enclosure. The playwright is known to have sought, and received, a guarantee that he would be compensated for any loss accruing to

36. See http://thomaspaine.org/aboutpaine/did-paine-write-these-quotes.html. The last statement is from an article entitled 'Thoughts on Defensive War' by an anonymous 'Lover of Peace', which appeared in July 1775 in the *Pennsylvania Magazine* (which Paine edited). The article was for a time thought to have been written by Paine. Though now believed to have been wrongly attributed to him, it continues to be quoted using his name.
37. Christopher Hitchens, *Thomas Paine's 'Rights of Man': A Biography* (London: Atlantic Books, 2007), 142.
38. Edward Bond, *Plays: 3* (London: Methuen Drama, 1987). See chap. 3 above for discussion of Shakespeare's play *Coriolanus*.
39. Tithes were taxes on various kinds of produce, the right to collect which was leased by the church authorities to private individuals for a fee.
40. See chap. 3 above.
41. See http://www.thewelcombehills.co.uk/the-lost-village-of-welcombe/.

him as a result of the scheme. On the other hand, he is also known to have said that he 'was not able to beare the enclosinge of welcombe'.[42] *Bingo* portrays Shakespeare as a conflicted and ultimately repentant collaborator in a brutal and exploitative society that is waging war against the poor. Bond says that he wrote the play because he thinks Shakespeare's predicament was similar to ours in the present day. 'He was a "corrupt seer" and we are a "barbarous civilization" . . . We believe in certain values but our society only works by destroying them, so that our daily lives are a denial of our hopes.'[43]

In 2012 a production of *Bingo* directed by Angus Jackson was performed at the Young Vic theatre in London, with Patrick Stewart in the role of Shakespeare. A review by Charles Spencer in *The Daily Telegraph* describes the play as 'a hatchet job on Shakespeare by the hard-left playwright Edward Bond'. 'It is a mean-spirited and reductive view of a writer most of us regard as a fount of wisdom, humanity and beauty', Spencer writes, and to see it is to be forced to endure 'arid enclosed acres of dramatic boredom'. He adds that an 'actor of Stewart's ability could play this one-dimensional role in his sleep and at times appears to be doing just that'.[44]

Guardian theatre critic Michael Billington was at the theatre on the same night, but evidently saw something quite different. For him, Bond's play 'is a guilt-ridden indictment of all poets and dramatists, himself included, for their exploitation of suffering and cruelty'. 'With extraordinary poetic economy, Bond evokes the horrors of Shakespeare's world. In place of Merrie England, we get a panoramic portrait of religious persecution, judicial severity and ubiquitous violence.' Patrick Stewart 'superbly reinforces Bond's vision by giving us a tragic Shakespeare, but also one alive to his own contradictions'. 'I have known Lears who have moved me less', Billington declares.[45]

Utopia: A discussion of 'utopia' in the twenty-first century needs to start with disambiguation. There are novels and short stories called Utopia, films and TV series called Utopia, and songs, bands and record labels called Utopia. Utopia is a computer game, a typeface, and many shops. User-Tested Optimized Practices in Action are UTOPIAs, as is the Utah Telecommunications Open Infrastructure Agency. As the name of a place, Utopia is home to people in

42. The basis of this information is the diary of Thomas Greene, who describes himself as Shakespeare's cousin. See *The Welcome Enclosure Dispute*, esp. Welcombe Records (1) and (27), available at: http://www.theshakespearerecords.com/welcombe-enclosure-dispute/.
43. Edward Bond, *Plays: 3* (London: Methuen Drama, 1987), 10.
44. Charles Spencer, '*Bingo*, Young Vic, review', *The Daily Telegraph*, 24 February 2012.
45. Michael Billington, '*Bingo* — review', *The Guardian*, 24 February 2012.

several countries — the largest an indigenous community in the Northern Territory of Australia, where the name Utopia is believed to be a corruption of *uturupa*, meaning 'big sand hill'.[46]

The word *uturupa* is likely to have been in use for millennia, while utopia has a much shorter history, which goes back to Thomas More's work *On the Best State of a Commonwealth and on the New Island of Utopia*, first published in Latin in 1516.[47] All usages of utopia retain at least some trace or echo of More's original sense of perfection in government and society, albeit with an ineradicable undertow of absurdity, as in his text. There exists a vast literature on the concept of utopia, and on the development and significance of utopian thinking within the domains of culture, theory and social practice. In that literature, as well as in popular discourse, utopianism is associated with hope, optimism, desire, imagination, experimentation and the impulse to make a better collective life.

It is also, of course, associated with naiveté — and worse. Utopians are daydreamers wasting their time in the pursuit of unattainable ideals. Or conversely, they are dogmatists making blueprints and then forcing the world to fit them. They are imperial adventurers, crusaders for civilisation, self-proclaimed island kings. They are privileged escape fantasists who need, in fact, to get out more. In 1868 John Stuart Mill coined the word 'dystopian' as the antithesis of utopian, and in 1967 an article in the *Listener* magazine applied the term to Aldous Huxley's *Brave New World* and George Orwell's *Nineteen Eighty-Four*, noting that these novels described 'not a world we should like to live in, but one we must be sure to avoid'.[48] However, it is often observed that utopia and dystopia may not be so distant. A vision of the best world generally tells us something about what the worst world looks like, just as a vision of a world we must be sure to avoid carries a message about the world in which we should aspire to live.

Utopia and dystopia have spawned further variants. Michel Foucault developed the concept of heterotopia to refer to the 'other places' in which difference is contained, but also enabled, within a social order.[49] Ernest

46. There are also other explanations of the name (which dates from the presence of European pastoralists in the area during the 1920s): see http://www.nma.gov.au/exhibitions/utopia_the_genius_of_emily_kame_kngwarreye/utopia. On this community, see further *Utopia*, Dir. John Pilger, Australia (2013).
47. See chap. 2 above and the references there cited.
48. B. F. Skinner, 'Visions of Utopia', *Listener* 77 (5 January 1967) 22.
49. See, e.g., Michel Foucault (Jay Miskowiec, trans.), *Of Other Spaces*, in *Architecture, Mouvement, Continuité* 5 (1984) 46, available at: https://foucault.info/documents/heterotopia/foucault.heteroTopia.en/.

Callenbach's *Ecotopia* helped to stimulate discussion of utopian thinking in the sphere of environmental activism.[50] And a vibrant tradition of feminist utopian (sometimes called feminotopian) fiction is traced from Christine de Pizan's *City of Ladies* through Charlotte Perkins Gilman's *Herland* to Marge Piercy's *Woman on the Edge of Time* and beyond, alongside which must also be set such feminist dystopias as Margaret Atwood's *The Handmaid's Tale*.[51] To be sure, writes China Miéville in the introduction to a quincentenary re-issue of More's text, utopia is ambiguous, chimerical and blood-stained. Yet, as these multiplying 'topias' seem to confirm, '[w]e can't do without [*Utopia*]. We are all and have always been Thomas More's children'.[52]

Human rights and the property question

The idea that human rights are the 'last utopia' was put forward in 2010 by Samuel Moyn.[53] In a review of Moyn's book, Robin Blackburn discusses its argument about the emergence and prospects of human rights as a worldwide movement, discourse and regime, and reflects that human rights 'can serve as a valuable watchword and measure'. But 'because inequality and injustice are structural, constituted by multiple intersecting planes of capitalist accumulation and realization, more needs to be said'. He continues: 'The plight of billions can be represented as a lack of effective rights, but it is the "property question" — the fact that the world is owned by a tiny elite of expropriators — that is constitutive of that plight.' And human rights 'cannot pose the property question relevant to the 21st century'.[54]

With its focus on the relatively (and in some parts, extremely) distant past in one country, this book has provided no basis for assessing whether Blackburn's remark about human rights and the twenty-first-century property question

50. Ernest Callenbach, *Ecotopia: A Novel* (New York: Bantam, new ed., 1990).
51. Christine de Pizan (Rosalind Brown-Grant, trans. and ed.), *The Book of the City of Ladies* (London: Penguin, 1999); Charlotte Perkins Gilman, *Herland* (London: Vintage, 2015); Marge Piercy, *Woman on the Edge of Time* (London: Penguin, 1976); Margaret Atwood, *The Handmaid's Tale* (London: Vintage, 2017).
52. China Miéville, 'Close to the Shore', in Thomas More, *Utopia* (London: Verso, 2016), 3, 6. This is not to suggest, of course, that every work now characterised as 'utopian' postdates the publication of *Utopia*. Christine de Pizan's text appeared in 1405.
53. Samuel Moyn, *The Last Utopia* (Cambridge, MA: Harvard University Press, 2010). See further chap. 1 above.
54. Robin Blackburn, 'Reclaiming Human Rights', *New Left Review* 69 (2011) 126, 137–38.

is correct. What it has attempted to show is that, if, or insofar as, that remark is correct, things might have been different. At a formative time and place in the development of the idea of human rights, the property question was posed and even made pivotal to the meaning of what were then termed the rights of man.[55] The relevant place and time were England in the 1790s. We have examined interventions in and around the 'Revolution controversy' (as Marilyn Butler has called it),[56] when English writers, politicians, and activists debated the significance of the French Revolution and its Declaration of the Rights of Man and the Citizen for their own country and the world.

The best known protagonists in this debate were, as they continue to be, Thomas Paine and Edmund Burke. The Revolution controversy is often portrayed as a disagreement between two camps divided along the lines of the two men's respective arguments for and against the rights of man. Our investigation has concerned itself with that disagreement and some of the other writers associated with it (Richard Price, Mary Wollstonecraft, John Thelwall, Hannah More, and Arthur Young), but in addition it has highlighted a third position. In the work of Thomas Spence, we have identified an outlook that took issue with both Paine and Burke, and did so in the name of an alternative vision of the 'real rights of man'. Spence is recognised today as a significant contributor to these discussions, and there is a growing literature on his work.[57] If, nonetheless, he remains relatively obscure, that is because for a long time he was either ignored or dismissed.

A book-length study of Spence appeared in 1927,[58] but it was not until later in the twentieth century that his thought became more widely considered. He and his circle were included as part of E. P. Thompson's narrative in *The Making of the English Working Class*, first published in 1963.[59] By Thompson's report, the English Jacobin movement of the 1790s produced 'two considerable theorists', who together 'reveal the tensions at its heart': one, Thelwall; the other, the 'revolutionist' Spence.[60] However, to the extent that Spence was

55. It is part of Moyn's argument in *The Last Utopia* that eighteenth-century discussions of the rights of man have no relevance to twentieth and twenty-first-century human rights, and should not be seen, in any sense, as their precursors. On this, see chap. 1 above.
56. See further chap. 5 above.
57. See, e.g., Alastair Bonnett and Keith Armstrong (eds.), *Thomas Spence: the Poor Man's Revolutionary* (London: Breviary Stuff, 2014), along with the references cited at the Thomas Spence Society website: http://www.thomas-spence-society.co.uk/.
58. Olive Rudkin, *Thomas Spence and his Connections* (London: George Allen & Unwin, 1927).
59. E. P. Thompson, *The Making of the English Working Class* (New York: Vintage, 1966), 161–63.
60. Ibid, 157, 161.

known during this period, it seems that the more prevalent view of him, and one to which Thompson himself alludes, was as a crank.[61] That at any rate was the assessment put forward by Thomas Knox in a paper about Spence published in 1977. For Knox, Spence was less a harbinger of modern radicalism than 'a mutation of the past'.[62] With his plan for vesting ownership of land in the parishes and his distinctive mix of eschatology and rationalism,[63] Spence secularised the millennium, but his 'was no more than the traditional dream of a local society of good husbandmen and moral economy'.[64]

In another publication of the same year, H.T. Dickinson spelled the point out. Spence 'concentrated all his attention on the agricultural sector of the economy just at a time when Britain was undergoing rapid commercial and industrial development'. '[U]tterly [failing] to recognize that industry could produce wealth far more rapidly than agriculture', he wished for 'a contented land of small peasant farmers'. 'Mines, factories and cotton mills had no place in Spence's vision of Britain's green and pleasant land.'[65] A second book-length study of Spence appeared in 1983, in which Mary Ashraf presented him in a light that could scarcely have been more different.[66] In Ashraf's telling, Spence was a proto-Marxist who 'may be said to have brought egalitarian democracy to the threshold of communism'.[67] Although concerned with agrarian relations, he had no attachment to the old ways, and 'no desire to restore the old peasantry'.[68] Instead, 'his theories gave the land question new content characteristic of transition towards the industrial age',[69] formulating 'a programme for a new economic system in the interests of the working classes'.[70]

Research on Spence since the later 1980s has emphasised the need to take him on his own terms, and while situating his work in a radical tradition with a past, present and future, scholars have mostly resisted characterisations of

61. Ibid, 161.
62. Thomas Knox, 'Thomas Spence: the Trumpet of the Jubilee', *Past and Present* 76(1) (1977) 75 (describing Spence as a 'radical crank').
63. On this, see chaps. 7 and 8 above.
64. Thomas Knox, 'Thomas Spence: the Trumpet of the Jubilee', *Past and Present* 76(1) (1977) 75, 98.
65. H.T. Dickinson, *Liberty and Property: Political Ideology in Eighteenth-Century Britain* (London: Weidenfeld and Nicholson, 1977), 267–68.
66. P.M. Ashraf, *The Life and Times of Thomas Spence* (Newcastle upon Tyne: Frank Graham, 1983).
67. Ibid, 26.
68. Ibid, 124.
69. Ibid, 125. For the idea that the 'roots of land nationalization can be traced back' to Spence, see also T. M. Parssinen, 'Thomas Spence and the Origins of English Land Nationalization', *Journal of the History of Ideas* 34(1) (1973) 135.
70. P.M. Ashraf, *The Life and Times of Thomas Spence* (Newcastle upon Tyne: Frank Graham, 1983), 26.

him as an early or primitive exponent of socialism or communism.[71] Not least that is because he never put forward, or sought to develop, a general critique of capitalism, still less a theory of historical change and eventual proletarian revolution. Malcolm Chase observes that Spence's critique focused on certain of the developments Marx would later discuss under the rubric of 'primitive accumulation', along with the 'wage contract, the cash nexus, and the materialistic concepts of success, failure, and happiness entailed on them'.[72] But if Spence is to be taken on his own terms, Chase and others do agree with Ashraf that his theories gave new content to the land question, and were firmly anchored in the emergent conditions of industrial capitalism. Thus, 'far from being some retarded throwback to pre-industrial, "traditional" society, agrarianism can — and indeed, must — be located precisely in the experience of labour during industrialization'.[73]

As Chase describes it, that experience engendered, on the one hand, a renewed appreciation of the productive agency of rural people in working the land. On the other hand, and more generally, the experience of labour during industrialisation also engendered a renewed sense of the importance of control over productive processes. Access to land seemed to offer the industrial working class a way of regaining something of the control they had lost, or were losing, over what was produced, how, when, where, and by and for whom. On Chase's account, the key issues were 'skill, security, independence, and status'. Behind the agrarian thinking of Spence was an awareness that '[s]ecurity was precarious, skill on the defensive, and status and independence were frequently beleaguered'.[74] It was not then just that the causes of inequality were seen as bound up with land monopoly. It was also that solutions to the problems thrown up by industrialisation were pursued in and through the land. At a time when the outcome of secular trends still seemed somewhat uncertain, demands for change to the system of landowning provided a

71. See, e.g., Alastair Bonnett, 'Spence and the Politics of Nostalgia', in Alastair Bonnett and Keith Armstrong (eds.), *Thomas Spence: The Poor Man's Revolutionary* (London: Breviary Stuff, 2014), 75, esp. 87.

72. Malcolm Chase, *The People's Farm: English Radical Agrarianism 1775–1840* (London: Breviary Stuff, 2nd ed., 2010), 161. On the connection between the sixteenth-century writings of Robert Crowley and this aspect of Marx's work, see chap. 2 above.

73. Ibid, 7. See also Noel Thompson, *The Real Rights of Man: Political Economies for the Working Class 1775–1850* (London: Pluto Press, 1998), 11 (arguing that Spence 'looked not to the reconstitution of an agrarian past but to an economy where commerce and manufacturing played a significant role').

74. Malcolm Chase, *The People's Farm: English Radical Agrarianism 1775–1840* (London: Breviary Stuff, 2nd ed., 2010), 7.

material basis from which to 'negotiate the form and future of industrializing society'.[75]

We have seen that Spence did not campaign for the restoration of customary rights of common. Rather, he envisaged an entirely new form of public ownership of land. In doing so, however, he drew on a long history and cultural memory of commoning practice and resistance to enclosure. This book has delved into something of that history and memory, as recorded in different periods and with reference to a variety of tropes. From More's man-eating sheep to Goldsmith's deserted village and Clare's fallen elm, the effects of the extinguishment of common rights were depicted in devastating terms. Historians warn us that the importance of enclosure relative to other contemporaneous developments bringing about social dislocation should not be overstated. The privatisation of land was only one element in a wider set of processes that were transforming life in the English countryside, and increasingly in the nation's towns and cities too, under conditions of emergent capitalism.[76] Nonetheless, it seems that contemporaries were not wrong to emphasise enclosure and use it as a metonym for all the rest. If in the 1860s Karl Marx could write of the dispossession of the peasantry as the 'point of departure' or 'economic original sin' of the capitalist mode of production, that is because it performed the crucial function of creating the 'free' wage-labourers without which there could be no such production.[77] Enclosure, as the reorganisation of land use, remodelling of landscape, and exclusion of agricultural producers from the land that wholly or partly provided their subsistence needs, was 'the basis of the whole process' and its most distinctive and conspicuous sign.[78]

Peter Linebaugh recalls that it was the extinguishment of rights of common and criminalisation of acts of commoning in the Prussian Rhineland that first set Marx on the path of his enquiry into political economy and class struggle.[79] In a series of articles written for the *Rheinische Zeitung* in 1842–3, Marx reported on debates in the Rhine Provincial Assembly about wood theft. The erosion of customary rights to take fallen wood and other forest resources had begun long before that time, but the legislation which was the

75. Ibid, 6, 13.
76. See, e.g., Ellen Meiksins Wood, *The Origins of Capitalism* (London: Verso, 2002), 109.
77. Karl Marx (Ben Fowkes, trans.), *Capital, Vol. 1* (London: Penguin, 1976), 873.
78. Ibid, 876.
79. Peter Linebaugh, 'Karl Marx, The Theft of Wood, and Working Class Composition: A Contribution to the Current Debate', *Crime and Social Justice* 6 (1976) 5, 6 (republished in Peter Linebaugh, *Stop, Thief!* (Oakland, CA: PM Press, 2014), 43).

outcome of these debates intensified the trend and served as a reminder that the criminal law was now at the service of forest owners. As Marx memorably put it, 'The wood thief has robbed the forest owner of wood, but the forest owner has made use of the wood thief to purloin the state itself.' In the process, Marx also wrote, the Rhenish legislators '[made] the right of human beings give way to that of young trees'. The triumph of commercial forestry put profit before people, and turned 'a customary right of the poor . . . into a monopoly of the rich'. Against this, he asserted the necessity of defending the 'poor, politically and socially propertyless', whose use-rights he identified with rights of the poor 'in all countries'.[80]

That enclosure caused hardship to commoners was not easy to ignore. However, in the argument of its advocates, this was the price to be paid for the modernisation and rationalisation of economic management to the benefit of all. Common lands and common rights were obstacles to progress, they said; to enable innovation and growth, indeed to ensure survival, landholders needed to be granted exclusive possession. Of course, that idea has not been confined to the early phases of capitalist development in Europe. Among more recent rearticulations, Garrett Hardin's 1968 article on the 'tragedy of the commons' is perhaps the most famous.[81] In explaining his thesis, Hardin invites readers to '[p]icture a pasture open to all'. 'It is to be expected', he goes on, 'that each herdsman will try to keep as many cattle as possible on the commons.' 'What is the utility *to me* of adding one more animal to my herd?', each will ask. Given that gains from the sale of animals are kept individually, while losses due to overgrazing are shared with others using the land, it will be reasoned that the most sensible course is to keep increasing herds — until the day arrives when all the cows die of starvation. Hardin uses this to illustrate the point that '[r]uin is the destination toward which all men rush, each pursuing his own best interest in a society that believes in the freedom of the commons'. As depicted by him, then, the commons are tragic in the sense that they lead inexorably to the degradation of shared resources; '[f]reedom in a commons brings ruin to all'.[82]

Thirty years after the publication of his original article, Hardin returned to the pages of *Science* to add the qualification that what he had described

80. Karl Marx, 'Proceedings of the Sixth Rhine Province Assembly', *Rheinische Zeitung*, No. 298, Supplement, 25 October 1842 (emphasis omitted), available at: http://hiaw.org/defcon6/works/1842/10/25.html.
81. Garrett Hardin, 'The Tragedy of the Commons', *Science* 162 (1968) 1243.
82. Ibid, 1244 (emphasis in original).

was the tragedy of an 'unmanaged commons'. It is freedom in an unmanaged commons that brings ruin to all, he now specified.[83] Certainly, a theme of much critical commentary and subsequent work had been the management or governance of common resources. For Elinor Ostrom, authors such as Hardin were too ready to assume that there was nothing users could do to save themselves because problems of non-cooperation were inherent in the logic of the commons. 'Instead of presuming that the individuals sharing a commons are inevitably caught in a trap from which they cannot escape', she writes, 'I argue that the capacity of individuals to . . . escape tragic outcomes' varies, so that the challenge for scholars is to expand understanding of relevant practice and how problems of non-cooperation are and are not resolved.[84] With that in mind, Ostrom's influential *Governing the Commons* brought together and analysed examples of successful and unsuccessful institutions for the management of shared resources (grazing land, but also forests, fisheries, irrigation systems and groundwater basins) in diverse settings, and developed from them an account of the variables affecting an institution's ability to assure long-term productive use. The general thrust was to raise, and suggest some answers to, the question of how best to frame policy on commons self-organisation and self-governance.

At the same time, Hardin's thesis also evoked another kind of response. For E. P. Thompson, Hardin not only failed to take into account the variable capacity of users successfully to manage common pool resources and escape tragic outcomes. He failed to take into account the whole nature of a commons. The English common of pasture to which his narrative alluded was not, as Hardin suggested, a right 'open to all'. Rights of common were local rights, and included the right to exclude strangers. Hence Thompson's widely quoted observation that enclosure made commoners 'strangers in their own land'.[85] As for the ruinous destination towards which all commoners supposedly rushed, Hardin ignored that the use of pasture lands was everywhere subject to detailed and regularly adjusted stints and other restrictions, backed up by community sanctions. While these did not always prevent overstocking, they put in place an orderly system far removed from the 'free-for-all' which Hardin described.[86] A related argument highlights that, where overstocking

83. Garrett Hardin, 'Extensions of "The Tragedy of the Commons"', *Science* 280 (1998) 682, 683.
84. Elinor Ostrom, *Governing the Commons* (Cambridge: Cambridge University Press, 1990), 14.
85. E. P. Thompson, *Customs in Common* (Pontypool: Merlin Press, 1991), 184. The phrase evokes an old trope, which we have seen, e.g., in the work of Spence (chap. 7 above).
86. E. P. Thompson, *Customs in Common* (Pontypool: Merlin Press, 1991), 108.

occurred, it was often less a manifestation of collective action problems than an active and deliberate assault on the commons.[87] By piling animals onto shared land, wealthy graziers made the case that the system of common rights did not work and should be replaced by a regime of private property, of which they would be beneficiaries.

If Hardin was heir to the English propagandists of Parliamentary enclosure and their Malthusian allies, what lends these discussions particular interest today is that the neoliberal nostrums of the decades following his intervention have been seen as unleashing a fresh, global wave of enclosures. And, with that, they have brought also a fresh appreciation of, and impetus for, local practices of commoning.[88] Thus, alongside the work of economists such as Ostrom and historians such as Thompson may be set the work of philosophers, geographers, sociologists, and others on the 'new enclosures' and 'new commons'. To touch on just a few relevant contributions, the Midnight Notes collective writes of how enclosures 'are not a one time process exhausted at the dawn of capitalism', but a 'regular return on the path of accumulation', latterly evident throughout the world in processes of privatisation, commodification, commercialisation, debt servicing, financialisation, gentrification, and individual responsibilisation.[89] In David Harvey's well-known formulation, the phenomena that Marx, following Adam Smith, associated with 'primitive' or 'original' accumulation are better conceptualised as instances of ongoing 'accumulation by dispossession'.[90] Regarding the heightened salience of accumulation by dispossession in the period since 1973, Harvey again cites patterns of privatisation of common property resources, commodification of biological and cultural forms, and (*inter alia*) suppression of indigenous and smallholder modes of production and consumption.[91]

To speak of the new enclosures is to connect these developments with a history of struggle against the predominance of exclusive ownership and big business, and to bring into focus the enduring and resurgent significance of

87. See, e.g., Simon Fairlie, 'A Short History of Enclosure in Britain', *The Land* 7 (2009), available at http://www.thelandmagazine.org.uk/articles/short-history-enclosure-britain.
88. Note, in the light of this literature, the words of caution expressed by Briony McDonagh and Stephen Daniels on the 'danger of casting the analytical net so wide as to thin the concept of enclosure beyond meaning' — a danger which they see as paralleled by the work of Hardin and others in which '[e]nclosure's antonym — the commons — has also been thinned beyond historical-geographical recognition as a sort of open access public space'. See Briony McDonagh and Stephen Daniels, 'Enclosure Stories: Narratives from Northamptonshire', *Cultural Geographies* 19(1) (2012) 107, 108.
89. 'Introduction to the New Enclosures', *Midnight Notes* 10 (1990) 1, 2.
90. David Harvey, *The New Imperialism* (Oxford: Oxford University Press, 2003), 144.
91. See ibid, chap 4.

older approaches to the organisation of economic life. One concept introduced by Maria Mies and Veronika Bennholdt-Thomsen to capture this is 'the subsistence perspective'.[92] Mies and Bennholdt-Thomsen recognise that any perspective which foregrounds subsistence is likely to be dismissed as romantic or even dangerous. On the other hand, they observe that it is part of the ideology of enclosure to denigrate non-market activity as backwardness, poverty and drudgery. They further observe that, in the face of great social dislocation, economic hardship, cultural dediversification and environmental destruction, that ideology can be, and is being, resisted by communities determined, as the authors put it, to 'reclaim the commons'.[93] Such initiatives are also the focus of writing and activism by David Bollier. For Bollier, new models of shared use and communal stewardship are a response to the 'silent theft' by which common wealth is being appropriated by corporate interests and turned into expensive commodities.[94] More than that, writes Massimo de Angelis, the defence and reinvention of commoning 'act as [a] "counter-enclosure" force' and a demonstration that 'around the issue of enclosures and their opposite — commons — we have a foundational entry point to a radical discourse on alternatives'.[95]

If in the present state of things only

I mentioned earlier Robin Blackburn's comment that human rights cannot pose the twenty-first-century property question, understood as a question about expropriation, ownership and the world we all share. It is worth pausing to note that that manner of framing the property question may itself be part of what is at issue. As Nicholas Blomley observes, a familiar feature of contemporary discussions is the 'depoliticisation' of property. For many people today, 'the crucial relation at the core of property' is 'that between the owner and the things owned', and there is no need to ask about the relations between owners and non-owners.[96] Likewise there is no need to interrogate the role of the state

92. Veronika Bennholdt-Thomsen and Maria Mies (Patrick Camiller et al., trans.), *The Subsistence Perspective* (London: Zed Books, 1999).
93. See, e.g., ibid, chap. 6.
94. See David Bollier, *Silent Theft* (New York and London: Routledge, 2002), *Think Like a Commoner* (Gabriola Island, BC: New Society, 2014) and other works.
95. Massimo de Angelis, *The Beginning of History: Value Struggles and Global Capital* (London: Pluto Press, 2007), 143, and Massimo de Angelis, 'Separating the Doing and the Deed: Capital and the Continuous Character of Enclosures', *Historical Materialism* 12(2) (2004) 57, 68. On this theme, see also Peter Linebaugh, *Stop, Thief!* (Oakland, CA: PM Press, 2014).
96. Nicholas Blomley, 'Remember Property?', *Progress in Human Geography* 29(2) (2005) 125, 126.

in underwriting those relations, the distant and recent acts of expropriation which lie behind them, and the circumstances in which forms of ownership that do not involve exclusive possession are currently being reasserted. But I have probably said enough about those matters, or certain of them. What remains now is to clarify my claim that if, or to the extent that, Blackburn is correct, the debates about the rights of man of 1790s England present a suggestive contrast, inasmuch as the property question did not there go unposed.

What kinds of questions, what kinds of issues, did proponents of the rights of man in the Revolution controversy raise when they argued for such rights? What did the rights of man signify to them? Our discussion has brought to notice two approaches, which can be referred to in shorthand as Paineite and Spencean. We have seen that, for Paine and others, the rights of man primarily signified popular sovereignty. They were the rights of the living against the manuscript-assumed authority of the dead — the right to choose government, to hold government to account, and to be governed on the basis that political authority derives from the people and always depends on their consent. Central to this was the abolition of aristocratic privilege, along with residual feudal institutions such as primogeniture. Realising the rights of man meant overcoming the old system of hereditary power, and installing a new system of representative government that, as Paine put it, would make every man a proprietor in government. Furthermore, Wollstonecraft argued, that popular proprietorship in government needed to include every woman.[97]

Yet if popular sovereignty was the primary significance of the rights of man in the work of their best-known proponents, it was not the only significance. As we have also seen, assertions of the rights of the living against the manuscript-assumed authority of the dead co-occurred with assertions of the rights of the living to live. These authors worried about the ill-effects of economic and social trends, and about the wretchedness and precarity that were being visited upon large sections of the poor. And whereas, according to Burke and other opponents of the rights of man, the remedy for that was harder work, greater frugality and, where shortfalls still remained, the discretionary benevolence of the rich, to supporters of the rights of man, subsistence was not a matter of charity, but of rights. 'I will advocate the Rights of Man', wrote Paine in introducing his proposals in *Rights of Man* for progressive taxation and social welfare.[98] No less than proprietors, said Thelwall in

97. See chap. 5 above.
98. Thomas Paine, *Rights of Man, Part II*, in Bruce Kuklick (ed.), *Paine: Political Writings* (Cambridge: Cambridge University Press, 2000), 155, 213. See chap. 5 above.

putting forward his ideas on fair wages, labourers have the right to maintain themselves in decency and plenty.[99]

Welfare and wages, then, were part of what these writers talked about when they argued for the rights of man. Anxious about the ambiguities of progress, they called for measures to redress or at least mitigate the destructive effects of what they and others mostly regarded as 'improvement', and used the rights of man to raise and justify that demand. The contrast with Spence comes into view when we recall that, rather than aiming at redress and mitigation, he presented a challenge to the system of private ownership in land itself. For him, the hardships and privations of the poor were not remediable by-products of Parliamentary enclosure and related developments. They were fundamental to the expropriation and monopolising of land. The nation's land was rightly the 'people's farm',[100] and the consequences of its loss could be rectified only through systemic change involving restitution. This certainly did not exclude, but instead, to his mind, necessitated political change of the kind urged by Paine and others, as it was a feature of what he termed 'the scrambling system' (everyone is invited to 'join in the scramble and catch that catch can') that the most powerful — the landlords — seized the government and kept it.[101]

Spence is not generally, or mainly, studied as a theorist of the rights of man. The scholarship on his work has mostly focused on the agrarian dimensions of his thought, along with his place in the activist circles of Newcastle and London, his intellectual development and the influences that shaped it, his modes of communication, his project for spelling reform, and his significance as a designer of tokens and coins. Nonetheless, it is striking that he expressed his ideas about land in the language of universal rights. The discovery in 2005 of a copy of his 1775 lecture outlining his land plan — believed lost until that point — helped to draw attention to this, confirming that the lecture had been entitled *Property in Land Every One's Right*.[102] Later (and always extant) editions of the lecture, published after the appearance of Paine's *Rights of Man*, carried the title *Rights of Man* and, eventually, *The Real Rights of Man*.[103]

99. See chap. 6 above.
100. Malcolm Chase, *The People's Farm: English Radical Agrarianism 1775–1840* (London: Breviary Stuff, 2nd ed., 2010), 1.
101. See Thomas Spence, *The Reign of Felicity* (London: T. Spence, 1796), reprinted in H. T. Dickinson, *The Political Works of Thomas Spence* (Newcastle upon Tyne: Avero, 1982), 41.
102. On the rediscovery of this lecture, see Alastair Bonnett, 'The Other Rights of Man: the Revolutionary Plan of Thomas Spence, *History Today* 57(9) (2007) 42.
103. See chap. 7 above.

Foregrounding, then, Spence's contribution as a writer about the rights of man, we might summarise his distinctive understanding of, and engagement with, these rights in terms of three aspects.

First, as Spence conceived them, the rights of man belonged with the effort to elucidate the conditions of oppression, and to transform those conditions. In literature about late eighteenth-century England, the word 'radical' is applied to dissidents across a wide spectrum from reformists to revolutionaries. But that usage should not be allowed to obscure the fact that Spence was a radical in the precise sense that he took as his goal change from the 'root' upwards.[104] As Chase explains, radicals of his sort sought out 'the roots of injustice', and developed analyses geared to the establishment of an economic and social order in which privilege was defunct.[105] We have seen that Spence criticised those whose vision of the rights of man he identified with a 'false Tree of Liberty' that would cause the multitude to rise up, and hierarchies and governments to be overthrown, while leaving oppression still to remain.[106] Importantly, however, his response was not to repudiate the rights of man. Rather, in criticising the failure of Paine and others to grapple with the roots of indignity and unfreedom, he advanced his own counter-vision of the 'real rights of man'.

Secondly, Spence's counter-vision had at its centre the right to subsistence. If his specific claim had to do with property in land, his more general point was that access to, and control over, the means of sustaining life was everyone's right. In this, he carried forward a tradition of connecting rights, humanity, and subsistence that is coeval with the threat to subsistence posed by the advent, or rather imposition, of market dependence. Long before the rights of man became a thing, men and women in sixteenth- and seventeenth-century England argued that they had the right to a livelihood, that the earth was there to support all human beings, and that it was wrong for the rich to monopolise its produce. We reviewed some writings along those lines in the initial chapters of this book.[107] It bears emphasis that the right to subsistence predates, and does not fit, the modern conceptualisation according to which

104. It seems that the term 'radical' in this sense itself dates from the late eighteenth century. See Timothy Morton and Nigel Smith, 'Introduction', in Timothy Morton and Nigel Smith (eds.), *Radicalism in British Literary Culture, 1650–1830* (Cambridge: Cambridge University Press, 2002), 1.

105. Malcolm Chase, *The People's Farm: English Radical Agrarianism 1775-1840* (London: Breviary Stuff, 2nd ed., 2010), 157.

106. See chap. 9 above.

107. See chaps. 2, 3 and 4 above.

rights are itemised as part of catalogues. The comments of Raj Patel in a study of twenty-first-century appeals to the right to subsistence are pertinent here. This 'isn't a call for a specific [right or] set of rights', he says. The point is to 'make . . . rights real', reset 'the terms of value', and assert the equal right of all to the 'stuff that [people] need' for a dignified life.[108]

Thirdly and finally, Spence worked with an account of the rights of man in which the rights of man were also the rights of particular people in particular places, and the rights of particular people in particular places were also the rights of man. Universal nature and local tradition did not appear in his writing as alternative justificatory schemas. Rather, both were reference-points in the articulation of social-systemic injustice. In a passage already partly cited in an earlier chapter, Christopher Hill writes that the 'rights of man are inevitably abstracted from the society in which they are conceived, and take the assumptions and property relations of that society for granted'. 'The state of nature gives the right answers', he adds, 'because it is peopled with abstractions.'[109] One may speculate with some confidence that Spence would have agreed with everything in that passage except the word 'inevitably'. It was the experience of expropriation to which his real rights of man were addressed, the daily dealing with social hierarchy which lent meaning to his state of nature. These phenomena were irreducibly local and demonstrably diverse, but they also connected those involved, and cast in relief the gap between shared humanity and real inequalities.

Eric Hobsbawm once described Paine as 'unforgotten',[110] and my very short story about Paine earlier in this chapter attests to that as well. Of course, we should not be surprised that, as between him and Spence, it is he who is remembered, his legacy that is fought over. The ignoring and dismissal of Spence began already in his own lifetime, while Paine's ideas about the rights of man formed part of the context in which the bourgeois revolution would go on to flourish and spread. Yet the Spencean approach, as I have termed it, has not been neutralised permanently. To the victims of capitalist modernisation, it still remains available — available to bread helmet man and his fellow demonstrators in Sanaa, available to the indigenous inhabitants of the place they did not name Utopia, available to the people for whom attendees at the Wellingborough Diggers' Festival were asked to make donations of food,

108. Raj Patel, *The Value of Nothing* (London: Portobello Books, 2011), 129, 122.
109. Christopher Hill, *Puritanism and Revolution* (London: Secker and Warburg, 1958), 116. See chap. 8 above.
110. Eric Hobsbawm, *Labouring Men* (London: Weidenfeld & Nicholson, 2015), 3.

available to all those who will never celebrate the launch of a new luxury housing development like the one on the site of the former Albion Mill. If, as de Angelis proposes, the new enclosures and new commons are a foundational entry point to a radical discourse on alternatives, so too, and relatedly, are the real rights of man.

In saying that, I need to acknowledge that, to some twenty-first-century ears, Spence's discourse will sound at times rather odd, replete as it is with visions, dreams, reveries and ancient prophecies. We have seen that, in an earlier era, Winstanley likewise located the origins of his communal subsistence project and law of freedom in a trance.[111] In the eighteenth century, as well as before then, critics of such people accused them of 'enthusiasm'. The primary meaning of enthusiasm was 'excessive' and 'vulgar' religious feeling and belief. It denoted the popular millenarianism that coexisted in the work of most enthusiasts with more rationalist and 'respectable' elements. But the term was also used with reference to the rebellious imagination, creative energy and subversive power of the multitude. As Jon Mee explains in a study of the 'dangerous enthusiasm' of William Blake, 'theories of the psychopathology of enthusiasm . . . [portrayed it as] a contagious disease capable of rapidly infecting the lower orders'.[112] In the case of Spence, the slur seems not to have stuck. Remonstrating with the judges during his 1801 trial for seditious libel, he claims to have declared: 'Are we never to expect a better State of Things than the present? . . . Must we be debarred from the Pleasures of the Imagination also? If in the present State of Things only we have Hope we are of all Creatures the most Miserable.'[113]

111. See chap. 4 above.

112. Jon Mee, *Dangerous Enthusiasm: William Blake and the Culture of Radicalism in the 1790s* (Oxford: Clarendon Press, 1992), 49. On anxieties surrounding the imagination in this period, see also John Barrell, *Imagining the King's Death: Figurative Treason, Fantasies of Regicide 1793–1796* (New York: Oxford University Press, 2000), esp. 5–44.

113. Thomas Spence, *The Important Trial of Thomas Spence* (London: A. Seale, 2nd ed., 1803), 9, reprinted in H. T. Dickinson, *The Political Works of Thomas Spence* (Newcastle upon Tyne: Avero, 1982), 92, 93.

Index

Note: *For the benefit of digital users, indexed terms that span two pages (e.g., 52–53) may, on occasion, appear on only one of those pages.*
Figures are indicated by *f* following the page number.

Abdullah, Khaled, 242*f*
accumulation by dispossession, 260; *see also* primitive accumulation
Adair, Douglass, 212*n*3
Adams, John, 97
agrarian law, 141–42, 167, 169–70, 199; *see also* Paine (*Agrarian Justice*)
aid-in-wages, 133, 135–36, 148–49, 150, 181–82; *see also* Speenhamland system
Albion, 151*n*144
Albion Flour Mill (Brisbane), 243–44, 265–66
Albion Mills (London), 121–23, 127
Alston, Philip, 4*n*10, 15–16
American Revolution, 13–14, 96, 97–98, 101–2, 111–12, 211–14
  and Burke, Edmund, 96
  and Paine, Thomas, 96, 111–12
  tree of liberty, 211–14
ancient constitution, 76–78, 80–81, 91, 92–93, 101–2, 104–5, 185–86, 187–89, 225–26, 227
Anderson, Perry, 208–9
Anievas, Alexander, 13*n*34
Arab Spring, 241–42
Arbuthnot, John, 159–60
Arendt, Hannah, 183–85, 190–91, 206–7
  and Burke, Edmund, 184–85, 206–7
  rights of man, 183–84, 190–91
  right to have rights, 183–84
Ashley, Isaac, 122*n*6, 122*n*7
Ashraf, Mary, 177*n*91, 177*n*93, 255–56
Atwood, Margaret, 252–53
Auricchio, Laura, 239

Ball, John, 45–47, 51–53, 68–70
banditry, social, 237
Barlow, Joel, 197–98
Barrell, John, 9, 126*n*23, 179*n*101, 266*n*112
Bates, Jack (aka Jack the Blaster), 1–3, 18
Batey, Mavis, 162*n*25
Beck, Glenn, 249
Becket, Thomas à, 48–49
Bellamy, Liz, 155*n*4, 161–62
Bennholdt-Thomsen, Veronika, 260–61
Berger, John, 8–9
Berlin, Michael, 122*n*5
Bernstein, Eduard, 202*n*105
Billingsley, John, 159–60
Billington, Michael, 251
Bindman, David, 100*n*26, 110*n*88, 110*n*90, 178*n*97, 179*n*99, 214*n*14
Bindoff, Stanley, 66–67
Bingo, 18–19, 250–51
birthrights, 4–5, 78–79, 82–83, 90, 93, 118, 189–90, 234–35; *see also* human rights, native rights, natural rights, rights of man
Black Act, 114, 150–51, 222–23
Blackburn, Robin, 253–54, 261–62
Blake, William, 7, 121–22, 150–51, 223, 266
Bliss, Lee, 63, 66–67
Blomley, Nicholas, 47*n*9, 163*n*32, 220*n*39, 261–62
Board of Agriculture, 163, 169
Bohstedt, John, 10*n*29, 123*n*12, 127*n*25, 129*n*34, 129*n*37, 137*n*84, 150*n*137
Bollier, David, 260–61
Bond, Edward, 18–19, 250–51
Bonnett, Alastair, 1*n*1, 1*n*3, 171*n*70, 171*n*71, 208*n*130, 254*n*57, 256*n*71, 263*n*102
Book of Orders, 62, 83, 123–24
Botting, Fred, 119
bread, 46, 58–59, 71–72, 85, 123–26, 128–29, 133, 137, 138–39, 241, 242, 243
  aid-in-wages tied to price of, 133; *see also* Speenhamland system
  bread helmet man, 241, 242*f*, 242–43, 265–66
  mourning loaves, 125–26, 242–43
  no living by bread alone, 58–59
  price rises, 23–24, 32–33, 62, 82–83, 123–26, 127–29, 130–32, 133, 138–39, 144–45, 166, 241–42; *see also* dearth
  riots, *see* food riots
  significance of, 71–72, 85, 128, 242
bread helmet man, 241, 242*f*, 242–43, 265–66
Brothers, Richard, 6–7

Brown, Lancelot 'Capability', 162, 231–32
Burke, Edmund, 3, 95–96, 99–108, 100*f*, 109–10, 111–15, 116, 118–19, 127, 135–37, 139, 142, 148–49, 164–65, 177, 184–89, 195, 196–97, 201–2, 203–4, 224–30, 232, 233, 239–40, 254, 262–63
  and Arendt, Hannah, 184–85, 206–7
  Ireton, Henry, compared to, 118, 201–2
  Letter to the Duke of Richmond, 226–27
  Letters on a Regicide Peace, 145
  and More, Hannah, 137, 139, 148–49, 164–65
  A Philosophical Enquiry etc., 107–8
  and Paine, Thomas, 96, 109–10, 111–15, 116, 118–19, 142, 148–49, 186–88, 190–91, 195, 196–97, 201–2, 232, 233, 239–40, 254, 262–63
  and Price, Richard, 99–100, 100*f*, 101–3, 104–5, 118–19, 186–87, 195, 224–25, 254
  Reflections on the Revolution in France, 3, 95–96, 99–105, 224–30
  and Spence, Thomas, 177, 197, 206–7, 254
  and Thelwall, John, 145, 148–50, 187–88, 190–91, 262–63
  Thoughts and Details on Scarcity, 135–37
  and Wollstonecraft, Mary, 105–8, 116, 188–89, 190–91
Bushaway, Bob, 222*n*48, 236*n*101
Butler, Marilyn, 96*n*7, 96*n*9, 237*n*109, 253–54
Byron, Frederick George, 116, 117*f*

Callenbach, Ernest, 252–53
capitalism, 7–8, 10–11, 12–13, 16, 17, 22, 66–67, 79–80, 84, 119–20, 140, 145, 160, 207–8, 255–57, 260
  commercial society, 7, 10, 140
  industrial revolution, 8, 79–80, 119–20, 124, 145, 221–23, 255–57
  transition debate, 7, 11, 17–18, 22, 67
  see also enclosure, proletarianisation
Chambers, John, 157–58
Chapman, John, 155*n*5
charity, 65–66, 106–7, 124, 136, 139, 141–42, 143–44, 148–49, 262–63
Charles I, 83–84, 86, 99–100, 220
Charles II, 102, 225
Charles I (unfinished play), 202–3
Chase, Malcolm, 255–57, 263*n*100, 264
citizenship, 4, 77, 103–4, 149–50, 183–84, 206–7, 226, 239–40
civilisation, 113–14, 139–42, 252
Claeys, Gregory, 7
Clare, John, 235–37, 238–39, 257
  The Fallen Elm, 236–37, 257
  The Moors, 236
  Nutting, 235–36
  The Village Minstrel, 236
Clarke, William, 73–74
coal, 221–23, 246
Cobham, 82–83, 87–88, 89, 245–46
Coleridge, Samuel Taylor, 215, 229–31, 232, 233
  Conciones ad Populum, 230–31
  pantisocracy, 230–31
  The Raven, 229–31, 233
Combe, William, 250–51
commercial society, *see* capitalism
common rights, *see* rights of common
commons, 7, 11, 24–25, 46–47, 49–50, 52–54, 55, 56–57, 58, 71–72, 82, 85–89, 90–91, 93–94, 150–51, 154, 155–60, 163, 165–66, 168, 169, 171–72, 175–77, 181–82, 215, 216–17, 220–21, 234–37, 240, 244–45, 246, 257–61
  common land, 7, 11, 24–25, 46–47, 49–50, 52–54, 55, 56–57, 58, 71–72, 82, 85–89, 90–91, 93–94, 150–51, 154, 155–60, 163, 165–66, 168, 169, 171–72, 175–77, 181–82, 215, 216–17, 220–21, 234–37, 240, 244–45, 246, 257–60
  commoning, *see* rights of common
  enclosure, *see* enclosure
  governance, 258–60
  'new commons', 260–61
  overstocking, 55, 259–60
  tragedy of the commons, 258–60
commonwealth, 26–30, 33–34, 49, 52–53, 60, 69–70, 90, 198–99, 217
  'commonwealths' government, 90
  concept, 26–27, 34–35, 49, 198
  Dudley, Edmund, on, 26–30, 217
  Harrington, James, on, 198–99
  More, Thomas, on, 33–34
  Tree of Commonwealth, 21–22, 26–31, 42, 214, 217–18, 219
Commonwealthmen (aka Commonwealthsmen), 21–22, 36–37, 42–43, 67
consumer protection, 62, 83, 123–24, 127–29, 135–36
  Book of Orders, 62, 83, 123–24
  repeal of statutory protections, 62, 123–24, 129, 135–36
  see also dearth, food riots
Cook, Elizabeth Heckendorn, 239
Cooper, Thomas, 197–98
Copley, Stephen, 162*n*28
Coppe, Abiezer, 89
Coriolanus, 63–66
Corvol, Andrée, 212*n*6
Coster, Robert, 88–89, 93–94, 182
Coventry, 46–48
Crawford, Patricia, 75*n*20
criminal law, 32, 33–34, 109–10, 113–15, 150–51, 177, 181–82, 222–24, 230–31, 240, 257–58
  Black Act, 114, 150–51, 222–23
  death penalty, 113–16, 181–82, 222–24
  sedition, 38–40, 46–47, 109–10, 177, 200, 215, 230–31, 266
  treason, 26–27, 177, 230–31, 266*n*112

wood-related offences, 222–23, 235–36, 240, 257–58
Cromwell, Oliver, 73–74, 75, 89, 94
Crowley, Robert, 21–22, 36–43, 47–48, 52, 65–66, 182, 256*n*72
Informacion and peticion etc., 38
Of Rente Raysers, 37
Of Unsaciable Purchasers, 37–38
The Way to Wealth, 38–40, 41, 47–48, 52, 182
Crowther, Mathew, 178*n*97, 178*n*98
customary rights, *see* rights of common

Daniels, Stephen, 215*n*16, 225*n*61, 227, 239, 260*n*88
Darwin, Erasmus, 121
Dawe, Philip, 212, 213*f*
de Angelis, Massimo, 260–61, 265–66
dearth, 23–24, 32–33, 60–66, 82–83, 123–32, 135–37, 138–39, 140–41, 144–45, 148–49, 150, 166, 182, 241–42
Book of Orders, 62, 83, 123–24
and Midland Rising, 57–59, 60–66, 182
and Revolution Controversy, 125–51
Smith, Adam, on, 130–32, 133–34, 135, 148
see also food riots, moral economy
Declaration of the Rights of Man and the Citizen, 4, 6, 13–14, 163–64, 183–84, 186, 196, 207, 231–32, 253–54
Defoe, Daniel, 191–92
de Lafayette, Marquis (aka Lafayette), 196–97, 200
democracy, 7, 175, 179–80, 182, 200, 206–7, 255
de Pizan, Christine, 252–53
depopulation, 26, 32, 36, 40, 42, 58, 60–62, 65–66, 153–54, 250
Dickinson, H.T., 255
Diggers (Civil War), 12, 69–70, 71–73, 82–92, 93–94, 182, 201–3, 220–22, 244–46
Coster, Robert, 88–89, 93–94, 182
Elmbridge Diggers Heritage Group, 244–45, 246
Iver, 88–89
Little Heath (Cobham), 87–88, 89, 245–46
Spence, Thomas, compared to, 182, 201–2
St George's Hill, 71–72, 82, 85, 87–88, 94, 245
The True Levellers Standard Advanced, 72, 85–86, 94, 245
Wellingborough, 88–89, 245–46, 265–66
Wigan Diggers' Festival, 246
Winstanley (film), 246
Winstanley, Gerrard, 71–73, 82–92, 93–94, 182, 201–2, 220–21, 245–46, 266
Diggers (Midland Rising), 56–62, 61*f*, 65–70
Dobson, Richard, 46*n*6, 69–70*n*91
Donnelly, F.K., 202*n*105, 205*n*118
Douglas, Jane, 214*n*15
Dudley, Edmund, 21–22, 26–31, 36, 42, 52–53, 65–66, 69, 214, 217–18, 219
The Tree of Commonwealth, 21–22, 26–31, 42, 214, 217–18, 219
Dyer, Christopher, 45*n*3
Dyer, George, 189–91, 197–98, 205–6
An Inquiry into the Nature of Subscription etc., 189–91
The Complaints of the Poor People of England, 205–6

Edward VI, 36–37
elections, right to take part in, *see* suffrage
Elmbridge Diggers Heritage Group, 244–45, 246
enclosure, 7–9, 11–12, 18–19, 24–26, 35–37, 40–42, 46–48, 49–51, 52–54, 55–57, 58, 59–63, 66–69, 79–80, 81–82, 83–85, 90, 92, 98–99, 117–18, 119–20, 154–60, 163–64, 165–70, 174, 176–77, 179–81, 192–93, 201–2, 203, 207, 214, 216–17, 220–21, 222–23, 235–36, 238–39, 240, 246–47, 250–51, 257, 258, 259–61, 263, 265–66
figurative, 18–19, 52–54, 106–7, 167–68, 170, 174, 207, 220–21, 236
materiality (hedges etc.), 24–25, 26, 47, 49–50, 52–54, 56–57, 58, 157, 163, 203, 214, 220
'new enclosures', 260–61, 265–66
Parliamentary enclosure, 8, 11, 98–99, 117–18, 119–20, 154–60, 179–81, 193, 235–36, 263
Young, Arthur, on, 163–64, 165–68, 169–70
see also commons, hedge-breaking, improvement, rebellion, rights of common
Engels, Friedrich, 208–9
English Civil War, *see* English Revolution
Englishmen, rights of freeborn, 12, 78, 104–5, 184, 185–86, 190–91, 196–97, 234–35
see also birthrights, native rights
English Revolution
Agreement of the People, 74–75, 81–82
Diggers, 12, 69–70, 71–73, 82–92, 93–94, 182, 201–3, 220–22, 244–46
Levellers, 12, 69–70, 72–73–
New Model Army, 72–74, 78–80, 81–82
Putney Debates, 72–82
Ranters, 72–73, 89, 202–3
'two revolutions', 72–73
engrossing (market practice), 23–24, 62, 123–24, 128–29, 131–32, 135–36
engrossment (farm size), 23–24, 25–26, 35–38, 40, 42, 55, 59, 79–80, 199, 200
enthusiasm, 266
estovers, right of, 24–25, 158, 220–21, 222–23, 240, 257–58
Euston Hall, 114–15, 231–32
Evelyn, John, 221–23, 231
execution, 26–27, 31–32, 51–52, 58, 65, 83–84, 86, 91–92, 99–100, 110, 114–16, 124, 150–51, 211–12, 220, 222–24, 240
regicide, 83–84, 86, 91–92, 99–100, 220
Tyburn, 223–24
Exodus, Book of, 85–86

Fairfax, Thomas, 94
famine, *see* dearth
Fifth Monarchists, 72–73
Firth, Charles, 73–74
fiscal seigneurialism, 55
Flowerdew, John, 48–50, 54
foldcourse system, 53, 54
food insecurity, *see* dearth
food riots, 56–66, 123–29, 132, 138–39, 144–45, 148, 149–50, 241–42, 242*f*
  moral economy, 123–24, 127–30, 132, 135–36, 148, 149, 150, 254–55
  mourning loaves, 125–26, 242–43
  price-setting *(taxation populaire)*, 62–64
  see also dearth
forest law, 215*n*19, 216–17, 222–23, 235–36, 257–58
Foucault, Michel, 252–53
Frankenstein, 119–20
Franklin, Benjamin, 97
freeborn Englishmen. *See* Englishmen
Freeman, Michael, 15–16
French Revolution, 3, 4, 6, 11, 13–14, 95–120, 125–27, 139–40, 145, 148–49, 163–64, 183–85, 186, 196, 201–2, 203–4, 207, 212–14, 233, 240, 253–54, 262–65
  Bastille, storming of, 99, 163–64, 233, 240
  Declaration of the Rights of Man and the Citizen, 4, 6, 13–14, 95–120, 163–64, 183–84, 186, 196, 207, 231–32, 253–54
  de Lafayette, Marquis (aka Lafayette), 196–97, 200
  Grégoire, Henri Jean-Baptiste (aka Abbé Grégoire), 212–15
  Revolution controversy in England, 3, 6, 11, 13–14, 95–120, 125–27, 139–40, 145, 148–49, 163–64, 184–85, 201–2, 203–4, 253–54, 262–65
  tree of liberty, 212–14
Frend, William, 197–98
Froissart, Jean, 46, 49–50, 51*n*24, 68–69
Fulford, Tim, 226*n*68, 236–37

Gainsborough, Thomas, 8–9
  Mr and Mrs Andrews, 8–9, 9*f*
  The Cottage Door, 9, 10*f*
Garrick, David, 225
Garside, Peter, 162*n*28
Gatrell, Vic, 223*n*52, 224*n*57
Gay, Edwin, 56
gender, 9, 83–84, 107–9, 137, 138, 158–59, 188–89
  enclosure, differentiated effects, 158–59
  roles, relations and stereotypes, 9, 83–84, 107–9, 137, 138, 158–59, 188–89
Genesis, Book of, 77–78, 175, 217
Gibberd, Graham, 122*n*4
Gillespie Brothers, 243
Gillray, James, 99–100, 100*f*, 101–2, 110, 111*f*, 117–19, 126*f*, 126–27, 143*f*, 143–44, 227*n*74
  Copenhagen House, 143–44, 143*f*
  Smelling out a Rat etc., 99–100, 100*f*, 101–2
  The Republican Attack, 126–27, 126*f*
  Tom Paine's Nightly Pest, 110, 111*f*, 118–19
Gilman, Charlotte Perkins, 252–53
glean, right to, 24, 46–47, 158
Glorious Revolution, 97–98, 101–2, 112, 194–97, 208–9, 222
Godwin, William, 6–7, 119, 197–98
Goldsmith, Oliver, 153–54, 161–62, 179–80, 197–98, 257
government, forms of, 90, 91–92, 113–14, 115–16, 140, 174, 181–82, 262, 263
  'commonwealths' *vs* 'kingly', 90, 91–92
  hereditary *vs* representative, 113–14, 115–16, 140, 262, 263
  limited significance of, 174, 181–82
  see also democracy, pantisocracy, popular sovereignty
Grafton, Duchy of, 114–15, 231–32
  Euston Hall, 114–15, 231–32
  and Paine, Thomas, 114–15, 231–32
grazing, right of, 24–25, 47, 55–56, 157–58, 165–66, 168, 176–77, 235–36, 246–47, 258–60
Grégoire, Henri Jean-Baptiste (aka Abbé Grégoire), 212–14, 215
Gurney, John, 71*n*4, 82*n*58, 89

Hadfield, Miles, 225*n*63
Halliwell, Miles, 246
Halme-Tuomisaari, Miia, 13–14
Hammond, Barbara, 133*n*52
Hammond, J.L., 133*n*52
Harcourt, first Earl, 161–62
Harden, David, 212*n*6
Hardin, Garrett, 258–60
Harrington, James, 198–200
Harris, Mary Dormer, 46–47*n*7
Harvey, David, 260
Hearts of Oak (song), 225
hedge-breaking, 47, 49–50, 53, 56–57, 58, 59–60, 203, 220
Heller, Henry, 13*n*34
Henry VII, 40, 55–56
Henry VIII, 26–27, 36–37, 48–49, 54–55, 66–67
Hexham, 234–35
Hill, Christopher, 24*n*8, 68*n*86, 71–73, 77*n*35, 79–80, 86*n*84, 87, 88*n*91, 93, 94, 182, 201–2, 206–7, 265
Hilton, Rodney, 13*n*32, 50–51, 68*n*87, 216*n*21, 238*n*113
Hindle, Steve, 56*n*41, 66–67, 82*n*59, 82–83
history, 'four stages' theory of, 140
Hitchens, Christopher, 250
Hobsbawm, Eric, 122*n*6, 122–23, 237, 265–66
Hoffmann, Stefan-Ludwig, 16
Holinshed's Chronicles of England, Scotland and Ireland, 48–49, 51–52, 219

Holstun, James, 55*n*32, 63*n*62, 66–67, 72*n*7, 79*n*43, 91*n*106, 92, 93–94, 181*n*108, 220*n*37, 220*n*40
Hood, Robin, *see* Robin Hood
Hopper, Andrew, 66–67
Hopper, Joshua, 246–47
Hoskins, W.G., 25*n*9
Howes, Edmund, 56–58, 59–60, 65–66, 68–69
human rights, 2–5, 12–17, 18–19, 183–84, 206–7, 253–54, 261–62
  origins, 13–17, 265–66
  relation to 18th-century rights of man, 3–5, 16–18, 184, 253–54, 261–62, 265–66
  right to have rights, 183–84
  Universal Declaration of Human Rights, 13–14
  see also natural rights, rights of man
humanity, 16–17, 26–27, 29–30, 31, 46, 52–53, 69, 93–94, 106–7, 116, 183–84, 188–89, 195–96, 204–6, 208–9, 233, 251, 264–65
Humphries, Jane, 158
Hunt, Lynn, 2*n*5, 5*n*13, 16–17, 18*n*53
Huxley, Aldous, 252

improvement, 8–9, 90–91, 102, 104–5, 106–7, 114–15, 141, 156, 160–64, 167–70, 174–75, 201, 221–22, 231–32, 236–37, 238–39, 240, 263
Inclosure Acts, 98–99, 155–56, 166; *see also* Parliamentary enclosure
inheritance, 17, 22–23, 101–2, 106–7, 112–14, 115, 117–18, 139–40, 141–42, 167–68, 169–70, 174, 175, 180, 184, 185, 187–88, 201–2, 208–9, 231, 233–34, 262
Ireton, Henry, 74–77, 80–82, 92–93, 118
Isaiah, Book of, 59, 60, 192–93, 197–98
Iver, 88–89

Jackson, Angus, 251
Janowitz, Anne, 190*n*44, 197
Jefferson, Thomas, 97
Johnson, Joseph, 105
Johnston, Kenneth, 6*n*17, 214*n*11
jubilee, 192–93, 207–8, 254–55

Keane, John, 114*n*114, 186*n*17, 231*n*83, 231*n*84
Kent, William, 162, 231–32
Kett, Robert, 49–52, 53–54, 67–68, 69–70
Kett's Rebellion, 47–56, 66–70, 182, 219–20
  Flowerdew, John, 48–50, 54
  Kett, Robert, 49–52, 53–54, 67–68, 69–70
  Kett's Demands. Being in Rebellion, 50–52, 55–56, 66–68, 69
  Mousehold Heath, 49–50, 53–54, 66–67, 69–70, 219
  Seymour, Edward, first Duke of Somerset, 50, 51–52, 55–56
  Tree of Reformation (aka Oke of Reformation), 50, 66–67, 219–20
king's coach, attack on, 125–27, 126*f*, 242

Knight, Richard Payne, 162
Knox, Thomas, 254–55
Koskenniemi, Martti, 5*n*12

labour, *see* wage-labour
Lafayette, *see* de Lafayette, Marquis
laissez faire, 122–23, 130–32, 133–37, 148, 149–50
land, 8–9, 11–13, 17–18, 22–26, 32–33, 37–38, 41, 51–52, 54–56, 62–63, 74–75, 83–84, 85–86, 90–91, 92, 93–94, 140–43, 153–54, 155–63, 165–70, 171–77, 179–82, 192–94, 197–202, 207–8, 222, 236–37, 239–40, 250, 255–57, 258, 263–65
  property-based model, 92, 181–82; *see also* enclosure
  rights-based model, 92, 93–94, 181–82; *see also* commons, rights of common
  tenure, forms of, 22–23, 26, 51–52, 55–56, 82, 157
landscape aesthetics, 8–9, 162, 227
landscape parks, 114–15, 153–54, 161–62, 222, 231–32, 236–37, 240
Laski, Harold, 6
Latin, 31–32, 35, 45–46, 51–52, 67–68, 212–14, 227–28, 252
lease-mongering, 23
Lee, Richard 'Citizen', 6–7, 197–98, 214
Levellers (Civil War), 12, 72–83, 90, 93, 118, 150–51, 182, 201–3, 205*n*120
  Lilburne, John, 72–73, 75, 81–82, 203, 205*n*120
  Overton, Richard, 77–78, 80–82, 93, 94, 203
  Paine, Thomas *et al.*, compared to, 118, 201–2
  Putney Debates, 72–82, 90, 92–94, 118, 201–2
  Rainborough (aka Rainsborough), Thomas, 75–77, 78, 81–82, 93–94, 118
  Sexby, Edward, 78–79, 93, 118
  True Levellers, *see* Diggers (Civil War)
  Walwyn, William, 77–79, 81–82, 203
  Wildman, John, 77–78
Levellers (Midland Rising), *see* Diggers (Midland Rising)
levelling, 59–60, 68–69, 102, 164–65, 186, 203–6, 227, 233–34
Leviticus, Book of, 192–93, 197–98
liberty tree, *see* tree of liberty
Lilburne, John, 72–73, 75, 81–82, 203, 205*n*120
Linebaugh, Peter, 150–51, 223*n*54, 223*n*55, 249, 257–58, 261*n*95
live, right to, 12, 88–89, 90, 93–94, 133, 139, 148–49, 150–51, 181–82, 262–63, 264–65
livelihood, *see* live, subsistence
living, rights of the, 111–12, 116–18, 149, 181–82, 195, 197, 262–63
Locke, John, 80–81, 92–93, 199–202
  and Burke, Edmund, 201–2
  Second Treatise of Government, 199–202
  and Paine, Thomas, 201–2
  and Spence, Thomas, 199–201

London, 1, 6, 26–27, 31–32, 45–46, 49–50, 72, 73–74, 82–83, 97, 121, 122, 125–26, 143–44, 177, 189, 194, 202–3, 214, 223–24, 242, 251, 263–64
London Corresponding Society, 143–44, 204–5
Longstaff, Jacky, 247*f*, 248
Luddites, *see* machine-breaking

MacCulloch, Diarmaid, 53*n*28, 66–67, 69*n*90
machine-breaking, 122–23
Macpherson, C.B., 81*n*55
Magna Carta, 77–78
Makdisi, Saree, 7, 205*n*119
Malthusian, 260
Manning, Brian, 80*n*47, 86
Manning, Roger, 24*n*8, 66–67
market, 7–8, 18, 23–24, 25, 33–34, 35–36, 50–51, 55–56, 62–63, 64, 69, 83, 85, 88–89, 93–94, 98–99, 123–24, 127–32, 133–37, 138–39, 144–47, 148–50, 168–69, 172–73, 175–76, 179–80, 181–82, 244, 260–61, 264–65
  compulsion, 7–8, 18, 62–63, 83, 88–89, 93–94, 98–99, 150–51, 180, 181–82, 235–36, 242, 260–61, 264–65
  labour, 133–37, 139, 145–47, 168–69, 175–76; *see also* proletarianisation
  land, 23–24, 50–51, 54, 55–56, 85, 172–73, 175–76, 179–81
  moral economy *vs* political economy (*laissez faire*), 123–24, 127–32, 133–37, 148–50
  provisions, 23–24, 33–34, 62–63, 64, 83, 123–24, 127–32, 135–37, 138–39, 144–45, 149–50, 181–82, 235–36, 242
  see also Book of Orders, capitalism, consumer protection
Marsden Rock, 1–2, 18
Marx, Karl, 22, 42–43, 99, 255–56, 257–58, 260
  Capital, 22, 42–43, 99, 255–56, 257
  On the Jewish Question, 207
  primitive accumulation, 22, 42–43, 255–56, 257, 260
  Rheinische Zeitung, 257–58
  rights of man, 207–8
  wood theft, 257–58
maypole, 214*n*14, 215–16, 229–30
McCalman, Iain, 6–7*n*18, 182*n*116, 201–3
McCrudden, Christopher, 14–15
McRae, Andrew, 35–36, 92*n*109
Mee, Jon, 205*n*118, 266
memory, 8–9, 12, 54, 69–70, 77, 88*n*93, 97–98, 123–24, 187–88, 193, 194, 203, 208–9, 214, 225, 230–31, 245–46, 257, 265–66
  collective memory, 8–9, 12, 54, 69–70, 77, 97–98, 123–24, 187–88, 193, 203, 208–9, 257, 265–66
  memorialisation, 8–9, 88*n*93, 97, 194, 214, 225, 230–31, 245–46
Midland Rising, 47–48, 56–70, 182, 192*n*60, 203, 219, 250
  and Coriolanus, 47–48, 63–66
  Diggers (aka Levellers), 56–62, 61*f*, 65–70
  Reynolds, John (aka Captain Pouch), 56–57, 58, 67–69
  Shakespeare, William, 47–48, 63–66, 250
  Tresham, Thomas, 58
  Wilkinson, Robert, 58–60, 67–69
Mies, Maria, 260–61
Miéville, China, 252–53
Mill, John Stuart, 252
millenarianism, 46–47, 191–92, 202–3, 207–8, 254–55, 266
Miller, Matthew, 244
minimum wage, 133–35, 148
Monahan, Sean, 249
monstrosity, 95–96, 99–101, 106–7, 118–20, 195
Montesquieu, Charles-Louis de Secondat, 197–98
Moore, Jason, 8*n*24
moral economy, 123–24, 127–30, 132, 135–36, 137, 148–49, 150, 254–55
More, Hannah, 127, 137–39, 164–65, 254
  and Burke, Edmund, 137, 139, 148–49, 164–65
  The Cottage Cook, 137
  and Paine, Thomas, 138
  The Riot, 138–39
  The Shepherd of Salisbury Plain, 138
  Village Politics, 138
More, Thomas, 21–22, 31–37, 42, 67–68, 155, 218–19, 252–53
  Utopia, 21–22, 31–36, 67–68, 155, 218–19, 252–53
Morton, Timothy, 202–3, 264*n*104
mourning loaves, 125–26, 242–43
Mousehold Heath, 49–50, 53–54, 66–67, 69–70, 219
Moyn, Samuel, 4–5, 14–15, 16*n*48, 253, 254*n*55
Muggletonians, 72–73
Murray, James, 197–98

native rights, 4–5, 12, 78, 104–5, 185–86, 190–91, 196–97; *see also* birthrights, Englishmen
natural rights, 4–5, 12, 18–19, 75–76, 80–81, 92–93, 102–4, 106–7, 112–14, 116–18, 138, 145, 171–72, 183–92, 193, 195–96, 205–9, 235–37, 240; *see also* birthrights, human rights, rights of man
nature, 8–9, 29–30, 41, 42, 45–46, 64, 76–77, 80–82, 95–96, 101, 104–5, 107–8, 112–13, 131–32, 134–35, 136, 140–42, 145–47, 149–50, 171–72, 174–76, 184–85, 189–91, 193, 196, 198, 199–200, 206–7, 232, 234–35, 265
  law of nature, 76–77, 80–81, 136, 140, 148–49
  natural rights, *see* natural rights
  natural world, 8–9, 42, 162, 199–200, 216–17, 232, 234–36
navy, *see* ships

Nedham, Marchamont, 81–82
Neeson, Janette, 8, 159, 160*n*16, 165*n*40, 165*n*44, 235*n*100
Neocleous, Mark, 119
Neville, Alexander, 48–49, 50, 51–54, 68–70, 219–20
Newcastle upon Tyne, 1, 170–71, 176–77, 201–2, 234–35, 237, 246–48, 247*f*, 263–64
  Philosophical Society, 170–71
  and Spence, Thomas, 1, 170–71, 176–77, 234–35, 237, 263–64
  Town Moor, 176–77, 201–2, 246–48, 247*f*
New Model Army, 72–74, 78–80, 82–83
Nişancıoğlu, Kerem, 13*n*34
Norman Yoke, 77–79, 85–86, 91, 93, 115, 187–88, 193–94, 196–97
North, Thomas, 63–64
Norwich, 49–50, 51–52, 53, 219–20
Nuneham Courtenay, 161–62
nutting, 234–36, 237–38

oak, 8–9, 50, 212–14, 215–16, 217–18, 219–20, 221–22, 225–30, 233, 236, 239–40
  associations, 212–14, 225–26
  and Burke, Edmund, 224–30
  Hearts of Oak (song), 225
  Major Oak, 215–16, 219
  royal oak, 225
  Tree of Reformation (aka Oke of Reformation), 50, 66–67, 219–20
Obama, Barack, 249
O'Brien, Pat, 243–44
Ogilvie, William, 167, 169–70, 180
O'Gorman, Frank, 110*n*87
open-field system, 24–25, 155, 156, 163, 235–36, 250
original accumulation, *see* primitive accumulation
Orwell, George, 252
Ostrom, Elinor, 258–59, 260
Overton, Richard, 77–78, 78*n*37, 80–82, 94, 203

Pacini, Guilia, 239
Paine, Thomas, 3, 5–7, 96, 109–19, 111*f*, 117*f*, 125–26, 127, 138, 139–44, 145–47, 148–50, 164–65, 169–70, 173–75, 177, 180, 185, 186–88, 190–91, 193–94, 195–98, 200, 201–2, 203–5, 206–7, 208–9, 231–34, 237–40, 248–50, 254, 262–64, 265–66
  Age of Reason, 140*n*98, 186–87, 248–49
  Agrarian Justice, 140–43, 149, 169–70, 174–75, 180, 196–97
  American Crisis, 249
  and Burke, Edmund, 96, 109–10, 111–15, 116, 118–19, 142, 148–49, 186–88, 190–91, 195, 196–97, 201–2, 232, 233, 239–40, 254, 262–63
  Common Sense, 248–49
  early life, 114–15, 186–87, 231–32
  Levellers, compared to, 118, 201–2
  Liberty Tree, 234
  Paine burnings, 109–10
  Rights of Man, 3, 5–6, 96, 109–19, 117*f*, 125–26, 138, 139–40, 149, 164–65, 173–75, 177, 186–88, 190–91, 195–98, 203–4, 232–34, 237–38, 248–50, 262–64
  and Spence, Thomas, 7, 173–75, 177, 180–81, 193–94, 197–98, 200, 238–40, 254, 262, 263, 265–66
  and Thelwall, John, 6, 143–44, 145–47, 148–50, 187–88, 190–91
  and Wollstonecraft, Mary, 115, 116, 118–19, 190–91, 254, 262
pantisocracy, 230–31
Parliamentary enclosure, 8, 11, 98–99, 117–18, 119–20, 154–60, 179–81, 193, 235–36, 263
Patel, Raj, 8*n*24, 18, 264–65
Paul, George Onesiphorus, 10
Peasants' Revolt, 45–48, 49–50, 51–53, 59–60, 68–70
  Ball, John, 45–47, 51–53, 68–70
  Tyler, Wat, 49–50
Perelman, Michael, 11
Petegorsky, David, 202*n*105
Peters (aka Peter), Hugh, 99–100
Pettet, E.C., 63–64
picturesque, 162
Piercy, Marge, 252–53
Pigott, Charles, 197–98, 214*n*12
Pilger, John, 252*n*46
Pitt, William the Younger, 95, 116, 118–19, 125–26, 133–35, 137, 148, 214, 215, 230–31
  anti-Jacobin measures, 126–27, 214, 215, 230–31
  minimum wage bill, 133–35, 148
  rights of man, 95, 116, 117*f*, 118–19
Plant, Ron, 243–44
Plutarch, 63–64
Pocock, John, 104*n*55
Polanyi, Karl, 11*n*31, 133, 148–49, 150
  Speenhamland system, 133, 148–49, 150
political arithmetic, 98–99, 163
political economy, *see laissez faire*
poor relief, 81–82, 106–7, 115–16, 132, 136, 140, 150, 159–60, 172–73
popular sovereignty, 4, 80, 98, 101–2, 117–18, 126–27, 139, 179–80, 183–84, 191–92, 195, 239–40, 262–63
Portland, Duke of, 234–35
prescription, 12, 101, 106–7, 108–9, 113–14
Price, Richard, 97–100, 100*f*, 101–3, 104–6, 112–13, 115, 116, 118–19, 163*n*30, 186–87, 189, 194–95, 197–98, 200, 224–25, 254
  and Burke, Edmund, 99–100, 100*f*, 101–3, 104–5, 118–19, 186–87, 195, 224–25, 254
  A Discourse on the Love of Our Country, 97–98, 99–100, 100*f*, 101–3, 104–5, 112–13, 186–87, 194–95, 254
  Observations on the Nature of Civil Liberty etc., 97
  Observations on Reversionary Payments etc., 98–99
  and Wollstonecraft, Mary, 105

Price, Uvedale, 162
price-setting, *see taxation populaire*
Priestley, Joseph, 197–98
primitive accumulation, 22, 42–43, 255–56, 257, 260; *see also* accumulation by dispossession
primogeniture, 106–7, 115, 117–18, 167–68, 233–34, 262
proletarianisation, 11, 26, 41, 42–43, 79–80, 84, 88–89, 92, 98–99, 120, 150–51, 157–60, 175, 181–82, 216–17, 240, 255–56, 257; *see also* enclosure
property, 2–3, 33–34, 36, 37, 41, 72–73, 74–82, 85–86, 87, 89, 90, 92–93, 95, 98, 107, 117–19, 142–43, 145–46, 149–50, 160, 163–64, 166, 167–68, 169, 170, 173, 174, 175–76, 179–80, 181–82, 198, 201–2, 203, 204–5, 207, 220, 222–23, 230–31, 232, 240, 253, 259–60, 261–62, 263
  common, *see* commons, rights of common
  'demon of property', 106–7, 118–19, 167–68
  'natural property' *vs* 'artificial property', 141, 142–43
  private property, 2–3, 33–34, 36, 37, 41, 72–73, 75–82, 85–86, 87, 89, 92–93, 95, 98, 107, 117–18, 142–43, 146–47, 149–50, 160, 163–64, 166, 167–68, 169, 170, 173, 174, 175–76, 179–80, 201–2, 203, 204–5, 207, 220, 222–23, 230–32, 240, 259–60, 261–62, 263; *see also* enclosure
  'property question', 253, 261–62
  qualification for participation in elections, 72–73, 74–79, 80–82, 90, 92–93, 118
  right to property, 2–3, 36, 72–73, 76, 80–81, 92–93, 163–64, 167, 201, 207, 231–32
  self-propriety, 78*n*41, 80–81
  'Tyranny of Property', 145–46
provisions politics, *see* moral economy, consumer protection, food riots
Putney Debates, 72–82, 90, 92–94, 118, 201–2
  Agreement of the People, 74–75, 81–82
  Clarke, William, 73–74
  Cromwell, Oliver, 73–74, 75, 89, 94
  Ireton, Henry, 74–77, 80–82, 92–93, 118
  Rainborough (aka Rainsborough), Thomas, 75–77, 78, 81–82, 93–94, 118
  Revolution controversy, compared to, 118, 201–2
  Sexby, Edward, 78–79, 93, 118
  Wildman, John, 77–78

Quakers, 72–73

radicalism, concept of, 264
Rainborough (aka Rainsborough), Thomas, 75–77, 78, 81–82, 93–94, 118
Ranters, 72–73, 89, 202–3
Reagan, Ronald, 249
rebellion, 28, 47–70, 129, 149, 182, 192*n*60, 203, 219–20, 250
  Cornish rebellion, 28
  Kett's Rebellion, 47–56, 66–70, 182, 219–20
  Midland Rising, 47–48, 56–70, 182, 192*n*60, 203, 219, 250
  rebellious traditional culture, 129, 149; *see also* food riots, moral economy
Reformation, Henrician, 54–55, 66–67
rent-racking, 23, 26, 32–33, 36, 37, 38–39, 40, 42, 50–51, 55, 80
Repton, Humphry, 162
Resnikow, Sylvia, 45*n*1
revolt, *see* rebellion
revolution, as turn, 233; *see also* American Revolution, French Revolution
Reynolds, John (aka Captain Pouch), 56–57, 58, 67–69
Richardson, Samuel, 16–18
rights, *see* birthrights, Englishmen, human rights, live, living, native rights, natural rights, right to have rights, land (rights-based model), rights of common, rights of man, suffrage, wage-labour (rights of labourers)
right to have rights, the, 183–84
rights of common, 24–25, 46–47, 55–56, 157–58, 165–66, 168, 176–77, 220–21, 222–23, 234–36, 237–38, 240, 246–47, 257–60
  estovers, 24–25, 158, 220–21, 222–23, 240, 257–58
  extinguishment, *see* enclosure
  gleaning, 24, 46–47, 158
  nutting, 234–36, 237–38
  pasture, 24–25, 47, 55–56, 157–58, 165–66, 168, 176–77, 235–36, 246–47, 258–60
  stinting, 24–25, 55, 259–60
rights of man, 1–2, 3, 4–6, 7, 11, 12–13, 95–96, 97, 102–4, 106–7, 108–9, 112–14, 115, 116–19, 125, 138, 139–40, 143–44, 146–47, 149, 150–51, 154, 164–65, 169–70, 171–72, 173–74, 176–77, 180–82, 183, 184–86, 188–92, 193–95, 196–97, 200–1, 203–4, 205–9, 214, 238, 240, 253–54, 261–66
  emergence, 1–2, 3, 5–6, 11
  meaning, 2–3, 96, 103–4, 112–14, 116–18, 138, 139, 149, 150–51, 173–74, 181–82, 200, 207–8, 238, 253–54, 262–65
  relation to human rights, 3–5, 16–18, 184, 253–54, 261–62, 265–66
  woman, rights of, 108–9, 205–6, 262
  see also human rights, natural rights, Paine (*Rights of Man*)
Ritson, Joseph, 237
Robin Hood, 215–16, 237–38
Rogan, Tim, 11*n*31
Roosevelt, Franklin D., 249
Rothschild, Emma, 130, 135
Rousseau, Jean-Jacques, 8–9

Royal Society, 221–22
Ruddick, William, 214*n*11
Rudé, George, 122*n*8
Rudge, Thomas, 159–60
Rudkin, Olive, 201, 254–55
Russell, Frederic, 48–49

Schlesinger, Arthur, 211*n*2, 212*n*4, 215*n*16
Schutz, John, 212*n*3
St George's Hill, 71–72, 82, 85, 87–88, 94, 245
St Matthew, 58–59, 233
Salle, Robert, 49–50
Sanaa, 241, 242*f*, 265–66
Saunders, Laurence, 46–48
Scheuermann, Mona, 137*n*83
sedition, 38–39, 46–47, 109–10, 177, 200, 230*n*77, 230–31, 266
Sexby, Edward, 78–79, 93, 118
Seymour, Edward, first Duke of Somerset, 50, 51–52, 55–56
Shakespeare, William, 47–48, 63–66, 216–17, 250–51
  A Midsummer Night's Dream, 216–17
  As You Like It, 216–17
  Coriolanus, 47–48, 63–66
  and enclosure, 250–51
  Macbeth, 216–17
  and Midland Rising, 47–48, 63–64, 65–66, 250
  see also Bingo
Sharp, Buchanan, 62–63, 64*n*69
sheep, 25, 32–33, 35–36, 42, 50–51, 53, 54–56, 60, 65–66, 155, 257
  'devouring men', 32–33, 35–36, 42, 155, 257
  wool trade, 25, 31–33, 35–36
Shelley, Mary, 119–20
Shelley, Percy, 202–3
ships, 127, 136–37, 202–3, 218, 225
  'prudent shipmaster', 127, 136–37
  Royal Navy, 221–22, 225
  ship-building, 218, 225
  shipwreck, 202–3
Slotte, Pamela, 13–14
Smith, Adam, 130–32, 133–34, 135, 136–37, 140*n*97, 148, 260
  Digression on Dearth, 130–32, 133–34, 135, 148
  'two Smiths', 135
Smith, Nigel, 88*n*92, 202–3, 264*n*104
Snell, Keith, 158*n*11, 160*n*17, 160*n*18
social banditry, *see* banditry
social contract, 180–81, 189–90
Somerset, Protector, *see* Seymour, Edward
Sotherton, Nicholas, 48–49, 51–52
Southey, Robert, 230–31
sovereignty, popular, *see* popular sovereignty
Speenhamland system, 132–33, 135–36, 148–49, 150, 181–82
Spence, Thomas, 1–3, 6–7, 18, 170–82, 191–94, 197–203, 205–6, 207–9, 214*n*14, 234–40, 247*n*23, 254–57, 259*n*85, 262, 263–66
  and Burke, Edmund, 177, 197, 206–7, 254
  coins and tokens, 177–80, 178*f*, 179*f*, 214*n*14, 263–64
  The Case of Thomas Spence, 177
  The End of Oppression, 173–74, 237–38
  A Fragment of an Ancient Prophecy, 238–40
  The Important Trial of Thomas Spence, 180–81, 200, 207–9, 266
  An Interesting Conversation, etc., 180–81, 192–93, 205–6
  land plan, 172–76, 177–78, 180–82, 191–93, 236–38, 254–55, 263–64
  life, 1–2, 170–71, 176–77, 180–81, 237, 263–64
  The Meridian Sun of Liberty, 174
  Newcastle Town Moor dispute, 176–77, 246–47
  and Paine, Thomas, 7, 173–75, 177, 180–81, 193–94, 197–98, 200, 238–40, 254, 262, 263, 265–66
  phonetic alphabet, proposal for, 170, 263–64
  Pig's Meat, 177–80, 197–201
  Property in Land Every One's Right, 170–73, 263–64
  The Real Rights of Man, 173, 191–92, 263–64
  The Reign of Felicity, 193–94, 263
  The Restorer of Society to its Natural State, 174, 175–77, 180–82, 205–6, 234–36
  The Rights of Infants, 172*n*72, 174–76, 200
  Spence's Songs, 18, 175–76
  Spensonia, 179–80, 191–93
  A Supplement to the History of Robinson Crusoe, 191–92
  and Thelwall, John, 174, 175, 254–55
  Winstanley, Gerrard, compared to, 182, 201–2
Spencer, Charles, 251
Sprigg, William, 198–200
Stafford, William, 182*n*116
Standish, Arthur, 218, 219, 221–22
state, 4, 11, 16, 22–23, 65–92, 112, 124, 149–50, 257–58, 261–62
Statute of Artificers, 133
Stedman Jones, Gareth, 10
Stern, Walter, 123*n*13, 125*n*19, 125*n*21, 128*n*32
stewardship, 37, 38, 41, 260–61
Stewart, Patrick, 251
stinting, 24–25, 55, 259–60
Stott, Anne, 137*n*80
Stoyle, Mark, 28*n*18
Stratford-upon-Avon, 63–64, 250
subsistence, 7–8, 12, 18, 62–63, 83, 88–89, 93–94, 98–99, 136–37, 150–51, 180, 181–82, 216–17, 235–36, 242, 257, 260–61, 264–65
  market compulsion, 7–8, 18, 62–63, 83, 88–89, 93–94, 98–99, 150–51, 180, 181–82, 216–17, 235–36, 242, 257, 260–61, 264–65

subsistence (*cont.*)
  right to subsistence, 12, 88–89, 136–37, 181–82, 264–65
  subsistence crises, *see* dearth
  subsistence perspective, 260–61
suffrage, 72–73, 74–82, 90, 92–93, 109, 118
  property qualification, 72–73, 74–82, 90
  Putney Debates, 72–73, 74–82, 118
  women, 75*n*20, 109, 117–18, 188–89
Swift, Jonathan, 199–200
'swinish multitude', 102–3, 118, 177, 197
Sylva, 221–23, 231

Tacitus, 186
Talbot, Gilbert, seventh Earl of Shrewsbury, 56–58, 59–60, 65–66
Tawney, R.H., 11, 46–47*n*7, 62–63, 67
taxation populaire, 62–64; *see also* moral economy
Thelwall, John, 6, 127, 143*f*, 143–47, 148–50, 168–70, 174, 175, 180, 187–88, 190–91, 204–5, 254–55, 262–63
  and Burke, Edmund, 145, 148–50, 187–88, 190–91, 262–63
  Copenhagen Fields, 143*f*, 147
  and Paine, Thomas, 6, 143–44, 145–47, 148–50, 187–88, 190–91
  Rights of Nature etc., 145–47, 187–88, 190–91, 204–5
  and Spence, Thomas, 174, 175, 254–55
  The Tribune, 144–45, 168–69, 187–88, 190–91
Thetford, 114–15, 231–32, 248–49
Thirsk, Joan, 26, 40*n*75
Thomas, Keith, 71*n*5, 90*n*104, 218*n*27, 225–26
Thomas Paine National Historical Association, 250
Thompson, E.P., 8, 114, 118, 123–24, 125–26, 127–29, 131–32, 135, 137*n*84, 148, 149–50, 201–2, 203*n*112, 204–5, 254–55, 259–60
  Black Act, 114, 222–23
  moral economy, 123–24, 127–29, 131–32, 148, 150
  on Paine, Thomas, 118, 149–50, 201–2, 233–34
  on Smith, Adam, 131–32, 135
Thompson, Noel, 256*n*73
Thompson, R.H., 178*n*97
tragedy of the commons, 258–60
treason, 26–27, 177, 230–31
tree of liberty, 211–15, 213*f*, 224, 227–28, 234, 238–40, 264
  British Tree of True Liberty, 227–28, 229*f*, 239–40
  celebration, 211, 214, 239
  'false tree of liberty', 238–40, 264
  history, 211–15
  Liberty Tree (song), 234
  maypole, links to, 215–16
  proscription, 215
  Tree of Liberty (shop), 214
trees, 12, 18–19, 21–22, 26–31, 42, 50, 66–67, 91–92, 161–62, 164–65, 167–68, 179–80, 211–40, 257–58
  'desperate tree of want', 219
  Great Replanting, 222
  'great tree still', oppression as a, 91–92, 220
  landscape design, 161–62, 167–68, 222, 231–32, 236–37, 240
  liberty tree, *see* tree of liberty
  literature, religion and ritual practice, in, 215–18, 225–26
  Major Oak, 215–16, 219
  maypole, 214*n*14, 215–16, 229–30
  royal oak, 225
  The Tree of Commonwealth, 21–22, 26–31, 42, 214, 217–18, 219
  Tree of Reformation (aka Oke of Reformation), 50, 66–67, 219–20
  'tree of Tyrannie', 91–92
  'trees of goodly appearance', 164–65, 231–32
  Tyburn tree (aka triple tree), 223–24
  see also oak
Tresham, Thomas, 58
Turner, Michael, 155*n*5, 156*n*6
turnpikes, 114–15
Twin Ocean Corporation, 244
Tyler, Wat, 49–50

Universal Declaration of Human Rights, 13–14
use-rights. *See* rights of common
utopia, 7, 21–22, 31–36, 66–67, 191–92, 218–19, 251–53, 265–66
  disambiguation, 251–52
  last utopia, human rights as the, 4, 14–15, 253
  More's *Utopia*, 21–22, 31–36, 42, 67–68, 218–19, 252–53
  Utopia (film), 252*n*46
  Utopia (Northern Territory, Australia), 251–52, 265–66
  utopianism, 7, 66–67, 191–92, 252–53

vagabondage, 26, 119–20
Valenze, Deborah, 158–59
Volney, Constantin François, 119–20, 197–98
vote, right to, *see* suffrage

wage-labour, 17, 26, 41, 79–80, 98–99, 120, 133–35, 136–37, 145–47, 150–51, 156, 157–60, 164–65, 175, 216–17, 240, 257, 262–63
  contract of employment, 136–37, 145–47, 255–56
  generalisation, 17, 41, 79–80, 92, 98–99, 120, 150–51, 156, 157–60, 164–65, 175, 216–17, 240, 257; *see also* proletarianisation
  minimum wage bill, 133–35, 148
  rights of labourers, 146–47, 149–50, 168–69, 174, 175, 262–63
Walsingham, Thomas, 45–46, 51–52, 59–60
Walter, John, 68*n*88, 148

Walwyn, William, 77–79, 81–82, 203
Warwickshire Diggers, *see* Diggers (Midland Rising)
Watson, Richard, Bishop of Llandaff, 140*n*98
Watt, James, 121
Wedderburn, Robert, 6–7
Welcombe, 250–51
Wellingborough, 88–89, 245–46, 265–66
Wells, Roger, 125*n*20
Whitbread, Samuel, 133–35, 148–50
Whittle, Jane, 22, 50*n*19, 51*n*23
Wildman, John, 77–78
Wilkinson, Robert, 58–60, 67–69
Williams, Raymond, 17–18, 161, 162
Williamson, Tom, 155*n*4, 161–62, 218*n*28, 222*n*46
Wilmot, Sarah, 160–61
Wilson, Kathleen, 170*n*69
Wilson, Nigel, 35*n*53
Winstanley, Gerrard, 71–73, 82–92, 93–94, 182, 220–21, 245–46, 266
  An Appeal to the House of Commons, 86
  A Declaration from the Poor Oppressed People etc., 220–21
  The Law of Freedom in a Platform, 89–90, 182
  A Letter to the Lord Fairfax, 87, 91
  The New Law of Righteousnes, 71–72, 83–85, 87, 182
  A New-yeers Gift, 86, 91–92, 220
  The True Levellers Standard Advanced, 72, 85–87, 94, 245
  A Watch-Word to the City of London, etc., 87–88
  Wigan, 82–83, 246
  Winstanley (film), 246
Wollstonecraft, Mary, 6, 105–9, 112–13, 115, 116–19, 167–68, 169–70, 180, 188–89, 190–91, 254, 262
  and Burke, Edmund, 105–8, 116, 188–89, 190–91
  Mary: A Fiction, 105
  and Paine, Thomas, 115, 116, 118–19, 190–91, 254
  and Price, Richard, 105
  A Vindication of the Rights of Men, 105–10, 118–19, 167–68, 188–89
  A Vindication of the Rights of Woman, 105, 108–9, 188–89, 262
women, 75*n*20, 107–9, 117–18, 137, 138, 158–59, 172*n*72, 188–89, 262
  enclosure, effects of, 158–59
  food riots, participation in, 137*n*84
  patriarchal ideology, 107–9, 117–18, 137, 138, 158–59, 188–89
  political exclusion, 75*n*20, 109, 117–18
  rights of woman, 108–9, 117–18, 262
wood, 24–25, 158, 218–19, 220–23, 235–36, 240, 257–58
  customary rights with respect to, 24–25, 158, 220–21, 222–23, 240, 257–58
  maiming, 222–23
  theft, 222–23, 235–36, 257–58
  woodland, *see* forest law
Wood, Andy, 42–43, 59–60, 66*n*74, 69–70*n*91, 94, 220*n*38
Wood, Ellen Meiksins, 12–13, 21, 67*n*84, 92–93, 257*n*76
Wood, Neal, 21, 22*n*4, 26–27*n*11, 31*n*36, 67
Woodhouse, Arthur, 73–74
Worden, Blair, 82*n*57, 203*n*112, 203–4
Wordsworth, William, 239–40
'world turned upside down', 35–36, 87–88
Worrall, David, 123*n*11, 211*n*1
Wrightson, Keith, 28*n*17, 41*n*76, 47, 62*n*57
Wyvill, Christopher, 118*n*128

Young, Alfred, 211*n*2
Young, Arthur, 131–32, 163–67, 231–32, 254
  Annals of Agriculture, 163, 165–66
  Board of Agriculture, 163
  A Plain and Earnest Address to Britons, 163–65
  Political Arithmetic, 163
  The Question of Scarcity etc., 166

9 780199 675456

The manufacturer's authorised representative in the EU for product safety is Oxford University Press España S.A. of el Parque Empresarial San Fernando de Henares, Avenida de Castilla, 2 – 28830 Madrid (www.oup.es/en or product.safety@oup.com). OUP España S.A. also acts as importer into Spain of products made by the manufacturer.

www.ingramcontent.com/pod-product-compliance
Lightning Source LLC
LaVergne TN
LVHW051155210926
848486LV00005B/281
* 9 7 8 0 1 9 9 6 7 5 4 5 6 *